"Good translations take risks and let you read a [   ] the first time. This irresistibly colloquial and energetic version of Christian Scripture keeps up a flow of linguistic vigor and sheds much fresh light: both the narratives of the Gospels and the arguments of the Epistles are presented with memorable vividness, and the rendering of the Book of Revelation is a genuine tour de force. There are definitely some high-risk decisions, but the overall impression is of a text that is wonderfully and confidently alive."

—ROWAN WILLIAMS, Anglican bishop, former Archbishop of Canterbury

"Now more than ever, when sacred texts are too often used as weapons of terror, there is a need to make the gospel message of love and justice accessible. Michael Straus does this in his translation of the New Testament. Michael's scholarship and passion brings the New Testament alive for a skeptical world in need of a trusting word."

—KELLY BROWN DOUGLAS, Dean of Episcopal Divinity School, Union Theological Seminary

"This is a pearl of great price."

—JAMES DIGGLE, Emeritus Professor of Greek and Latin, University of Cambridge

"There is no question that we live in an age when words matter. They have the power to inspire and to incite, to create and to destroy, to mobilize and to suppress. Straus has taken a text that has done all of this throughout its history and has given it fresh expression, nuanced meaning, and befitting urgency. At times he chooses literal accuracy, and at times he takes poetic license, all the while remaining faithful to original context and intent, even as he attempts to capture its relevance for this present age. This translation is not only elegantly innovative, but it also brims with the vigor and revolutionary spirit so present at the moments of its original composition. It is a gift apt for an age when words matter supremely."

—JAVIER A. VIERA, Vice Provost, Dean of the Theological School, Drew University

THE NEW TESTAMENT

June 2019

for David Bentley Hart,

w: R deepest admiration for
your compellingly original
and indeed gutsy explorations
of the ofttimes obscure and yet
powerful draw of the Greek NT,
not only in your masterful handling
of the deceptively lucid John
but your willingness to allow
"bad Greek" to remain that way,
for truth's sake. Accept this
humble book in that light,

Michal.

THE NEW TESTAMENT

A 21st CENTURY TRANSLATION

Translated by Michael Straus

The New Testament: A 21ˢᵗ Century Translation

Translation © Michael Straus (2019),
from texts published as B. Aland, K. Aland, J. Karavidopoulos,
C. M. Martini and B. M. Metzger (eds.), *The Greek New Testament* (5ᵗʰ edition)
(Stuttgart: German Bible Society, 2014);
Institute for New Testament Textual Research (ed.),
Novum Testamentum Graece (28ᵗʰ edition, 3ʳᵈ corrected printing)
(Stuttgart: German Bible Society, 2014); and M. A. Robinson and W. G. Pierpont,
The New Testament in the Original Greek
(Southborough: Chilton Book Publishing, 2005).

Wipf & Stock
An Imprint of Wipf and Stock Publishers
199 W. 8th Ave., Suite 3
Eugene, OR 97401
www.wipfandstock.com
paperback isbn: 978-1-5326-4876-2
hardcover isbn: 978-1-5326-4877-9
ebook isbn: 978-1-5326-4878-6
Manufactured in the U.S.A.

The SymbolGreekU and NewJerusalemV fonts
used in this work are available from
www.linguistsoftware.com/lgku.htm
+1-425-775-1130.

Illustrations: Anna Pipes
Design: Practical People
Notes on the type:
Set in Amster by Francisco Gálvez

TABLE OF CONTENTS

TRANSLATOR'S PREFACE

My goal in this translation has been to bring some fresh turns of phrase to the gospels, histories, letters and revelatory texts already familiar to English-speaking readers and listeners, not least because they are the source of a number of sayings and stories embedded in our language by virtue of the long dominance of the King James Version of the Bible. Anyone undertaking a new translation necessarily works in the shadow of the King James because even though the Hebrew and Greek texts available at the time had their flaws, the quality of the English – the lion's share of which comes from William Tyndale's individual translation – can hardly be improved upon. Some later translations relying on better materials have thus improved the accuracy of the text but rarely the rhythm and force of the style.

There are of course also a number of exceptional modern translations. I appreciate in particular J. B. Phillips' translations of the letters and Reynolds Price's of certain gospels, both writers retaining a deep respect for the texts while varying their approaches, the one freely using common English phrases and the other adhering to Greek's at times staccato strangeness.[1] I likewise admire Robert Alter's uniquely creative and at the same time faithful translations of Old Testament texts.[2]

My general view is that translations that reflect an individual translator's own way of writing or speaking are the most successful in conveying the corresponding style and personality of a given author. Sometimes that's not always a plus factor, of course, as might be seen in David Bentley Hart's recent translation, where he admittedly writes in "bad English" in an effort to convey what he considers "bad Greek."[3] I get his theory, but

---

1   B. Phillips, *Letters to Young Churches* (New York: The Macmillan Company, 1952); R. Price, *Three Gospels* (New York: Simon & Schuster, Inc., 1996).

2   R. Alter, *The Five Books of Moses: A Translation with Commentary* (New York: W. W. Norton & Company, 2004); R. Alter, *The Book of Psalms: A Translation with Commentary* (New York: W. W. Norton & Company, 2007); R. Alter, *The Wisdom Books: Job, Proverbs and Ecclesiastes: A Translation with Commentary* (New York: W. W. Norton & Company, 2010).

3   D. B. Hart, *The New Testament: A Translation* (New Haven: Yale University Press, 2017).

the result is predictably clunky, obscure and more of interest for academic study than enjoyment by general readers. At the same time, translations born of committee efforts are generally lifeless and bland, reflecting no one's style but rather the homogenized result of multiple linguistic as well as doctrinal compromises. Notable failures in this category include the Revised Standard Version and its numerous progeny, whose dominant usage should not be confused with quality.

While as a general matter I believe it is possible to preserve in translation the sense, mood and character of a text, there are also inherent limits to conveying all of an original language's subtleties. Greek, for example, is a particle-loving language and is thus liberally sprinkled with tiny words that often function more as structural signposts than as translatable signifiers. This is in large part because Greek sentences and paragraphs depend not so much on word order as on inflected forms. English, on the other hand, does rely on word order for meaning. One major translation task is therefore to adhere to relatively normal English word order without losing some of the ambiguities and complexities found in oftimes lengthy and even convoluted Greek sentence structures.

Moreover, given the inescapable underlay of Ancient Greek's centuries of usage in epic, lyric, history, rhetoric and drama, as well as in everyday life and commerce, it is often unclear how much of that background context must be considered in trying to find an apt English equivalent to the Koine Greek of the New Testament. But even if classical or historical meanings are considered it is at best challenging to know for certain what nuances were preserved in the language at the time the texts were written.

I also found it essential to consider the Hebrew Scriptures – or more often in this case, the Greek Septuagint version of those books. It is clear, for example, that by and large the New Testament writers were deeply familiar with them. Indeed, Old Testament references and allusions as well as paraphrases and direct quotations permeate the entire New Testament, albeit in some instances (such as the Letter to the Hebrews) more than others. I have footnoted many of these references accordingly. And in places where the writers presupposed the reader's familiarity with the myriad personages of the Hebrew Scriptures (such as in the long genealogy that opens Matthew's Gospel), I added pithy descriptions of those figures on the theory that the implicit historical facts might not always be brought to mind.

To a great extent it is misleading to use terms such as "Old" and "New" in referring to the two broad divisions of the Bible as commonly presented. The earlier writings are subject to multiple ways of being categorized, such as by reference to Law, History, Prophets, Wisdom and similar groupings. Nor is there general agreement as to the ordering of those works, with considerable variance between the structure of the Hebrew and Christian Bibles as well as within the Christian canon itself, *e.g.*, whether to include any of the so-called Apocryphal books, something that still divides Protestant, Catholic and Orthodox communities. That is why I prefer to think of the Gospels, the Acts of the Apostles, the Letters and Revelation as a possible way to group works that follow on but are not in discontinuity with all that came before.[4] Of course, this isn't the place to re-write religious or literary history and I therefore also use "Old" and "New" as the form of shorthand they've become. But I also opted for "New Covenant" rather than "New Testament," both because it is a more accurate translation of the relevant Greek word and because it focuses on the relational nature of what was being established. Where I found it helpful I've therefore also tried to reflect both in language and references the diverse ways in which the New Covenant writers saw continuity and fulfillment of the Old in the New.

As would any translator, I always faced uncertainty which English word to select from within the range of permissible meanings. Even against the background of earlier usage, there is no straight-line path from the ways in which words and concepts such as goodness, excellence, virtue, wickedness or justice were used in Greek classical literature (with its own context of religious and philosophical thought), or the Septuagint translation of the Hebrew Scriptures, to the ways in which they were used, adopted or modified by those writing during the 1st century as the Christian community began its formation. And it bears keeping in mind that nearly all these writers (Luke being the most likely exception) were themselves Jews.

The vocabulary and grammar of the New Covenant texts also reveal these writers to have a wide range of educational, cultural and literary backgrounds – some writers perhaps simply dictating their memories, others drawing on years of rabbinical studies, and others steeped in Hebrew, Latin and Greek history and literature. I do not pretend to be fully confident that I have

---

4 I haven't taken note for present purposes of further subdivisions that can be made, such as the "Synoptic Gospels" as separate from John's Gospel, or Paul's Letters as separate from others, and variations on those themes.

sufficiently conveyed the meanings of such terms as "righteousness," "time-lessness," "judgment," "word/logos," "works," "faith," "sin," "ransom" or even "body," "soul" and "spirit." Solutions such as the sometimes elaborate strings of modifiers found in the Amplified Bible may highlight the difficult choices but do not resolve them.

Notwithstanding, uncertainty doesn't mean inaccessibility or even ob-scurity. Any shifts and developments in a word's meaning over time or by its appropriation within a new context remain, in my view, subordinate to the shared dilemmas, passions and distresses of human experience over time, *all* of which can be expressed in any language. What I mean is that a good trans-lation can and should provide a reader of the translated text with essentially the same intellectual and emotional responses as the original would have to a reader of that text. For me the goal of translation is to reach below "surface" dissimilarities of language in order to convey "those deep-seated universals, genetic, historical, social, from which all grammars derive...."[5] A successful translation therefore does not seek to recover what George Steiner calls "the lost Vulgate of Eden," but it also rejects the "monodist" position that real translation is impossible.[6]

It is also important to distinguish among different sorts of translation issues. The Greek text sometimes reflects the writer's own observations of events and reporting of speech, but at other times reflects a writer's effort to put into words what he perceived to be God's thoughts and words, *i.e.*, understanding himself to be inspired, quite literally, by the Holy Spirit. In such instances I tried to infer, imagine and/or intuit what might have been the thoughts, images and emotions that inspired the original writer and then sought to present them in English, building on the Greek text as at least an indicator of that first animating inspiration. Does that mean that I fairly caught the sense of that inspiration, or farther still that my translation of such passages is somehow likewise inspired? I'm happy to leave all that for someone else to decide. Either way, I did not consider myself free to find new truths or beliefs in these sacred texts on grounds that I might be "inspired" to find such meaning. It's sufficient for theolo-gians to argue about matters of faith, justification, judgment and the like without a translator purporting to wade into such debates with a wholly novel word choice.

---

5   G. Steiner, *After Babel* (3rd ed.) (Oxford: Oxford University Press, 1998), 76-7.
6   *Id.* at 65, 77.

I therefore did not consider it my job to resolve such issues but rather to provide a penumbra of meanings without departing from the core of what can faithfully be derived from the Greek itself. Inspiration, in that sense, for me meant thoughtfully and at times imaginatively considering the underlying message that a given writer sought to convey and then trying to present it in a way that same writer might have appreciated were he to read it in English today. That isn't too difficult in dealing with pure narrative. The harder choices come in books like the Letter to the Romans, which treats of such weighty questions as the freedom of the will, the nature of evil, the deathly consequences of sin, the history and future of Israel, the resurrection of the dead and like matters. Will differences among the Protestants, Roman Catholics or Greek Orthodox on these issues be resolved by one or another translation choice? I seriously doubt it. But one shouldn't add fuel to the fire. In order to respect a range of legitimate interpretations I therefore tended not to use the same English word every time I translated a given word in Greek.

Here's an example of what I mean. A number of Greek words build on a common root that may variously be translated as "righteous," "just," "upright," "rectified" or "vindicated." The English words chosen might thus alternatively suggest individual actions, divine imputation, some form of judicial acquittal, or compliance with ritual demands. It follows that the choice of words to express such concepts in English may, depending on the context, give rise to differing doctrinal emphases on such essential questions as the nature of forgiveness, redemption and propitiation. I therefore tried to allow for such possibilities as the text could fairly allow. I did so in part because I am suspicious of doctrines that rely overmuch on one or another choice within a given range of meanings. In other words, I tended to take a "both/and" rather than "either/or" approach.

The same was true in translating certain genitival constructions, notably passages that could be read to say that salvation is obtained through the subjectively genitive "faith of Jesus" (*i.e.*, by operation of his own faith and obedience), or the objectively genitive "faith in Jesus" (*i.e.*, by operation of one's own faith and trust). I don't view these alternatives as mutually exclusive, however. If anything, the expansiveness of the genitive construction in Greek has the virtue of legitimately embracing both understandings. I consider this a positive form of ambiguity and therefore alternated between the options, a choice that may well be unsatisfactory to partisans on either side of the debate.[7]

Apart from this, how should one translate certain lyrical passages such as those in the Letter to the Colossians that describe Jesus in what can fairly be called non-literal, impressionistic or spiritually abstracted language? Passages, for example, that refer to him as "the radiant image of the invisible God, the offspring of Heaven, the firstborn of all creation," embodying "the whole plenitude of divine perfection"? Such images cannot be limited by words and I therefore often dispensed with standard grammatical forms and punctuation as a way of signaling the limits of language.

Consider too how daunting it is to deal with the prologue to the Gospel of John. The King James has it thus: "In the beginning was the Word, and the Word was with God, and the Word was God. The same was in the beginning with God." But here is how I translated the same opening verses: "The Word existed before all Time, timelessly present with God and himself true God. He was with God at the outset."

The original Greek is quite simply written and the King James is a highly defensible literal rendering, one that has in fact been followed by virtually all other translations. Yet the meaning of the words remains elusive. I must have revised my translation dozens of times before settling on the current version, ultimately taking considerable liberty in word usage and phrasing. It's the portion of the book I'm probably least satisfied with, and it legitimately remains open to criticism. For me the chief obstacle was in dealing with John's use of the past tense "was" when speaking of a being who by definition exists beyond time. So even though I tried to convey the sense of the Word/Logos as "timeless" it was nearly impossible not to use temporal references, such as that the Word "existed" before all time or "was" with God from the beginning.

I'm not defending the way I've handled it and the past tense "was" and "existed" do appear in the Greek itself. I'm simply noting that this passage *par excellence* proves my point that sometimes the best one can hope for is to choose words that at least allusively suggest the mystery that writers like John or Paul felt when they set pen to paper. In other words, if Paul or John understood themselves to be inspired by the Holy Spirit, then a translator

7   *Compare, e.g.,* R. B. Hays, *The Faith of Christ* (2nd ed.) (Grand Rapids: Eerdmans, 2002) with J. D. G. Dunn, *The New Perspective on Paul* (Grand Rapids: Eerdmans, 2008); *see generally* M. F. Bird and P. M. Sprinkle (eds.), *The Faith of Jesus Christ: Exegetical, Biblical and Theological Studies* (Peabody: Hendrickson Publishers, 2010).

owes it to the text to seek words suggestive of that inspiration.[8]

One compelling and alternative way to deal with John's prologue is that chosen by Dr. Hart, whose translation of the same two opening verses reads thus: "In the origin there was the Logos, and the Logos was present with GOD, and the Logos was god; this one was present with GOD in the origin."

One immediately sees the varied ways he deals with the language, including by means of orthographic distinctions. Dr. Hart carefully identified the multiple meanings of the core Greek word "logos" and further analyzed the fraught theological issues at stake in how it was used in the so-called Trinitarian Debates of the 4th century. Recognizing the limitations of translating "logos" into a single word (as it were), he ultimately decided the best course was to appropriate the transliterated Greek itself rather than rendering "Logos" as "Word" or something else. He correctly observed that translating it as "Word" would do little more than replicate the King James and therefore not add much to our understanding that wasn't already there.[9]

The difficulty of the passage, as he and others have noted, is that no single word in English can possibly capture the fullness of the Greek word "logos." Yes, it means "word" but it also means "speech," "declaration," "thought," "reason" or variants on those. Dr. Hart also explains that at the time of John's writing the word likely carried with it an implied reference to, and possible rebuttal of, Platonist metaphysics and/or incipient Gnostic heresies, none of which would be readily apparent to most English readers. And Dr. Hart identifies a further series of complexities in the passage whereby certain grammatical aspects might give rise to uncertainty whether John is referring to "God" or "God Most High" or to "a god."[10] These he addressed orthographically with variations on large and small capital letters, an ingenious solution but one requiring something of a road map (which he also provides).

My point in focusing on this particular passage is that it exemplifies the pitfalls of overly literal renderings. They can be deceptively simple and there-

---

8   *See* 1 *Timothy* 3:16.

9   Hart, *op. cit.* at 533-37 (separately written as "A Note on the Prologue of John's Gospel
    – *An Exemplary Case of the Untranslatable*").

10 *Id.* at 168, note a. These words would not have been written with an initial capital
    letter in the original. The same of course is true for "logos" and "Logos." The small
    and capital letter distinctions found in later Greek writings are therefore themselves
    interpretations of meaning without clear textual justification. But I admit that I've
    freely alternated between small and capital letters myself, in particular in dealing
    with highly abstracted terms.

by mask the nuances and more complex and profound meanings that the words seek to convey. But as I said, I'm not completely happy with my own resolution of these issues. I opted principally to focus on what I see as the "time versus timelessness" aspects of the opening verses, *i.e.*, to emphasize what is perhaps but one of multiple senses embedded in the text. I recognize the risk of doing so in that the other senses may thus become less emphasized. But that's also the virtue of readers having multiple translations available to consult, where other aspects of the verses can be explored.

More generally, a Biblical text presents particular challenges in those places where it purports to speak *not* as the voice of its specific writer but as the voice of the one speaking to/inspiring that writer. Hans-Georg Gadamer argues that the "usual function of writing [lies] in its referring back to some original act of saying...."[11] The challenge would thus be in divining the nature and substantive content of that "original act." In that sense the translation of a Biblical text may require more poetry than science.

This is among the reasons I haven't felt governed by a particular theory or school of translation. In other words, I don't rely on an overarching rule that the text should be translated "literally," or "word-for-word," or with "dynamic equivalence," or "thought-for-thought," or "paraphrastically," or "idiomatically." For better or worse, I tried to find something of each of those approaches that would allow me to respond to the nature of a given book, letter or individual passage rather than force the text to fit a preconceived translation theory.

For example, sometimes the text *is* plain - as in the factual reporting of a sea voyage and shipwreck - and presenting it in a reasonably literal way will best capture the sense of the original. But sometimes the text is obscure, telegraphic or even convoluted, as can be the case with some of Paul's argumentation. Yet at other times the writing is elevated, abstract and laced with spiritual terms that reflect the writer's effort to convey in words experiences or thoughts that have no clear linguistic let alone physical equivalent. Hence the language can be metaphorical, allusive and imprecise, yielding more to poetry than prose.

I therefore found it better to try to figure out what the nature of a given passage was - whether visual or poetic, factual or conceptual - and treat it accordingly. At times I found it necessary to reconfigure the text in a way I

---

11   H.-G. Gadamer, *The Relevance of the Beautiful and Other Essays* (Cambridge: Cambridge University Press, 1986), 141-42.

thought it might have been had it first been written in English. That occasionally meant reducing some of the text to footnotes where the writer had interjected parenthetical observations that might otherwise interrupt the flow of the work. Paul tended to do this frequently, with thoughts that seem to have occurred to him in the middle of another thought the way they can while one is speaking – something that argues in favor of many of the letters being dictated to an amanuensis rather than first generated by writing. One such example was his comment to Timothy that he might try drinking a little wine from time to time to help settle his stomach, a thought that comes in the middle of another thought. Footnotes are admittedly a modern form of dealing with such interjections, but one that I hope is useful in that context.[12]

Without at all purporting to assume the poet's mantle, I took my admittedly eclectic approach analogously to the task John Dryden set for himself in his translation from Virgil:

> I thought fit to steer betwixt the two extremes of paraphrase
> and literal translation; to keep as near my author as I could,
> without losing all his graces, the most eminent of which are
> in the beauty of his words…. I have endeavor'd to make Virgil
> speak such English as he would himself have spoken, if he had
> been born in England, and in this present age.[13]

That sometimes required my adding words as aids to meaning. I take some comfort in Martin Luther's defense when he was criticized for adding the adverb *allein* (the German word for "alone") to his translation of Romans 3:28, even though the word does not appear in any known Greek text. A plain English rendering would be, "We know that a person is justified by faith apart from works of the Law." As per Luther it reads something like, "We know that a person is justified *solely* by faith/by faith *alone*, apart from works of the Law." Luther took the challenge as the opportunity to state his

---

12   Where a descriptive footnote is mine rather than the writer's I generally show it as a "translator's note." I also used Greek or Hebrew fonts for various names and places where translating or transliterating them might diminish their force. I therefore left them in the original form but also add my own indication what the word means "in English," a phrase clearly not in the original.

13   Virgil, *Aeneid* (J. Dryden, trans.) (New York: P. F. Collier and Son, 1909), 64, available at http://oll.libertyfund.org/titles/virgil-the-aeneid-dryden-trans.

governing approach to translation in such circumstances:

> I also know that in Romans 3, the word *solum* is not present in either the Greek or Latin text ... [but] it conveys the sense of the text – if the translation is to be clear and accurate, it belongs there.[14]

At times I also used anachronistic language, thus updating persons or settings in the parables to the present time as a way of keeping them lively; or quoting from Shakespeare or Milton as a means of universalizing the thoughts presented. At other times I simply appropriated the King James for certain passages so perfectly written or so embedded in our minds and culture that it would be either futile or arrogant to change them. And on other occasions – particularly with the Book of Revelation – I dispensed with normal English grammar and usage, used musical scores, or translated the Greek into languages other than English, all in aid of the admittedly impossible task of conveying what the writer himself states are sights and sounds that words cannot convey of a setting filled with people and creatures speaking and singing in myriad tongues.

Ultimately my aim is not to compete with let alone supplant other translations so much as to shed light on passages that may otherwise seem obscure; capture aspects of the man Jesus' personality as presented distinctively in the Gospels; convey in relatively plain language Christian doctrine and experience as related in Acts and the Epistles; and reflect the atemporal nature of the Book of Revelation. My goal has therefore been to arrive at the English translation I felt best captured the sense either of a particular Greek word or passage, avoiding the overly-literal where the text itself is far from plain.

At the same time I hope this translation is more accessible to the ordinary reader than what can be the daunting format of so-called "authorized" versions – I mean this work, in other words, to be user-friendly. That's one reason I eliminated verse numbers and sometimes even chapter numbers, none of which appear in the original Greek text but are simply later additions included for greater ease of reference. One goal is thus for the texts to

---

14   M. Luther, *On Translating: An Open Letter* (G. Mann, trans.) (Project Wittenburg, 1995), 9, also available at https://archive.org/stream/anopenletterontr00272gut/ltran11.txt.

read more novelistically in the case of the Gospels, as historical narrative in the case of the Acts, recognizably as letters in the case of the Epistles, and fluidly in the case of John's Revelation.

I also made a conscious effort not unduly to subordinate distinctive aspects of a particular writer's style. That explains some of the formal differences among the several books, such as my use of more action vocabulary in Mark; elevated and almost abstract language in John; stream-of-consciousness elements in Revelation; paragraph-long sentences in the letters to the Ephesians or Colossians; or even italics to suggest handwriting where Paul states that he himself is writing all or part of a letter. In other words, it's no accident that each of the books reads somewhat differently in style. Even so, at the end of the day this translation probably reveals more about my own writing style and manner of speech than it does about the authors'. But I don't presume to have captured all there is to convey or to have met all legitimate scholarly demands, let alone to have presented a volume acceptable for liturgical use.

Now, as far as acknowledgments go, it's impossible to know where to start let alone where to end. This translation is the product not only of my studies in both Attic and Koine Greek but also and more importantly of decades of immersion in the Bible itself. It is the product as well of a loving family, who both tolerated and supported my studies and writing time. To go beyond that would shortchange someone, I'm sure. I therefore find it more than sufficient to close with the unpayable debt I owe in thankfulness to Philippa, Philippa and Marc.

Michael Straus

GOSPELS

ACCORDING TO MATTHEW

1

This is the genealogy of Yeshua, the Messiah, the son of David, the son of Abraham. Abraham was father to Isaac by his wife Sarah in their old age, according to God's promise. Isaac was father to Jacob and Jacob to Judah and his brothers. Judah fathered the twins Perez and Zerah incestuously by Tamar his Canaanite daughter-in-law, mistaking her for a whore. Now Perez was father to Hezron, then Hezron to Aram, Aram to Amminadab, Amminadab to Nahshon and Nahshon to Salmon. Salmon fathered Boaz by Rahab, the harlot of Jericho, and Boaz fathered Obed by Ruth the Moabite. In turn, Obed was father to Jesse and Jesse to David the King.

David then fathered Solomon by Bathsheba, the wife of Uriah the Hittite, first committing adultery with her and then procuring Uriah's death. For his part, King Solomon was father to Rehoboam by Naamah the Ammonite. King Rehoboam, under whom the kingdom split in two, was father to Abijah; King Abijah to Asa by his wife Micaiah, granddaughter of David's rebel son Absalom; King Asa to Jehoshaphat, who suppressed the worship of idols; King Jehoshaphat to Joram, who married Athaliah, the Baal-worshiping daughter of wicked King Ahab and his wife Jezebel; King Joram to Uzziah, who was struck by leprosy for transgressing the Temple altar; King Uzziah to Jotham, who did right in God's sight; King Jotham to Ahaz, who sacrificed his children in the fire; King Ahaz to Hezekiah, who restored the Passover Festival to Israel; King Hezekiah to Manasseh, who practiced witchcraft and set up in the Temple an idol he himself had made; King Manasseh to Amon, who did evil and was assassinated in his palace; King Amon to Josiah, who renewed Israel's covenant with God; and King Josiah to Jechoniah and his brothers about the time the people were taken captive and exiled to Babylon.

But after they were taken to Babylon, King Jechoniah fathered Salathiel and Salathiel fathered Zerubbabel, who laid the foundations of the Second Temple. Zerubbabel fathered Abiud, Abiud Eliakim, Eliakim Azor, Azor Zadok, Zadok Achim, Achim Eliud, Eliud Eleazar, Eleazar Matthan and Matthan Jacob. Now Jacob was father to Joseph, Mary's husband, and Yeshua – the Anointed One – was born of Mary.

So it was that fourteen generations passed between the time of Abraham and David and another fourteen from David to the captivity in Babylon and another fourteen from the time of the captivity until the coming of the Messiah.

Yeshua's own genesis was as follows.

While his mother Mary was engaged to Joseph but before they had sex with one another, Mary became pregnant – and that by the Holy Spirit. Her fiancé Joseph was a just man, unwilling to expose her to public shame and disgrace. Instead, he thought he could secretly release her from her pledge. But while he was trying to figure out what to do an angel of the Lord came to him in a dream and said, "Joseph, son of David, don't be afraid to marry Mary. She's with child by the hand of the Holy Spirit and will bear a son. You will name him יֵשׁוּעַ (which in English means 'he will save'), because he will rescue his people from their sins."

All of this happened to fulfill the word of the Lord through his prophet – Watch! A virgin will be with child and bear a son and people will call him עִמָּנוּאֵל[1] (which in English means God is with us).[2] Once he woke up Joseph did as the angel commanded and took Mary into his house yet did not have sex with her until after she had given birth to a son, whom he named Yeshua.

---

1   *Isaiah* 7:14, 8:8.
2   *Isaiah* 8:10.

2

This Yeshua was born in Bethlehem of Judea during King Herod's reign. At some point after his birth certain Magi, men of the Orient steeped in the movements of the stars, came to Jerusalem and asked around, "Where is the child born King of the Jews? We've seen his star ascendant in the eastern quadrant and have come to worship him."[3] But when King Herod heard this he was agitated – indeed, so was all Jerusalem with him. Once Herod had gathered all the nation's chief priests and scribes he asked them where the Messiah was to be born. They responded, "In Bethlehem of Judea, just as the prophet wrote –

> And you, Bethlehem, in the land of Judah,
> are by no means least among the rulers of Judah,
> for a leader shall emerge from you
> and he will shepherd my people Israel."[4]

Herod summoned the astrologers to meet with him in private, at which point he pressured them to tell him precisely when the star began to appear. Then he sent them off to Bethlehem and directed them, "Investigate this matter of the child carefully. Let me know once you've found out who and where he is, because I'd like to come worship him too." The wise men heard the king out and left. As they travelled, the star they had seen in the eastern sky went ahead of them until it stood over the child's abode.

The wise men eagerly followed the star's guiding and rejoiced on entering the house it led them to. There they saw the child with Mary his mother and, kneeling before him, they worshiped. Then they opened treasure boxes they had brought with them, presenting him with gifts – gold, frankincense and myrrh.[5] But in a dream the wise men were given divine warning not to return to Herod. They therefore left Bethlehem by an alternate route, heading straight back to their own country.

Once they had left, an angel of the Lord again appeared to Joseph in a dream and instructed him, "Rise up! Take the child and his mother

---

3   *See Numbers 24:17.*
4   *Micah 5:2; 2 Samuel 5:2.*
5   *Psalms 45:8; Song of Songs 3:6, 5:5; 1 Kings 10:2; Proverbs 7:17.*

and flee into Egypt.[6] Herod will be out looking for the child with an aim to kill him. So just stay put until you hear from me." Joseph packed up that night, took the child and his mother and escaped to Egypt, planning to live there at least until Herod died. In this way the word of the Lord through the prophet was fulfilled, to wit, I called my son out from Egypt.[7]

Herod of course went crazy when he found out the Magi had slipped by him. In a fury he ordered his men to murder all the babies in Bethlehem and its surrounding villages aged two years and under, based on the time frame he'd exacted from the star-gazers. So too was the word of Jeremiah fulfilled –

> A cry was heard in Rama,
> > great wailing and lamentation,
> Rachel weeping for her children,
> > refusing to be consoled, for they are gone.[8]

But once Herod was dead the Lord's messenger again appeared in Joseph's dreams and directed him, "Rise, take the child and his mother and head back to Israel. Those who sought to kill the child are themselves now dead." So Joseph gathered his belonging and returned with his family to the land of Israel. Yet he was afraid to settle in Judea again because he'd been warned by God in another dream that it was still a danger zone with Archelaus having assumed the kingship after Herod. Joseph therefore changed course and headed instead for the Galilean District, settling in the backwater village of Nazareth. This too fulfilled a word of the prophets that the Messiah would be known as a man from Nazareth.[9]

3

During this same period John was preaching and baptizing in the wilderness regions of Judea saying, "Turn back from your ways – the kingdom of Heaven is come near."

---

6   *Exodus* 5:22-23.
7   *Hosea* 11:1.
8   *Jeremiah* 31:15.
9   *Cf. Judges* 13:5; *Isaiah* 11:1

This is just what Isaiah spoke about when he wrote,

A voice cries out in the desert –
  "Prepare the way of the Lord, straighten his paths!"[10]

Now John himself wore clothes woven of camel's hair, tying them on his waist with a leather belt, and he fed himself on locusts and wild bees' honey. People from Jerusalem and indeed from all around Judea and the Jordan region came to be baptized by him in the Jordan River as they confessed their sins.

But when John saw many of the Pharisees and Sadducees on their way to be baptized he said, "You're a serpents' brood – who warned *you* to flee from the wrath to come?[11] You'll need to lead changed lives if you want to confirm your repentance. Oh and don't get the idea that it's enough to say, 'we've got Abraham as our father.' The truth is God can bring forth children to Abraham from the pebbles on this river bank. I'm telling you the axe is poised above the root of the trees. Every tree that fails to yield healthy fruit will be cut down and tossed to the fire. And yes, I'm immersing now you in water so you'll turn from your ways – but someone more powerful than I is following me and I'm not worthy so much as to carry his sandals. *He* will baptize you in the Holy Spirit and with fire. He has his winnowing tools in hand, ready to cleanse the threshed grain, gathering the wheat into the storehouse and burning the chaff with a fire that can't be put out."

Then Yeshua came down from Galilee to the Jordan River to be baptized by John. Yet John faced him down.

"I'm the one who needs to be baptized by you, not the other way around – so why are *you* coming to me?"

"Let it go for now. It's fit that we observe ritual propriety."

John yielded to him.

But the moment Yeshua was baptized, even as he came up from the water, the Heavens were split and John saw the Spirit of God descending, lighting on Yeshua gently as a dove, all as a voice from Heaven spoke, This is my beloved Son, in whom I am well-pleased.[12]

---

10   *Isaiah* 40:3.
11   *Malachi* 3:1.
12   *Psalms* 2:7; *Isaiah* 42:1.

4

The Spirit then led Yeshua into the wilderness to be tested for a time by the Accuser of the Brethren. He fasted there forty days and forty nights.[13] Hungry as he was for food, it was just then the Prince of This World approached with a challenge.

"If you're really the Son of God then turn these stones to bread."

Yeshua countered with a verse, "Man doesn't survive on bread alone but by every word that comes from the mouth of God."[14]

Then the Prince of Darkness whisked him away to the Holy City, stood him on the Temple's parapet and tempted him, "Prove to everyone you're really the Son of God - jump! As the Scriptures tell us,

> He will command his angels to protect you,
>   suspending you in the palms of their hands -
> your feet won't even touch the stone."[15]

Yeshua rebuked him again, "Don't provoke the Lord your God."[16]

Taking him once more, the Adversary set him atop the highest mountain and gave him a view of the kingdoms of the world in all their glory, promising Yeshua, "I will give all these things to you, if only you will bow down and worship me."

But yet again Yeshua rejected him, "Get out of my sight, Satan. You know the Scriptures - You will worship the Lord your God and serve him alone."[17]

Then the Wicked One left him as swift angels swept to his side, tending to his needs.[18]

After this, Yeshua heard that John had been arrested. He therefore withdrew to Galilee where, leaving Nazareth behind, he settled in Capernaum-by-the-Sea in the lands first given to the tribes of Zebulon and Naphtali. He thus fulfilled Isaiah's prophetic word,

---

13   *Exodus* 24:28; *Deuteronomy* 9:9, 18.
14   *Deuteronomy* 8:3.
15   *Psalms* 91:11-12.
16   *Deuteronomy* 6:16; *cf.* W. Shakespeare, *Macbeth* 1.3.123-26.
17   *Deuteronomy* 6:13; *Joshua* 22:5.
18   *1 Kings* 19:5-8.

> Bright dawn broke along the Via Maris
> across from Jordan,
> a light shining on those who sat in darkness,
> there among the tribes of Zebulon and Naphtali
> there under the shadow of death
> there among those of Upper Galilee.[19]

From that point on Yeshua began to preach and he urged the people, "Turn from your ways - the kingdom of Heaven has drawn near."

Walking by the Sea of Galilee Yeshua saw two brothers casting throw-nets, they being fishermen. These were Simon (nicknamed Πέτρος, which transliterated into English is Peter but in Greek means "the Rock") and Andreas. He said, "Come with me and I'll make you fishers of men." They quickly left their nets behind and followed him. Walking a bit further along the shore he saw another two brothers, Jacob and John, sons of Zebedee. They were mending nets in a boat with their father when Yeshua called them to join as well. Right away they left their boat - and their father too - and followed him.

Yeshua went all around Galilee teaching in its synagogues, preaching the good news of the kingdom to the people and healing them of every kind of sickness and disease. He also became famous throughout the entire Syrian region, where they carried to him people with diverse illnesses and diseases, some suffering in constant pain as well as people who were demon-possessed or epileptic or paralyzed - and he healed them all. Not surprisingly, a major crowd began to follow him everywhere, with people streaming in from Galilee, Decapolis, Jerusalem and the Trans-Jordan.

5

Seeing the multitudes gathered, Yeshua went up to the hill country west of the Sea of Galilee. Once he'd found a good place to sit his disciples gathered to listen and he shared with them freely, teaching lessons like these:

"You who are now downcast and oppressed, lift up your heads - God

---

19   *Isaiah* 9:1-2.

will give you the kingdom of Heaven! You who mourn will be comforted[20] and you the humble will inherit the Promised Land.[21] Do you hunger and thirst for God's righteousness? He'll give you your fill.[22]

And blessed are you who show mercy, because he will be merciful to you.[23] So too, the pure in heart will see God.[24] Peacemakers - you'll be known as God's children.[25] Happy are those who bear the marks of persecution, because theirs is the kingdom of Heaven. The fact is, you should consider yourselves fortunate when people revile and oppress you, slandering you for my sake. When that happens rejoice and be glad, because your reward is great in Heaven - they persecuted the prophets before you in just the same way.[26]

"You are the salt of the Earth but if salt loses its strength and becomes tasteless, what good is it? It's good for nothing other than to be thrown out and trampled underfoot.[27] You are the light of the world - and a city perched on a hilltop cannot be hidden.[28] No one would light a candle and then dump a bushel of grain on it. No, you'd put it on a candlestick and let it shine throughout the house. So don't hide your light but let it shine before all mankind. That way they'll see your good deeds and give glory to your heavenly Father.

"I don't want you to think I've come to destroy the Law or the Prophets. Far from it - I've come not to destroy but to fulfill. Listen to me carefully: Heaven and Earth may well pass away but not a single · - not one ink stroke - shall disappear from the Law until all things are fulfilled. Therefore whoever dispenses with the least of these commandments and teaches people to do the same will be called least in the kingdom of Heaven, while whoever both observes and teaches them will be called the greatest. My point is that unless in God's eyes your righteousness exceeds that of the scribes and Pharisees, you will not enter the kingdom of Heaven.

---

20   *Isaiah* 61:2.
21   *Psalms* 37:11.
22   *Psalms* 16:15, 42:1-2, 107:9; *Isaiah* 41:17, 55:1-2.
23   *Psalms* 18:25-26.
24   *Deuteronomy* 6:5; *Psalms* 24:3-5.
25   *Psalms* 34:14; *cf.* W. Shakespeare, *Henry VI, Part 2,* 2.1.35.
26   *E.g., Jeremiah* 20:2; *2 Chronicles* 24:21.
27   *Cf. Genesis* 19:26; *2 Kings* 2:20.
28   *Isaiah* 2:1.

"You've heard it was said to those who lived in past times, don't mur-der[29] and that anyone caught doing so would face judgment. But I'm tell-ing you anyone who's angry with his brother will also stand condemned.[30] Indeed, if anyone says to his brother רֵיקָא (which in English means numb-skull), he will answer to the Sanhedrin. And whoever calls his brother a fool risks the smoldering fires of גֵּי הִנֹּם (which in English means the Valley of Hinnom).[31]

"Therefore if you're on the way to take your gift to the altar and real-ize your brother has something against you, hold off presenting your gift and first go set things right with your brother – after that you can offer your gift to God.[32] If you are sued, settle the case quickly. Otherwise, the odds are you'll run into the plaintiff on the road, he'll haul you before a judge, the judge will hand you over to the bailiff and the bailiff will throw you in jail. I'm telling you if that happens you won't get out of there until you've paid the last penny.

"It's true that Moses told the people, don't commit adultery.[33] But I'm telling you that as soon as you've looked at someone else's wife with a mind to sleep with her you've already committed adultery in your heart.[34] This being the case, if your right eye is leading you into scandal take it out and throw it away. Isn't it better for you to lose one part of your body than to have your whole self cast into the fire? So likewise if your right hand is causing you up to stray cut it off and toss it. It's *clearly* better for you to lose one part of your body than have your whole self burnt in Gehenna's flames.

"Moses *did* add that if anyone wishes to divorce his wife he must pro-vide her with a divorce decree.[35] But I'm saying that anyone who divorc-es his wife other than for unfaithfulness pushes her to commit adultery, because anyone who marries a woman who's been unlawfully divorced commits adultery with her.

"Again, you've heard the ancients were told, don't swear falsely but

---

29   *Exodus* 20:13; *Deuteronomy* 5:17.
30   *Cf. Leviticus* 19:17-18.
31   And which, transliterated into Greek as Γέεννα and then again into English, some-times reads Gehenna. *See Jeremiah* 7:31; 2 *Kings* 23:10.
32   *Isaiah* 1:10-17; *Jeremiah* 8:8-11; *Amos* 5:21-24; *Micah* 6:6-8.
33   *Exodus* 20:14; *Deuteronomy* 5:18.
34   *Exodus* 20:17.
35   *Deuteronomy* 24:1.

give over to the Lord all that you've promised.[36] Yet now I'm telling you categorically – don't swear any oath *at all*, not 'by Heaven,' not 'by God's throne,' not 'by the Earth' (that being God's footstool)[37] and not 'by Jerusalem' (since that's the city of the Great King).[38] Don't even swear by your own head, because you can't turn one hair white or black. Instead, when you give your word just let it be 'yes, yes' or 'no, no.' Anything more than this comes from the Evil One.

"You've also heard you should repay an eye for an eye and a tooth for a tooth.[39] But I say, don't resist an evildoer. If someone punches you on the right side turn to him your left. If someone asks for your shirt give him your jacket as well. If someone dragoons you into going a mile with him, go two. Lend to those who find they must borrow – don't turn away someone in need!

"Now, you've also heard you should love your neighbor[40] and hate your enemy.[41] But I say to you, love your enemies and pray for those who persecute you.[42] As God's children you should be like your Father in Heaven: he causes the sun to rise on the evil as well as the good, the rain to fall on the just as well as the unjust. If you love those who love you do you think you deserve a medal? Don't men of the world do that too? And if you only greet your brothers, what's so special about that? Don't the Goyim do the same? But *you* – you must be all embracing in your love and holy, even as your Father in Heaven is holy.[43]

6

"Be careful you don't put on a show of your piety for everyone to see. If you do, then you'd better enjoy it now because you've forfeited any reward from my Father in Heaven. Instead, whenever you do something charitable don't tell everyone what you're up to – that's what the hypocrites do, publicizing their gifts to the rest of the congregation, putting up

36 *Leviticus* 19:12; *Numbers* 30:3; *Deuteronomy* 23:22.
37 *Isaiah* 66:1.
38 *Psalms* 48:2.
39 *Exodus* 21:24; *Leviticus* 24:20; *Deuteronomy* 19:21.
40 *Leviticus* 19:18.
41 *Psalms* 139:21-22.
42 W. Shakespeare, *Macbeth* 3.1.90-93.
43 *Leviticus* 11:45, 19:2, 20:26; *Deuteronomy* 18:13

billboards on the highways, always seeking praise from men. They have their reward. But whenever you're moved to donate money or goods don't let your left hand know what your right is doing. Make your donations anonymously – and don't worry, your Father, who sees what goes on in secret, will vouchsafe your reward.

"Whenever you pray don't be like the hypocrites. They make it a point to pray where everyone can see them – and I mean not just in the assemblies but out in the town square and on street corners as well. They too have their reward. But whenever *you* pray go into an inner room of your house, lock the door and pray to your Father in secret – and your Father, who sees all that happens, even the hidden things, will reward you.

"And when you pray don't babble on the way the Goyim do, thinking the more they talk the more they'll be listened to. Don't be like them. There's nothing you need that your Father doesn't know about ahead of time. So pray like this –

> Our Father, who art in Heaven,
>   hallowed be thy name;
> Thy kingdom come, thy will be done,
>   on Earth as it is in Heaven.
> Give us this day our daily bread;
>   And forgive us our trespasses,
> as we forgive those who trespass against us.
>   And lead us not into temptation,
> but deliver us from evil.
>   For thine is the kingdom and the power and the glory,
> forever and ever, amen.

If you forgive those who do you wrong your Father in Heaven will also forgive you. But if you don't forgive others their sins neither will your Father forgive yours.

"And whenever you fast don't be all gloomy like the hypocrites. They hide their faces with ashes or dirt so everyone will see they're fasting. I'm telling you, they have their reward. But when you fast, anoint your head with oil and scrub your face. That way no one will know you're fasting – no one other than your Father who sees in secret, that is, and he will guarantee your reward.

"Don't heap up riches for yourselves on Earth, where moths and rust can eat away at them or thieves break in and steal. But store up for yourselves treasures in Heaven, where moths can't devour and rust can't corrode, where thieves can't break in and robbers can't steal, because wherever you keep your treasures that's where your heart will be.[44] You gather light by focusing - so if you focus your eyes on what's good and true your soul will be filled with light. But if you eye what's evil you darken the soul - and if darkness hides in your soul how great must that darkness be!

"No one can serve two masters. He will hate the one and love the other or honor the one and scorn the other. You cannot serve both God and Money. That's why I'm telling you not to worry yourselves to death what you'll eat or what you'll wear. Isn't the soul more than food, the body more than the clothes it wears? Look at the birds that fly through the skies. They don't plant crops or harvest them or store them in a barn - and yet your Father in Heaven makes sure they have food to eat. Aren't you worth a lot more than they are? And besides, where does all your worrying get you? Worrying won't make you live longer.[45]

"As far as clothing is concerned, learn something from wildflowers, how they grow. They don't work, they don't weave, and yet Solomon in all his glory was never draped with such finery. If God so adorns the grass of the field, which is here today and gone tomorrow, how much more will he clothe you, you faithless people! That's why I say you'll just get ulcers with all your worrying, all your 'What are we going to eat? What are we going to drink? What are we going to wear?' That's what the Goyim fret about all day. Just remember what I've told you - your Father in Heaven knows everything you need. Therefore seek out first the kingdom of God and his righteousness and all these things will be provided you. And don't anguish about what tomorrow will bring. Tomorrow will bring its own worries. Sufficient for the day is the evil thereof.

7

"Don't condemn other people or you may end up condemned yourself. After all, you'll be judged by the same standards you apply to others, mea-

---

44   *Cf.* W. Shakespeare, *Henry VI, Part 2,* 2.1.19-20.

45   *Cf. Psalms* 39:5.

sure for measure by the same yardstick you use on them. Are you so focused on that splinter in your brother's eye that you can't see the log stuck in your own? And how can you say to him, 'Here, let me take that splinter out of your eye,' when the log is still blocking your sight? You hypocrite - first remove the log from your own eye and then you'll see clearly enough to take the splinter out of your brother's.

"Don't mix what's holy with what's not.[46] You wouldn't cast pearls before swine, after all, because they'd first grind them underfoot then turn and tear you to pieces.

"Ask and it will be given to you; seek and you will find; knock and it will be opened to you. For everyone who asks receives; whoever seeks finds; and the door is opened to all who knock. Would any one of you give a stone to your daughter if she asked for bread? Or a rattlesnake if your son asked for a fish? You're corrupt by nature yet still know how to give good gifts to your children -so how much more does your Father in Heaven know how to give good things to *his* children?

"Whatever you want other people to do for you, do the same for them *- and right there you have all the Law and the Prophets!*

"Take the road less travelled. There's a 10-lane crowded highway leading straight to destruction, but the path to Heaven's Gate is straightened with suffering and few there are who find it.

"Keep an eye out for false prophets. To all outward appearances they're mild as sheep but on the inside they're ravenous wolves. You'll know them by their fruits - you can't pick grapes from thorns or figs from thistles. Every good tree yields healthy fruit but every bad tree, rotten.[47] By the same token you don't harvest rotten fruit from a good tree or healthy fruit from a bad tree. But every tree that doesn't yield healthy fruit will be cut down and thrown to the fire.[48]

"You'll know the bad ones through and through by the fruit they bear. That's why not everyone who says to me 'Lord, Lord' will enter the kingdom of Heaven but only those who do the will of my Father in Heaven. Many will say to me in that day, 'Lord, Lord, didn't we prophesy in your name and didn't we cast out demons in your name and didn't we perform many miracles in your name?' But I will tell them the plain truth -

---

46   *Leviticus* 22:2-16.
47   W. Shakespeare, *As You Like It,* 3.2.116.
48   *Isaiah* 5:1-7.

'I never knew you. Depart from me, you workers of iniquity.'[49]

"Anyone who hears these words of mine and does what I say can well be compared to a practical man building his house on a rock foundation. Rain and floods may come, gale winds may beat on the house, but it won't fall because it's founded on the rock.[50] On the other hand, whoever hears what I'm saying but doesn't heed my words is like the fool who built his house on sand. When the rain and floods came and the storms with them they beat on the house until it fell, and great indeed was its fall."

Yeshua ended this series of talks at that point, leaving the crowds overwhelmed, speechless, astounded by his teaching. Why? Because unlike their own scholars, he taught them with authority,.

8

When he left the hill country large crowds trailed him. And as he walked along the way a leper rushed up to him, knelt down and said, "Lord, if you want to you can cleanse me from this disease."

Reaching out his hand Yeshua touched him[51] and said, "I do wish it – be cleansed!" And immediately the leprosy disappeared.

Then Yeshua said to him, "See that you don't tell anyone – just get yourself straight to the Temple and offer the gift that Moses required,[52] as a testimony to the priests."

When he entered Capernaum a Roman centurion called out to him and said, "Lord, my young servant has been horribly injured and now lays paralyzed and suffering in our house."

"I will go there and heal him."

"No, Lord. I'm not worthy to have you under my roof. Just speak the word and my servant will be healed. You see, I know all about obedience because I'm subject to higher authority myself. I have soldiers under my command who also obey me – I tell one soldier 'Go!' and he goes, another 'Come!' and he comes, or my servant 'Do this!' and he does it."

---

49   *Psalms* 6-8.
50   *E.g., 2 Samuel* 22:2, 32, 47; *Psalms* 28:1, 30:2.
51   *Cf. Leviticus* 5:3; *see generally Leviticus* 13 and 14.
52   *Leviticus* 14:10 ff.

Hearing this Yeshua marveled and said to his followers, "I'm telling you the truth, I've not found such great faith as this before, no, not in all Israel. Many will come from the East and from the West[53] to feast in the kingdom of Heaven with Abraham, Isaac and Jacob, but the sons of the kingdom will be cast into outer darkness. And there will be weeping and gnashing of teeth."

Then he said to the centurion, "Go, let it be to you in accordance with your faith." And the boy was healed that very hour.

Yeshua then went to Peter's house, where he saw Peter's mother-in-law abed, sick with fever. He touched her hand, the fever left her immediately and she got up and waited on them. When evening came the people brought many who were possessed by demons. He cast the spirits out with a word and also healed the badly ill. Thus was fulfilled the word of the prophet Isaiah,

He alone took on our weakness and bore our diseases.[54]

When Yeshua saw the crowds gathering around him after these healings he ordered his people to take him across to the other side of the sea. But before he could leave one of the scribes approached him and said, "Teacher, I wish to follow you wherever you go."

"Foxes have dens and birds of the air have nests, but the Son of Man has no bed to call his own."

Another of his disciples said to him, "Lord, let me first stand vigil with my father until his death."

"No, follow me now – and let the dead bury their own dead."[55]

His disciples then followed him, embarking together in the boat. Yet once they had crossed halfway a sudden squall whipped winds across the shallow sea, washing waves over the boat. But Yeshua lay slumbering in the stern.

Rousting him his disciples cried out, "Lord, save us! We're about to die!"

"What are you afraid of, you people of such little faith?"

Then he got up and ordered the wind and the waves to cease.

---

53 *Psalms* 107:3; *Isaiah* 43:5, 49:12.
54 *Isaiah* 53:4.
55 *Numbers* 6:6-7; *Leviticus* 21:11.

A spreading calm fell over the sea. His men were stunned, terrified really, wondering, "What kind of a person *is* this whom even the winds and the sea obey??"[56]

When they arrived at the far shore they started to enter the land of the Gadarenes, but two demoniacs came down from the hillside tombs and blocked Yeshua's path. These were men totally gone from their senses, fiercely violent, so fearsome that none could safely pass. They screamed at him, "Son of God! What are *you* doing here?! Have you come to torment us before it's time?"

Now, a herd of pigs was feeding a far distance from them and the demons urged him persistently, "If you're going to cast us out of these men then at least send us to the herd of pigs."

"Go!"

So the unclean spirits freed the men and entered the pigs, whereupon the herd flung itself over a sharp sea bank, perishing in the waters below. The swineherds fled back to their village and told everyone what had happened - at which point the townspeople raced out to run Yeshua off, shouting "Get the Hell out of here and leave us alone!"

9

Yeshua therefore got back in the boat and returned to his own hometown. Then and there they brought a cripple to him, borne on a pallet bed. When he saw their faith Yeshua said to the man, "Cheer up, my child, your sins are forgiven."

However, some of the scribes who heard him said to themselves, "This man is a blasphemer, nothing but a heretic!"

But Yeshua knew what was in their hearts and asked, "Why do you harbor evil thoughts? Tell me, which do *you* think it's easier for me to say - 'your sins are forgiven'? or 'rise up and walk'? You need to know that the Son of Man has power on Earth to forgive sins."

Turning then to the crippled man he said, "Rise now! Pick up your pallet and walk back home." Standing straight the man headed right back to his house. When they saw this the crowd turned fearful, yet

---

56   *Job* 38:8-11; *Psalms* 65:5-8, 89:8-9.

glorified God for having given such power to mankind.

As he left the place, Yeshua spied a revenuer named Matthew collecting customs duties and said, "Follow me." So he got up from his desk and followed him.

Later, when Yeshua and his disciples were having dinner at Matthew's home, a number of high-rollers and other sinners also showed up to break bread. When the Pharisees saw them they said to the disciples, "What's this? How is it your teacher is eating with money grubbers and miscreants?"

But Yeshua himself responded, "Healthy people don't need a doctor, just sick ones. You need to learn what the prophet meant when he said, I want mercy not sacrifice,[57] because I haven't come to call the righteous but the sinners."

Then John's disciples approached him and asked, "Why is it that we and the Pharisees fast often but your disciples don't bother to fast at all?"

"Should the children of the bridegroom mourn while he's with them?[58] However, before long the bridegroom will be taken away from them[59] and then they will fast. No one patches up an old coat by sewing an unshrunken patch onto it because the added piece will pull at the old cloth and tear a worse hole. It's the same idea with wine – no one pours new wine into worn-out wineskins because it will cause them to burst open and then you'll lose the wine *and* the wineskins. That's why they put new wine into new wineskins, preserving both."

As he was speaking, the president of the local synagogue came up to him and knelt beseeching him, "My little girl is at the point of death – but if you would just come and touch her, I know she'll live."

Yeshua went with him, his disciples tagging along. But as he went a woman who'd heard what the synagogue leader had said came up from behind Yeshua[60] and touched the tassel of his garment[61] – she'd been suffering 12 years with prolonged menstrual bleeding and thought to herself, "If I can but touch him, or even his clothes, I'll be healed."

At that Yeshua whirled around and when he saw her said, "Cheer up, daughter, your faith has made you well." And indeed the woman

---

57 *Hosea* 6:6.
58 *Hosea* 2:12.
59 *Isaiah* 53:8.
60 *Cf. Leviticus* 15:25 ff.
61 *Numbers* 15:38-39; *Deuteronomy* 22:12.

was healed from that moment.

Yeshua continued on. Reaching the elder's house he saw a death scene complete with pipers and mourners, the whole house thrown into turmoil. Yet he said to them, "Clear out of here! This girl isn't dead - she's just sleeping." They all mocked him as a fool. But after the crowd was gone Yeshua went inside, took hold of the girl's hand and she sat right up. And so his fame spread across that whole region.

When he left there two blind men followed after crying out, "Have mercy on us, Son of David!"

Back at Matthew's house he said to the two of them, "Do you believe I can make this happen?"

"Yes, Lord."

He touched their eyes and said, "Then let it be to you according to your faith." And right then their eyes were opened wide up. Yet Yeshua warned them sternly, "See that you don't let anyone know about this." But they went out anyway and advertised him to everyone they ran into, all throughout the area.

As Yeshua walked on the people brought him a man possessed by a mute spirit. Once Yeshua had set him free from that demon the man began to speak. The crowd around him was astonished and said, "It's never been seen like this before in all of Israel." But the Pharisees said, "This man must be casting out demons by the power of their Prince."

Yeshua continued his journeys through every town and village teaching in their synagogues and preaching the good news of the kingdom, healing the people from any sort of sickness and disease. As he watched the crowds he felt deep compassion for them, seeing them beaten down, helpless, confused - much like sheep without a shepherd to guide them.[62] And so he said to his disciples, "The crop is ripe to harvest but there are hardly any workers around. You must pray the master of the harvest to send his laborers out to the field."

---

62   *Numbers* 27:17; *I Kings* 22:17; *Ezekiel* 34:5; *Zechariah* 11:16.

10

After that Yeshua summoned his twelve disciples and gave them authority over unclean spirits, that they might cast them out, and power to heal all manner of sickness and disease. These are the names of the twelve apostles. First, Simon, also called Peter; then Andreas his brother; Jacob the son of Zebedee; John his brother; Philip; Bartholomew; Thomas; Matthew the customs officer; Jacob the son of Alphaeus; Thaddeus; Simon from Qana; and Judas from Kerioth, who also betrayed him.

Yeshua gave orders to these twelve as he sent them out, telling them, "Stay off any road that would take you into foreign territory and also don't go into villages where you're likely to find Samaritans[63] – go instead to search for the lost sheep of the House of Israel.[64] As you go, tell people 'the kingdom of Heaven is come near.' Heal those who are weak, raise the dead, cleanse lepers, cast out demons. You've received freely, give freely as well. Leave your gold or silver or copper coins at home, don't bring a backpack filled with extra shoes and clothes and don't go buying a new walking stick. Why? Because a worker is entitled to a meal.[65]

"Whenever you go into a town or village ask around to find out who is a suitable host and stay in that home until you leave. And when you enter such a home, let your greeting be שָׁלוֹם עֲלֵיכֶם – or in English, 'Peace be upon you.' If the household is inclined to receive you, let your peace remain upon it; but if not, let your peace return to you. If no one will receive you or hear your words then when you leave that house and city, shake off the dust from your feet. I'm telling you that when Judgment Day comes that city will have it worse than Sodom or Gomorrah.[66] "I'm sending you out like sheep into a pack of wolves – so be shrewd as snakes[67] yet pure as doves. But also don't be naïve. The chances are that people will hale you before their courts[68] or even flog you in their

---

63   *2 Kings* 17:24-41.
64   *Jeremiah* 50:6.
65   *Deuteronomy* 25:4.
66   *Deuteronomy* 32:32; *Isaiah* 1:10; *Lamentations* 4:6; *Ezekiel* 16:46-57.
67   *Genesis* 3:1.
68   *Deuteronomy* 16:18.

congregations. You will be taken to stand in front of kings and princes, for my sake, in order to be witnesses to them and to the nations. But when you are handed over don't anguish about what you're going to say or how you're going to say it. You'll be given the words you need at the time you need them.[69] After all, it's not so much you who are speaking but the Spirit of your Father speaking through you. But brother will betray brother even to death, and a father his child, and children will rebel against their parents and have them put to death. Everyone will hate you because of my name, but whoever holds out to the end will be saved. If you're persecuted in one city, flee to another. You can be sure you won't have made the rounds of all the cities of Israel by the time the Son of Man comes.[70]

"The disciple doesn't rule over his teacher and neither does a servant rule over his master. It's enough for the disciple to be *like* his teacher or the servant *like* his master. If they've already called the master of the house בַּעַל זְבוּב - which in English means 'Lord of the Flies'[71] - what worse can they say about the members of his household? So don't be afraid of them.

"There's nothing hidden but won't be revealed, no hiding place so secret it won't be found. Whatever I say to you in the nighttime, speak in the daylight; and whatever your ears have heard, shout from the rooftops. Oh and don't be afraid of those who can kill the body - they can't kill the soul. Fear instead the one who can destroy both body and soul in Gehenna's unquenchable fire.[72] Don't two sparrows go for a penny? Yet not one of them can fall to the ground without your Father knowing.[73] The truth is that even the hairs on your head are numbered. So don't be afraid - you're worth a lot more than sparrows.

"Whoever acknowledges me in front of other people will I acknowledge before my Father in Heaven. But whoever denies me in front of other people will I deny before my Father in Heaven.[74] Don't have it in your mind that I've come to blanket the world in peace. My coming doesn't bring peace, but a sword. What I mean is that because of me a

---

69   *Exodus* 4:12.
70   *Daniel* 7:13.
71   *2 Kings* 1:2-3, 6, 16.
72   *Psalms* 34:9, 89:7; *Isaiah* 8:13-14.
73   *Cf.* W. Shakespeare, *Hamlet* 5.2.219-220.
74   *1 Samuel* 2:30.

man is set against his father and a daughter against her mother and a daughter-in-law against her mother-in-law, such that a man's enemies are those of his own household.[75] Whoever cares for father or mother more than me is not worthy of me and whoever cares for son or daughter more than me is not worthy of me.[76] Whoever will not bear her cross and follow after me is not worthy of me. Whoever treasures her life in this world will lose it, but whoever loses her life for my sake will gain it, even life that cannot be lost.

"Whoever receives you receives me and whoever receives me receives him who sent me. Whoever receives a prophet as a prophet will have a prophet's reward[77] and whoever receives a righteous man as a righteous man will have a righteous man's reward. And what if someone gives just a cup of cold water to one of these little ones because he is my disciple? I'm telling you, he won't lose his reward."

11

Once Yeshua had given these instructions to his disciples, he left to teach and preach in his own cities. Now John, still bound in prison, heard about the Messiah's deeds and sent his own disciples to ask Yeshua, "Are you the one who is to come or should we be waiting for someone else?"

"When you go back to John tell him what you've seen and heard – that the blind see again, the crippled walk, lepers are cleansed, the deaf hear, the dead are raised and the poor have the good news preached to them[78] – and blessed is he who is not offended by me."

Continuing on his way, Yeshua began to talk to the crowd about John, "What did you go out to the wilderness to see? A reed shaken by the wind? But tell me, why did you go? Were you hoping to see some spectacle? Maybe someone wearing haute couture? Hardly – those people live in kings' palaces. Tell me, you went to see a prophet, didn't

---

75   *Micah* 7:6.
76   *Deuteronomy* 33:9; *Exodus* 33:26-29.
77   *1 Kings* 17:8-24; *2 Kings* 4:8-37.
78   *Isaiah* 35:5, 61:1-2.

you? And indeed you saw not just a prophet but much more than a prophet, because John is the very one of whom it was written,

> Watch! I am sending my messenger out
> before your appearing,
> to prepare your way ahead of you.[79]

"Listen to this truth: no one greater than John the Baptizer has yet been born of women. Even so, the least one in the kingdom of Heaven is greater than he.[80] From John's days until now people had to force their way into the kingdom of Heaven, and zealous people have indeed grabbed hold of it. That's because all the prophets and the Law prophesied until John. But if you are able to take it in, this man is Elijah, who shall come.[81] Whoever has ears, let him hear. But what can I compare this people to? It's like children in the marketplace calling out to one another and saying,

> 'We played the flute for you but you didn't dance;
> we sang a dirge but you didn't mourn.'

"John came neither eating nor drinking and they said, 'He's demon-possessed.' And now the Son of Man comes both eating and drinking and they say, 'Look! There's a glutton and a drunk, a friend of users, cheaters, six-time losers.'[82] Yet wisdom is justified by her deeds."

Then Yeshua began to reproach the cities where so many of his miracles were performed, because they refused to turn from their ways. "Alas for you, Chorazin, alas for you, Bethsaida. If the mighty deeds done in you had been done in Tyre and Sidon they would've long since repented in sackcloth and ashes.[83] I tell you that Tyre and Sidon will better endure the Day of Judgment than you. And you, Capernaum, do you think you'll be exalted to Heaven?[84] No, I say you'll be cast down to the underworld. If the great miracles performed in you had been

---

79   *Exodus* 23:20; *Malachi* 3:1.
80   *Zechariah* 12:8.
81   *Malachi* 4:5-6.
82   *Cf.* B. Dylan, *Subterranean Homesick Blues* (1965).
83   *Isaiah* 23; *Ezekiel* 26-28; *Amos* 1:9-10; *Jonah* 3:6.
84   *Isaiah* 14:13-14.

performed in Sodom it would be standing to this day. And so I tell you that Sodom will have an easier time of it in the Day of Judgment than you will.[85]

"I praise you, Father, Lord of Heaven and Earth, because you've hidden these things from the wise and learned but revealed them to children - for so it pleased you. All things have been given me by my Father. No one has known the Son except the Father and no one has known the Father except the Son, and those to whom the Son may wish to reveal him.

> "Come unto me, all you that labor and are heavy laden,
>   and I will give you rest.
> Take my yoke[86] upon you, and learn of me;
>   for I am meek and lowly in heart:[87]
> and you shall find rest unto your souls.[88]
>   For my yoke is easy,
> And my burden is light."

12

One Sabbath Yeshua happened to walk through some grain fields. Since his disciples were hungry, they started to pluck some of the ripe grain off the stalks. When the Pharisees saw this they said to Yeshua, "Look! Don't you see your disciples are violating the Sabbath laws?"

But he replied, "Don't you know what David and his soldiers did when they were hungry, how they went into the House of the Lord and ate the sanctified bread, something forbidden to David as well as his men but set aside for the priests alone?[89] Or maybe you haven't considered that according to the Law priests don't violate the Sabbath when performing their Temple duties?[90] What you're missing here is that

---

85 *Deuteronomy* 32:32; *Isaiah* 1:10; *Lamentations* 4:6; *Ezekiel* 16:46-57.
86 *Jeremiah* 2:20; *Lamentations* 3:27.
87 *Isaiah* 42:2-3; *Zechariah* 9:9.
88 *Jeremiah* 6:16.
89 *1 Samuel* 21:1-6; see *Leviticus* 24:8.
90 *Numbers* 28:9-10.

something greater than the Temple is in your presence. If you had only understood what these words mean – I want to see mercy, not sacrifice[91] – you wouldn't go blaming the guiltless, because the Son of Man is also Lord of the Sabbath."

Having crossed back into Galilee he entered one of the local synagogues. It chanced there was someone at worship that day whose hand had been withered by a wasting disease. Some of the leaders asked Yeshua, "Is it lawful to heal on the Sabbath?" – seeing if they could find something to charge him with.

But he answered them with another question, "Suppose you had a sheep and it fell into a pit on the Sabbath. Would you leave it there or lift it out to rescue? And how much more valuable people are than sheep! So yes, of course it's lawful to heal on the Sabbath."

Then he said to the man, "Stretch out your hand!" He did so and his hand returned to normal that very moment.

At that the Pharisees left the scene to plot against Yeshua, trying to figure out how they might kill him. But he knew their thoughts and departed, a large crowd following him. He healed all who came to him. But he also warned them not to reveal him openly to others, so that Isaiah's prophecy might be fulfilled,

> Behold the servant whom I've chosen, my beloved one,
> > in whom my soul is well pleased;
> I will put my Spirit upon him
> > and he will proclaim God's justice to the nations.
> He will not strive neither will he shout,
> > nor will anyone hear his voice in the town square.
> He won't so much as crush a bruised reed
> > or quench a smoldering wick
> until the day he emerges victorious in judgment.
> > And the nations will put their hope in his name.[92]

Then the people brought a blind man to him, one who was also demon-possessed and mute. But Yeshua healed him too, so that once dumb he now spoke, once blind he now saw. The crowd was pretty

---

91   *Hosea* 6:6.
92   *Isaiah* 42:1-4.

much beside itself and said as one, "Can this be anyone *other* than the Son of David?"

But when the Pharisees heard that they said, "He couldn't cast out demons unless he did so with the power of Beelzebub, the Prince of Demons."

Knowing their thoughts Yeshua told them, "Every kingdom divided against itself must fall and any city or household divided against itself cannot stand. So if Satan casts out Satan he is divided against himself. Why then does his kingdom still survive? And if I cast out demons by the power of Beelzebub then by whose power do your sons cast them out? Therefore they will be your judges. But if I am casting out demons by the Spirit of God, then be sure that the kingdom of God has come upon you.

"Think about it: how can anyone enter into a strong man's home and snatch his goods unless he first binds the strong man? Once he does that he can freely steal everything the man has. Whoever isn't with me is against me and whoever doesn't gather with me scatters. That's why I say that every sin or cursing word will be forgiven people except for blasphemy against the Spirit – that will never be forgiven. So if anyone speaks a word against the Son of Man it will be forgiven him. But if anyone should slander the Holy Spirit he will not be forgiven it, neither in this age nor the age to come.

"Either make the tree good and its fruit good or the tree rotten and its fruit rotten, because a tree is known by its fruit. You serpent's brood – how can you, being evil, say anything good? The mouth speaks whatever flows in abundance from the heart. Therefore a good man brings forth good things from the good stored within him, but an evil man evil from his wicked storehouse. I tell you that at the Judgment Day people will have to answer for every idle word they speak – because by your words you will be justified and by your words condemned."

Some of the scribes and Pharisees responded, "Teacher, we want to see a sign from you."

"A wicked and adulterous people require a sign, but no sign will be given it save the sign of Jonah the prophet. Just as Jonah was in the belly of the sea-monster three days and three nights[93] so too will the Son

---

93 *Jonah* 1:17.

of Man be in the depths of Sheol three days and three nights.[94] The men of Nineveh will stand up in judgment against this people and condemn it, because *they* turned from their ways at the preaching of Jonah and, I assure you, there is more than Jonah here. The Queen of Sheba will also rise up in judgment against this people and condemn it, because she came from the far ends of the Earth to hear Solomon's wisdom[95] and, again, one greater than Solomon is here.

"When the unclean spirit leaves someone it wanders about in dry places seeking a place to rest, but doesn't find it. He then says to himself, 'I will return to the home I left.' When he gets there he finds the place empty, swept clean and fit for habitation. He next grabs seven other spirits even filthier than he and they take up residence there – and that man ends up in worse shape than when he started. So it will be with this wicked people."

While he was still speaking to the crowd, his mother and brothers stood outside, hoping to catch a word with him. Someone came and told Yeshua, "Your mother and your brothers are standing outside, wanting to speak to you."

"Who is my mother and who are my brothers?" Stretching his hand out to his followers he said, "Look! These are my mother and my brothers! For whoever does the will of my Father in Heaven, he is my brother and sister and mother."

13

Later that day Yeshua left the house and taught by the sea. But the crowds gathering around him were so large that he had to get into a small boat, push a bit offshore and teach them from there while the people stood on the beach to listen. He spoke to them of many things – but he did so by way of parables, analogies and similes, such as this one:

"A man went out to sow seeds. As he sowed some of the seeds fell alongside the road, where birds swooped down and snatched them away for food. Some other of the seeds fell on rocky ground, where the soil

---

94   *Jonah* 2:2.
95   *1 Kings* 10:1-13.

was thin at best. Those seeds sprouted too quickly because there was no depth to the soil. So once the sun had risen and scorched the plants with its heat they withered and died for lack of roots. Yet some other seeds fell among the thorns and thistles and these grew up strangled. But some of the seeds fell on rich soil and grew to yield fruit, some 30, some 60 and some even 100 times as much as others. May whoever has ears hear what I say."

Afterwards his disciples said to him, "Why do you speak to them in parables?"

"You have the benefit of knowing the secrets of the kingdom of Heaven, but that knowledge hasn't been given to them. It follows that whoever has, to him more will be given, even to the point of overflowing; while whoever lacks, even that which he has will be taken away. That's why I speak to them in stories and proverbs – because even though they see, they don't perceive and even though they hear, they don't take it in and therefore don't understand. And so Isaiah's prophecy is being fulfilled in them,

> You will hear with the ear but not understand
> > and see with the eyes but not comprehend.
> For the caul has fattened around this people's heart,
> > their ears grown heavy of hearing,
> their eyes shut to sight –
> > lest they see with their eyes
> and hear with their ears
> > and understand in their heart
> and turn to me and be healed.[96]

But blessed are your eyes because they see and your ears because they hear.[97] I tell you truly that many prophets and just men longed to see what you see and hear what you hear, but did not.

---

96   *Isaiah* 6:9-10.
97   *Proverbs* 20:12.

"Listen therefore while I explain the tale of the sower. If anyone hears the message of the kingdom but doesn't let it penetrate, the Wicked One comes and snatches away what had been sown in his heart. He's like the seeds by the roadside. And then there are people who hear the word and receive it eagerly with joy. But that's only for the time being, because they aren't very deep inside. As soon as they face pain or persecution for the sake of the gospel they get offended and fall away. So they're like the seeds that fell on rocky ground. And what about the seeds that fell among the thorns and thistles? That's a portrait of people who hear the gospel but let the cares of ordinary life as well as the lure of riches crowd out the word, and thus they become unfruitful. And then of course there are people who hear the word and understand it. They are like seeds planted in good soil because they grow and mature and yield fruit for the kingdom, some of them 30 times as much as others, some 60 and some 100."

Then he gave them another illustration.

"The kingdom of Heaven is also like a man who planted healthy seeds in his tilled field. But while his workers were sleeping an enemy of his snuck in, sowed weeds among the planted grain and then left. When the wheat grew up so did the weeds that were mixed in the furrows. The landowner's workers came to him and said, 'Didn't you sow good seed in your field? How come it's now full of weeds?' He said to them, 'It's not your fault – some enemy of mine did this.' The workers asked, 'Do you want us to pull the weeds now?' But he said, 'No, you can't look into the seeds of time and say which will grow and which will not.[98] Just let them keep growing together until the harvest. Then I'll tell the reapers to gather the weeds first and bundle them up to be thoroughly burned, and only afterwards to harvest the wheat and bring it into my granary.'"

Again he explained things in another parable:

"The kingdom of Heaven is like a mustard seed that a man planted in fertile soil. As you know, it's the tiniest seed there is. But once it grows into a tree it's the greatest of them all, spreading wide its branches, welcoming the birds of the sky to build their nests."[99]

He also made this comparison:

"The kingdom of Heaven is like a bit of yeast a woman kneads into three large measures of flour, causing the whole loaf to rise."

---

98 *Ecclesiastes* 11:6; *cf.* W. Shakespeare, *Macbeth* 1.3.58-59.
99 *Ezekiel* 17:23, 31:6; *Daniel* 4:10-12, 20-22.

Thus spoke Yeshua in figurative form, speaking to the masses by way of illustrations alone. And so the prophet's word was fulfilled,

> I will open my mouth in parables
> and tell of things hidden
> since the foundation of the world.[100]

Leaving the crowds behind, he returned to the household then hosting him. His disciples gathered around him again and asked him to explain the tale of the weeds in the field. So he said:

"The Son of Man is the one who sowed good seeds in the field; the field is the world itself; and the seeds are the children of the kingdom. But the Devil is the sower's enemy and the weeds are *his* children. Therefore the harvest is the end of all time and the harvesters the angels of God. Just as the weeds were gathered and burned with fire so it will be at the Last Judgment: the Son of Man will send his angels to gather out from his kingdom the lawless as well as any who cause others to fall. They will toss them into a fiery furnace, where there will be wailing and gnashing of teeth. But then those whom God has justified will shine forth like the sun in the kingdom of their Father. Let whoever has ears hear.

"And the kingdom of Heaven is also like treasure buried in a field. If someone knew it was hidden there he would in sheer joy take everything he owned to the marketplace, sell it and go buy that land.

"Again, if you want to understand the kingdom of Heaven think of a jeweler on the watch for precious pearls. If he finds one perfect pearl he'll trade away his others just to buy it.

"I can also compare the kingdom of Heaven to a dragnet cast into the sea, where it snags every type of fish. Once it's pulled up and hauled to shore the fishermen sit down to gather the good fish into their baskets and toss the rotten aside. That's what will happen at the end of the age when the angels separate the evil ones from the midst of the righteous and toss them into a fiery furnace - there will be wailing and gnashing of teeth."

Then Yeshua asked them, "Do you understand everything I've said?"

"Yes!"

"So it is that anyone schooled in the teachings of the kingdom is like a

---

100   *Psalms* 78:2.

homeowner who reaches into his treasure box and brings out good things old and good things new."

Once he had finished sharing these lessons Yeshua headed back to his childhood village, where he taught the people in their synagogue, leaving them so perplexed and amazed that they questioned themselves, "Where did he get all this wisdom and power? Isn't he just the local builder's son? And isn't that his mother Mary? And aren't those his brothers Jacob and Joseph and Simon and Judas? And aren't his sisters all right here with us? Just where did he get all this?" And they found him deeply offensive.

But Yeshua said to them, "It seems that a prophet is honored everywhere except in his own town and by his own family." So because of their lack of faith he couldn't do much for them in the way of miracles.

14

During this same time Herod the Tetrarch of Judea heard the news about Yeshua and said to his servants, "This man must be John the Baptist risen from the dead and that's why he has the power to work such miracles!"

Herod, you see, had arrested John and thrown him into prison at the behest of his half-brother Philip's ex-wife Herodias, whom he took and married even though John had told him repeatedly, "You cannot have that woman."[101]

Herod was willing to kill John for her sake but was also afraid of the people, because they held John to be a prophet. When Herod's birthday

---

101 *Leviticus* 18:16.

celebration came around, however, Herodias sent her teenage daughter in to dance among the guests. The girl pleased Herod, so much so that he swore her a gift of anything her heart desired. But having been put up to the whole thing by her mother, she demanded of Herod – "Give me now the head of John the Baptist on a silver platter."

Herod was struck to the heart at this, but he gave in to her because he'd sworn an oath with everyone around the banquet table watching and listening. Dispatching his men, he therefore had John beheaded in the prison. The head was brought up on a platter, given to the girl, and she in turn gave it to her mother. Then John's disciples came and asked for his corpse, which they duly buried, afterwards coming to inform Yeshua.

When Yeshua heard what had happened he left that region by boat, heading toward a wilderness area where he could be alone. But when the people heard he had gone they left the city and followed in his direction on foot. When he got there he found a great multitude already waiting for him. He felt compassion for them and healed any that were sick. But by the time mid-afternoon rolled around his disciples told him, "We're in a desert place and the time is now far gone – send the crowd back to town so they can try to buy some food for themselves before the markets close."

"There's no need for them to go. Just give them what you have."

"We don't have anything here except five loaves of bread and two fish."

"Bring me whatever you've got."

He then made the people sit down on the grass. Having taken the five loaves and two fish in his hands he lifted his eyes to Heaven and blessed the food, breaking and passing it to his disciples, who then distributed it to the people. There were around five thousand men there, plus women and children, and they all ate and were satisfied – yet they still had enough leftovers to fill twelve baskets.[102]

Right after that Yeshua pressed his men to get into the boat and go ahead of him to the opposite shore while he stayed behind to disperse the people. Once the crowd had gone he went up the mountain to pray. When night fell he was there alone. By that time the boat was pretty far distant from the land, yet struggling against a contrary wind with the waves beating harshly against it. They were still out there rowing around 4 or 5 in the morning when Yeshua came striding toward them

---

102   *2 Kings* 4:42-44.

on the surface of the sea. When the disciples saw him they screamed in terror, frightened to death, thinking they saw a ghost. But right away Yeshua called out to them, "Chill! It's just me. Nothing to be scared about."

Peter shouted back, "Lord, if it's really you, command me to come to you on the water."

"Come!"

Getting out of the boat Peter walked on the water to Yeshua – but then he focused on the strength of the wind and took fright, at which point he lost his footing and began to sink, crying out, "Lord, save me!"

Instantly Yeshua reaching out, grabbed Peter's hand and lifted him back up – "What little faith you have! Why did you think twice?"

Once they were both back in boat the wind softened. The men in the boat worshipped him, saying "Truly you are the Son of God!"

Having finally crossed the sea they landed in the district of Gennesaret. When the local people recognized him they sent around to their neighbors to bring all the sick to him, praying they might just touch the hem of his garment. And as many as touched were fully healed.

15

After this, certain Pharisees and scribes came to Yeshua from Jerusalem and asked him, "How is it your disciples don't follow the traditions the forefathers handed down? Don't you know your disciples don't wash their hands before they sit down to a meal?"

"How is it you use your *own* traditions as a way to ignore the commandment of God? For example, God told you to honor your father and your mother[103] and whoever speaks evil to his parents must surely die.[104] But you say 'anyone is free of his duty to support his parents if he tells them that whatever he would've given them has already been dedicated to the Temple.' You thereby nullify God's commandment with your own. What hypocrites! Isaiah had it right about you when he said,

---

103 *Exodus* 20:12; *Deuteronomy* 5:16.
104 *Exodus* 21:7.

> This people honors me with their lips
>> but their heart is far from me.
> It's useless for them to worship me as long as they
>> teach as doctrine the commandments of men."[105]

Summoning the mass he said, "Listen and learn. It isn't what people take into their mouths that makes them unclean, it's what comes out of them."

His disciples said, "Don't you realize you've offended the Pharisees by saying that?"

"Any plant my Father in Heaven hasn't planted[106] will be torn up by the roots. Let them be – they are blind guides guiding the blind and if the blind lead the blind they'll both fall into a ditch."

But when Peter asked him to explain his saying Yeshua exclaimed, "You still don't get the message? Doesn't everyone know that the food you put in your mouth passes through the system and in due course is flushed down the toilet? But whatever is spoken by the mouth has its seed in the heart and *that's* where you find things that contaminate people – because out of the heart come wicked thoughts, murders, adulteries, perversions, thefts, perjuries, slanders. Those are the things to be worried about, not whether someone washes his hands before he eats."

Withdrawing from that place Yeshua moved up to southern Lebanon, to the coasts of Tyre and Sidon. A local Canaanite woman met up with him and cried out, "Lord, have mercy on me, you Son of David – my daughter is horribly tormented by demons!"

He ignored her.

His disciples urged, "Send her away!   She keeps following us and screaming."

Finally Yeshua said to the woman, "I've been sent to the lost sheep of the House of Israel, none others."

She persisted, falling in worship before him and begging, "Lord, help me!"

"But it would be wrong for me to take bread from the children's mouths and throw it to the little dogs."

"True Lord, but even dogs are allowed to eat scraps that fall from the

---

105 *Isaiah* 29:13.
106 *Isaiah* 60:21, 61:3.

master's table."

"O woman, you have great faith! Let it be to you as you wish." And her daughter was healed that very hour.

Moving on from there Yeshua came back to the Sea of Galilee, where he set himself a place on the hillside to continue his teaching. A great multitude came, bringing with them people who were lame or blind or deformed or mute, along with many others like them, laying them before Yeshua's feet. And he healed them all, leaving the crowd speechless in their amazement when they saw the dumb speak, the crooked go straight, the lame walk and the blind see.[107] And they gave glory to the God of Israel.

Yeshua then called his disciples to himself and said, "I am moved in my heart for these people because they've already stayed with me for three days and haven't gotten anything to eat. I don't want them starving lest they faint dead away on the road home."

"Where are we supposed to get food in this wilderness to feed such a large crowd?"

"How much bread do you have?"

"Seven loaves and a couple of fish."

Having ordered the people to sit down on the ground he took the seven loaves and the few fish and once he had said grace he broke and gave the food to his disciples, who then gave it to the crowd. Everyone ate and was full, yet they still had seven baskets full of crumbs and broken pieces left over. That was after four thousand men had finished eating – and we're not even counting the women and children. So having dismissed the multitude they embarked and sailed over to the shores of Magdala.

16

Once there, both the Pharisees and Sadducees approached to test him, demanding he show them a sign from Heaven.

But he said, "You have a saying, 'red sky at night, sailor's delight; red sky at morning, sailor take warning.' How is it you can read the signs in the sky but can't read the signs of the times? A wicked and adulterous people seeks a sign, but no sign will be given it other than the sign of Jo-

---

107 *Isaiah* 35:5-6.

nah." So they left him and went away.

Now it happened that when they crossed over on the boat his disciples had forgotten to take any bread with them. But Yeshua said to them, "See that you watch out for the leaven of the Pharisees and Sadducees." So they argued among themselves about what he meant, supposing it was because they hadn't brought any bread.

Knowing what they were thinking Yeshua asked, "What are you faithless people fighting about? You think I'm speaking about the bread you didn't bring along? Do you *still* not get it? Is it really possible you've already forgotten about the five loaves that fed five thousand, or how many basketsful were left over? Or about the seven loaves and the four thousand and how many basketsful you had left then? Don't you see I'm not talking about bread but about the leaven of the Pharisees and Sadducees?"

Then they understood he wasn't telling them to watch out for yeast that makes bread rise but to beware of the leavening effects of the teaching of the Pharisees and Sadducees.

When Yeshua came next to the region around Caesarea Philippi he asked his disciples, "Who do people say the Son of Man is?"

"Some say John the Baptist, others say Elijah, while some say Jeremiah or one of the other prophets."

"Yes but *you*, who do you say I am?"

Simon Peter said, "You are the Messiah, the Son of the living God."

"Blessed are you, Simon, son of Jonah, because flesh and blood did not reveal this to you but my Father which is in Heaven. People have nicknamed you 'the Rock' – well, I tell you I will build my faithful people on a foundation of living stones so that the very gates of Hell[108] will not prevail against it. And I will give you the keys of the kingdom of Heaven, such that whatever you prohibit on Earth will be judged so in Heaven and whatever you rule lawful on Earth will be judged so in Heaven." Then he ordered the disciples not to tell anyone he was the Messiah.

At that point Yeshua began to explain to his disciples how he needed to go to Jerusalem – where he would suffer many things at the hands of the elders, the chief priests and the scribes and be killed, yet be raised up on the third day.

But on hearing this Peter reproached him, "God forbid! That will never happen to you!"

---

108 *Isaiah* 38:10.

"Get behind me, Tempter! You're a stumbling stone to me - you have your mind set on the things that men care about, not on God's concerns."

Then he said to his disciples, "If anyone wants to come after me let him leave his own path, take up his cross and follow me. Whoever wishes to preserve his life will lose it but whoever lets go his life for my sake will find it. What good does it do anyone to gain the whole world but lose his soul? Or what would anyone give in exchange for his soul?[109] But the Son of Man will come in the glory of his Father together with his angels and repay each person according to what he has done. And I tell you in truth, some of those standing here now will not taste death until they see the Son of Man coming in his kingly power."

17

Six days later Yeshua took Peter, Jacob and his brother John up to a high mountain. They were by themselves and Yeshua was transformed before them, his face as the sun in radiant brilliance, his clothes as if white light[110] - and not only that but Moses and Elijah appeared to them, conversing with Yeshua.

Peter said, "Lord, it's divine being here! Let me build three tabernacles in this place - one for Moses, one for Elijah and one just for you!"

But before he'd finished speaking a glowing cloud overshadowed them and a voice from within the cloud spoke, "This is my Son, whom I love. He pleases me greatly - listen to him!"[111]

When they heard that the disciples trembling fell down in fear. But taking hold of them Yeshua said, "Stand up, don't be afraid." Slowly raising their eyes they saw no one else, save Yeshua.

Once they had descended the mountain Yeshua commanded them, "Don't tell anyone what you've seen until after the Son of Man is raised from the dead."

But the disciples asked him, "Why then do the scribes say Elijah must come beforehand?"

---

109 *Psalms* 48:7-9.
110 *Exodus* 34:29-35.
111 *Exodus* 24:15-18.

"Indeed, Elijah must come and reconcile everything.[112]   But I'm telling you Elijah has already come – yet they didn't recognize him and instead did whatever they wanted to him. So too the Son of Man will suffer at their hands."   Then the disciples understood he was speaking about John the Baptist.

As they approached the multitude a man came forward and knelt down before Yeshua saying, "Lord, have mercy on my son – he's tormented all the time but worst of all when the moon is full. He's overtaken, collapses in fits, often tumbling into a fire or if not there, then a river or a lake. I carried him to your disciples but they couldn't do a thing to help him."

"What a twisted and faithless people this is! How long do I have to stay here and put up with you? But bring the boy to me."

Yeshua then took charge of the demon, casting him out and healing the boy that very moment. His disciples came up to him afterwards and asked, privately, "What went wrong? Why couldn't we cast him out?"

"It's because you have such little faith – if you had but the faith of a tiny mustard seed you could tell this mountain 'Move from here to there!' and it would. In truth, nothing would be impossible to you. Even so, to cast out this particular type of demon you'd need to fast and pray."

When they had gathered around him Yeshua said to his disciples, "The Son of Man will soon be delivered into the hands of men. They will kill him, but he will be raised up on the third day." And hearing this they were deeply distressed.

When they arrived back in Capernaum the people responsible for collecting annual Temple dues came up to Peter and said, "Your Teacher hasn't paid the half-shekel he owes."[113]

"No way – I'm sure he has!"

When Peter got back to the house but before he could speak Yeshua asked him, "What do you think, Simon – do the kings of the Earth collect dues and taxes from their children or from strangers?"

"From strangers."

"Quite right – and in that case the children are free. However, we don't want to offend anyone, so go down to the sea and cast a line. Take the first fish you hook, open its mouth and there you'll find a silver shekel. Give it to them to cover both your dues and mine."

---

112   *Malachi* 4:26.
113   *Exodus* 30:11-16; *2 Kings* 12:4; *2 Chronicles* 24:6, 9.

18

About that time the disciples asked Yeshua, "How can we tell who is the greatest in the kingdom of Heaven?"

Setting a little child in their midst he said, "Unless you turn from your ways and become as children there's no way you'll enter the kingdom of Heaven. And whoever accepts a lower place in life, like this child, will be greatest in the kingdom of Heaven. Whoever receives one such child in my name receives me. But whoever causes one of these little ones who believe in me to trip and fall would've been better off if a millstone had been hung around his neck and he were drowned in the open sea - yes, there are bound to be things that trip people up and alas for the world when they come - but you don't want to be the one who does the tripping. That's why I said earlier that if your hand or your foot is causing you to stumble you're better chopping it off and tossing it away. Isn't it better to suffer through life crippled or lame than be thrown whole to the flames of Moloch?

"And be sure you don't look down your nose at one of these little ones - believe me when I tell you their guardian angels stand watch for them before the face of my Father in Heaven. The Son of Man has come to save the lost, so think about this - if a man had 100 sheep and one were to wander off, don't you think he'd leave the 99 behind and seek out the lost one? And then when he finds it, won't he rejoice over it more than all the 99 that didn't wander off? Just so, it's my Father's will that none of these little ones be lost.

"And how should you deal with each other? Suppose your brother does you wrong - take it up directly with him alone.[114] If you can straighten things out, then you've won your brother back again. But if he won't listen to you take one or two of your friends along so you can prove what happened by the word of two or three witnesses.[115] If he also runs roughshod over them then give him still another chance by bringing the matter before the whole congregation. Yet if he defies the whole group you have no choice but to treat him no better than a renegade or a Goy.

---

114 *Leviticus* 19:17.
115 *Deuteronomy* 19:15.

"Whatever you collectively prohibit on Earth will be what is prohibited in Heaven, as will whatever you judge to be permitted. And so I tell you that if any two of you are of one mind concerning the things you pray for, it will be granted them by my Father in Heaven – because wherever two or three of you gather together in my name, I am there in your midst."

Then Peter said to him, "How many times do I have to put up with my brother when he constantly does me wrong? Maybe as many as seven times?"[116]

"No, not just seven times – but 70 times seven.[117]   In that way the kingdom of Heaven is like an earthly king who wanted to settle accounts with his servants. As he began reconciling the amounts they brought someone in who owed the king 10,000 talents – like a billion dollars.[118] Since there was no way he could pay the money back the king ordered him sold into slavery along with his wife and his children. Likewise he ordered the man's property to be liquidated and all the proceeds handed over. But the servant fell prostrate at the king's feet, begging him, 'Lord, in your longsuffering mercy be patient with me and I will pay you back.' The king was moved with compassion for his servant, forgiving and releasing him from all his debts.

"But that servant then went out and found a fellow servant who owed him 100 denarii – let's call it a few hundred dollars – and grabbed him by the throat, choking him and saying 'pay up!' Then that fellow servant fell before him and begged him, 'In your longsuffering mercy be patient with me and I will pay you back.' But he refused and, worse still, had him thrown into debtors' prison until he could find a way to pay back the last penny. When the other servants learned of this they were deeply grieved and reported to the master all that had taken place. Then the king summoned the man and said, 'You wicked servant! You begged my forgiveness and I absolved you of all your debts – how could you not forgive your fellow servant the same?' And so the king turned him over to the torturers, until payment was made. The same will happen to you if you don't each forgive one another's sins from the heart."

---

116   *Proverbs* 24:16.
117   *Genesis* 4:24.
118   *Cf. Esther* 3:9.

19

When Yeshua had finished these teachings he left Galilee and came to that part of Judea that lay beyond the Jordan River. A great multitude followed him and he healed them there.

Some Pharisees came to test him and asked, "Is it lawful for someone to divorce his wife for any reason he comes up with?"

"Haven't you read that at the outset God created the human race both male and female?[119] That's why a man leaves his father and mother and is physically joined to his wife, the two uniting as one flesh.[120] In other words, they are no longer two but one. So people should not separate those whom God has yoked together."

"But why then did Moses command that a man should give his wife written notice of divorce when he releases her?"[121]

"Moses allowed you that because your hearts were still hardened, but that's not the way things were from the beginning. What I'm saying to you is that if someone divorces his wife for any reason other than her having sex with someone else and then marries another, he's committing adultery too."

His disciples were perplexed.

"If that's the way things are then we're better off not getting married at all!"

"I'm not at all saying you shouldn't get married. But if you prefer to remain single, you're also free to do so. Look, some men have no choice in the matter because they've been castrated or are just incapable of sex, but others have chosen to abstain from marriage for the sake of their labors for the kingdom of Heaven. So if you feel called to be celibate, be celibate."

Thereafter the people brought their children to him, seeking him to lay hands on and pray for them. But when the disciples blocked them Yeshua said, "Don't stop them but let them come to me, for the kingdom of Heaven is made of just such as these." Then having laid hands on them, he departed.

---

119   *Genesis 1:27, 5:2.*
120   *Genesis 2:24.*
121   *Deuteronomy 24:1.*

Another man came to him and asked, "Teacher, what good deed should I do to lay hold of life that endures?"

"What prompts you to come to *me* to learn what is good? Isn't only the One good? But if you're seeking life without end, well then of course you need to guard the commandments."

"Which ones?"

"Don't murder. Don't commit adultery. Don't steal. Don't lie on the witness stand. Honor your father and your mother.[122] And, of course, Love your neighbor as yourself."[123]

"I've kept all those! Is there anything else I need to do?"

"If you would be wholly complete sell all your goods and give the money to the poor. Believe me, you'll have treasure in Heaven. And then come, follow me." But when he heard that last commandment the young man shuffled away in grief, because he had vast wealth.

Seeing this Yeshua told his disciples, "The fact is, it's difficult for someone burdened with riches to enter the kingdom of Heaven. A rich man would find it easier to thread a rope through the eye of a needle than to enter the kingdom of God."

That totally shocked the disciples.

"So who *can* be saved??"

"Well," he said, fixing his eyes on them, "God can do what seems impossible to men."

Peter piped up, "Look, we've given up *everything* to follow you! So where do we stand?"

"You needn't worry. Because you've kept close to me all along the way you will be with the Son of Man in the resurrection. And when he sits on his throne in glory you will sit on your twelve thrones, judging the twelve tribes of Israel.[124] Even now, anyone who has left his home or his brothers or his sisters or his father or his mother or his children or his lands for my name's sake will receive 100 times as much back – and inherit eternal life. But know this: many who are now in first place will be last and many in last place first.

---

122 *Exodus* 20:12-16; *Deuteronomy* 5:16-20.
123 *Leviticus* 19:18.
124 *Cf. Daniel* 7:9-14, 22, 27.

20

"That's why the kingdom of Heaven can be compared to a landowner who went out at 6:00 AM to hire workers for his vineyard. After negotiating with the workers to pay them a silver denarius as their day's wage he sent them out to the field. But around 9:00 AM he saw a group of others hanging out in the town square, still looking for work. He said to them, 'If you're willing to go work in my vineyard I'll pay you a fair wage.' And so they agreed. He did the same again when he passed through the square, finding unemployed workers at noon and at 3:00 PM. He even came across some men standing idle at 5:00 PM.

Amazed at them he asked, 'What's the matter with you, hanging around all day and not working?'

'We'd have been happy to work but no one hired us.'

'Head out to my vineyard in that case!'

"When evening came the landowner asked his foreman to call the workers in and pay them each their wages, starting with the last group and ending with the first. The men who came at the 11th hour each received a silver denarius. Seeing this the men who had started work first thing in the morning figured they would be getting more – but when they were each paid a silver denarius as well they took to muttering against the landowner.

'Hey, these johnny-come-latelies only worked for an hour! But now they're getting paid the same as us even though we wore ourselves out working the whole day, plus which it was very hot out there!'

'Friends, are you accusing me of injustice? Didn't you negotiate with me for a denarius? Take what's yours and get out of here. It's in my heart to give these last men just as much as I gave you and yet you're telling me I can't do whatever I want with my own money? Are you envious of them just because I'm kind?'

So it is that the last will be first and the first will be last."

On the way up to Jerusalem Yeshua took the Twelve aside and told them, "It's time now for us to enter Jerusalem, where the Son of Man will be handed over to the chief priests and scribes, who will condemn him to death and turn him over to the heathen to be mocked, whipped and crucified – but on the third day he will be raised up."

At that point Jacob's and John's mother came to Yeshua, bringing her sons with her. She knelt before him seeking what he could do for them.

"What would you like me to do?"

"I want my boys should sit with you in your kingdom, one on the right and one on the left."

To her he said, "You have no idea what you're asking," and to them, "You think you can drink the cup[125] I'm about to drink?"

"We can!"

"You may well drink from my cup, but to sit at my right hand and my left? That's not mine to give except to those for whom my Father prepared it."

But when the other ten heard this they were furious with the two of them. So Yeshua called them all together and said, "You know that the goyische rulers oppress their own people, lording it over them, and their strong men are nothing but bullies. It has to be the opposite with you. If any of you wants to be high up let him become everyone's servant and if any of you wants to be first in rank let him become slave to the rest – just the way the Son of Man didn't come to be waited on but to serve, even to give his own life to pay the ransom for many."[126]

When they left Jericho a huge multitude came with them. Two blind men sitting by the side of the road heard Yeshua was passing by and shouted out, "Son of David, have mercy on us!"

People in the crowd told them to shut up, but that just made them shout all the more.

"LORD!! Son of David! Be merciful to us!"

At that Yeshua stopped and called to them, "What is it you wish of me?"

"Oh Lord – open our eyes!"

Touched by them he touched their eyes.

Instantly they saw, then followed him.

---

125 *Isaiah* 51:17; *Jeremiah* 25:17 ff; *Ezekiel* 23:3 ff.
126 *Isaiah* 52:13-53:12.

21

When they had drawn near Jerusalem, getting as far as the village of Beth-phage in the vicinity of Mount Olive, Yeshua sent out two disciples, directing them as follows: "Go into the village opposite you and right off you'll see a donkey tied up and her young colt alongside her.[127] Untie them both and bring them here to me. If anyone tries to stop you or asks what you think you're doing, just tell them 'the Lord needs these animals.'"

And so they went, all this happening in order that these words of the prophet might be fulfilled,

> Tell the daughter of Zion –
>   Watch how your king comes to you,
>   humbly, seated on a pack animal,
>   the mere colt of an ass."[128]

The disciples did as Yeshua had instructed them, leading both the donkey and her colt back. They spread their cloaks on the animals and Yeshua sat on the colt. Most of the multitude going with them spread their own cloaks along the road,[129] while others cut down branches from the trees and spread them in the road as well. And the whole crowd – those parading in front of Yeshua as well as those following behind – cried out singing,

> הוֹשִׁיעָה נָּא – which means Save us! – Son of David.
>   Blessed is he who comes in the name of the Lord,[130]
>   Hosanna in the highest!

When he entered Jerusalem the whole city was in turmoil, with people wondering aloud, "Who is this??" Some in the crowd said, "He's the prophet Yeshua, come out from Nazareth of Galilee."

Then Yeshua went straight to the Temple.[131] First he shoved out the

---

127 *Genesis* 49:11.
128 *Isaiah* 62:11; *Zechariah* 9:9; see *2 Samuel* 16:1-2.
129 *2 Kings* 9:13.
130 *Psalms* 118:25-26.
131 *Malachi* 3:1.

people who were using it as a marketplace to buy and sell their goods and then went after the people changing foreign currencies,[132] along with those who sold doves to be sacrificed,[133] turning their tables upside down and tossing their chairs into the street. He justified his actions with these quotations from Scripture:

My house will be called a house of prayer,[134]
yet now you've made it a den of thieves.[135]

But while he was in the Temple the blind and the lame came to him – and he healed them there.[136] When the chief priests and scribes saw the wonders he performed in the Temple and heard the little children crying out "Hosanna to the Son of David," they flew into a rage and demanded, "Aren't you listening to what these children are saying? How can you permit them to say such things?!"

"Yes, of course I hear them, but haven't you read in the Psalms that I've prepared for myself praise to come from the mouths of babes and sucklings?"[137] Then leaving them he went out to the city of Bethany, where he spent the night sleeping in a courtyard.

On his way back to the city early the next morning Yeshua was hungry. Spying a lone fig tree ahead on the road he found when he got to it that in fact it only had leaves on it.[138] So he said, "You'll never grow fruit again!" And indeed, right away the fig tree withered.

When the disciples saw this they were stunned.

"Did you see how the tree dried right up?"

"Believe me, if you have faith and don't waiver you can not only do the same to a fig tree but even say to this mountain, 'be ripped from the ground and tossed to the sea,' and it will happen. Indeed, if you pray believing, then anything you ask you'll receive."

Once he had gotten to the Temple the chief priests and elders of the people approached him while he was teaching and asked, "Where did you get the authority to do the things you're doing?"

---

132 *Exodus* 30:13.
133 *Leviticus* 5:7, 12:8.
134 *Isaiah* 56:7.
135 *Jeremiah* 7:11.
136 *2 Samuel* 5:8.
137 *Psalms* 8:3.
138 *Micah* 7:1.

"Let me first ask you a question and if you answer it then I'll answer you. Where did John get his authority to baptize, from Heaven or from men?"

That created a problem because even though they debated back and forth among themselves what to answer, they couldn't agree. Their reasoning was, "Well, if we say 'from Heaven' he'll just ask us, 'so why didn't you believe him?' But if we say 'from men' then we'll have to deal with the crowd and we're afraid of them because they think John was a prophet." So they decided to simply tell Yeshua they didn't know the answer.

So he said, "Then I can't explain to you where I get the authority to do what I do either. But let me get your thoughts about something else. There was a man who had two children and he asked the first one, 'Son, would you mind going out to the vineyard today to do some work?' But the kid said, 'No, I don't feel like it.' However, later on he had regrets, changed his mind and went out to work. In the meantime the man had asked his second child the same thing and this boy said, 'Yes sir!' But he didn't do a thing. Tell me then, which of these two did what his father asked?"

"The first, of course."

"That's why gamblers and whores will enter the kingdom of God ahead of you, because John came to you showing the way of righteousness[139] and you didn't believe him while the pimps and thieves did. Worse still, you did nothing even though you saw them trust John and turn from their ways.

"And listen to this allegory. A landlord planted a vineyard, installed a safety fence around it, dug the foundations for a wine press, built a watchtower, let it out to some tenant farmers and started off on a journey.[140] When harvest time came around he sent his servants over to collect his rent in kind. But the tenants grabbed the servants and beat one, killed another and stoned the third. So this time he sent out yet more servants but they dealt with them the same way. Finally he sent them his own son saying, 'When they see my son they will hide their faces in shame.' But instead when the farmers saw him they said to themselves, 'This is the heir! Let's kill him right now[141] and take his inheritance.' Seizing him they dragged him outside the vineyard and murdered him. Just what do you think the lord of the vineyard will do to

---

139 *Proverbs* 8:20.
140 *Isaiah* 5:1 ff.
141 *Genesis* 37:20.

those men when he shows up at the vineyard?"

"He'll rain hellfire on those wicked men and let the vineyard out to other farmers, who will pay over to him his share of the harvest in due season."

"Then haven't you also read in the Scriptures where it says,

> The stone the builders rejected has now become
> the chief cornerstone of the building –
> a marvel done by the Lord, a wonder to our eyes?[142]

That's why I tell you the kingdom of God will be taken away from you and given to a people who will yield him its fruits in due season. Whoever stumbles on this rock will be broken in pieces and whomsoever it falls upon will be crushed."[143]

When the chief priests and Pharisees heard these parables and stories they knew he was speaking about them and though they sought a way to have him arrested, they also feared the people, who took him to be a prophet.

22

Yeshua continued speaking to them by way of comparisons and illustrations.

"I can liken the kingdom of Heaven to an earthly king who prepared a wedding feast for his son. He sent his servants out to help his invited guests travel to the wedding – but the invitees said they didn't want to come after all. So the king decided to give it another shot, summoning another group of trusted servants to tell the invited guests in the king's name – 'Look, I've prepared a midday feast for you and have already slaughtered the fatted oxen. Everything is ready, so come and dine!' But they ignored the king's messengers again, some heading to their own farms and others off to do business elsewhere.

"But some of them did worse, waylaying the king's servants and beating

---

142 *Psalms* 118:22-23; *Isaiah* 28:16.
143 *Isaiah* 8:14-15; *Daniel* 2:34-35, 44-45.

them to death. When he learned of this the king was beside himself with rage and sent soldiers out to destroy those murderous men and burn their city to the ground. That done, he summoned more of his servants and told them, 'The wedding feast is still ready but the people I invited were weighed in the balance and found wanting. Therefore go instead to the highways and by-ways, grab whomever you find and invite *them* to the wedding.' The servants rode out to spread the good news through each village and farm, gathering up all they could find, both sinners and saints, and thus filled up the wedding table.

"But when the king entered the banquet hall he noticed one of the guests didn't have on proper wedding attire. So he asked him, 'Friend, how did you get in here without being properly dressed?' The man had no answer. Then the king ordered his guards, 'Bind him hand and foot and cast him into outer darkness, where there will be wailing and gnashing of teeth[144] – for many are called but few are chosen.'"

The Pharisees then took counsel to figure how to entangle Yeshua in his own words. They first sent their pupils along with some of the Herodians to ask him, "Teacher, we know you are honest and sincere, teaching God's ways in truth, not worrying about what other people think or giving preference to one person over another. So give us your opinion – does the Law permit us to pay a poll-tax to Caesar or not?"

Yeshua saw the malice behind the question.

"I know you don't really have a question for me – you're just acting out a rôle here, tempting me. But show me the money."

They handed him a silver denarius.

"Whose image is that? And whose name's on the coin?"

"Caesar's."

"Well then give back to Caesar what's Caesar's and to God what's God's." They were dumbfounded when they heard that, and left.

That same day some Sadducees came to him. They don't believe there's any resurrection of the dead and therefore posed this query:

"Teacher, Moses taught us that if anyone dies childless his brother should marry the widow and thereby raise his brother's dead seed to life.[145] Well, there were once seven brothers living among us. The eldest got married but died childless, so his brother duly married the widow. The same thing hap-

---

144 *Zephaniah* 1:7-8.
145 *Deuteronomy* 25:5; see *Genesis* 38:8.

pened with him, then the third brother, then all the way down to the seventh. Once all seven brothers had died their wife died too. So tell us, when they are raised from the dead which of the seven will have her to wife?"

"It's no wonder you've fallen into heresy – you don't know the Scriptures or the power of God. Don't you know that in the life to come people don't marry but are like the heavenly angels? And is it possible you haven't read God's word to you concerning the resurrection of the dead – I am the God of Abraham and the God of Isaac and the God of Jacob[146] – therefore he is not the God of the dead but of the living."

When the multitude heard that teaching they were overjoyed, but when the Pharisees saw he had boxed in the Sadducees they gathered together and had an expert of their own, well-trained in Moses, test him with this question – "Teacher, what's a major commandment in the Law?"

"Thou shalt love the Lord your God with all thine heart, and with all thy soul, and with all thy mind.[147] That's the principal commandment. But the second is like it. Thou shalt love thy neighbor as thyself.[148] Everything in the Law and the Prophets depends on these two commandments."

With the Pharisees assembled around him Yeshua then asked them a question.

"Tell me what you think about the Messiah – whose son is he?"

"David's son."

"How then can David, inspired by the Spirit, call him lord? As he said,

> The Lord said to my lord,
>   'Sit down at my right hand
> until I lay your enemies
>   beneath your feet.'[149]

So how can Messiah be his son if David calls him 'lord'?"

No one had an answer for him – and after that exchange no one had the nerve to ask him another question.

---

146 *Exodus* 3:6, 15, 16.
147 *Deuteronomy* 6:5.
148 *Leviticus* 19:18.
149 *Psalms* 110:1.

23

Then Yeshua spoke to the crowd and his disciples together.

"The scribes and Pharisees sit in the chairman's seat left by Moses,[150] therefore heed and observe whatever instructions they give. But don't *do* the things they do, because they don't practice what they preach. Instead, they're content to load heavy cargos onto someone else's shoulders without lifting a finger to help them. Pretty much everything they do they do to be seen by others, like wearing Bible-verse wristbands[151] or lengthening the fringes of their prayer shawls.[152] They love it when they're seated at the head of the table, given the best seats at the synagogue, embraced in the town square and hailed as 'Reverend!' by other men. But I don't want you to revere one another. You have but one Teacher and you are all brothers. So don't name someone 'Papa' on Earth – you have but one Holy Father and *he's* in Heaven. And don't be made masters – you have but one Master, the Messiah. As I've told you, the greatest among you will be your servant and whoever exalts himself will be brought low, while whoever humbles himself will be lifted on high.[153]

"But woe to you, scribes and Pharisees, hypocrites! You shut the door to Heaven in the face of those trying to enter. You don't go in yourselves and yet prevent others. Woe again to you, scribes and Pharisees, hypocrites! You devour widows' homes and justify yourselves with lengthy prayers. For this you'll suffer the greater judgment. And woe to you, scribes and Pharisees, hypocrites! You circle the globe to make one convert and once you've roped him in you make him twice the child of Hell that you are.

"Oh you blind guides of the blind! You say if someone swears by the Temple it doesn't get him anywhere, but if he swears by the Temple gold then he's bound. What kind of blind fools are you? Do you think the gold is more precious than the Temple that sanctifies it? It's the same when you say that someone who swears by the altar is bound to nothing, but if he swears by the gift he presents on the altar then he's in debt. Are

---

150 *Deuteronomy* 17:19-13.
151 *Cf. Exodus* 13:9; *Deuteronomy* 6:8.
152 *Numbers* 15:38.
153 *Ezekiel* 21:26.

you sightless to see that the altar sanctifying the gift is greater than the gift? But whoever swears by the altar swears by it and all that is on it and whoever swears by the Temple swears by it and he who dwells therein and whoever swears by Heaven swears by it and the throne of him who sits upon it.

"Woe I say to you, scribes and Pharisees, hypocrites! You tithe mint and dill and cumin[154] but forget about the weightier portions of the Law - justice, mercy, faithfulness.[155] You would have done better paying attention to those and forgetting about your spice tithes. You are leaders without vision, straining a gnat from your soup[156] but gulping down a camel.[157]

"Woe to you, scribes and Pharisees, hypocrites! You take care to wash the outside edges of cups and other vessels but inside they're full of stolen goods and waste. You purblind Pharisee, wash the inside first and then worry about keeping the outside clean.

"Yet alas, scribes and Pharisees, you hypocrites! You're just like freshly plastered tombs - nice enough to look at from the outside but inside filled with dead men's bones and every kind of filth. So by your outward appearance people think you are righteous but inside you're full of hypocrisy, utterly lawless.

"Alas for you, scribes and Pharisees. You hypocrites build the tombs of the prophets and adorn the graves of the righteous and say 'if *we* had lived in the time of our forefathers *we* wouldn't have shed the blood of the prophets, as they did.' Thus you bear witness against yourselves, that you are the sons of those who murdered the prophets. Fill then the measure of your forefathers' sins. You snakes, you viper's brood, do you think you can escape a fiery judgment? To show a way out I will send you prophets and wise men and scholars, but even so you'll kill some, crucifying them, others you'll beat in your synagogues and others you'll drive from city to city - all so that on you may fall all the righteous blood spilled on the Earth,[158] from the blood of righteous Abel[159] to the blood of Zechariah the son of Barachiah, whom you slew between the Temple and the altar.[160] Truly I tell you, all these things shall come upon this people.

---

154   *Cf. Leviticus* 27:30.
155   *Micah* 6:8.
156   *Leviticus* 11:20-23.
157   *Leviticus* 11:4.
158   *Lamentations* 4:13.
159   *Genesis* 4:10.
160   *2 Chronicles* 24:20-22.

"Jerusalem, Jerusalem, you who murdered the prophets and stoned those I sent to you – how often I longed to gather up your children as a hen gathers chicks under her wing,[161] but you would not.[162] Behold, your house is left to you desolate.[163] And I tell you, you will not see me henceforth until you say, Blessed is he who comes in the name of the Lord."[164]

24

As Yeshua left the Temple he saw his disciples pointing out the various structures in the Temple compound.

"Are you really fixated on all that? I'm telling you this will all be torn down with not one stone left on top of another."[165]

Once he was back on Mount Olive[166] his disciples approached him separately and asked, "When will that happen? Is there a sign we need to watch for so we'll know you are soon to appear? And when will *everything* come to an end?!"

"Watch out you don't get fooled, because many people will come in my name saying 'I'm the Messiah,' deceiving many. You will hear the din and clamor of wars. But don't let that frighten you – this has to occur but it's not the end yet. One nation will rise up against another nation, one kingdom against another kingdom, and there will be famines and earthquakes from place to place. And yet those are just the first birth pangs. You'll be handed over for suffering, even death, and be the off-scouring of all nations for my name's sake. Many people will take offense, hating one another, betraying one another. Many false prophets will appear on the scene and lead people off the path.[167] And because lawlessness will increase, what once were charitable hearts will grow cold. But whoever stays fast to the end will be saved. And once the good news of the kingdom has been preached throughout the whole inhabited world as a witness to every nation, then shall the end come.

---

161 *Psalms* 17:8, 91:4; *Isaiah* 31:5.
162 *Isaiah* 30:15.
163 *Ezekiel* 10:18-19, 11:22-23; *Jeremiah* 12:7.
164 *Psalms* 118:26; see *Zechariah* 12:10.
165 *Cf. Micah* 3:12; *Jeremiah* 7:12-14.
166 *Cf. Ezekiel* 11:23.
167 *Daniel* 11:41.

"But when you see the loathsome and desolate horror that Daniel the prophet spoke about set up in the holy place[168] – if you are reading this, be sure you understand what I'm saying[169] – then whoever's in Judea better flee to the mountains and whoever's on a rooftop better not go back down to get things out of his house and whoever's out in a field better not turn back to grab his coat. But alas for those who are pregnant or still nursing their babies in those days. And pray that your flight not be in the wintertime or on the Sabbath, because there will be dreadful anguish in the world of a sort never seen from the beginning of creation until now nor ever will be seen again.[170]   If those days were not shortened no one would be saved. But they will be shortened, for the sake of the elect.

"Even if anyone says to you at that time, 'Look! Here's the Messiah!' or 'There he is!' – don't believe her. There will be false messiahs and false prophets all displaying great signs and wonders to the point where – if it were possible – even the elect might be deceived. But listen! I've told you about all this ahead of time! So again, if someone says to you, 'He's in the desert!' – don't go there. Or 'He's in a secret place!' – don't believe him, because as lightning flashes from East to West that's just how the Son of Man will appear. And wherever there's a corpse you'll find birds of prey.[171]

"Now, right after the suffering that takes place in those days the sun will go dark and the moon won't shine. Even the stars will fall from the sky and the forces that hold the Earth together will come apart.[172]   But *that's* when you'll see the banner of the Son of Man in the sky.[173]   All the tribes of the Earth will mourn, beating their breasts[174] when they see the Son of Man coming in the clouds of Heaven in power and great glory.[175] He will send his angels out with a mighty trumpet call[176] to sweep up his elect from the four corners of the Earth and from one end of the sky to the other.[177]

"Learn the parable of the fig tree. When its branches become tender

---

168 *Daniel* 9:27, 11:31, 12:11; *cf. 1 Maccabees* 1:54.
169 *Daniel* 12:10.
170 *Daniel* 12:1.
171 *Job* 39:30.
172 *Isaiah* 13:10, 34:4; *Jeremiah* 4:28; *Ezekiel* 32:7; *Joel* 2:10; *Amos* 8:9; *cf. Micah* 3:6.
173 *Isaiah* 11:12; 49:22.
174 *Zechariah* 12:10-14.
175 *Daniel* 7:13-14.
176 *Isaiah* 27:13.
177 *Deuteronomy* 30:4; *Zechariah* 2:6.

and shoot forth leaves you know Summer is on its way. So when you see all these things happening you'll know it's near, right at the doorstep. I can tell you as well that this race of people will not pass away until all these things are fulfilled.

"Heaven and Earth may dissolve but my words will never pass away. As far as just when those days will be? No one knows the day or the hour – not the angels in Heaven not even the Son but only the Father – but I *can* tell you that as it was in the days of Noah so will it be with the coming of the Son of Man. People were eating, drinking and making merry in the days before that cataclysm, right up to the day Noah entered the ark.[178] And they had no idea that a flood was coming until it swept them off the face of the Earth. So too will it be with the coming of the Son of Man. Two people will be grinding wheat in a mill when one is taken and the other left behind.

"Be like a watchman, because you don't know what day your Lord will return. If the homeowner had known the time of night the thief was coming he would've been on the lookout and not let him break into the house. That's why you need to stay ready – because the Son of Man will come just when you don't expect him.

"Who is that faithful servant, prudent and wise, someone the master has placed in authority over his other servants to distribute food to them at the proper time? Blessed is that servant whom his lord finds at his post when he arrives. I'm telling you, he'll make him master of the house. But if an evil servant says in his heart, 'my master is taking his own sweet time,' starts to beat up his fellow servants and then go out on the town with a bunch of other drunks – well, his master will show up on a day he doesn't expect him, at a time he doesn't know, and will cut him to pieces, sending him off to share the fate of the rest of the hypocrites, where there will be weeping and gnashing of teeth."

---

178 *Genesis* 9:20.

25

He then continued with other parables and analogies.

"At that time the kingdom of Heaven will be compared to ten maidens who took their lamps and went out to greet the bridegroom. Five of them were wise but five were foolish. The foolish ones brought their lamps but forgot to bring any oil while the wise ones not only brought their lamps but also took vessels filled with oil. When the bridegroom ended up taking more time than they expected all ten nodded off and fell asleep. But in the middle of the night there was a shout – 'Here's the bridegroom! Go out to meet him!'

"Then all the maidens rose up and each trimmed her lamp. But the foolish ones said to the wise, 'Give us some of your oil because our lamps are starting to go out.' Yet the wise answered, 'Can't do it – if we share ours with you there won't be enough for both of us. Run into town and buy more for yourselves from the shopkeepers.' While these went off shopping the bridegroom came and those who were ready went in with him to the wedding feast. But then the gates were shut, so that when the foolish maidens finally showed up and clamored for the bridegroom to open the doors he refused them, saying 'I don't even know who you are.' Watch therefore because you don't know the day or the hour.

"It's also just like a man who summoned his servants before leaving on a voyage and entrusted his goods to them. To one he gave five bags full of silver, to another two and to another one – to each according to his skill set – and then left. The servant with five bags of silver promptly put his capital to work through trade and investments. In due course he doubled the money, as did the servant with two bags of silver. But the servant who had received one bag of silver hid it under a mattress. After a good deal of time had passed the servants' master returned and wished to settle accounts with them. The one who'd received five bags of silver brought back ten saying, 'Master, you entrusted me with five bags of silver and look, I've earned you another five as well.' The master said, 'Well done, my good man! You were faithful to me with a few things and will now have rule over many. Enter therefore into the joy of your lord.' And likewise the man who had two bags of silver came back to the master with four and he too was commended and entrusted with greater treasures, enjoying his lord's good graces.

"But when the man who had hidden his one bag of silver came forward he said, 'Master, I knew you to be rapacious, harvesting from farms where you hadn't sown any seed, calling in loans you never made – so I was afraid of what you might do to me when you returned and therefore hid your silver under the mattress, where I knew it would be safe. So here it is – take what's yours.'

But the master answered him, 'You wicked and lazy servant! You say you knew me to harvest crops I haven't sown and collect on loans I never made? If you really believed that you would *at least* have put my money in a savings account and gotten me some interest on it.' He then said to another servant, 'Take this bag of silver from him and give it to the one who has ten, because to everyone who has more will be given, even to excess, but those who have little will lose even the little they have. And as for this worthless servant, cast him into outer darkness, where there will be weeping and gnashing of teeth.'

"When the Son of Man comes in the grandeur of his glory along with all his angels he will sit on his throne with all peoples gathered before him.[179] Then he will separate one from another, just as a shepherd separates the sheep from the goats, placing the sheep at his right hand and the goats at his left. The king will say to those on his right, 'Come, you who are blessed by my Father, inherit the kingdom prepared for you from the foundation of the world. When I was hungry, you fed me; thirsty, you gave me something to drink; a stranger, you treated me like one of your own; naked, you clothed me; sick, you comforted me; imprisoned, you visited me.'[180] But the justified answered, 'Lord, when did we ever see you hungry and nourish you, or thirsty and give you water? When did we find you a stranger and welcome you in, or naked to clothe you? And when did we see you weak or in jail and come to your aid?' But the king explained to them, 'In truth, whenever you did any of this for one of the least of these brothers of mine you did it for me.'

"Then will he say to those on his left, 'Go away from my sight, you who are cursed, to share in the timeless fire prepared for the Accuser and his demon angels. When I was hungry you gave me nothing to eat; thirsty you left me parched; a stranger you rejected me; naked you left me shivering and homeless; sick and in prison you left me to languish alone.' But then they will say, 'Lord, we never would have left you hungry or thirsty or wandering or naked or weak or in prison and not come to your aid!' Yet the king will

---

179 *Daniel* 7:14; *Zechariah* 14:5; *Joel* 3:1-12.
180 *Isaiah* 58:7.

say, 'As often as you failed to show mercy to the weakest of these my brothers, so often did you fail me.' And so these departed agelessly to sorrow but the righteous agelessly to live."[181]

26

Once Yeshua had completed his teachings[182] he said to his disciples, "It's just two more days to the start of the Passover festival, where the Son of Man will be handed over to crucifixion."

Then the chief priests and elders of the people gathered together at the palace of the High Priest, a man named Caiaphas, and plotted how to catch Yeshua in a trap and have him arrested and condemned to death. The High Priest cautioned, "But not openly at the festival, lest we cause a riot among the people."

While Yeshua was staying in Bethany at the house of Simon the leper, a woman came to him bearing an alabaster flask filled with the rarest of myrrh, anointing his head as he dined. But when the disciples saw what was happening they were angered and said, "What's the reason for such waste? These spices could've been sold for a lot of money, a gift to the poor!"

"Why are you giving her a hard time? She has performed a righteous deed for me. You will always have the poor with you but won't always have me - she has prepared my body for burial with this myrrh and I promise you that wherever this gospel is preached throughout the whole world what she has done will also be told, as a memorial to her."

Then Judas, the man from Kerioth and one of the Twelve, left to go see the chief priests, asking them, "What are you willing to give me if I hand Yeshua over to you?" They settled on 30 pieces of silver[183] and from the time the deal was struck he looked for the right moment to betray.

On the first day of the Feast of Unleavened Bread the disciples came to Yeshua and asked, "Where would you like us to prepare your Passover meal?"[184]

"Go into town and say to so-and-so, 'The Teacher says, "My time

---

181 *Daniel* 2:12.
182 *Deuteronomy* 32:45.
183 *Zechariah* 11:12; cf. *Exodus* 21:32.
184 *Exodus* 12:1-25; *Leviticus* 23:5-8; *Numbers* 9:3.

draws near. I will eat the Passover meal at your place, together with my disciples.'"

The disciples did as Yeshua directed them and so made ready the meal. Once evening had come, he reclined at the table with the Twelve. While they were eating he said, "Here's the truth - one of you's going to sell me out."

Great grief fell on them, each in turn asking, "It isn't me, Lord, is it?"

"Whoever dipped his hand in the dish with me, that's the one who will turn me in.[185] Yes, the Son of Man must go, as it is written, but woe to that man whose hand is in the works - he'll wish he'd never been born."

Then the traitor Judas said to him, "Surely you don't mean me, Rabbi?" "So you say."

As they ate, Yeshua took the unleavened bread and, after giving praise to God, broke it and gave to each of his disciples saying, "Take, eat, this is my body." Taking the cup and likewise giving thanks he shared it with them, saying, "Drink from this cup, all of you - it is my covenantal blood, shed for many for the forgiveness of sins.[186] And listen to me carefully. I will not drink of this fruit of the vine from now until that day I drink it anew with you in the kingdom of my Father."

After they had sung a hymn[187] they went out to Mount Olive, where Yeshua told them, "Tonight you will all fall away because of me, as it's been written,

>   Strike the shepherd
>   and the sheep of his flock will be scattered.[188]

Yet after I've been raised I will go ahead of you into Galilee."

But Peter stood him down and said, "I don't care if the rest of these guys turn their backs on you, I never will!"

"You think so? The fact is, you'll run from me three times before the rooster crows."

"No way - even if it kills me I'll never deny you."

So said they all.

Then Yeshua went with them to an enclosed place called Gethsemane

---

185 *Psalms* 41:9.
186 *Exodus* 24:8; *Isaiah* 53:10; *Jeremiah* 31:31-34.
187 *Psalms* 136.
188 *Zechariah* 13:7.

and said, "Rest here while I go pray."

Taking Peter and Zebedee's two sons with him he went, and he began to suffer with dread, filled with anxiety.[189]

"My soul is veiled with grief, crushed down, even to the point of death. Stay here, friends, watch with me."

Going somewhat further past them he fell prostrate as he prayed, "My Father, if there is another way, let this cup pass from me - nevertheless it's your will I seek, not my own."[190]

But when he came back to his three disciples he found them asleep. He said to Peter, "Are you so weak you couldn't watch with me for even one hour? Watch and pray, lest you fall into temptation - the spirit may be willing but the flesh is weak."

So again a second time he went aside to pray, "My Father, if this cup cannot pass unless I drink from it, your will be done."

Coming again to them he found them slumbering, their eyelids heavy with sleep. He let them be and a third time went to pray these same words. Returning to his disciples he said, "Sleep on and take your rest. The hour is near when the Son of Man is betrayed into the hands of sinners."

A little later he said, "Time to wake up! The turncoat approaches."

And indeed even as he spoke those words Judas, one of the Twelve, came along with a large crowd carrying swords and staves, men sent by the chief priests and scribes of the people. The quisling had given them a sign to watch for - "Whomever I greet with a kiss, that's the man you need to arrest."

Judas stepped quickly up to Yeshua and said, "Peace, Rabbi," greeting him with a kiss on the cheek.

"Friend, what brings you here?"[191]

At that they grabbed Yeshua and arrested him. But one of the disciples drew his sword and sliced the ear off the High Priest's servant. Yeshua turned to him and said, "Sheathe your sword. Whoever lives by the sword will die by the sword. Don't you realize I could call on my Father at any time and he would send twelve legions of angels to defend me? But then how would the Scriptures be fulfilled?"

Yeshua turned to the mob around him and said, "You came out with

---

189 *Isaiah* 53:3.
190 *Psalms* 55:1-8.
191 *Psalms* 55:12-14.

swords and staves to seize me, as though I were some rebel to be subdued – yet I was with you every day in the Temple teaching and you didn't bother to arrest me then. But all this is happening to fulfill what the prophets have written."[192]

At that the disciples abandoned him and fled.

The guards led Yeshua to the High Priest's house, where the scribes and elders were already gathered. But Peter followed at a safe distance, up to the courtyard, where he sat down with the palace workers to watch the end. Meanwhile, the chief priests and the whole Sanhedrin had been out trying to suborn perjurers to testify against Yeshua with the goal of having him put to death. But they were having a hard time finding any to come forward, until finally they got two[193] false witnesses to say that he'd said, "I can tear down God's Temple and built it back up in three days."

Caiaphas confronted Yeshua, "What's your response to that accusation?"

He kept silent.[194]

"But I charge you by the living God to tell us – *are* you the Messiah, the Son of God?"[195]

"The words are in your own mouth – and henceforth you'll see the Son of Man seated enthroned at the right hand of the Almighty, coming in the clouds of Heaven."[196]

The High Priest tore his cloak in two[197] and cried out, "He cursed God! What do we need with more witnesses? You've heard the blasphemy yourselves. What say you?"

The judges said, "He deserves to die for this."[198]

At that they all spat in his face and took turns punching and slapping him as they taunted, "Prophesy to us, 'Messiah,' which one of us is hitting you now?"[199]

Peter stayed outside huddled in the courtyard, when one of the servant girls came up and said, "Weren't you also with Yeshua the Galilean?"

But he swore up and down to them all, "I don't know who you're

---

192   *Isaiah* 53:12.
193   *Numbers* 35:30; *Deuteronomy* 17:6, 19:15.
194   *Isaiah* 53:7.
195   *2 Samuel* 7:14; *Psalms* 2:7.
196   *Psalms* 110:1; *Daniel* 7:13.
197   *Leviticus* 11:10.
198   *Leviticus* 24:10-23.
199   *Isaiah* 50:6.

talking about."

Yet another maid spied him through the gate and shouted, "That man was with Yeshua of Nazareth!"

Then he cursed all the more – "Damn you, girl! I'm telling you I don't know the man!"

But a short time later some others standing nearby confronted Peter, "In truth you *are* one of his men – your hick accent gives you away."

Peter even cursed himself swearing, "Let God strike me dead if I'm lying – I don't know him!"

Immediately the rooster crowed and Yeshua's words came back to Peter – "Before the rooster crows you will deny me three times." So Peter left, weeping bitterly.

27

At dawn the chief priests and elders of the people counseled how they might put Yeshua to death. Handcuffing him, they handed him over to Pilate, the Governor of Judea.

There and then Judas saw that Yeshua was condemned and bewailed his own treason. He tried to return the 30 pieces of silver to the chief priests and elders as he confessed, "I have sinned, betraying innocent blood."

But they said, "That's not our problem – see to it yourself."

Throwing the silver back into the Temple,[200] he departed to hang himself. But the chief priests took the silver and said, "This is blood money – it isn't lawful to put it in the Temple treasury." After considering what to do they used the money to buy the Potter's Field, where strangers are buried. That's why to this very day that place is known as the Field of Blood. So too this word of Jeremiah the prophet was fulfilled,

> I took the thirty pieces of silver,
> > the price they put on Israel's priceless one,

---

200 *Cf. Zechariah* 11:13.

and bought a potter's field
just as the Lord commanded me.[201]

When Yeshua was brought before Pilate he asked him, "Are you the king of the Jews?"

"Is that what you say?"

And Yeshua said nothing to the many charges brought against him by the chief priests and the elders.

So Pilate said to him, "Haven't you heard all the things you're accused of?"

But still he answered not a word, leaving Pilate taken aback.

Now it had become a custom at the Passover feast for the Governor to release to the people one of his prisoners, whomever they should pick. At that time he had chains on a particularly notorious man, one Barabbas. Pilate therefore summoned the crowd and asked them which of the two they wanted released, Barabbas or Yeshua. He knew, you see, that the rulers had handed Yeshua over *not* because he'd done anything wrong but because they were jealous of him. And as Pilate sat at the judgment seat his wife approached him – "Don't have anything to do with this just man! I've already suffered enough in a dream I had about him."

But the chief priests and elders stirred up the people to ask for Barabbas, leaving Yeshua to die. So when the Governor asked them which of the two they chose they shouted, "Barabbas!!"

"But what shall I do with Yeshua, the one you call Messiah?"

"Crucify him!"

"Why? What evil has he done?"

Yet they cried out all the more, "Crucify him!"

When Pilate saw he wasn't getting anywhere but was in fact making matters worse, to the point where he almost had a riot on his hands, he took a bowl of water and washed his hands[202] in front of the whole crowd, saying, "I am guiltless of this blood. See to it yourselves."

Then all the people said, "His blood is on us and on our children."[203]

Pilate therefore released Barabbas to them and delivered Yeshua to be crucified, first flogging him.

---

201 *Zechariah* 11:12-13; *Jeremiah* 18:1-2, 32:6-9.
202 *Deuteronomy* 21:6-9; *Psalms* 26:6, 73:13; W. Shakespeare, *Macbeth* 2.2.43-44, 57-60 and 5.1.53-55.
203 *Jeremiah* 26:8-9.

After that the Governor's soldiers took Yeshua to the guardhouse, where the whole cohort was stationed, to make sport of him. First stripping off his clothes they put a scarlet cloak around him. Having woven thorns, they crowned his head and for a scepter placed a reed in his right hand. Then they knelt down before him in mockery intoning, "All hail, King of the Jews!" After spitting on him they took the reed from his hand and beat his head with it. And when they had had their fun they took off the scarlet mantle, dressed him back in his own clothes and led him off to be crucified.

As they went out the soldiers found a man from Cyrene, Simon by name, and pressed him into service carrying Yeshua's cross. When they came to the placed known as גֻּלְגָּלְתָּא — Skull Hill in English - they gave him wine mixed with bile to drink as a sedative. But when he had tasted it he refused. Having stripped him of his clothes and placed him on the cross, the soldiers rolled dice to divide his garments among them, that the word of the prophet might be fulfilled,

> They divided my garments among themselves
> and cast lots for my cloak.[204]

Once seated they kept guard over him. They also wrote down the charge against him and posted it on a sign above his head - "This is Yeshua, king of the Jews."

He was crucified between two bandits, one on his right and one on his left. Passersby cursed him, shaking their heads.[205]

"You who would destroy the Temple and build it back in three days, save yourself - and if you're really the Son of God why don't you just come down now off the cross?"

The chief priests, the scribes and the elders likewise ridiculed him.

"He saved others but he can't save himself. If he's the king of Israel, let him come down now from the cross and we'll believe in him. He trusted in God, let him deliver him if he delight in him,[206] for he said, 'I am the Son of God!'"

Even the thieves on either side mocked him in the same way.

---

204 *Psalms* 22:18.
205 *Psalms* 22:7.
206 *Psalms* 22:8.

But about the sixth hour darkness fell across the face of the Earth, lasting to the ninth hour. And at the ninth hour Yeshua cried out with a loud voice saying אֵלִי אֵלִי לְמָה שְׁבַקְתָּנִי - which in English means, My God, my God, why have you abandoned me?[207]

Some of those watching said, "He's calling upon Elijah!"

One of them quickly grabbed a sponge, wrapped it around a stick, soaked it in sour wine and offered him to drink.

But others just said, "Let be - let's see if Elijah comes to save him."

Then a soldier took a spear and pierced his side, whence flowed water and blood.[208]

Having called out once more with a strong voice, Yeshua yielded up his spirit. And at *that* the inner Temple curtain was rent from top to bottom,[209] the Earth convulsed, boulders split, tombs broke open.[210]

But when the centurion and those with him guarding Yeshua felt the earthquake and saw all that occurred, they yelled in terror, "Truly this *was* the Son of God!"

Many women watched all this from afar, the same who followed Yeshua out of Galilee, ministering to him, among them Mary from Magdala and Mary the mother of Jacob and Joseph, as well as the mother of Zebedee's two sons.

As evening neared a wealthy man from Rama came by, Joseph by name. He too had become one of Yeshua's disciples. Having seen what occurred he approached Pilate, imploring the release of Yeshua's corpse. Pilate ordered it given him. Taking the body Joseph wrapped it in fine linen and laid it in his own stone tomb, freshly hewn. Having done so, he rolled a huge boulder in front of the opening and left. But Mary Magdalene and the other Mary stayed behind, sitting themselves down opposite the tomb.

On the next day - the day following Sabbath preparations - the chief priests and the Pharisees gathered before Pilate and said, "Your Excellency, we remember that while he was still alive that fraudster said, 'I will rise up after three days.' Order therefore that the tomb be sealed until three

---

207 *Psalms* 22:1.
208 *Psalms* 22:14-17.
209 *Exodus* 26:33.
210 After Yeshua's resurrection the bodies of many long-dead prophets sleeping in those tombs were raised up, left their graves and entered the holy city, where they appeared to many.

days pass, lest his disciples come and steal him away and tell the people 'He is raised from the dead!' – so that the last lie becomes greater than the first."

Pilate said to them, "Take some of my guards and make it as sure as you wish." And thus they secured the tomb, sealing the slab and posting a guard.

28

In the waning night following the Sabbath, with dawn of the week's first day approaching, Mary Magdalene and the other Mary came back to see the tomb. But a sharp quake shook the ground and – behold! – an angel of the Lord descended from the sky, rolled the stone away from the tomb and sat on the rock. His countenance was as lightning, his garments as snow.[211]

In terror the tomb guards trembled, toppling over as dead. But turning to the women the angel said, "Don't fear – I know you seek Yeshua, who was crucified. He's not here! He has risen, just as he told you he would. Come see for yourselves the place he was laid. Then quickly run to tell his disciples, 'He has risen from among the dead and goes ahead of you into Galilee, look for him there.' That's your message, now go!"

They ran racing from the grave in a tremor of joy. But of a sudden Yeshua himself stood in their path to greet them.

"Peace!"

They fell prostrate before him and took hold of his feet.

But he assured them, "Fear not, but go tell my brothers to leave for Galilee and there they too will see me."

As the women went on their mission some of the tomb guards rose back up and went into the city to tell the chief priests all that had happened. Having gathered the Sanhedrin and the elders the chief priests decided to give a good deal of silver to the soldiers and directed them, "Go tell people that his disciples came during the night and stole the body away while you were sleeping. And if anyone brings charges against you before the Governor, don't worry, we'll protect you from harm." Having

---

211 *Daniel* 7:9, 10:6.

been bribed they did as instructed. Their tale spread widely among the people and is current to this very day.

In the meantime the eleven remaining disciples left Jerusalem for Galilee, heading to a mountain Yeshua had specified. When they saw him there they worshipped – but some were confused about what was happening. Then Yeshua told them, "All power in Heaven and on Earth has been given to me. Go therefore and make disciples of all nations,[212] baptizing them into worship of the Father and of the Son and of the Holy Spirit, teaching them to hold fast all things I have commanded you. And behold! I am with you always, even to the end of the age."

---

212 *Daniel* 7:14.

ACCORDING TO MARK

1

This is the beginning of the good news of Jesus Christ, the Son of God – and it was just as the prophets had written.

> Listen up!
> I am sending my messenger ahead of you
> to lay out the walkway[1] –
> he will be a voice shouting in the wilderness:
> "Prepare ye the way of the Lord!
> Straighten out his paths!"[2]

At that time John was in a desert area immersing people in water and proclaiming his baptism as one of repentance, leading to the forgiveness of sins. The whole land of Judea came out to him, as well as all Jerusalem, and they were dipped by him in the Jordan River, confessing their sins. Now John wore the simplest of clothes, nothing but a tunic woven of camel's hair tied at the waist with a leather belt. He ate nothing but insects and wild honey. But he called out to the people –

---

1   *Malachi* 3:1
2   *Isaiah* 40:3

"Someone much mightier than I is coming and I'm not even worthy to bend down to untie his shoelaces. So yes, I am baptizing you with water but he will bathe you in the Holy Spirit."

Just then Jesus came from Galilean Nazareth and was baptized by John in the River Jordan. The moment he came up from the water he saw the sky split apart and the Spirit descending, lighting on him gently as a dove. Then a voice spoke from the Heavens, "You are my beloved son, in whom I delight."[3]

Instantly, the Spirit thrust Jesus out to the desert. He wandered there in the wilderness 40 days while the Accuser tested his strength. He even made his bed among wild beasts. Even so, he had angel servants watching to protect him.

John was arrested about then, at which point Jesus went into Galilee and started announcing God's good message.

"The exact moment has come and the kingdom of God is near - turn now from your ways and have faith in this gospel."

Then one day, as Jesus walked alongside the Sea of Galilee, he saw Simon and his brother Andrew, fishermen casting their nets into the sea. So Jesus said to them, "Come along with me! I'll turn you into fishers of men." They dropped everything, left their nets and followed him. A little farther down the beach he saw two more fishermen, James and his brother John, sons of Zebedee, sitting in their boat knitting their nets. He called them too and they dropped everything to follow Jesus, this time leaving their father in the boat with the hired help.

The five of them entered Capernaum, where Jesus attended the synagogue every Sabbath day and taught. People were amazed at his teaching because he taught them authoritatively, unlike their local rabbis. But there was a man in their synagogue possessed of an unholy spirit, and when he saw Jesus he screamed.

"Aaay! Are you after us now, Jesus Nazarene? Have you come to destroy us? I know well who you are - you're God's Holy One!"

Jesus stopped the evil spirit in its tracks.

"Muzzle it - and come out of him!"

The unclean spirit threw the man into convulsions, bellowed and shrieked but finally left him. The witnesses were stunned, perplexed as they argued among themselves.

---

3   *Genesis* 22:2; *Psalms* 2:7.

"Who is this man, with such new and powerful teaching? He bosses the unclean spirits around and they *obey* him!"

So Jesus quickly became famous all throughout Galilee. After that exorcism Jesus left the synagogue for Simon and Andrew's house, bringing James and John along as well. However, Simon's mother-in-law was lying sick in bed with a fever and they implored him on her behalf. Jesus went inside, took her hand and lifted her up, at which point the fever left her. And right away she got up to serve them.

When evening came and the sun had set people brought everyone to him who was sick or demon-possessed. Indeed, the whole city crowded against the door. Then and there he healed any who were afflicted, however varied the diseases. He also cast out many demons – but didn't let the demons speak, because they knew who he was.

Still nighttime yet dawn approaching Jesus left the house for a lonely spot, where he prayed. Shortly Peter and his friends went looking for him. When they'd found him they said, "Everyone around here is seeking you out!"

"Then we need to head in the direction of the outlying villages so I can preach there too – that's the very reason I've come!"

And thus he went preaching in synagogues all throughout Galilee, casting out demons along the way. At one point a leper called out to Jesus and begged as he knelt before him, "If it's your will, you can heal me."

Jesus was moved with compassion for the man and reaching with his hand he touched his skin.

"It is indeed my will – be healed!"

The leprosy left the man the very moment Jesus spoke, and he was cleansed. But Jesus took him aside to give him a stern warning.

"Take care you speak to no one about this but go instead to the Temple to present an offering of purification, just in the way that Moses commanded, as a witness to those who are there."[4]

Yet as soon as the man left he began to tell everyone what had happened and the word spread quickly, so much so that Jesus could no longer go openly into any city and had to stay in more remote spots. But that didn't stop people from coming to him anyway from all directions.

---

4   *Leviticus* 14:2-32.

2

Jesus next moved on to Capernaum, where the crowd heard he was staying in a home. So many gathered inside the house so quickly that there wasn't room for any more, not even outside the doorway, as all listened to him share his teaching.

And while he was teaching four men came carrying a paralytic. When they weren't able to get near Jesus because of the crowd they went up on the roof, pried off the roof tiles and lowered the man down lying on a sick bed. Jesus saw their faith and spoke to the paralyzed man.

"My child, your sins are forgiven."

But some members of the scribal class were sitting there as well and started murmuring in their hearts.

"Why does this man speak such blasphemies? Only God can forgive sins, no one else."

Yet Jesus knew instantly in his spirit what they were thinking.

"Why are you in such turmoil in your thoughts? Which do you think it's easier to say, 'your sins are forgiven' or 'get up, pick up your cot and walk?' But you need to know that the Son of Man has power on earth to forgive sins and so" – turning now to the paralytic – "I say to you, get up, pick up your pallet and go your way to your own home."

Immediately the man got up, grabbed his pallet and walked out in front of everyone. They were astonished and gave the glory to God.

"We've never seen anything like this!"

Once again Jesus went walking along the sea with a whole crowd of people following after him, hanging on his every word. Along the way he saw Levi, Alphaeus' son, collecting fees in the customs office.

"Follow me!"

Levi jumped right up and followed him. As Jesus was reclining at dinner later in Levi's house many of his fellow tax collectors – plus plenty of other sinners too – joined him and his students at the table (by now he had a large number of acolytes). Seeing Jesus with miscreants and moneygrubbers the scribes and Pharisees said to the disciples, "How can he eat and drink with scoundrels and rakes??"

But Jesus heard them.

"People who aren't sick don't need a doctor, just those who are.

The point is, I'm not here to call good people to repentance, just sinners."

It was also the case that both John's disciples and those of the Pharisees fasted on a regular basis. So the scribes then said to Jesus, "Why is it that John's and the Pharisees' followers fast but yours don't?"

"Why would the sons of the bridegroom fast while the bridegroom is with them? It's just not possible. But when the day comes that the bridegroom is snatched from them, then they'll fast. No one is going to make a patch of unshrunk cloth and sew it onto an old coat because all that happens is the new cloth pulls against the old cloth and tears it. Same thing with wine. No one is going to pour new wine into old wineskins because the new wine will burst the old wineskins and you'll lose not only the wine but the wineskins as well. So instead, put new wine into new wineskins."

Jesus and his disciples happened to be walking through a wheat field one Sabbath day. As the disciples passed along they plucked the heads of wheat. The Pharisees were watching and challenged Jesus on this.

"Look! Your people are doing something that's forbidden on the Sabbath!"

"Haven't you ever read what David did once when he and his men were hungry, how he entered into the house of the Lord during the time of High Priest Abiathar and ate the holy bread that was there? And not only that but David gave some to his friends.[5] Listen to me – the Sabbath is there for man's benefit, not the other way around. Just so, the Son of Man is also lord of the Sabbath."

3

Jesus went again into the synagogue and a man was there whose hand was withered away. But the Pharisees were keeping an eye on him to see if he would heal on the Sabbath, in which case they would bring charges against him. Nevertheless, Jesus spoke to the man with the withered hand, "Stand here in the middle."

Then he asked those around him, "Should we do good on the Sabbath or evil, save a life or kill someone?"

---

5   *I Samuel* 21:1-6.

But they all just kept silent. Jesus glared at them in anger, deeply grieved by the hardness of their hearts. He turned instead to the man.

"Stretch out your hand!"

He stretched it out and his withered hand became healthy and whole, just like his other. But the Pharisees left immediately and began to plot with the Herodians how they could find a way to arrest Jesus and destroy him.

At that point Jesus and his men withdrew to the seaside as an immense crowd from Galilee followed them, as well as a multitude of people from Judea, Jerusalem and Idumaea, from the lands across the Jordan and even from Tyre and Sidon, all having heard of the marvelous things Jesus had done.

Jesus asked his disciples to outfit a small boat for him so the crowd wouldn't press against him too hard. He had healed so many by then that he was nearly in danger of being crushed by people falling over themselves trying to touch him, hoping to be healed of their suffering.

And when those possessed by evil spirits saw Jesus they beat their way down toward him, screaming "You are the Son of God!"

But he shut them up, commanding them not to reveal him so openly.

Then Jesus ascended a nearby mountain, where he called to himself those whom he had chosen. Once they were there he appointed twelve to be his core followers and sent them to preach, also giving them power to heal the sick and cast out demons. These were Simon, whom he also called Peter; Zebedee's sons James and John, whom he named Sons of Boanerges, which means Sons of Thunder; Andrew; Philip; Bartholomew; Matthew; Thomas; Alphaeus' son James; Thaddeus; Simon the Canaanite; and Judas, a man from Kerioth, who betrayed him.

They came next to someone's home and once again a spreading crowd gathered, so much so that it was impossible for Jesus and his disciples to find time to grab a bite to eat. When his friends saw how things were going they tried to prevail on Jesus to leave, being worried because people were saying, "He's gone nuts." Moreover, some scribes who had come down from Jerusalem said he was demon-possessed himself and only able to cast out evil spirits by the power of the Prince of Demons.

Jesus called them over to reason with them, using illustrations.

"How can Satan cast out Satan? And if a kingdom is divided against itself, how can it avoid destruction? Or if a house is divided against itself, how can it stand? And if the Devil were to rebel against himself and split up his kingdom, he'd be done for. No one is going to break into a strong man's house to steal his goods without first tying the man up. Only then will he be able to steal whatever he wants from him. And be sure of this: you can be forgiven for any kind of sins and blasphemies save this one thing – someone who blasphemes against the Holy Spirit cannot be forgiven, not in this world, not in the next."

Jesus told them this because they had said, "He's demon-possessed."

Around then his mother and his brothers came and waited outside the house, sending someone in to call for Jesus. The crowd seated about Jesus told him, "Your mother, your brothers and your sisters are outside waiting for you."

"Who is my mother and who are my brothers?" Looking at those sitting in a circle around him he said, "Here is my mother and here are my brothers – for whoever does the will of God, he is my brother and my sister and mother."

4

Jesus moved on again and began to teach along the seaside. Increasing numbers gathered to be with him – they sat on the shore while he stepped into his boat and taught them from offshore. He spoke using a multitude of stories and examples, for such was his manner of teaching.

"Listen – a sower went out to sow. As he sowed some of the seed fell by the roadway and birds came and gobbled it up. Some other seed fell on stony ground. With little soil in the shallow ground it sprang up quickly. When the scorching sun beat down these plants dried up for lack of deep roots. Some other seed fell among thorn bushes and as the thorns grew they crowded the plants, choking them – so they bore no fruit. But some seed did fall on fertile soil and as the plants grew their fruit abounded as much as 30, 60 or even 100 times over. Whoever has ears, let him hear."

When he was alone those who were with him, including the Twelve, asked him about this image.

"It's been given to you to understand the secret of the kingdom of God, but everything remains in parables to those who remain outside, who even though they see with their eyes will not understand, nor hearing with their ears comprehend, nor turning from their ways be forgiven their sins.[6]

"Or maybe you too didn't understand this homespun illustration? And if not, how will you grasp all the others? The sower is the one who spreads the word of God. Those by the side of the road are the ones who hear the word but quickly have it snatched from their hearts by the Devil. Those on rocky ground are like people who hear the word and immediately take it into their hearts with joy – but they lack inner depth and so when trouble comes calling on account of the gospel they instantly get offended and wither away. Those among the thorns are the ones who hear the word but let the cares of the moment and the deceitfulness of wealth and all the rest of the things that people run after enter their lives and choke the word, and so they become unprofitable. But those who receive the word on the fertile soil of their hearts *do* become fruitful, some of them 30 times as much as others, some 60, some even 100.

"Does anyone hide a lamp under a basket or stick it under the couch? Don't people instead put it on a lampstand? Nothing is hidden that will not be revealed nor anything secret that will not come to light. If anyone has ears, let her hear.

"And pay attention when you listen. Whatever measure you use to measure things out, that's how they will be measured back to you. To you who hear, more will be given. And catch this: whoever has will be given more, but whoever has next to nothing will lose even that.

"Listen again, here's what the kingdom of God is like. Picture a man who plants seed in the ground, then sleeps and rises again daytime and night. Meanwhile, the seed sprouts and matures – but how? He has no idea. The earth on its own yields first the stalk then the head then the full kernel. And as soon as the wheat is ripe the man thrusts in his sickle, because it's harvest time.

"I'll describe the kingdom of God another way. Let's compare it to a mustard seed. When it's planted in the ground it's by far the tiniest seed in the whole earth, but once it grows up it becomes the greatest of all trees in the field, so much so that the birds of Heaven find shelter in its mighty branches."[7]

Jesus shared many such similes and analogues with them, to the degree

---

6   *Isaiah* 6:9-10.
7   *Ezekiel* 17:23.

they were able to hear them. Yet though he spoke to the larger crowd only by
way of parables, he also explained everything to his disciples once they were
alone.

That same day once evening had come he said, "Let's cross over to the
other side of the sea." After Jesus had sent the crowd back on home the
disciples joined him in the ship, and some other small boats came along as
well. But as they sailed a full gale arose. Wind-driven waves crashing over the
gunwales nearly swamped the boat. Yet Himself lay sleeping like a babe on a
pillow, peacefully calm on the stern-most thwart of the ship.

So they rousted him shouting, "Rabbi! Don't you give a damn we're
about to die?!"

Shaken awake he chastised wind and sea: "Silence! And be still."

The wind ceased and a spreading calm quelled the whole sea.

"What were you so scared about? Don't you have any faith?"

Then they were scared indeed, asking themselves, "Who is he *really* –
that even the wind and the sea do what he says??"

5

Finally they landed on the other shore, near the hilltop town of Gadara, one
of the Ten Cities. But as soon as Jesus disembarked a demon-possessed man
accosted him. This man had lost his mind and now dwelt among the tomb-
stones of the dead. No one could catch let alone bind him. They had tried a
number of times but even if someone managed to get handcuffs on him he
was always able to break loose and smash them to pieces – the bottom line
is that no one had the strength to control him. Day and night he wandered
through the mountains and about the graves, screaming and cutting himself
all over with sharp stones.

But the moment he saw Jesus from afar off he raced to him and knelt
down, crying out, "What's now between me and you, Jesus, Son of the Most
High God? I beg you, by God, do not torment me!"

He said this because Jesus had already commanded the spirit to leave
the man.

"What's your name anyway?"

"Call me 'Thousands!' There are as many of us here as in a Roman legion."

And he begged Jesus not to send them all far away. It happened that a herd of pigs was grazing there on the hillside and so he urged, "Send us to the pigs and we'll possess them instead."

Jesus quickly gave them leave to do so. These unclean spirits then left the man and entered the pigs, the whole herd running headlong down the hillside straight to the sea, some two thousand of them drowning in the waves. Now, the pigs' herdsmen fled and told everyone in town and country what had happened.

They all ran out to see it for themselves, yet when they got to Jesus they now saw the madman - this same one who'd had thousands of demons possessing him - seated, clothed and fully in control of himself. And they were scared to death. Those who'd witnessed everything told them all about the unclean spirits and the pigs. But the villagers' reaction was to beg Jesus to get out of town. So Jesus returned to his ship.

The man who had been demon-possessed wanted to follow along with Jesus. But Jesus wouldn't let him.

"Go back to your own home and your own people and tell them what a marvelous thing the Lord has done, having great mercy upon you."

The man therefore left and began to tell everyone all throughout the Ten Cities what Jesus had done for him - and the people were dumbstruck with awe.

Right after that, Jesus crossed back by ship again to the other side, where a large crowd had gathered to be with him there by the shore. Jairus, one of the synagogue's rulers, rushed up to Jesus, and when he saw him threw himself down at his feet, begging him.

"My little daughter is dying. If you will just touch her with your hands I know she'll be healed and live."

Jesus went with him and a big mob followed along as well, crowding in on him as he went. Now there was a certain woman in the throng who had been suffering from menstrual disorders for twelve years. She had tried going to many doctors, wasting all her money on them and only getting worse, not better. But she had heard about Jesus and therefore snuck up behind him in the crowd and touched his clothes because she thought to herself, "If I can just touch his clothes I'll be all well."

The instant she did so she felt the flow of blood stop and knew by the feel of her own body she was free of her suffering. But that same instant Jesus also sensed that healing power had gone out of him and he spun around in the crowd.

"Who touched my clothes?"

His disciples questioned him, "Can't you see everyone pushing all around you? So how can you possibly ask 'who touched me?'"

But gazing around at everyone he spied the woman who did this. And she was afraid and shook because she knew what had happened inside her. Yet she approached, fell at Jesus' feet and told him the whole story.

"Daughter, it is your faith that has saved you. Go in peace and be healed from this plague."

Just as Jesus was speaking to the woman someone came from the synagogue ruler's house and told the man, "Your daughter is dead. Why are you bothering the rabbi?"

Jesus ignored them.

"Don't worry," he told the synagogue ruler, "just hold onto your faith."

Jesus wouldn't let anyone follow further on with him other than the ruler, Peter, James and James' brother John. When Jesus came to the man's house he saw that everyone there was in turmoil, crying and wailing.

"Why are you all troubled and grieving? The child isn't dead, she's just sleeping."

They ridiculed Jesus at this so he threw them all out of the house and, taking the girl's father and mother with him as well as his friends, he went to the room where the child lay. Reaching out his hands to her he commanded, טְלִיתָה קוּמִי - which in English means, "Get up little girl."

The girl got up right away and walked around. She was twelve years old. And they were all astonished beyond imagining. Yet he instructed them not to say anything to anyone but simply give the girl something to eat.

6

He soon left that region and headed to his own village, his disciples following him. On the Sabbath he went to the local synagogue and started to teach, but many hearing him were shocked.

"Where's all this coming from, such wisdom he's been given, such power in his hands? Isn't this just Mary's son, a carpenter, and the brother of James, Joseph, Jude and Simon? And aren't his sisters all here with us?"

So they found him offensive.

"Prophets are honored everywhere except in their hometowns and by everyone other than their fellow villagers and relatives."

He was amazed at their lack of belief and wasn't able to do anything especially powerful there, just laying his hands on a few sick people and healing them. After that, he went to some of the neighboring villages and taught there. And he also started sending his disciples out two by two, giving them power over evil spirits and telling them to take to the road with nothing but a walking stick – no bread, no backpack, not a dime in their pockets – just wearing sandals and the clothes on their backs.

"Whatever house you enter, stay there until you leave that town. But if there's someplace that won't have you or even listen to you, just leave and wipe the soil from underneath your feet on the way out as a witness against them. I'm telling you that Sodom and Gomorrah will have an easier time of it in the Day of Judgment than they will."

The disciples went right out and preached that men should turn from their evil ways. They cast out many demons and anointed many of the sick with oil, and the sick were healed.

Now by this time Jesus had become quite well known and soon King Herod heard about him. People said he must be John the Baptist raised from the dead on account of the mighty deeds he was doing. Others said he was Elijah and still others that he was a prophet, or was at least like one of the prophets.

"No, it's John. I had his head cut off but now he's risen from the dead."

Herod, you see, had arrested John and put him in prison because Herod had gone ahead and married his brother Philip's wife, Herodias, even though John had told him it was wrong – "It's against the Law of Moses for you to take your brother's wife."[8] So, not surprisingly, Herodias had it in for John and would've loved to kill him but she couldn't persuade Herod to do so, the reason being that Herod was afraid of John, knowing he was a just and holy man, and protected him.

---

8   *Leviticus* 18:16.

Frankly, Herod had been at a loss how to handle John. But once he heard him speak he decided he'd better keep him alive. Yet Herodias found an opportune moment for vengeance on the day Herod threw a feast for himself to celebrate his birthday, inviting his rich friends, his military commanders and all the leading lights of Galilee, so she procured her own daughter to dance the dance of the seven veils before him. Herod and his friends were so aroused by her dancing that Herod said to the girl, "Ask me what you will, and it's yours."

He even swore an oath to her, "Ask me anything, to the half of my kingdom, and I'll give it to you."

So the girl spoke aside to her mother, "What should I ask for?"

"The head of John the Baptist."

The girl went back to the king all eager, "I want the head of John the Baptist right away – and have them bring it on a silver platter."

The king was grief stricken at this but would not break his oath, not with all his friends sitting around him, and thus gave in to her, immediately calling for the executioner and commanding him to bring John's head. The soldier left and straightway beheaded John in the prison, brought his head on a silver platter and handed it to the girl, who gave it to her mother. When John's disciples heard what had happened they collected the body and buried it in a tomb.

Then Jesus' disciples gathered together again with him and told him about all the things they had done and all the things they had taught. Jesus said to them, "Let's find someplace quiet, somewhere apart, so you can rest up a bit," because the crowd around them was coming and going all the time and they had no chance to rest and hardly time to eat.

They took ship to a desert spot. But many people saw them leave and many knew who he was, so they sped afoot from all the local villages and got there ahead of Jesus, waiting for him to come. When Jesus arrived he saw the crowd and was moved with compassion for them, because they were like sheep without a shepherd. He began to teach them many things, but it was getting on in the day and his disciples became concerned.

"This is a desert spot and it's already getting late. Tell the people to leave and go to the nearby farms and villages to buy some bread for themselves, because they have nothing to eat."

"So give them something to eat."

"Where are we supposed to get the money to buy food for all

these people?"

"How much bread do you have? Go find out."

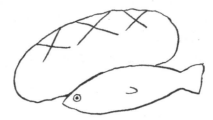

"Five loaves of bread plus two fish."

Jesus directed everyone to sit down picnic style on the pale grass. The people arranged themselves together in groups of 50 or 100. Taking the five loaves and two fish Jesus looked up to Heaven and blessed and broke the bread, giving the pieces to his disciples to distribute to the people. He did likewise with the two fish, sharing portions with everyone. All of them ate until they were full – five thousand men ate food there, yet when they were done there were still twelve baskets left over, filled with leftover pieces of bread and fish.

Thereafter Jesus pressed his disciples to get into the boat and cross over to Bethsaida, but he stayed behind to disperse the crowd. Once he had taken leave of them he went off to a mountainside to pray. By well into the night the ship was off in the middle of the sea, while Jesus remained alone on the land.

He could see the disciples far off toiling as they rowed, the wind being against them, so around 3 or 4 in the morning he strode toward them, walking on the sea with a mind to pass right by them. When they saw him walking on the water they thought it was a ghost and screamed – they all saw him and were thrown into distress.

But right away he calmed them.

"Cheer up, don't be so scared, it's only me!"

Then he climbed into the boat with them and the wind immediately stopped. They were dumbstruck, nearly out of their minds with fright and confusion. The truth is, they hadn't really understood what had happened with the loaves of bread, because their hearts were still calloused.

Once they finished crossing they anchored at Gennesaret. But as soon as they landed everyone knew who he was and ran all through the surrounding villages to carry the sick on pallets and bring them to wherever they found Jesus. So it was that wherever he went, whether to a village or a city or just out in the countryside, people laid the sick before him, begging him that they might touch just the hem of his garment. And as many as did touch were healed.

7

Then some of the Pharisees and scribes came down from Jerusalem to see Jesus. They criticized him because they saw some of his disciples eating bread without first washing their hands. Now, the Pharisees, indeed all observant Jews, held to the tradition of the forefathers, diligently washing their hands before eating as a form of ritual purity. For example, if they've just come from the market square, they will not eat until they've first washed their hands. And they observe a number of other traditions of like sort concerning the washing of drinking cups and pitchers, copper kettles and even anything they sit on. Therefore the Pharisees and scribes questioned Jesus.

"Why is it your disciples transgress the tradition of the forefathers, eating bread with impure hands?"

"It's plain that Isaiah was prophesying about you hypocrites when he said, 'These people honor me with their lips but their hearts are far from me. It's useless for them to worship me, teaching as doctrines the commandments of men.'[9] The truth is, you set God's commandments to one side, holding instead to the traditions of men, such as those concerning the washing of cups and pitchers and you do many other such things.

"Let's be honest – you're setting aside God's commandments in order to safeguard your own. For example Moses said, Honor your father and

---

9   Isaiah 29:13.

your mother[10] and Whoever speaks evil to his father or mother, let him be put to death.[11] But you say that if a man says to his father or mother קָרְבָּן - which in temple worship refers to a sacrificial offering - he's freed from a Biblical obligation to support his parents on the pretext that he's already dedicated some funds to the temple. You let your own interests trump his duty to his parents, thereby nullifying the commandment of God. And you do plenty of other things just like that."

Then Jesus spoke to the surrounding people.

"Listen carefully to me, all of you, and be sure you understand what I'm saying. Nothing that comes from outside someone can make him impure once it's entered him, only those things he brings forth from within. If you have ears to hear, hear me."

Once he got back to the house and was away from the crowd his disciples asked him what that saying meant.

"Don't you understand either? Don't you know that nothing that enters people from outside can corrupt them because it doesn't go into their hearts but simply through the bowels thence to the toilet?[12] It's what comes from *inside* people that makes them impure - for evil lurks in the hearts of men and thence come perversions, thefts, murders, adulteries, greed, deviltry, treachery, lechery, hexes, blasphemy, hubris, folly. All such evil comes from within and it's these that make people impure."

Jesus next travelled up to the Lebanese coasts of Tyre and Sidon. He stayed at someone's home, hoping the word wouldn't get out, but it was impossible for him to escape people's notice. And so it was that a certain woman whose daughter had an unclean spirit heard about Jesus, came to him and fell right at his feet. She was Greek, from the Syrophoenician region, and she begged Jesus to cast the demon out from her child.

"Let the children first eat their fill. It would be wrong to take their bread away and toss it to the dogs."

"True, m'lord, but the puppies beneath the table can still feast on the scraps."

"For that wise word go in peace. The demon has now left your daughter."

Indeed, when the woman returned home she found the evil spirit had

---

10   *Exodus* 20.12.
11   *Exodus* 21.17.
12   In saying this, Jesus made all foods pure.

already gone out of the girl - and there she was lying peacefully upon her bed.

Leaving those borders Jesus soon came again to the Sea of Galilee, in the midst of the Ten Cities. The people brought a deaf mute to him and pleaded with him to touch the man with his hand. Jesus took him aside away from the crowd, put his fingers into his ears and, having first spit on his hands, touched the man's tongue.

Then lifting his eyes up to Heaven Jesus sighed a deep sigh and said to the man אֶפְּתָח - which in English means, "Be opened!"

Instantly his ears were opened, the chains on his tongue were broken and he spoke with perfect clarity. Jesus ordered the people not to say anything about this to anyone. But as often as he told them not to, they blazed it about all the more. And they were astonished, simply beside themselves.

"He does all things well, even making the deaf to hear and the dumb to speak."[13]

8

By then there was a huge crowd around Jesus, but the people lacked food. Jesus called his disciples over.

"I'm deeply moved for these people - they've now stayed by me for three days despite having nothing to eat! Yet many of them have come from far off and if I send them away hungry some may faint along the way."

"But how can anyone feed them bread in the wilderness?"[14]

"How much do you have?"

"Seven loaves, that's it."

Jesus ordered the crowd to sit down upon the ground. Lifting up the seven loaves he blessed and broke them, giving the pieces to his disciples to set before the people, and they did so. They also had a few fish. So Jesus blessed these as well and ordered them distributed. After the people had eaten their fill it turned out there were still seven basketsful of crumbs

---

13   *Isaiah* 35:5.
14   *Exodus* 16:1 ff.

left over. After these four thousand people had eaten, Jesus dismissed them. He then promptly took ship with his disciples and came to region of Dalmanutha.

The Pharisees came out to meet him once again and started to argue with him, asking for a confirming miracle from Heaven in an effort to tempt him. Jesus groaned in his spirit deep with sorrow.

"Why do you seek such a sign? I'm telling you, you're not going to be given one."

So he left them then and there. Getting back aboard ship he crossed once more to the other side of the sea. But the disciples forgot to bring extra food with them and had no more than one loaf of bread in the boat. Jesus took the occasion to teach them another lesson, warning them to "Watch out for the leaven of the Pharisees and of Herod." They tried to figure out what he meant by that, concluding it was just that they hadn't brought along any bread.

But Jesus knew what they were thinking.

"Don't you understand? Are your hearts still that hard? Even though you have eyes, can't you see? And even though you have ears, can't you hear? Don't you remember? When I broke the five loaves for the five thousand, how many basketsful did you gather of the crumbs?"

"Twelve...."

"And when I broke the seven loaves for the four thousand, how many basketsful did you take up then?"

"Seven...."

"So how is it you don't understand now?"

They next landed at Bethsaida, where the people brought a blind man to Jesus and begged him to touch him. Taking the blind man by the hand Jesus led him out of the village. Spitting into the man's eyes and laying his hand upon him Jesus asked whether he saw anything. Looking up, the man said, "I see people but they look more like trees walking around."

Then Jesus laid his hands on the man again and his eyesight came into focus - his vision was fully restored and he saw everything with perfect clarity. Jesus sent him back to his home.

"Don't go back to the village. Don't even speak to anyone from the village."

Leaving there, Jesus and his disciples made it to the villages of Caesarea Philippi. As they walked along the road he questioned them.

"Who do people say I am?"

"John the Baptist, but some say Elijah and still others say one of the prophets."

"But who do *you* say I am?"

Peter spoke up.

"You're the Messiah!"

But Jesus warned them not to say anything to anyone about him. He began to teach them, explaining that the Son of Man must suffer many things, being rejected by the elders and the chief priests and the scribes, and that while he would be killed, after three days he would rise up again.

This much Jesus spoke quite clearly. But taking him aside Peter began to reproach him about it. Yet Jesus shut Peter down, turning from him toward his other disciples as he said, "Get thee behind me, Satan, for your mind is not set on God's cares, but those of men."

Jesus then gathered the multitude along with his disciples to shed more light on the subject.

"Whoever wishes to come after me, let him deny himself, take up his cross, and follow me. Whoever wants to save his life, will lose it. But whoever lets go his life for my sake and the sake of the good news of God will save it. What good is it for someone to gain the whole world but suffer the loss of his soul? What could anyone even give in exchange for his soul? I tell you that whoever is ashamed of me and my words before this adulterous and sinful generation, so too will the Son of Man be ashamed of him when he comes with the holy angels in the glory of his Father."

9

Then Jesus said to them, "Truly, there are some of those present who will not taste of death until they see the kingdom of God coming in power."

Just six days later Jesus took Peter, James and John climbing up a high mountain where they could be alone and he was transformed before them, his clothes shone gleaming, incandescent, snow-white beyond what any earthly bleach could make them. Then Elijah and Moses appeared to them, speaking to Jesus.

Peter said, "Rabbi, it's good that we're here - let's build three tabernacles, one for you and one for Moses and one for Elijah."

He had no idea what he was talking about. He only spoke out because they were all so afraid. But at that point a cloud cast a shadow over them and a voice spoke from the cloud.

"This is my beloved Son, pay heed to him."

They quickly looked around but there was no one there anymore, save Jesus only. As they descended the mountain Jesus warned them not to tell anyone what they had seen, at least not until the Son of Man was risen from among the dead. So they kept it to themselves. Even so, they debated among themselves what he could possibly mean about his rising from the dead. Finally they asked him, "Why do the scribes say Elijah first must come?"

"Elijah must indeed come first and restore everything,[15] even as it is also written about the Son of Man that he must suffer many things and be scorned. But I'm telling you that Elijah has already come and they did to him whatever they felt like, just as it was written about him."[16]

When Jesus got back to the rest of his disciples he saw a large crowd already gathered around and scribes arguing with them. But when the people saw Jesus they were stunned by his radiance[17] and rushing toward him hailed him. Then he asked the disciples, "What were you all arguing about?"

But before they could answer, someone from the crowd interjected.

"Teacher, I carried my son to you because he is possessed of a mute spirit and whenever the spirit overtakes him it throws him to the ground, foaming at the mouth and gnashing his teeth, and then he becomes stiff as a board. So I begged your disciples to cast the spirit out of him but they weren't strong enough."

"O faithless generation! How much longer must I stay with you? And how much longer put up with you? Bring the boy to me."

They brought him. But as soon as the spirit saw Jesus it tore at the boy and cast him to the ground, foaming at the mouth. Jesus spoke to his father, "How long has he been like this?"

"Since he was a child. Lots of times the spirit will throw him into the fire or into the sea, trying to kill him. But if you can, then help us, have

---

15 *Malachi* 4:5-6.
16 *Psalms* 22:1-18; *Isaiah* 53:3.
17 *Exodus* 34: 29-35.

mercy on us!"

"If you can but have faith all things are possible."

"I *have* faith, Lord, but you must help me where I lack."

When Jesus saw that the people all came running he took command of the evil spirit.

"You deaf and dumb spirit, I order you to leave this boy, never to return!"

After screaming and throwing the boy into convulsions one last time, the demon departed. Yet the boy looked to be dead, so much so that many said he *was* dead. But laying hold of his hand Jesus lifted the boy and he stood up.

When Jesus got back to the house his disciples asked him privately, "How come we weren't able to cast this one out?"

"There's no way to get rid of this type of demon without prayer and fasting."

Leaving there they passed through Galilee, but Jesus didn't want anyone to know. He explained to his disciples, "The Son of Man will be betrayed into the hands of men and they will kill him. Yet though he die, he will rise again on the third day."

But they didn't understand what he was saying and were afraid to ask him what he meant. He moved on to Capernaum and spoke to the Twelve again once they had gotten to the house.

"So what is it you were arguing about on the way here?"

They wouldn't answer, because they'd been fighting with one another over which of them was the most important. But Jesus knew their thoughts and sat them down.

"If anyone wants to be first, he will be last, the servant of all."

Then he stood a little child in the midst of them and taking him in his arms said, "Whoever receives such a child as this in my name receives me and whoever receives me receives not me, but him who sent me."

Then John said, "Teacher, we saw someone casting out demons in your name but he wasn't following along with us so we stopped him – because he wasn't one of us."

"Don't prevent him – whoever isn't against us is for us. Understand that there's no one who has power to act in my name who can easily speak evil of me – and I will be sure to reward anyone who lets you drink a drink of water in my name as one of the Messiah's. But whoever offends any of these little ones who believe in me would be better off if he'd had a millstone hung around his neck and been plunged in the sea. So if your hand leads you to offend, cut it off – you do better to enter life crippled than with two hands depart for the ceaselessly burning valley of Gehenna, where the maggots never die and the fire is unquenched.[18] Just so, if your foot causes you to stumble, cut it off – as I said, you're better going lame into life than with two feet be cast into Gehenna's unending blaze, where the maggots never die and the fire is unquenched. And even if it's your eye that hinders you, pluck it out – better again to go one-eyed into the kingdom of God than with two eyes be thrown to fiery Gehenna, where the maggots never die and the fire is unquenched.

"Everyone must be seasoned in the fire, and all burnt sacrifices are seasoned with salt.[19] Salt is a good thing – but if salt becomes unsavory how will you season things then? Have salt within yourselves and be at peace with one another."

10

Jesus left there shortly and came to the region of Judea by the far side of the Jordan River. And again a crowd gathered itself around him. As was his custom, he taught them. Then the Pharisees asked, testing him, "Is it lawful for a man to divorce his wife?"

"What did Moses command you?"

"Moses permitted a man to draft a writ of divorce and send her away."[20]

"He wrote that commandment to you only because of the hardness of your heart. But from the beginning of creation, he made the human race male and female;[21] so when a man leaves his father and mother he is joined to his wife and the two bodies become one[22] – they are no lon-

---

18   *Isaiah* 66:24.
19   *Leviticus* 2:13.
20   *Deuteronomy* 24:1,3.
21   *Genesis* 1:27.
22   *Genesis* 2:24.

ger two bodies, but one. What God has yoked together no man should split apart."

Once they were back in the house again his disciples asked him about this matter.

"Whoever divorces his wife and marries another is committing adultery against her. And if a wife divorces her husband and marries someone else she too commits adultery."

Then some parents brought their children so that Jesus might touch them – but the disciples blocked them. Jesus was angry at that and ordered, "Let the children come to me and don't hold them back, for of such is the kingdom of God – I tell you no one is able to enter the kingdom of God unless he's willing to receive it as would a little child." Then he took the children in his arms and having laid his hands upon them blessed them.

As they were going along the road a certain man rushed up to Jesus and knelt down before him asking, "Good Teacher, what should I do to inherit enduring life?"

"Why are you calling me good? No one is good, other than God alone. And you know the commandments: Don't commit adultery, don't murder, don't steal, don't be a lying witness, don't cheat the working poor, honor your father and mother."[23]

"Teacher, I've obeyed all those since I was a little child."

Then Jesus looked at him intently, and loved him.

"In that case you're only missing one thing: Go now, give whatever wealth you have to the poor – and don't worry, you'll have treasure in Heaven. Then, having taken up your cross, come back and follow me."

But the man was overcome with grief at Jesus' word and left weeping, because he owned many things. Gazing around, Jesus said to his disciples, "How hard it is for people who have wealth to enter the kingdom of God!"

But the disciples were stunned by his words, so Jesus tried explaining it to them again.

"Children, it's just very difficult for people who trust in money to enter into the kingdom of God. It would be a lot easier to thread a ship's hawser through the eye of a needle than for a rich man to enter the king-

---

23   *Exodus* 20:12-16; *Deuteronomy* 5:16-20, 24:14.

dom of God."

Then his friends were truly at a loss and said to one another, "In that case how can anyone be saved?"

"Impossible for men to do? Yes, but not with God - everything is possible with God."

Peter quickly said to him, "Look, we've left everything behind to follow you."

"And truly I tell you there's no one who's left his home, his brothers, his sisters, his father, his mother, his wife, his children or his lands all for my sake and the sake of the gospel who won't have a hundred times as many homes, brothers, sisters, mothers, children and lands in this life - along with suffering of course - and timeless life in the world to come. But many that are first shall be last and the last first."

They were now well on the road up to Jerusalem, Jesus going before them. But they were still in some confusion based on recent events and above all, fearful. Taking the Twelve aside Jesus tried to explain once more what was soon to happen.

"Listen up! We are going up to Jerusalem and the Son of Man will be betrayed to the chief priests and scribes. They will condemn him to death, handing him over to the uncircumcised. They will ridicule him, spit on him, whip him with lashes and finally kill him - but, on the third day he will rise up!"

Then James and John, the sons of Zebedee, approached Jesus and asked, "Teacher, we would like you to grant us whatever we may ask."

"And just what is it you want me to do for you?"

"Grant that when we sit down with you in glory one of us will be at your right hand and the other at your left."

"You have no idea what you're asking. Do you think you can drink the cup that *I* drink, or be baptized with the baptism that *I* am baptized with?"

"Yes we can."

"Then you will indeed drink the cup I drink and be baptized with my baptism. But to sit at my right and at my left? That it isn't mine to grant - it goes to those for whom it has been prepared."

When the other ten heard this they were indignant toward James and

John, so Jesus explained what he meant.

"You need to understand that those who sit as rulers among the nations lord it over them and the men in power oppress the people. But that's not the way it will be with you. Whoever wants to be great among you, he will be servant to all. And whoever wants to be first among you, he will be slave to all. Even the Son of Man did not come to be served but to serve, and to give his life as ransom for many."

Then Jesus and his disciples entered Jericho, passing through with a large crowd following them. As they left the city, blind Bartimaeus, the son of Timaeus, sat begging by the side of the road. When he heard that Jesus the Nazarene was there he began to shout and cry, "O Son of David, Jesus, have mercy on me!"

People in the crowd tried to hush him up. But he just shouted louder and louder, "David's Son, have mercy on me!!"

Jesus stopped dead in his tracks and ordered him to be brought. So they called the blind man, telling him, "Cheer up! He's asking for you, get up now." Casting his cloak aside he arose and came to Jesus.

"What is it you want me to do for you?"

"O my Master, would that I might see again!"

"Go then, your faith has healed you."

Instantly the blind man saw once more and he too followed Jesus on the way.

11

When they had gotten as far as Bethpage and Bethany, near Jerusalem and looking toward Mount Olive, Jesus sent two of his disciples on a mission.

"Go into the village opposite you and as soon as you enter you'll see a donkey's colt, one no one has ever sat upon. Loose him and bring him to me. If anyone asks you what you're doing just tell them that the Lord needs him, and he'll send you right on your way."

So they left and found the colt tied up by the outside gate where two roads cross and set it loose. Some of the bystanders said to them, "What do you think you're doing unhitching that animal?" They answered just as Jesus had told them and the people then let them go ahead.

They brought the colt to Jesus, laying their cloaks over it, and upon it sat Jesus.[24] Many people spread their own cloaks on the road, while others cut down branches from the trees and strew them along his way. Both those who walked ahead and those who walked behind cried out.

"Hosanna! Blessed is he who comes in the name of the Lord![25] And blessed be the future kingdom of our father David, Hosanna in the highest!"

Jesus then entered Jerusalem and came to the Temple precincts. But evening approached and, having looked around the city, Jesus retired to Bethany with the Twelve. As he left for Jerusalem the next day, he was hungry. Seeing a fig tree in the distance with its leaves in bloom Jesus went to it in the hope of finding some green figs on it – it being still too early for ripe figs – but when he got there he found not even those, just the leaves. Jesus commanded the tree, "Let no one eat your fruit, not ever." And his disciples heard him.

Once Jesus had entered Jerusalem again and gotten to the Temple precincts he began to toss out anyone there who was selling and buying things. First he overturned the counting tables of the moneychangers and the seats of those who sold pigeons and then he prevented anyone from carrying any vessels through the Temple area. He also explained to them why he did what he did.

"Isn't it written, My house shall be called a house of prayer for all nations?[26] But now you've made it a den of thieves."

The chief priests and the scribes heard what had happened and began to look for a way to destroy Jesus. They feared him, however, because the whole crowd was overwhelmed by his teaching.

Once it was evening Jesus left again to go outside the city. Passing by on the road the next morning the disciples saw the fig tree had already withered from the roots up. Having recalled the prior incident Peter said to Jesus, "Look, Rabbi, the fig tree you cursed has withered away."

---

24   *Zechariah* 9:9.
25   *Psalms* 118:25-26.
26   *Isaiah* 56:7.

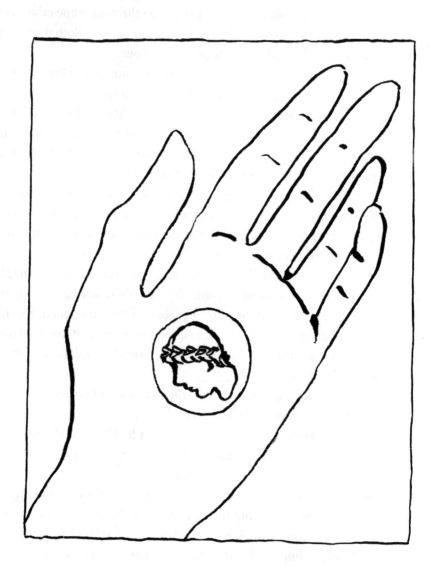

"Have faith in God. I'm telling you if you were to say to this mountain, 'Be gone, be tossed to sea,' and weren't of two minds about it but believed that what you asked for would happen, so it would be. Understand me - whatever you ask for when you pray, believe it is yours and it shall be. But when you stand to pray, if you have anything against anyone, forgive, so that your Father in Heaven may forgive you your sins - because if you do not forgive others neither will your Father in Heaven forgive you your trespasses."

And so Jesus came again into Jerusalem. As he walked in the Temple precincts the chief priests and the scribes and the elders approached him and asked, "By what authority do you do these things? Or who gave you this authority to do them?"

"Let me ask you one thing and if you answer then I'll tell you by what authority I do the things I do. John's baptism - was it from Heaven or was it from men? Answer me that."

They debated among themselves how to respond: "If we answer him, 'from Heaven,' he'll say, 'so why didn't you believe him?' But if we say, 'from men...?'" Well, they were afraid of the people if they said that because all the people held John to be a true prophet. So they simply said, "We don't know."

"Well then, neither will I tell you by what authority I do these things."

12

After this he began to speak to them by way of parables, like this one.

"A man planted a vineyard. He built a wall around it, dug foundations for the wine press, let it out for lease to tenant farmers and then left on a long journey. When harvest time came he sent one of his servants to the farmers to bring him back fruit from the vineyard. But, seizing the man, the farmers flogged him and sent him away empty handed. Yet again the owner sent them one of his servants. The farmers bashed him in the skull and abused him. Then he sent a third servant, but this man they killed. And they did the same to many others he sent, killing some, beating others. The owner had yet one son, whom he loved. As a last resort he sent him to his tenants saying, 'Surely they will honor my son.' But when the farmers saw him they said to themselves, 'This is the heir – let's kill him and his inheritance will be ours.' And so grabbing him they killed him and tossed his body outside the vineyard. What then will the lord of the vineyard do? He'll return to wipe those farmers out and give the vineyard to others. Haven't you read this scripture – The stone that the builders rejected has now become the cornerstone; this is the Lord's doing and it's a miracle in our eyes?"[27]

Then they looked for a way to seize him (but they feared the crowd), because they knew this parable was directed at them. They went away themselves but sent some of the Pharisees and Herodians over next, trying to catch him in his words.

When these came to Jesus they said, "Teacher, we know you are truthful and don't cater to anyone and that you teach people God's path with complete honesty, paying no regard to anyone's status. Tell us then, are we permitted to pay taxes to Caesar or aren't we?"

But perceiving their hypocrisy Jesus said to them, "Why do you keep tempting me? Bring me a silver coin so I can look at it."

When they had brought one he asked, "Whose image and inscription is that?"

"Caesar's."

"Then hand over to Caesar what's Caesar's and to God what's God's." And they marveled at him.

Next came the Sadducees – they think there's no life after death – and asked him, "Teacher, Moses told us that if a brother dies leaving a widow behind but no children his surviving brother should marry her and raise up a line of children for his late brother.[28] Now, it happened once that there were seven brothers. The first got married but died without any children, so one of his brothers married the widow. But he died without heirs as well. Same with the third brother. In due course all seven had her and died, none leaving children. Finally she died too. Here's the question: whose wife will she be in the next life when they are all raised from the dead, since she was married to all seven of them?"

"You're way off base with that! Don't you know your Bible or the

---

27   *Psalms* 118:22-23.
28   *Genesis* 38:8; *Deuteronomy* 25:5-6.

power of God? Don't you know that when people are raised up from the dead they don't get married but are like the angels in Heaven? And as for the dead being raised, have you forgotten what God said to Moses from the burning bush – I am the God of Abraham, and the God of Isaac and the God of Jacob?[29] So he is not the God of the dead, but of the living. You are therefore deep in error."

Then one of the scribes who had heard Jesus reasoning with the Sadducees and knew he had answered well approached him with this question, "What is the chief of all the commandments?"

"The first of all the commandments is this, Hear, O Israel, the Lord our God, the Lord is one.[30] And thou shalt love the Lord your God with all your heart, and with all your soul, and with all your mind, and with all your strength. This is the first commandment. And the second is like it: You will love your neighbor as yourself.[31] There is no commandment greater than these."

"Teacher, you have spoken well and truly, for God is one and there is no other God besides him.[32] And to love him with all your heart and all your thoughts and all your soul and all your strength, and to love your neighbor as yourself? Well yes indeed, that is far greater than any burnt offerings and sacrifices."[33]

Jesus saw that he answered wisely and told him, "You are not far from the kingdom of God."

After that, no one dared ask Jesus anything.

Teaching at the Temple Jesus inquired of the people, "Why is it that the scribes call Messiah the 'Son of David'? After all, David himself speaking by the Holy Spirit said, The Lord said to my Lord, 'Sit on my right hand, until I make your enemies your footstool.'[34] If David calls him Lord then in what way is he his son?"

And the multitude of people heard him with joy as he continued in his manner of teaching.

"Watch out for the scribes, because they love to walk around in long

29   *Genesis* 3:6, 15, 16.
30   *Deuteronomy* 6:4-5; *Joshua* 22:5.
31   *Leviticus* 19:18.
32   *Deuteronomy* 4:35, 6:4; *Isaiah* 45:21.
33   *I Samuel* 15:22; *Hosea* 6:6.
34   *Psalms* 110:1.

robes and be embraced in the market squares. They want the best seats in the synagogues and seats of honor at the feasts. But they devour widows' homes and for a pretext recite long prayers – they shall have the greater judgment."

Sitting down opposite the Temple treasury Jesus watched how the multitude cast their money into the pledge box, the rich casting in plenty. But one poor widow dropped in two cents. Summoning his disciples Jesus shared this insight: "If you want to know the truth, this poor widow has just put more into the treasury than everyone else! They all gave out of their surplus but she in her poverty gave everything she had, even all her life's goods."

13

As they left the Temple one of his disciples said, "Teacher, look at how glorious the stones are, how grand all the buildings!"

"You're impressed by these big buildings? There isn't one stone on stone that won't be thrown down."

Once he was seated back at Mount Olive, across from the Temple Mount, Peter, James, John and Andrew asked him privately, "Tell us, when will these things happen? And what's the sign we should watch for, telling us that all this will come to an end?"

"Don't let anyone deceive you. Many will come in my name saying, 'It is I!' And they will trick many people. But when you hear the sound of wars and rumors of wars, don't panic – that has to happen – it's not the end. One nation will rise up against another nation, kingdom against kingdom, and there will be earthquakes in many places and famines and suffering. These are just the beginnings of sorrows.

"So watch out for one another. They will hand you over to the courts and beat you in the synagogues. You will stand before rulers and kings for my sake, as a testimony to them. Yet the good news of God must first be preached to all peoples. When they come to take you away, don't plan or worry ahead of time what you're going to say. Whatever comes to you at that time, speak it, because it's not you who's speaking, but the Holy Spirit. But a brother will betray a brother, even so will a father his son, and children will rebel against their parents,[35] even to put them to death. You will be hated by everyone for my name's sake, but whoever holds fast to the end will be saved.

"Let whoever reads this understand what I'm saying: when you see the creature spoken of by Daniel the prophet holding place where it is forbidden - the horror, desolate and loathsome[36] - then those in Judea must flee to the mountain and those on the rooftops not come back down into the house, not even to go inside and gather their belongings. Just the same with those in the fields - they mustn't turn back even to grab their coats. Those days will be full of sorrow for those who are pregnant and for those still nursing. Only pray that you don't have to flee in the bitterness of winter. For those days will be days of pain, pain like there hasn't been seen from the time God made the world until now, nor ever will be.[37]

"If God were not to shorten those days no one would survive. But for the sake of those he has chosen, he will shorten them. And if anyone should say to you then, 'Look! Here's the Messiah!' or 'Look! He's over there!' - don't believe them. False Messiahs and false prophets will pop up all over the place performing miracles and wonders in order to deceive - if it were possible - even the chosen ones. So you watch out - I've told you all this ahead of time.

"In those days, after all that pain, the sun will be darkened and the moon will not shed its light.[38] Even the stars in the sky will fall and powers in the Heavens be tossed to and fro.[39] But it's *then* that they'll see the Son of Man coming in the clouds[40] in all of his power and glory. He will send his angels out to gather up the chosen ones from the Four Winds,[41] from the far reaches of the Earth to the far reaches of Heaven.[42]

"Let me give you a comparison to a fig tree that should help. When

---

35   Micah 7:6.
36   Daniel 9:27.
37   Daniel 12:1.
38   Isaiah 13:10.
39   Isaiah 34:4.
40   Daniel 7:13-14.
41   Zechariah 2:10.
42   Deuteronomy 30:4.

its branch is tender and shoots forth its leaves, that's how you know it's
nearly summertime. Same here – when you see all these things starting to
happen you'll know the time is near, right at the door. I promise you this
generation won't pass away until all these things are done. Heaven and
Earth may pass away, but my words will not. However, no one knows the
day or hour when all this shall happen, not even the angels in Heaven, not
even the Son! Only the Father knows. Watch, take heed, pray! Because
you don't know when this time will come.

"It's like a man who takes a trip, leaving his household in the hands
of his servants, giving them all instructions what to do and appointing
a foreman to keep watch. You need to keep watch as well because you
don't know when the master of the house will return – in the evening, at
midnight, when the rooster crows, or at dawn, lest coming unexpected
he finds you fast asleep. I'm saying the same thing to you that I say to
everyone – Watch!"

14

The festival of Passover and Unleavened Bread was beginning in two days
and the chief priests and the scribes tried to figure out how they could
trap, seize and kill him, "but not," they said, "on the Feast Day itself, lest
the people start a riot."

While Jesus was having dinner in Bethany at the house of Simon, a
leper, a woman came in carrying an alabaster flask filled with the purest
of scented spikenard, a precious ointment. Breaking open the flask she
anointed Jesus' head. Some of those dining with Jesus got upset and said
to themselves, "What a waste of chrism! It could've been sold for a good
year's wages and the money given to the poor."

And they scolded her.

But Jesus scolded *them*.

"Leave her alone! Why are you making trouble for her? She's done
something fine here. You will always have the poor with you and whenever you are moved to do so you'll be able to help them. But you won't

always have me here. She has done what she could for me, anointing my body with oil for the burial. I tell you truly that wherever in the whole world this good news is preached that which she has done will also be spoken of, as a memorial to her."

Then Judas, the man from Kerioth and one of the Twelve, went to the chief priests in order to betray Jesus to them. They were overjoyed when they heard him and offered to pay him silver for his treachery, so Judas looked for a way to hand Jesus over.

On the first of the festival, the day the Passover lamb was to be sacrificed, Jesus' disciples said to him, "Where do you want us to go to make arrangements to eat the Passover meal?"

He sent out two of his disciples.

"Go into the city and someone carrying a pitcher of water will meet you. Follow him. Go where he takes you and say to the innkeeper, 'The Teacher says, "Do you have a private room where I can eat the Passover meal with my disciples?"' He will show you a large room upstairs where you can lay out the Seder table."

His disciples left and went into the city, where everything happened just as Jesus had said it would. And thus they got ready for the Passover meal.

At sundown Jesus came with the Twelve. While they ate, reclining as freemen, Jesus said, "One of you eating with me will betray me."[43]

Then they began to grieve and first one asked him, "Is it I?"

Then another, "Is it I?"

"It's one of you Twelve, one who dips his hand with me in the bowl. The Son of Man must go, as is written about him. But woe to that man who betrays him. It would have been better for him never to have been born."

And as they ate Jesus took unleavened bread. Having blessed it he broke and gave it to them saying, "Take, eat. This is my body." Taking the cup he gave thanks and passed it to them. And they all drank from it. Then he said, "This is my blood - the blood of a new covenant[44] - which is poured out for many. I tell you truthfully I shall not drink of the fruit of

---

43 *Psalms* 41:9.
44 *Jeremiah* 31:31.

the vine again until the day I drink it anew in the kingdom of God."

Once they had sung a hymn, they went out to Mount Olive.

"Tonight you will all be offended because of me, for so it is written, Strike the shepherd and the sheep will be scattered.[45] But after I am raised from the dead I will go ahead of you into Galilee."

Peter quickly said to him, "Even if everyone else is offended, I'll never be."

"Yet today, this very night before the rooster crows twice, you'll deny me three times."

Peter protested all the more, "I'm telling you that even if I'm put to death with you, I'll never deny you."

So said they all. Then they came to an orchard known as Gethsemane.

"Stay here while I go off to pray."

Taking Peter and James and John with him, he began to be dismayed, in utter distress.

"My very soul is covered with grief, filled with deathly sorrow.[46] Stay here, friends, watch with me."

Going a little off to the side he fell on the ground and prayed that if it were possible the time might not come, saying אַבָּא (which in English means father), "Everything is possible for you: take this cup from me. Yet not as I wish, but as do you."

Then he returned and found them sleeping.

"Simon, are you really asleep? Weren't you strong enough to watch with me for even one hour? Watch and pray so you don't fall into temptation, because the spirit is willing but the flesh is weak."

Going off again he prayed the same as before. Then he returned a second time and found them sleeping, their eyes being heavy. And they didn't know how to answer him. Then he went off again a third time, saying, "Sleep on and rest. It's done. The time has come. The Son of Man is betrayed into the hands of sinners."

And after that he said, "Wake up! Let's go - look now, the traitor is at hand."

Right then, even as he spoke, Judas appeared, one of the Twelve.

---

45 *Zechariah* 13:7.
46 *Psalms* 42:5, 11 and 43:5.

He had with him a large crowd armed with swords and clubs and along with them the chief priests and the scribes and the elders. The double-crosser had given them a sign: "Whomever I kiss, that's the one. Seize him – and don't worry, you can safely take him away."

As he approached Jesus he said, "Rabbi, rabbi" and kissed him. Then they grabbed Jesus by the arms and took him away. One of those standing by drew his sword and laid into the servant of the High Priest, hacking his ear off.

But Jesus spoke out, "Are you coming after me with swords and clubs as you would a thief? Day after day I was with you in the Temple precincts, teaching, and you didn't go after me then. But now the scriptures must be fulfilled."

Then all his friends fled away, leaving him behind.

One of the young men following Jesus wore nothing but a linen cloth draped around his body. The men tried to grab him but when they did he slipped out of it and fled away naked.

Then they led Jesus to the High Priest, where all the chief priests and elders and scribes had gathered together. Peter followed him from far off, to just outside the High Priest's palace, and he sat with the servants warming himself by the fire. The chief priests and the whole Sanhedrin scouted around for someone to testify against Jesus in order to put him to death. But they couldn't find anyone. They did come up with plenty of people to give false testimony, of course, but the problem was that none of them agreed with the other in the lies they gave. For example, a couple of the lying witnesses said, "We heard him say 'I will destroy this temple made by hands and on the third day build another one without hands.'" But no one else's testimony agreed with theirs.

Then the High Priest stood up in the middle of everyone and challenged Jesus straight out, "Aren't you going to say anything? What about these accusations they're making against you?"

But Jesus stayed silent, answering not a word.[47]

So again the High Priest confronted him.

"*Are* you the Messiah, Son of the Blessed?"

"I am. And you will see the Son of Man sitting enthroned at the

---

47 *Isaiah* 53:7.

right hand of power[48] and coming with the clouds of Heaven."[49]

Then the High Priest tore his clothes and cried out, "What need do we have of more witnesses?! You've heard this blasphemy – what say you?"

And they all judged him worthy of death. Some spat on him while others covered his face and punched him, mocking as they said, "Prophesy!"

Even the servants slapped him.

Now Peter was still outside below the palace when one of the High Priest's serving girls came by. Seeing Peter warming his hands she said to him, "You too were with Jesus the Nazarene!"

But he denied it.

"I don't know him. I don't even know what you're talking about."

Then he went outside into the forecourt and the rooster crowed. But the maidservant saw him again and told all those around, "This man is one of them, I tell you he *is*!"

And again Peter denied it.

But a little while later the bystanders said, "No, we can tell you are one of them. You're from Galilee, your accent gives you away."

Peter began to curse and swear, "I don't even know this person you're talking about!"

The rooster crowed a second time and Peter remembered what Jesus had said to him: "Before the rooster crows twice you will deny me three times." And he burst into bitter tears.

15

First thing in the morning the chief priests with the elders and the scribes conferred with one another and assembled the Sanhedrin. Then having bound Jesus they handed him over to Pilate.

Pilate asked him flat out, "Are you the King of the Jews?"

---

48 *Psalms* 110:1.
49 *Daniel* 7:13.

"Do *you* say so?"

Then the chief priests threw many accusations against him. So Pilate challenged him again, "Aren't you going to answer? They're accusing you of all sorts of evil things."

But Jesus answered nothing,[50] such that Pilate marveled.

Now it was the custom at the Feast for Pilate to set one prisoner free, whomever the people desired. There was a certain prisoner named Barabbas. He had incited a rebellion against the government and now lay in chains with his fellows, murderers all. The people began to clamor, urging Pilate to release someone this time just as he always had before.

"Is it your wish that I release to you the King of the Jews?"

He said this because he knew the chief priests had only handed Jesus over out of envy. But the chief priests stirred up the mob, pressing them to ask for Barabbas rather than Jesus.

"What then am I supposed to do with the man you call King of the Jews?"

"Crucify him!"

"Why? He's done nothing wrong."

Yet they cried out all the more, "Crucify him!"

Pilate wished to please the crowd and so he set Barabbas free, ordered that Jesus be whipped and then delivered him to be crucified.

The soldiers first led Jesus away from the courtyard to their headquarters, the Praetorium, and called together their whole cohort. There they dressed Jesus in a crimson robe and crowned him with a crown of thorns they had woven. They began to salute him, saying, "Hail, King of the Jews!" They whipped his head with a reed, spat on him and bowing their knees pretended to worship him. When they were through mocking him they took off the crimson robe and dressed him back in his own clothes.

Then they led him out to be crucified. As they went the soldiers grabbed hold of a certain man named Simon - a Cyrenian, the father of Alexander and Rufus - who was passing by on his way in from the countryside and they forced him to carry Jesus' cross. And so they brought Jesus to a place called גָּלְגָּלְתָּא - which in English means Skull Hill. They gave him wine to drink, mixed with myrrh. But he wouldn't drink it.

It was 9:00 in the morning when they crucified him. They took his clothes

---

50   *Isaiah* 53:7.

and divided them among themselves, rolling dice to see who would get what.[51]
The accusation against him was written down and posted above his head –
"King of the Jews." Two thieves were crucified along with him, one on his right
side and one on his left. Thus was the scripture fulfilled, He was counted as a
sinner.[52]

People passing by scoffed at him, shaking their heads and saying, "So! You
said you could destroy the Temple and build it back in three days? Try saving
yourself – come down from the cross."

The chief priests and the scribes mocked him in the same way, saying to
one another, "He healed others but he can't save himself.[53] Let this Messiah,
King of the Jews, come down now off the cross so we can see and believe in
him." And the two thieves crucified with him scorned him as well.

But darkness fell upon the whole land[54] from noon to 3 in the afternoon.
At that hour Jesus cried out with a great cry saying אֵלִי אֵלִי לְמָה שְׁבַקְתָּנִי – which in
English means "My God, my God, why have you forsaken me?"[55]

When some of those standing by heard it they said, "Look! He's calling
for Elijah!" And one of them ran up with a sponge soaked in vinegar, held on a
reed, and handed it up to Jesus to drink saying, "Let him be. Let's see whether
Elijah will come to take him down."

Jesus cried with a loud voice and breathed out his last.

Then the Temple curtain split in two from top to bottom.

When the centurion who stood there heard him cry out and die like that
he said, "Truly, this man was the Son of God."

Some women watched from afar off – Mary Magdalene, Mary the mother
of young James and of Joseph, and Salome – all followers and servants of Jesus
from the time he was in Galilee, as well as many other women who came up
with him to Jerusalem.

Because the Day of Preparation for the Sabbath would begin at sunset,
Joseph of Arimathaea – an honorable council member who himself yearned
for the kingdom of God – daringly went to Pilate and begged leave to take the
body of Jesus. Pilate could hardly believe that Jesus was already dead so he

---

51   *Psalms* 22:18.
52   *Isaiah* 53:12.
53   *Psalms* 22:7-8.
54   *Exodus* 10:22.
55   *Psalms* 22:1.

summoned the centurion and examined him to find out how long ago he had died. Once the centurion had confirmed the death Pilate allowed Joseph to remove the body. After buying fine linen Joseph took Jesus' body down from the cross, wrapped it, laid it in a tomb hewn out of the rock and had a great stone rolled across the entrance to seal it. And Mary Magdalene and Mary the mother of Joseph saw where Jesus was laid.

16

After the Sabbath, Mary Magdalene, Mary the mother of James, and Salome bought spices so they could come to anoint him. On the first day of the week, very early in the morning and just as the sun was rising, they went to the tomb. Along the way there they said to one another, "Who will roll the stone away from the tomb for us?"

But when they got to the tomb, looking up they saw that the stone had already been rolled away. And it was very large. When they entered the tomb they saw a young man seated on the right side, dressed in a white robe - and they were scared out of their wits.

But he said to them, "Don't be afraid. You're looking for Jesus the Nazarene who was crucified. But he's not here, he is risen! See for yourselves, there's the place where his body was laid. Go now, tell his disciples - and Peter - that he's gone ahead of you into Galilee. You'll see him there, just as he said you would."

So they fled from the tomb, trembling yet ecstatic. But they didn't tell anyone yet, because they were still frightened.[56]

Now, having risen from the dead and while it was still early on the first day of the week, the first person Jesus appeared to was Mary Magdalene, out of whom he had cast seven unclean spirits. She then ran to tell those who had been with Jesus, even as they still mourned and wept. But they didn't believe her when she told them that Jesus was alive and that she herself had seen him.

Soon after that, Jesus appeared in another form to two of them as they walked in the countryside. Then they went to tell the rest - but the others

---

56   Translator's note: certain manuscripts end Mark's account at this point.

didn't believe them either.

Finally, Jesus himself appeared to the eleven as they were dining and reproached them for their lack of faith and the hardness of their hearts, having disbelieved those who had seen him after he was raised up.

Then he left them with these words.

"Go out to all the world, preach the good news to every creature. Whoever believes and is baptized will be saved. But whoever doesn't believe will be judged. And these signs will follow those who believe – in my name they will cast out demons, they will speak in new languages, they will take up poisonous serpents. If they drink any deadly thing it will not harm them. They will lay their hands on the sick and the sick will get well."

When he had finished speaking to them the Lord was taken up into Heaven, where he sat down enthroned at the right hand of God. But the disciples went right out to preach everywhere, the Lord working with them and giving strength to their words through the signs that followed them.

Amen.

ACCORDING TO LUKE

Dear friend of God, many people have set their hands to compile various narratives of the multitude of deeds done among us, taking down memories from those who were eyewitnesses from the outset, servants of the word as preached. Having now investigated the facts and with the benefit of such materials, I thought it would be useful for me as well carefully to edit the accounts, writing them down for you in an orderly way to provide you with a full understanding as well as confidence in the oral instruction you've received.

1

During the time Herod ruled as king over Judea there was a priest by the name of Zechariah,[1] a member of the priestly order of Abijah.[2] His wife was named Elisheva[3] and she too was a descendant of Aaron, the first High Priest.[4] They were both faithful in their service before God, observing blamelessly all the commandments and statutes of the Lord. But they

---

1   Which in English means "God has remembered."
2   1 Chronicles 24:10.
3   Which in English means "God's oath."
4   Exodus 6:23.

were by now well advanced in years and had no children, Elisheva being barren.

Zechariah's priestly order was one of the 24 established by King David and he served at the Temple in weekly rotation with the others. It was the custom to choose by lot one of the priests on daily duty to offer incense within the Holy Place. On a certain day the lot fell on Zechariah. At the hour of the offering all the people waited outside praying, while he went within. But while he was inside an angel of the Lord appeared to him, standing at the right of the golden altar of incense – and Zechariah was in turmoil, fear falling over him. But the angel said, "Don't be afraid, Zechariah, your prayers have been heard: your wife Elisheva will bear you a son and you will name him Johan.[5] He will be your pride and joy and many will be overjoyed at his birth. He will be mighty in the sight of the Lord, drinking neither wine nor liquor[6] but filled with the Holy Spirit from the time he leaves his mother's womb. He will turn many of the Children of Israel back to their God, going out before him in the spirit and power of Elijah, turning the hearts of the fathers to their children[7] and the disobedient to the wisdom of the righteous, all to make ready a people prepared for the Lord."

"How can that be? I'm way old and my wife's no younger."

"I am Gabriel[8] and stand in the presence of God, who sent me to speak to you and proclaim this good news.[9] But watch! You are now silenced, made mute till the day the child is delivered because you doubted my words, which by their very nature will come true at the appointed time."

Meanwhile the congregation waited outside, astonished that Zechariah was taking so long to finish his tasks. Yet when he finally emerged he was unable to speak and they discerned he had seen a vision in the Temple. He confirmed this by making signs to them but otherwise remained speechless. Nevertheless, he stayed on duty for the rest of his designated week and then went home. Soon thereafter his wife Elisheva became pregnant. She kept herself secluded for five months, saying "Thus has the Lord been gracious to me, deigning to look upon me and remove my reproach in the eyes of men."

---

5   Which in English means "God is gracious."
6   *Numbers* 6:2-3.
7   *Malachi* 4:6.
8   Which in English means "God is my strength."
9   *Cf. Daniel* 9:21-27, 10:13.

In the sixth month of Elisheva's pregnancy God sent the angel Gabriel to the Galilean village of Nazareth to visit a girl named Miriam.[10] She was then engaged to be married to a man named Josef,[11] a linear descendant of King David. Entering her home the angel said, "*Ave Maria, gratia plena, Dominus tecum. Benedicta tu in mulieribus.*" But she was perplexed by his words, not understanding what kind of greeting that might be.

Then the angel spoke to her again: "Fear not, Miriam, because you have found favor before God. And watch! You will conceive in your womb and give birth to a son. You will call his name Yeshua, or Jesus.[12] He will be great, known as the Son of the Most High, and the Lord God will give him the throne of his father David.[13] He will rule over the house of Jacob forever and his kingdom will have no end."[14]

"How will that happen, since I've never had sex?"

"The Holy Spirit will descend on you, the power of the Most High over-shadow you - and he that is born of you will be called holy, the Son of God. Now look! Your kinswoman Elisheva has conceived a child in her old age, she who was called barren. Therefore nothing the Lord declares shall be impossible."

"Behold the handmaid of the Lord. Be it unto me according to your word."

And so the angel departed from her.

During those days Miriam arose and went quickly into the hill country of Judea, to the town where Zechariah lived. When she entered his house she greeted her cousin - but the moment Elisheva heard Miriam's voice the child leapt in her womb for joy. Then being filled that moment with the Holy Spirit Elisheva called out to Miriam, "*Benedicta tu in mulieribus et benedictus fructus ventris tui!* And how is it that the mother of my Lord should visit me? For behold, at the sound of your greeting in my ears the child leapt for joy in my womb. And blessed is she who believed that all the Lord had promised would occur."

Miriam responded in song[15] -

---

10   Which in English means "bitter waters."
11   Which in English means "the Lord will increase."
12   Which in English means "savior."
13   *Isaiah* 9:6-7.
14   *Daniel* 2:44, 7:13-14.
15   https://www.youtube.com/watch?v=3YHf3CtEi8E.

"My soul doth magnify the Lord,
and my spirit hath rejoiced in God my Saviour.
For he hath regarded the low estate of his handmaiden:
for, behold, from henceforth all generations shall
call me blessed.
For he that is mighty hath done to me great things;
and holy is his name.
And his mercy is on them that fear him from
generation to generation
He hath shewed strength with his arm;
he hath scattered the proud in the imagination
of their hearts.
He hath put down the mighty from their seats,
and exalted them of low degree.
He hath filled the hungry with good things;
and the rich he hath sent empty away.
He hath helped his servant Israel, in remembrance of
his mercy;
As he spake to our fathers, to Abraham, and to his seed
for ever."

Thereafter, Miriam stayed with Elisheva about three months before returning to her own home..

Now when Elisheva's pregnancy had gone full term she gave birth to a son. When all her friends and relations heard of it they rejoiced with her, giving thanks and praise to the Lord for the mercies shown to her. On the eighth day, the day for the child to be circumcised, they were prepared to name him after his father, Zechariah. But Elisheva protested and said, "He shall be named Johan."

"But none of your relatives has that name!"

So they signaled to the boy's father to find out what he thought the name should be. Asking for a wax tablet Zechariah inscribed, "His name is Johan." Just then as they all marveled at this his tongue was loosed and he opened his mouth to sing the praises of God, causing awe to fall on those present. And indeed as soon as these events became known throughout the surrounding areas of Judea the neighbors were abuzz, guarding all this in their hearts with the thought, "What sort of child will he be? Because the hand of the Lord is clearly upon him."

And thus Zechariah, filled with the Holy Spirit, prophesied about his
son in this hymn –

> "Blessed be the Lord God of Israel,
>> because he has come to help and has redeemed
> his people.
>> For he has raised up a horn of salvation for us
> in the house of his servant David,
>> as he spoke through the mouth of his holy prophets
> from long ago,
>> that we should be saved from our enemies,
> and from the hand of all who hate us.
>> He has done this to show mercy to our ancestors,
> and to remember his holy covenant —
>> the oath that he swore to our ancestor Abraham.
> This oath grants that we, being rescued from the
>> hand of our enemies,
> may serve him without fear, in holiness
>> and righteousness
> before him for as long as we live.
>> And you, child, will be called the prophet of the
> Most High.
>> For you will go before the Lord to prepare his ways,
> to give his people knowledge of salvation
>> through the forgiveness of their sins.
> Because of our God's tender mercy
>> the dawn will break upon us from on high
> to give light to those who sit in darkness
>> and in the shadow of death,
> to guide our feet into the way of peace."

And so the child grew, becoming strong in the Spirit as he dwelled in
the Wilderness of Judea until the day he was openly revealed to Israel.

2

Now during this same time Caesar Augustus issued a census decree requiring the registration of all those living in the Empire. This was the first census taken while Quirinius was Governor of the Syrian Province[16] and everyone went to his ancestral village to be registered. Josef came down from Galilean Nazareth to his family's home in Bethlehem, the city of David, because he was of the house and lineage of David, there to be registered along with his pregnant wife Miriam. Her pregnancy came fully due while they were in Bethlehem and she gave birth to a first-born son, wrapping him in swaddling clothes and laying him in a feeding trough for his cradle because there was no room for them inside the local inn.

It was the time of year for pasturing sheep. The shepherds were therefore out in the open fields and the hillsides guarding their flocks at night when an angel of the Lord appeared to them and the glory of the Lord shined around them. The shepherds were struck dumb with fear but the angel said to them, "Don't be afraid – I come bringing you good news and great joy for the whole nation because today a Savior was born to you in the city of David – he is the Lord and Messiah."

And at those words the Host of Heaven filled the skies praising God and singing [17]

When the angels left them and departed to Heaven the shepherds said to one another, "Let's cross over to Bethlehem and see for ourselves this advent the Lord has revealed to us!" They raced there quickly and finding Miriam and Josef together with the child as he lay in a manger they repeated all they had been told concerning the child. Everyone who heard their story marveled at what the shepherds told them, but Miriam kept it all in her heart, pondering their words. The shepherds then returned to their flocks, glorifying and praising God as they went for all they had seen and heard.

The child was circumcised on the eighth day and they named him Jesus, all as the angel had declared while he was still in the womb.

When Miriam's time of purification was fulfilled in accordance with

---

16   Josephus, *Antiquities of the Jews*, Book XVIII, ch. 1, § 1.
17   https://upload.wikimedia.org/wikipedia/commons/5/53/Handel_-_messiah_-_17_glory_to_god.ogg.

the law of Moses[18] she and Josef brought Jesus to the Temple to be presented to the Lord – as it stands written in the Law, Let every male born of the womb be called holy to the Lord.[19] And they came as well to redeem the child in accordance with the Law, offering the only sacrifice they could afford – a pair of turtledoves or maybe two young pigeons.[20]

The day they came to make their offering a local man named Simeon was led by the Holy Spirit to show up at the Temple as well. He was a just man, devout, waiting with great expectation for the Consolation of Israel, having been told by the Spirit in a vision that he would not die until he had seen the Lord Messiah himself. When Jesus' parents walked through the door to fulfill the Law's customs, he took the child in his own arms and praised God like this –

> "Lord, now lettest thou thy servant depart in peace,
> according to thy word,
> For mine eyes have seen thy salvation,
> Which thou hast prepared before the face
> of all people;
> A light to lighten the Gentiles, and the glory of your
> people Israel."[21]

Jesus' father and mother were astonished at his words. But Simeon continued on in prophecy

> "Behold, this child is set for the fall and rising against of
> many in Israel;
> and for a sign which shall be spoken against;
> (Yea, a sword shall pierce through thy
> own soul also,)
> that the thoughts of many hearts may be revealed."

Now Anna, a prophetess and the daughter of Phanuel, a member of the tribe of Asher, was in the Temple then as well. She was well near ancient, having lost her husband some 84 years earlier after only seven years

---

18   *Leviticus* 12:1-4.
19   *Exodus* 13:2, 12, 15.
20   *Leviticus* 12:8.
21   *Isaiah* 49:6.

of marriage, continuing throughout her widowhood in deep devotion to the Lord, not ceasing to pray in the Temple and to fast whether day or night. She too entered the Temple at just that moment and gave thanks to God, speaking to all those waiting for the deliverance of Israel.

When Jesus' mother and father had completed all required by the Law they returned to their own village, Galilean Nazareth. There the child grew in strength and became filled with wisdom, the grace of God resting upon him.

Each year, Josef and Miriam went up with their friends and relatives to spend Passover in Jerusalem. Once Jesus turned 12 they brought him along as well, as was the Jewish custom for boys who reached that age. At the end of the festival the group from Nazareth headed back with Josef and Miriam, assuming that Jesus was somewhere in the caravan, probably with others his age.

Unbeknownst to them, however, Jesus had stayed behind in Jerusalem on his own. But after a day on the road his parents still hadn't seen him and therefore started asking their kin and other travelers whether anyone knew where he was. No one did, so Josef and Miriam panicked and turned back to Jerusalem, desperately seeking Jesus.

After scouring the city for three days they finally found him in the Temple, seated in the midst of a group of scholars, both listening and asking questions, confounding all who heard him with his knowledge and keen responses.

But his parents didn't know what to do when they saw him so Miriam challenged him –

"Jesus, how could you do this to us? Your father and I have been out of our minds looking for you!"

"Why? Didn't you know I had to be at work with my Father?"

They had no idea what he was talking about. Yet he returned thereafter with them to Nazareth, remaining obedient to his parents, growing in wisdom as well as age and finding favor with both God and the people.

3

It was during the fifteenth year of Tiberias' reign as Caesar that the word of God came to Johan, son of Zechariah, while he lived in the desert. Pontius Pilate had become procurator of Judea during this period, with Herod Antipas ruling as tetrarch over Galilee, his brother Philip over Ituraea and the region of Trachonitis, and Lysanias over the Abilene district. And at this same time Annas and his son-in-law Caiaphas served as high priests.

Johan went throughout the whole region surrounding Judea announcing a baptism for the forgiveness of sins. This was as in the words of the prophet Isaiah, written long before –

A voice of someone calling out in the desert:

> 'Prepare the way of the Lord,
> straighten out his paths!
> For every gorge will be filled,
> every mountain and hill leveled,
> the crooked ways straight and
> the rough roads smooth.'
> Then shall everyone see the salvation of God.[22]

Johan was blunt with the crowd that came out to be baptized by him.

"You snakes! Who warned you to flee the coming wrath? But if you seek forgiveness then do some good deeds to show you really are repentant. And don't start thinking to yourselves, 'We'll be fine because Abraham is our father.' Not so. God could raise up children for Abraham from the stones lying in front of you. But he's already set the axe to the root of the trees and any tree that doesn't bear good fruit will be cut down and tossed to the fire."

The people asked him, "What then shall we do?"

"Any with two jackets should give one away and those with food should likewise share."

Some taxmen asked at their baptism, "What should *we* do?"

"Don't collect more than what people owe."

Then some soldiers said, "What about us?"

---

22   *Isaiah* 40:3-5.

"Don't shake people down and don't blackmail them – just be happy with your wages."

The people listened with great expectation, wondering in their hearts whether Johan himself might be the Messiah. But he disabused them of that notion.

"I may be baptizing you with water but the one who's coming after me is more powerful than I, so much so that I'm not even worthy to help him unlace the thongs of his sandals. When he comes he'll immerse you in the baptismal fire of the Holy Spirit. He has a winnowing tool in his hand, ready to sweep clean the threshing floor, gathering the wheat to his storehouse but burning the chaff with unquenchable fire."

Johan preached the good news to the people with these and many other exhortations. But he leveled charges against Herod the tetrarch on account of what he did with Herodias, who was his sister-in-law until Herod took her for his own; and Johan indicted him for many other crimes and misdemeanors. Having had enough, Herod had Johan arrested and thrown in jail – yet not before all the people who came to Johan had been baptized, and Jesus as well. But as Jesus prayed coming up from the water Heaven itself was opened and the Holy Spirit descended in the bodily form of a dove, lighting upon him as a voice booming from above spoke, "You are my Son, my Beloved, in whom I am well pleased."

Then this same Jesus set out on his public ministry, being around 30 years old[23] and the son – or so people understood – of Josef, who in turn was descended from Heli, Matthat, Levi, Melchi, Jannai, Josef, Mattathias, Amos, Nahum, Esli, Naggai, Maath, Mattathias, Semein, Josech, Joda, Joanan, Rhesa, Zerubbabel, Salathiel, Neri, Melchi, Addi, Cosam, Elmadam, Er, Yeshua, Eliezer, Jorim, Matthat, Levi, Simeon, Judah, Josef, Jonam, Eliakim, Melea, Menna, Mattatha, Nathan, David, Jesse, Obed, Boaz, Sala, Nahshon, Amminadab, Admin, Arni, Hezron, Perez, Judah, Jacob, Isaac, Abraham, Terah, Nahor, Serug, Reu, Peleg, Eber, Shelah, Cainan, Arphaxad, Shem, Noah, Lamech, Methuselah, Enoch, Jared, Maleleel, Cainan, Enos, Seth and Adam, who himself came from God.

4

---

23   *Numbers* 4:3, 23, 43, 47.

Filled with the Holy Spirit Jesus returned from the Jordan region. He was then led by the Spirit into the wilderness, where he was tested 40 days by the Accuser. He ate not at all during those days and when they came to a close he was virtually starving. At that point of weakness the Devil said to him, "You're the Son of God – why don't you just turn these stones into bread?"

"Because man does not live by bread alone."[24]

Whisking Jesus to Jerusalem the Tempter set him at the edge of the Temple's pinnacle and said, "You're the Son of God – jump! But don't worry, he's commanded his angels to watch over you[25] so that, caught in their hands, you won't even touch ground."[26]

"Don't tempt the Lord your God."[27]

Finally, leading Jesus to a mountain peak Satan flashed before him all the kingdoms of the world and promised, "I can deliver you their power and glory – it's mine to give to whomever I wish – so it's all yours if you will but worship me."

"Thou shalt worship the Lord your God and him only shalt thou serve."[28]

When these temptations came to an end the Devil left him, albeit just for a season.

Then Jesus headed back to Galilee in the power of the Spirit and as he began to teach in the synagogues his fame spread throughout the whole region, the people praising him. In due course he came to his native village of Nazareth and on Saturday as was his custom he went to shul. At the appropriate time in the service he stood up to read. When they handed him the scroll of the prophet Isaiah he unrolled it to the day's appointed text –

> The Spirit of the Lord rests upon me:
>> he has anointed me to preach
> good news to the downtrodden –
>> healing the brokenhearted,
> proclaiming freedom for the captives,
>> giving sight to the blind,

24   *Deuteronomy* 8:3.
25   *Psalms* 91:11.
26   *Psalms* 91:12.
27   *Deuteronomy* 6:16; *cf.* W. Shakespeare, *Macbeth* 1.3.123-26.
28   *Deuteronomy* 6:13.

> granting deliverance to the oppressed,
>   all in the year of the Lord's good grace.[29]

Then he rolled it back up, handed it to the shamas and sat down. With the eyes of all piercingly upon him he proclaimed, "Today this scripture is fulfilled in your ears!" Witnessing his testimony the whole congregation was amazed at the graceful words that flowed from his lips, yet they said, "Isn't this just Joe's boy?"

But Jesus replied, "I suppose you'll use this proverb on me, 'Physician, heal yourself.' Or perhaps you'll ask me, 'Why don't you do the same things here we've heard you did in Capernaum?' Well, the truth is that a prophet gets no respect in his own hometown. It was the same in the days of Elijah. There were many widows at the time in Israel because it hadn't rained for three and a half years[30] and famine lay hard on the land. Even so, Elijah wasn't sent to help any of them, just one poor widow in Zarephath, a small village between Tyre and Sidon.[31] And the same held true in Elisha's time. Israel was filled with lepers but he only healed the one man Naaman, and him a Syrian to boot!"[32]

When the people heard that they flew into a rage, gathered as a mob and ran Jesus out of town, pushing him to the edge of a cliff outside the city where they aimed to throw him off. But he turned around and passed through their midst, continuing on his way.

From Nazareth Jesus went back to Capernaum of Galilee. He spent the Sabbath days instructing the people, to the point where they were frankly astonished as they saw the authority in his words. But there was a man in the congregation who was possessed of a filthy and demonic spirit. On hearing him the demon cried out, "What are you doing here, Jesus Nazarene?? Have you come now to destroy us? Because I know *exactly* who you are, you're the Holy One of God."

But Jesus chastised the spirit –

"Shut up! And come out of this man!"

The demon first threw the man to the ground and then left him, yet did him no further harm in the process. All of this terrified the people and they said to one another, "What kind of voice is this?! He commands

---

29   *Isaiah* 61:1-2.
30   *Daniel* 7:25, 12:7; *Revelation* 11:2-3, 12:6, 12:14, 13:5.
31   *1 Kings* 17:8-24.
32   *2 Kings* 5:1-27.

the evil spirits with power and authority and they obey." And so spread Jesus' renown throughout that whole region.

Once he had left the synagogue Jesus entered Simon's house, where he found Simon's mother-in-law suffering from a raging fever. The family appealed to him on her behalf. Jesus stood over the woman and commanded the fever to cease, which it instantly did. In fact, so quickly was the woman healed she as much as jumped up then and there to host and serve her guests.

By sunset that day the people had brought to Jesus anyone who had any kind of sickness from any kind of disease. He laid his hands on each individual and healed them all – and not only that but cast demons out of many of them, the evil spirits screaming as they fled, "You are the Son of God!" But Jesus squelched them from speaking any more, because they knew him to be the Anointed One.

At daybreak Jesus left for a place of solitude. The crowd searched him out anyway and pressed him to stay.

"I can't," he said. "I've got to share the good news of the kingdom of God with other towns as well – indeed, that's the very reason I've been sent!"

And so he continued preaching throughout the synagogues of Galilee.

5

A large crowd followed Jesus to the edge of Lake Gennesaret to hear him teach. But there was barely any room for him to stand. Looking around he saw two ships beached along the shore sitting empty, the fishermen having gotten out to wash their nets. Jesus climbed into one of the boats (Simon's to be precise) and had him push it out a bit from the land. There he sat on a thwart to teach the people.

Once he'd finished the lessons Jesus asked Simon, "Why don't you put out to sea now and try casting your nets into deeper waters to see what you can catch?"

"We spent the whole night out there already, dropping and hauling nets until we were wiped out and we still didn't catch a thing. But Master, if that's your word to us, we'll cast out again."

And so they did, this time hauling in such a multitude of fish their nets were strained to the point of breaking. Signaling to their business partners in the other boat they asked them to come and give a hand. But as they loaded the catch together the weight was so great that it threatened to sink both boats! When Simon saw what was happening he fell at Jesus' knees and begged him, "Get away from me, Lord! Don't you know I'm a sinner?" And all of the rest, including his partners Jacob and John, Zebedee's sons, were likewise fearful, seeing the magnitude of the haul.

But Jesus said to Simon, "You needn't be afraid - from now on you'll be catching men not fish." Then they brought their boats back to land and left them there, following Jesus instead.

As they came to one of the towns in the area a man covered head to toe with skin disease saw Jesus and prayed prostrate before him, "Lord, I know you're able to heal me if you wish."

Reaching out Jesus touched the man and said, "I do wish it - be cleansed!" Instantly the disease left him. But Jesus told the man not to run around telling everyone, directing instead, "Show yourself first to a priest, bringing the offering commanded by Moses as evidence to them of your cleansing." Even so word spread quickly and massive crowds gathered from all around both to hear Jesus and be healed of their diseases. In all this, Jesus still took whatever chance he could to withdraw to some quiet places to pray.

Now one day as he was teaching, a number of Pharisees and teachers of the Law were seated to hear him, having come from villages all over Judea and Galilee and out from Jerusalem as well - and the healing power of Yahweh was upon Jesus.

Others came as well, one group carrying a paralytic with them. However they couldn't find any way to get into the building where Jesus was speaking and so they clambered up to the roof, pried off a bunch of the tiles and lowered the paralyzed man down on a stretcher right in the middle of the crowd by Jesus. When Jesus saw their faith he said to man, "My friend, your sins are forgiven you."

But on hearing that, the scribes and Pharisees started to quarrel and debate among themselves, "What kind of heresy is this!? Isn't God the only one who can forgive sins?"

Jesus perceived their doubts and asked, "Why are your hearts so troubled? Do you think it's easier to tell someone crippled like this,

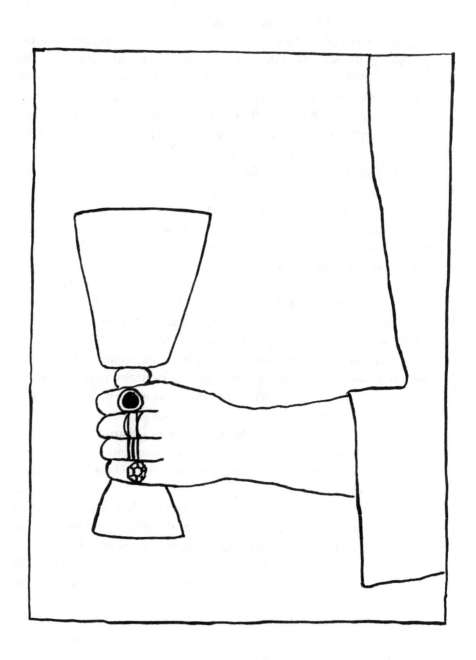

'Your sins are forgiven,' or to tell him 'Get up and walk?' But I want you to know that the Son of Man has power on Earth both to forgive *and* to heal!"

Then Jesus turned to the paralyzed man and said, "Stand up! Take that stretcher and walk back home." And at that the man who had lain a paralytic stood straight, picked up his pallet and left on his own two legs, praising God all the way to his village. Then something like terror mixed with glee seized everyone who saw it - awestruck, they glorified God and said, "We've seen incredible things today!"

As Jesus walked along sometime after these events he observed a man named Levi busy collecting taxes.

"Hey you! Come follow me!"

Levi got right up from his desk to follow Jesus, leaving all his papers behind. That night Levi hosted a major feast for Jesus in his home, inviting all his friends to join - and not just those colleagues who skimmed taxes for the Romans but a whole bunch of other greedy people. Yet when the Pharisees and scribes saw this they groused to the disciples, "What's with you eating and drinking with such people?!"

Jesus overheard them.

"Healthy people don't need a doctor, just the sick. That's why I haven't come to call the righteous to repent, just the sinners."

"Fair enough, but why do Johan's disciples pray and fast all the time just like us Pharisees yet your disciples eat and drink?"

"Do you expect wedding guests to fast at the wedding feast while the bridegroom is with them? But soon enough the bridegroom will be snatched away from them and for sure they'll fast in those days. Let me give you this comparison. No one patches an old coat with cloth torn off a new one - not only won't the new cloth match the old but you'd wreck the new coat when you tear out a patch. And it's the same idea with wine. No one pours new wine into old wineskins because the new wine will burst the old leather and you'll lose both the wine *and* the wineskins. You have to pour new wine into new wineskins. Nevertheless, people who are used to drinking old wine don't want to try the new because they're happy enough with the old."

One Sabbath day as Jesus and his disciples passed through a sown field, the disciples, being hungry, plucked the standing grain, rubbed it in their hands to blow away the chaff and ate the wheat berries. Some of the Pharisees saw it and confronted them. "How dare you break the Sabbath like this?"

But Jesus asked them, "Haven't you read in the Scriptures what David did when he and his friends were hungry? How he entered the House of God, took the Bread of the Presence and ate it, both he and his men, something only priests were allowed to do? My point is that the Son of Man is also Lord of the Sabbath."

On the ensuing Sabbath Jesus again entered the synagogue to teach. There was a man there who had a withered right hand. The scribes and Pharisees kept a close eye on Jesus to see if he would heal on the Sabbath – their purpose was to find some charge to bring against him. Jesus knew their plans but even so he said to the man with the withered hand, "Get up and stand here in the middle of the room." And so he did. Jesus then turned to the congregation and asked, "Is it lawful to do good on the Sabbath or do harm, to save a life or destroy it?" As he gazed on the people he spoke to the man, "Stretch out your hand!" He did so and the crippled hand was restored to health with his other. But the rulers were filled with senseless rage and plotted what they might do to Jesus.

Thereafter he went to the hill country to pray and stayed all night in supplication to God. When daybreak came he called his disciples to himself and selected twelve of them, whom he named to be emissaries: Simon (a/k/a Peter), his brother Andrew, Jacob, John, Philip, Bartholomew, Matthew, Thomas, Jacob the son of Alphaeus, Simon (nicknamed the "Zealot") and Judas, a man from Kerioth, who became a traitor.

Once Jesus descended with them back to the plain he found a huge crowd of his followers waiting there together with many others who had flowed in from the whole of Judea, including Jerusalem. Besides them there were yet others who had travelled in from the Lebanese coasts of Tyre and Sidon. They had all come to listen to Jesus, certainly, but also to be freed, healed of all their diseases, released from the torment of unclean spirits. And so the people crowded in on Jesus to touch him, for he was radiant with the healing power of God.

Then Jesus lifted his gaze to his disciples and expounded –

"Blessed are you poor for yours is the kingdom of God. You hunger now but will be filled. You weep now but later will laugh. People hate you, I know. But when they scorn you and toss you out, spitting on your name for the sake of the Son of Man - that's when you are most blessed! I'm telling you to rejoice in that day, even jump for joy, because your reward will be great in Heaven. Why? Because that's the same way their fathers treated the prophets.

"Yet woe to you who revel in wealth! You've gotten all the joy you'll ever have - full now but hungry later, laughing now but weeping later. And watch out if everyone fawns on you. Why? Because that's the same way your fathers treated the false prophets.

"So listen carefully: love your enemies and do good to those who hate you, laud those who curse you, pray for those who mistreat you. If someone smacks you across the face offer her the other side. And if someone swipes your jacket don't hold back your shirt. If someone panhandles you give him cash. And if someone rips you off don't call the cops. The rule of thumb is to deal with people the way you'd like them to deal with you. After all, if you love the people who love you is that something special? Even sleazy people do as much. And what credit are you entitled to if you only lend to people you can get the money back from? Believe me, loan sharks do the same. I want you to love your enemies and do them good, to lend to those who can't repay you. Do *that* and your profit will be great in Heaven because you will be children of the Most High, who is kind to the ungrateful and the wicked. Therefore be merciful just as your Father is merciful.

"Judge not and you shall not be judged: condemn not and you shall not be condemned: forgive and you shall be forgiven: give and it shall be given unto you; good measure, pressed down, and shaken together, and running over, shall men give into your bosom. For with the same measure that you mete withal it shall be measured to you again."

Then Jesus gave them a number of illustrations.

"Can a blind person guide a blind person? Won't both fall into a ditch?

"Is a student greater than his teacher? Yet when fully instructed he will be like his teacher.

"How is it you can spot a speck in your brother's eye but don't notice the blot in your own? And how is it you say to your brother, 'let me pick out this splinter from your eye' when you can't see the log in yours? You hypocrite! Get rid of your own defects and then you'll see clearly enough to help your brother with his.

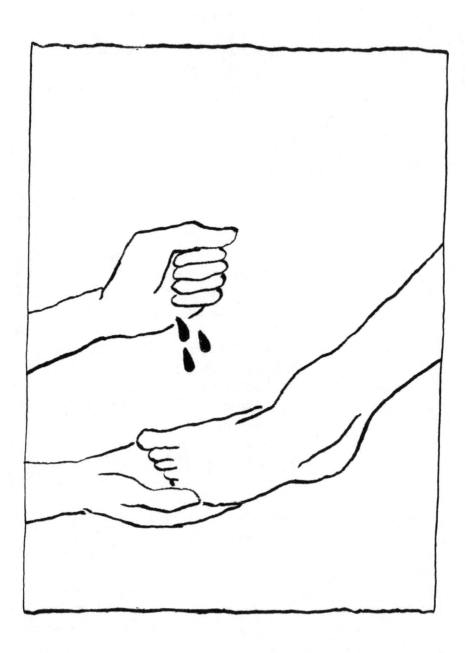

"I'm telling you good trees don't bear rotten fruit and rotten trees don't bear good fruit. That's why you can tell a tree by the fruit it bears – people don't gather figs from thorns neither harvest grapes from brambles. My meaning is this: A good man out of the good treasure of his heart brings forth that which is good; and an evil man out of the evil treasure of his heart brings forth that which is evil: for of the abundance of the heart his mouth speaks.

"So why do you call me 'Lord, Lord' but don't do what I tell you? Let me compare someone who listens to my words and does what I say to the woman who built her house by digging deep into the ground to lay the foundation on bedrock. That way when the floods came and the river rose to beat against the house it couldn't shake it because it was built well. In contrast, anyone who hears my words but doesn't do what I say is like the man who built *his* house on the soil, not bothering with foundation stones. When the waters rose and dashed against the house it collapsed in a seeming instant – and great was its ruin."

7

When Jesus finished these teachings, words the people had needed to hear with their own ears, he went back to Capernaum. It happened that the local Roman centurion had a highly trusted slave, one very dear to him, but the lad had fallen grievously ill and lay at death's very doorstep. Now, the centurion had heard tell about Jesus. He therefore sent some of the Jewish elders to intercede with Jesus in the hope he might heal the boy. When they reached him they pressed him earnestly, telling him that "the man who asks this of you is worthy of your help – he loves the Jewish people and even built us a synagogue at his own expense!"

Jesus started on the way to accompany them but while he was still pretty far away from the house some of the man's friends came with this message from the centurion: "Lord, you needn't come yourself to my aid! In truth, I'm not worthy of your presence in my home, which is why I didn't presume to approach you myself but sent elders of your own people instead. But just say the word and I know my servant will be healed. I too am someone in the chain of command. I've got people over me who tell me what to do and I've got people under me who follow my orders. I can tell one soldier, 'Go!' and he goes or 'Come!' and he comes, just as I tell my servant, 'Do this!' and he does it."

Jesus was astonished when he heard this, turned to his crowd of followers and said, "I haven't found anyone in all of Israel with that kind of faith!" And when the centurion's friends got back to his house they found the sick boy alive and well.

The next day Jesus visited the nearby village of Nain, a few miles south of Mount Tabor, with his disciples and a sea of followers trailing along. As they approached the city gate they were met by a massed procession of mourners leaving the town, bearing with them a widow's only son. When the Lord saw the boy's mother his heart went out to her.

"Woman, weep not."

Then Jesus stopped the pall bearers in their tracks, touched the coffin and commanded, "Son, wake up!" At that the dead arose and began to speak. Jesus handed him back to his mother as a godly terror fell on all those who saw what had happened. But they glorified God saying, "This is the Great Prophet, now risen among us[33] – for God has visited his people!" So Jesus' fame continued to spread throughout Judea and all surrounding regions.

As all this was occurring Johan's disciples reported the events to him. Johan then sent two of his men to Jesus to ask whether he was in fact the one they'd been expecting or whether they should still be looking for someone else. When they reached Jesus he was in the midst of the people, healing many from their diseases and afflictions, casting out demons and granting sight to the blind. Jesus said, "Tell Johan what you've seen and heard – the blind recovering their sight, the lame walking, the lepers cleansed, the deaf hearing, the dead raised back to life, the poor receiving God's good news. And blessed is the one who is not offended in me."

After Johan's messengers had left Jesus explained about him to the crowd.

"What did you think you were seeing when you went out to the desert places? A reed shaken by the wind? But tell me – why did you go? Were you hoping to see some spectacle? Maybe someone wearing fancy clothes? Hardly – those people live in kings' palaces. But you went to

---

33   *Deuteronomy* 18:15.

see a prophet, didn't you? And indeed you saw not just a prophet but much more than a prophet, because Johan is the very one of whom it was written,

> Watch! I am sending out my messenger
>> before your appearing,
> to prepare your way ahead of you.[34]

Listen to this truth: no one greater than John has yet been born of women. And yet, the least one in the kingdom of Heaven is greater than he."[35]

When the tax collectors and other sinners heard this they praised God, because they had all been baptized by Johan. But the Pharisees and doctors of the Law rejected Johan's baptism, turning their backs on God's will for them.

Then Jesus continued.

"To what then shall I compare the people of this generation? They are like children in the market calling out to one another,

> 'We played the flute,
>> but you didn't dance.
> We sang a dirge,
>> but you didn't mourn.'

So it is that Johan came neither eating nor drinking and you say, 'He's demon-possessed.' The Son of Man came both eating and drinking and you say, 'Look! There's a glutton and a lush, a friend of shysters and tricksters' – yet wisdom is justified by her deeds."

Around then one of the Pharisees decided to ask Jesus over for dinner and he went. As Jesus reclined at the table one of the local whores walked in. She had heard that Jesus would be dining there and had gone and bought an alabaster jar, filling it with ointment of myrrh. Standing by Jesus' feet she wept; with shed tears she washed; with hair let down she dried; and with her lips she kissed his feet as she anointed them with myrrh.

---

34   *Exodus* 23:20; *Malachi* 3:1.
35   *Zechariah* 12:8.

When Jesus' host saw what the woman did, he thought to himself, "If this man were a real prophet he would've known this girl for the slut she is and never let her touch him like that."

But Jesus knew his thoughts.

"Simon, I have something to say to you."

"Say on, teacher."

"Two people owed money to a certain creditor. The first owed him $5000 and the second $500. Neither had enough money to pay him back but he discharged both of them, forgiving the loans. Tell me then, who will love him the most?"

"I would guess the one who owed him the most."

"And you would be right. But Simon don't you see? When I entered your home you didn't give me so much as a drop of water to wash my feet, yet this woman wet my feet with tears and dried them with her own hair. You didn't greet me with a kiss, but from the time she walked through the door she hasn't ceased to shower my feet with kisses. And you didn't anoint my head with oil, but she anointed my feet with myrrh. I'm telling you this for your own good – her sins, which are great, are forgiven because she loved greatly. But someone who is forgiven little loves little."

Then Jesus turned to the woman and said, "Your faith has saved you. Go now in peace."

Hearing that, the rest of those around the table said to themselves, "Who *is* this man, forgiving sins as he does?"

8

Then Jesus strode through every Judean village and farm to spread the good news to the country folk there as he preached and proclaimed the kingdom of God. The Twelve went with him, as did a number of women who had been healed from their ills and freed from evil spirits, among them Mary Magdalene with seven devils in her pen, Joanna the wife of Herod's steward Chuza, Susanna, and many others, all ministering to Jesus out of the goods they had.

And as a large crowd gathered of people coming in from one town after another Jesus shared a parable.

"A sower went out to sow his seed. In the process some of the seed fell along the roadside, where people trampled it or let it be snatched as devouring birds swooped down. Some other seed was scattered on the rocks, where it sprouted spiny and stiff, lacking sufficient moisture. Other seed drifted among the brambles, where the plants arose tangled in thorns, choking in the enveloping dark. But the rest of the seed fell on fertile soil and blossomed with fruit in du season, sometimes 100 times over. So listen – and hear what I'm saying!"

But his disciples didn't really follow the story and therefore asked him later what he meant.

"It's open to you to learn things about the kingdom of God that used to be hidden – but for others they're just figures of speech and though they see they see not, though they hear they cannot understand.[36] So here's what this illustration is all about. The seed is the word of God. The image of seed dropped by the roadside represents people who hear the word but have it snatched from their hearts by the Devil, lest they believe and be saved. Seed on the rocks concerns those who hear the word and at first receive it with joy, but are rootless, holding onto their faith for a bit but withering when trouble comes calling. And seed fallen among thorns describes people who hear the word but let the worries and wealth of the world weave webs in their hearts, choking all growth. But those who take the word in and hold it fast with good hearts and true, these are like the fertile ground, where the seed yields fruit in their lives through faith and patience.

"No one takes a lamp and hides it under a basket or puts it under the bed. They put it on a lampstand so someone coming into the house can see where she's going. There's nothing secret that won't come to light and nothing hidden that won't become known. Therefore take heed to what I'm saying – whoever has will receive and whoever lacks will lose even what he thinks he has."

It was about this time that Jesus' mother and brothers came to see him, but they couldn't get through the crowd.

Someone passed the word to Jesus, "Your mother and brothers are out there wanting to see you."

"But my mother and brothers are already here! They are all those who hear the word of God and act on it."

Shortly thereafter Jesus said to his disciples, "Let's take ship and

---

36   *Isaiah* 6:9-10.

cross this lake." As they sailed Jesus soon fell asleep. But a whirling wind swept the waves, swamping the boat to its peril. Rousting Jesus, the men called, "Master! Master! We're about to die!" Sleep gone from his eyes, Jesus upbraided the wind and the waves, and so the storm dispersed and the waters lay still. But then he chided the disciples as well, "What's with you, where's your faith?" That stunned them so much that they puzzled among themselves, "Who is this man, after all, that he bosses around the wind and waves and they obey?!"

They sailed on, reaching the land of the Gerasenes on the far shore opposite Galilee. As they disembarked a certain man of the city came out to confront Jesus. This man was demon-possessed, for a long time dwelling neither in house nor home but among the tombs, naked and untamed. The local people had often caught the man and tried to guard him bound in chains and irons. Yet each time they did so he broke free and the evil spirits then drove him back out to the wilds.

But when the man came to Jesus he fell at his feet and screamed, "O son of the most high God – are you come for me now? But I'm begging you Jesus, *don't torture me!*" – because he was ordering the unclean spirit to come out of the man.

"What's your name?"

"Legion," he answered, because a host of demons had entered him.

Now there happened to be a herd of pigs nearby, grazing on the mountainside. The demons begged Jesus not to hurl them to the Abyss but rather allow them to enter the swine. He granted them leave to do so. But when the wraiths had left the man and possessed the pigs, the herd bolted rushing headlong over the cliff, plunging to the sea, drowning in the surf.

When the herdsmen saw what had happened they fled to tell the tale in town and country. Mobs ran out to see what was going on. And there at Jesus' feet sat the demonized man now fully clothed and in his right mind. Yet once the townspeople had seen and heard how the man had been healed they (and indeed all those in the surrounding Gerasene region) were smitten with fear. So they told Jesus to leave them be.

Jesus therefore got back into the boat ready to sail off. Before he left, however, the man out of whom the demons had been cast begged to be able to go with him. But Jesus said, "Go back instead to your own home and tell everyone what God has done for you." And so he went off preaching and proclaiming throughout the whole city what Jesus had done.

When Jesus arrived back to Galilee he found a throng awaiting him in expectation, among them a synagogue ruler named Jairus. The man fell prostrate at Jesus' feet beseeching him to come to his home because his only daughter, aged but 12, was sick and nearing the end. As Jesus walked with the man the crowd clogged around him. Among the multitude was a woman who'd been suffering for 12 years from prolonged menstrual bleeding, nearly from the onset of puberty. All the money she could muster had gone to doctors, yet she found none who could heal her. But she pressed through the swarm from behind Jesus and managed to touch the tassels of his garments – and her flow of blood stopped in a second. At that Jesus said, "Who just touched me?"

Everyone around him denied it but Peter added, "You're hemmed in by this horde and you're asking who touched you?"

"I know when healing power has gone out from me – that's what I mean when I ask who touched me."

Realizing she could not escape his notice, the woman came and fell trembling before Jesus, confessing her illness before all but also testifying how she'd been healed in an instant. Then he said, "Daughter, it is your faith that has made you whole. Go in peace."

As he spoke someone approached coming from the synagogue ruler's house and told him, "Your daughter has died. Trouble the Master no more."

But Jesus heard and said, "Don't be afraid, just keep faith and she will be healed."

Jesus continued on into the house, not allowing anyone to enter with him save Peter, John, Jacob and the girl's father and mother. He found the whole household wailing, beating their breasts in mourning. Yet he said, "Cease this weeping – she's not dead but only sleeping."

They all jeered him, knowing full well the girl was dead. But taking hold of her hand Jesus called out, "Child, wake up!" At that her spirit returned and she sat right up. Then Jesus ordered them to give her something to eat. Her parents were, well, shocked out of their minds – but he told them not to say a word to anyone.

9

After this took place Jesus brought his disciples together and granted them authority over all devilish spirits and the power to cure diseases. Then he dispatched them to proclaim the kingdom of God and heal the sick, telling them, "Don't take anything with you as you go on your way, not a walking stick or a backpack, no silver, no bread, not even an extra shirt. Don't go hopping from house to house in a given town but just stay where you first lodge and then leave from there. But if you're rejected in any village shake the dust off your feet on the way out as a record held against them." And so they travelled as itinerants from town to town preaching the good news and healing people wherever found.

News of this came to Herod the tetrarch. Yet he was at a total loss what to think, with some people saying it was Johan risen from the dead, others that Elijah had appeared and still others that this was one of the ancient prophets. But Herod said, "I cut John's head off – so who is this man, such things I'm hearing about him?!" Then Herod looked for a way to see Jesus.

Once the disciples got back from their travels they recounted for Jesus all the things they'd done. Then he gathered them and withdrew quietly to a town named Bethsaida. But the crowd learned of it and pursued him. Still, he welcomed them, speaking to them of the kingdom of God and mending any in need.

As the day drew to a close the Twelve made a suggestion to Jesus.

"Disperse the people so they can go to the nearby farms and hamlets and find food and lodging – it's late and we're in a desert out here."

"Then give them some bread."

"We've got no more than five loaves and two fish. Worse than that we don't have enough money to go buy food for everyone even if we wanted to – we're looking at 5,000 men and who knows how many women and children!"

"Just have them split up in groups of around 50 and take a seat."

So they did, reclining as though ready to dine. Then Jesus took the five loaves and two fish and lifting his eyes to Heaven blessed and broke them, giving the pieces to his disciples to distribute to the flock. Everyone ate until fully satisfied, yet when they were all done there were still twelve basketsful of fragments left over.

After this Jesus went off by himself to pray. Then he summoned his disciples with a question.

"Who do people say that I am?"

"John the Baptist, although some say you're Elijah and others one of the prophets of old."

"But *you*, who do you say that I am?"

"God's Anointed," said Peter.

Jesus cautioned them not to tell that to anyone else, for this reason –

"The Son of Man must suffer many things and, once tested, be rejected by the elders and rulers and scribes, even put to death – but on the third day he will be raised up. Therefore if anyone wants to come along after me let him deny himself, take up his cross and follow me, day by day. Anyone who tries to preserve his life will lose it but whoever yields his life for my sake will save it. What good is it, after all, for someone to win the whole world but end up losing his soul? And if anyone is ashamed of me and my words the Son of Man will find shame in him when he comes in his glory and that of his Father and the holy angels. But I can tell you for sure that some of those standing here right now won't taste death until they've seen the kingdom of God."

Around eight days later Jesus took Peter, John and Jacob and went into the hill country to pray. But as he prayed his very aspect changed, his garments gleamed transcendent white and of a sudden two men appearing spoke with him – Moses and Elijah, robed in splendor, telling him of his exodus from the world and things soon to happen in Jerusalem.

Peter and the others slept through it all. But once sprung awake they glimpsed Jesus in his glory even as the two with him vanished from sight. When they were gone Peter blurted, "Master, it's a good thing we were here to

see this! Let's build three shrines on the spot, one for you, one for Moses and one for Elijah," having no idea what he was talking about. But even as Peter spoke a cloud descended shadowing over them and a voice speaking from the cloud said, "This is my Son, my Elect, my Beloved – listen to him!"

When the voice ceased and the cloud lifted they saw Jesus standing alone. But they kept all this to themselves during those days, telling no one else what they had seen.

When they came down from the mountain the next day they were met by a sizable crowd and a man shouted out from the midst, "Teacher!! I beg you come, look kindly on my child, my only child! Some spirit seizes him without warning, he screams, he foams at the mouth, he's torn and tossed to and fro, he's almost never at peace. I brought him to your disciples to cast this demon out but they couldn't do it."

"What a faithless and crooked generation this is! And how much longer do I have to put up with you? Yet, bring your boy here." But as Jesus began to pray for the child the fiend seized and twisted him, throwing him to the ground convulsing - whereupon Jesus stopped the unclean spirit, healed the boy and restored him back to his father. The crowd went wild, overwhelmed by the glory and grandeur of God.

And while they all marveled Jesus took his disciples aside and told them, "Open your ears to what I am telling you now - the Son of Man is about to be betrayed into the hands of men." But they couldn't grasp his full meaning and the Lord obscured it from them lest they perceive it. More than that, they were even afraid to ask him what he meant when he said such things.

About that time the disciples began to speculate which of them would be the greatest once they got to Heaven. Jesus knew what they were thinking in their hearts and so he brought a young child over to stand by him and said, "Whoever receives this child in my name receives me and whoever receives me receives the one who sent me - just so, it is the least among you who is the greatest."

Then John said, "Master, we saw someone casting out demons in your name and we stopped him because he wasn't one of our followers."

"No need to do that - whoever's not against us is for us."

The time now approached for Jesus to ascend back to Heaven and so he fixed his purpose on heading to Jerusalem. He sent messengers ahead who entered a Samaritan village to prepare the way of the Lord. But the villagers saw that he was set toward Jerusalem and wouldn't have him. When Jacob and John saw that they said, "Lord, shouldn't we rain down fire from the skies, destroying them just like Elijah did?"

Reproving them Jesus said, "That's not who we are."

So they simply went to another village. As they walked along the road someone came up to Jesus and said, "I'll follow you wherever you go."

"Foxes have dens but the Son of Man has nowhere to lay his head."

Then Jesus said to another man, "Follow me."

"I will, but first let me give my father a proper burial."

"Let the dead bury their dead – but you, come proclaim the kingdom of God."

Then another person said, "I will follow you, Lord, but first I've got to say goodbye to my family."

"If you've set your hand to the plow but look back over your shoulder you won't do well in the kingdom of God."

10

After this Jesus commissioned another 70 or so helpers, giving them instructions as he sent them out two-by-two to the towns and villages along his path.

"The harvest is plenteous but the workers are few. Pray to the master of the harvest and ask him to send more workers out into his field. Go out now – but remember you're just sheep among the wolves. Don't carry a wallet or a knapsack or even extra sandals and don't say 'hi' to anyone along the road. Yet once someone lets you into their home bless it by saying, 'Peace be upon this house.' If a child of peace lives there your peace will remain on him but if not it will return to you. Don't flit around from place to place but remain in that house eating and drinking with them and sharing their goods, because a workingman is entitled to his wages. Likewise, if you enter a town and the people welcome you, eat whatever kind of food they put in front of you – heal any diseases they may have and tell them, 'The kingdom of God has drawn near to you.'

"Now on the other hand, if you enter a town and they reject you then walk into the middle of the main street and tell them, 'On our way out of town we're going to wipe off any of the dust that's still clinging to our feet. Why? As a charge against you, because the kingdom of God drew near and you walked away.' Believe me, Sodom will have an easier go of it in that Day than will that city. And woe to you as well Chorazin, and to you Bethsaida, because if the miracles that were done in your town had been done in Tyre and Sidon they would've long since turned from their sins, bewailing them, seated in sackcloth and ashes. That's why it will go better for them in the Judgment Day than it will for you. And you, Capernaum - not only won't you be exalted to Heaven, you'll be cast down to Hell!

"Whoever listens to you listens to me and whoever rejects you rejects me and whoever rejects me rejects the one who sent me."

These 70 returned in joy saying, "Lord, even the spirits obey us in your name!"

"I saw the flash of Satan falling lightning-bright from Heaven. I've given you power to trample down snakes and scorpions and control over every power of the Enemy - so nothing's gonna harm you, not while I'm around. Even so, don't rejoice that the demons are subject to you. Rejoice instead that your names are inscribed in Heaven."

As he spoke this Jesus rejoiced in the Holy Spirit and said, "I give you all the glory, Father, Lord of Heaven and Earth, because you've allowed these truths to remain hidden to the wise and clever but revealed them to the simple and foolish, for so it seemed good to you. All things have been entrusted to me by my Father - but no one knows who the Son is except the Father nor who the Father is except the Son and those to whom the Son reveals him."

He then spoke privately to his disciples.

"Blessed are the eyes that see what you are seeing. Many prophets and kings longed to see the things you are seeing but did not and to hear the things you are hearing but did not."

Thereafter a scholar of the Law stood up to question Jesus.

"Teacher, what should I do to inherit life never ending?"

"What does the Law say? How do you read it?"

"Thou shalt love the Lord your God with all thine heart, and with all thy soul, and with all thy might and with all your mind - and your neighbor as yourself."[37]

"You've spoken with truth - do this and you'll live."

But he wanted to get an edge on Jesus and pressed the point with another question.

"So who is my neighbor?"

"A certain man went down from Jerusalem to Jericho but highwaymen surrounded him on a lonely stretch of road, stripped him of everything he had and beat him, leaving him half-dead on the ground. Now a priest chanced to come by on his way back home after serving at the Temple, but

---

37   *Deuteronomy* 6:5; *Joshua* 22:5; *Leviticus* 19:18.

when he spied the man lying there he skirted around him, passing to the other side of the road. After that a Levite came on the scene. Although at first he drew near the hapless victim he then crossed over and bypassed as well. At last a Samaritan journeyed by on a mule and when he saw the man he was touched in his heart, moved with compassion for him. Dismounting, he bound the man's wounds and poured soothing oil on them to ease the pain, giving him wine to drink as well. He then lifted the man onto the animal and, walking beside it, led him to the nearest inn, where he continued to care for him. The next day he gave the innkeeper more than enough money to tend to the man as he convalesced and said, 'Please care for him. I will stop by again on my way back and if you've spent more than this, count on me to reimburse you.' So let me ask you, which of these three proved neighbor to the man?"

"The one who showed him mercy."

"Then you should do likewise."

As Jesus continued on he came to the mountain hamlet of Bethany, where he was welcomed in as a guest by a woman named Martha. This Martha had a sister named Mary who liked to sit right by Jesus to catch his every word. But while Jesus taught and Mary listened Martha took on the burdens of cooking and cleaning and waiting on everyone. When she'd had about enough of this she came up to Jesus and said, "Lord, doesn't it bother you that my little sister here leaves all the work to me? Tell her to pick herself off the ground and come help me."

"Martha, Martha. You've let yourself be taken with many cares. Mary's focused on the one important thing - don't take that away from her."

11

Jesus had gone off apart to pray one day and when he had finished, one of his disciples asked whether he would teach them to pray as well, just as Johan had done with his followers. He gave them this model -

"Father, may your name be ever blessed! We pray your kingdom may come amongst us, that your will be done here on Earth as it is in Heaven. We ask that you give us day by day the things you know we need. And Lord, forgive us our failings, for we too forgive those who've failed us. But keep us from the snares of the Evil One – deliver us from all temptations."

Then he explained what it means to pray.

"Think about what would happen if one of you were to go to a friend's home in the middle of the night, knock on the door and say something like this, 'We've got a guest who just came to our house from his travels on the road but we're short of food – can you lend us a few loaves of bread?' He might then call out the window, 'I can't help you – I've already locked and barred the door and I, my wife and kids are all in bed, so it's just too much trouble.' True, he might not want to get out of bed to help you just because he's your friend, but believe me if you keep knocking he'll finally get up and give you whatever you need thanks to your shameless persistence. That's why I'm telling you to ask and it shall be given you; seek and you shall find; knock and it shall be opened unto you. For everyone that asks receives; and he that seeks finds; and to him that knocks it shall be opened.

"Or think about it this way. If your son asks you for bread are you about to give him a stone? or if he asks for a fish, a snake? or an egg, a scorpion? Look – you're basically bad people but even *you* know how to give good gifts to your children. So how much more will your Father in Heaven give the Holy Spirit to those who ask him?"

On one occasion Jesus was casting out a spirit of muteness and as the demon left the dumb spoke, astonishing the crowd. But some of the people murmured, "He's casting out spirits by grace of the Prince of Demons!" Others, tempting him, asked to see a sign from Heaven.

Piercing their thoughts Jesus said, "Every kingdom divided against itself collapses and a house divided falls. If Satan wars against himself how can his kingdom stand? You say I exorcise by his power but by what power do your own sons cast them out? Let them be your judges. But if I cast out fiends by the Finger of God know then for sure that the kingdom of God has come upon you. Think about a mighty man – when he's fully armed and guarding his own mansion all his goods are safe. But if someone stronger comes along and overpowers him he'll seize his weapons and his property for himself and distribute as he sees fit.

"So hear this – whoever's not with me is against me and whoever doesn't gather with me scatters.

"And learn this lesson as well – when a foul spirit leaves someone it wanders in waterless lands seeking surcease but finding none. Then it says to itself, 'I'm going to go back to the house I left.' And when it returns it discovers the place swept clean, neat and tidy. So it corrals seven wraiths more wicked than it ever was and they all move in together – and that person ends up worse off than he was in the first place!"

When he spoke these words a certain woman shouted out from the crowd, "Blessed is the womb that bore you and the breasts that nursed you!"

"No – blessed instead are those who hear the word of God and keep it."

As the crowd began to swell around him, Jesus said, "This is a malignant generation – it looks for a sign but no sign will be given it save that of the prophet Jonah. Just as Jonah himself was a sign to the people of Nineveh so too will the Son of Man be to this generation. Indeed, the Queen of Sheba will rise up and condemn the people of this generation because she travelled from remote parts of the globe to hear the wisdom of Solomon and now look – someone greater than Solomon is among you! It's just the same with the men of Nineveh. They will arise in condemnation against this generation because they turned from their wicked ways at the preaching of Jonah and now you have someone greater than Jonah.

"No one hides a light bulb in the basement but screws it into a lamp so people coming and going can see their way. The body's lamp is the eye and if your eye is focused your whole body will be radiant. But if your eye is evil the body is dark. Be careful therefore that the light in you is not darkness. And if your whole body is full of light, leaving no part in darkness, it will shine as if lit by lightning."

At that point a member of the Pharisaical sect invited Jesus to lunch at his house and he went. But the Pharisee expressed surprise that Jesus didn't wash his hands with ceremony before he sat down to eat.

"You Pharisees wash the outside of the cups and plates but inside you're filled with greed and malice. What fools! Didn't the one who created the outside make the inside as well? But open your hearts and give to the poor – then all will be cleansed. And yet I fear for you Pharisees because you parse tithes of mint and rue and every herb but pass by the justice and goodness of God. You ought to have seen to those without neglecting the others. But you love the best seats in the synagogues and greetings in the marketplace. You're like unmarked graves – people don't even know they're walking over them."

One of the teachers of the Law complained to Jesus that he was insulting them, provoking this response.

"You scholars are also in peril. You burden people with weights too heavy to bear but don't lift a finger to help them. Woe to you, because you built the tombs of the prophets your own fathers killed. You thereby ratify their deeds – they killed the prophets while you build the tombs. Thus spoke the Wisdom of God: I will send them prophets and messengers. They will kill some and persecute others,[38] to the end that the blood of all the prophets slain from the beginning of time may fall on this generation, from the blood of Abel to the blood of Zacharias, who was cut down between the altar and the sanctuary. I tell you this generation will have to answer for all these crimes. And more than that, you keen students of the Law have taken away the key to knowledge, neither opening the door yourselves nor letting others go in."

Even as Jesus turned to leave the scribes and Pharisees continued to press him with hostility, barraging him with multiple questions, lying in wait to catch him in a trap.

12

Pretty soon thousands and thousands of people started gathering around Jesus (so many in fact they almost trampled one another). Speaking in the first instance to his inner circle of followers, Jesus told them to "watch out for the kind of pretense you see in the Pharisees. It can work like leaven does, expanding throughout the whole group. But anything that's been covered up will be opened and what's now hidden will become known to all. It's the same with anything you've spoken in the darkness: it will come to light. And what you've whispered in someone's ear will be shouted from the rooftops. I'm telling you this as friends.

"And don't be afraid of those who can destroy your bodies but afterwards have nothing more they can do to you. I'll tell you what to fear – fear him who can toss you to Hinnom's smoldering fires *after* you're dead! I mean it. Fear him.

"You can buy five sparrows for a nickel these days but God keeps his

---

38　*2 Chronicles* 24:18-19.

eye on every one of them. He even tracks the number of hairs on your head. So don't lose any sleep - you're worth a lot more than a few sparrows.

"Let me put it this way. If anyone stands by me in front of other people then the Son of Man will stand by him in the presence of God's angels. And if someone says something against the Son of Man, well, he can be forgiven that. But if he scoffs at the Holy Ghost, he'll have nowhere to run.

"Now, the time will come when you'll have to defend yourselves before synagogue rulers or other authorities - but don't plan out ahead of time what you're going to say. The Holy Spirit will let you know what to say when you need to say it."

Someone in the crowd piped up, importuning Jesus, "Teacher, tell my brother he has to share his inheritance with me."

But he answered, "Is it up to me to tell you how to divide your wealth?"

Then he warned the people, "Flee greed! Your lives are more than the things you own. Let me tell you about a rich man whose farm had a bumper crop. He thought to himself, 'What am I going to do now, since my barns and silos aren't big enough to store all this extra grain? I think I'll just tear down the silos, build bigger ones and gather the wheat in along with my other goods. Then at last I'll be set for life and can just eat, drink and be merry.'[39] But God said to that man, 'You idiot! Tonight's the night you die - and who will get the things you've hoarded then?' That's what happens to someone who piles up treasure for himself but is not rich toward God."

Then he asked his disciples, "Do you understand now why I told you not to fret your soul over what you'll eat, what clothes you'll wear? Your life is more than food, your body more than apparel. Haven't you noticed the crows? They don't plant. They don't harvest. They don't have barns. They don't have silos. But God feeds them anyway[40] and you're a lot more important than a bunch of crows! And is any of you able to add an hour to his life by worrying how short it is? So if fretting can't change something as small as that how can you worry yourselves out of the bigger problems of life?

---

39   *Sirach* 11:18-19.
40   *Job* 38:41; *Psalms* 147:9.

"Consider the lilies of the field, how they grow – they don't go to work and they don't spin in circles, yet Solomon in all his glory wasn't clothed as well as they. If that's how God graces grass that's here today and gone tomorrow then how much more will he clothe you, you doubting Thomases! Stop acting like the Goyim, always worrying about what you'll eat and what you'll drink. Your Father *knows* you need all that. Seek his kingdom instead and all the rest will be added to you. And don't worry, little flock, it's the Father's pleasure to give you the kingdom. Therefore sell all you have, give the money to the poor and sew wallets for yourselves that will never wear out. You need to store your treasure in Heaven, where no thief can steal nor any moth devour – because where your treasure is there will your heart be also.

"Keep your clothes nearby and your flashlights at hand, and be prepared as those waiting for their master to return home late from a party, ready to open the door at his knock and welcome him back. Blessed are those servants who on his return their lord finds busy at their posts. He will put on an apron, bid them sit down and serve them dinner himself. If he doesn't get back until midnight or even three in the morning yet finds them still awake and waiting, then blessed are those servants indeed. Understand also that if the guardian of the house had known ahead of time when a thief was coming he'd have been on his guard and prevented anyone from breaking in. You therefore need to be ready as well because you don't know when the Son of Man will come."

Peter asked Jesus, "Is this parable for us or those outside our inner circle?"

"Let me put it this way – to whom do you think the master will entrust all his goods? It's the one he finds on the job apportioning to the other servants their daily bread, even in the moment the master comes home unexpectedly. He will bless that servant, giving him rule over all that he has. But if that servant should think to himself, 'my master is taking his own sweet time getting back' and begin to beat the rest of the staff, both men and women, gorging himself with food and getting drunk, then his lord will appear on a day unlooked for and at an hour unknown and will cut that servant in half, treating him as the faithless. Therefore the servant who knew the will of the lord but neither prepared himself nor obeyed his master's wishes will be treated harshly. The one who was ignorant of his will and acted badly will be punished as well, but with fewer blows. For unto whomsoever much is given, of him shall be much required: and to whom men have committed much, of him they will ask the more.

"I've come to purify the Earth with fire – and I would it were already kindled! But I have a baptism yet to be baptized with and am pressed within myself until it be accomplished. Do you think I've come to bring peace on Earth? Not so. I've come to divide the world, with three against two in one house and two against three in another, father against son and son against father, mother against daughter and daughter against mother, mother-in-law against daughter-in-law and she against her."

Then he said to the masses, "When you see a cloud rising in the West you say right away, 'there's a storm coming,' and right you are. And when the southern wind blows you say, 'a heat wave is coming,' and so it is. How two-faced you are! You can read the signs of land and sky but not the season that's upon you.

"Can none of you judge justly? Let's say you're on your way to court with someone who's sued you on a loan. Make it a point to settle with him before you get there. Otherwise you'll get haled before the judge, where she'll rule against you and hand you over to the bailiff, who will toss you in jail. And if *that* happens you won't get out until you've paid the last penny."

13

With the people still gathered around Jesus, messengers came running to tell him news about some Galileans whom Pilate had slaughtered as they made their sacrifices and then mixed their blood with that of their offerings.[41]

"Do you think those Galileans were worse sinners than the rest of the Galileans just because that was their fate? Not so. Unless you turn from your ways you'll be cut down just as they were. Same with those 18 people who were crushed when the Tower of Siloam collapsed. Do you think they were guilty of worse evils than anyone else in Jerusalem? But no, if you don't repent you'll be destroyed just like them."

---

41   *Cf.* Josephus, *Antiquities of the Jews*, Book XVIII, ch. 1, § 1, and Book XX, ch. 5, § 2.

Then he gave them this parable.

"A certain man had a fig tree planted in his vineyard but when he looked for fruit on it there was none. He told his farm manager, 'Listen, I've been watching this tree for three years now and it still hasn't borne any fruit. Cut it down – why take up good space on the land?'[42] But the manager said, 'Boss, I think it's worth giving it another year. Let me dig holes around the perimeter, fertilize it with manure and see how it does. If it's still not yielding fruit next year then we'll cut it down.'"

On a following Sabbath Jesus was teaching in one of the synagogues when a woman came in all bent in two. She'd been oppressed by an evil spirit for the past 18 years and it had crippled her so much she couldn't stand straight. When Jesus spied her in the back of the room he called her over, laid hands on her and said, "Woman! Be free!" Instantly she straightened right up and shouted with glory to God.

Yet the synagogue president flew into a rage because Jesus had healed on the Sabbath. More than that, he scolded the people: "You've got six working days each week. Come get healed on any of those, but *not* on the Sabbath!"

But Jesus scolded *him*.

"You false front! Don't all of you untie your oxen and donkeys from their stalls on the Sabbath and lead them to eat and drink? And you're telling me I can't release this daughter of Abraham, this woman bound 18 years by the Devil??"

Jesus' opponents were thereby put to shame; but the people glorified God for the wonders he did.

"What's the kingdom of God like," he continued, "what's a good comparison? It's like a mustard seed a man planted in his garden. It grew to a tree, the birds of the air nesting in its branches. And it's also like yeast folded by a woman's hands within a lump of dough, causing the whole loaf to rise."

Then he walked on, teaching as he passed through village and town, making his way to Jerusalem. Along the way someone asked him, "Lord, will only a few people be saved?"

"Fight your way in through the narrow gate, because many will try to enter but won't have the strength. Otherwise, once the owner of the house rises and shuts the door and you're left outside knocking to be let in, he'll say, 'I don't know where you're from.' And you'll say, 'But Lord,

---

42 *Isaiah* 5:7.

we've dined in your presence and you've taught in our streets!' Yet he'll say again, 'I don't even know where you come from – depart from me, all you who work evil.' And so there will be wailing and gnashing of teeth when you see Abraham, Isaac and Jacob and all the prophets in the kingdom of God but yourselves cast out. Indeed, still others will come from North, South, East and West to sit down and feast in the kingdom of God – because the last will be first and the first will be last."

Right after that some of the Pharisees came to warn Jesus, telling him, "Leave this area – we've learned that Herod is out to kill you."

"Go back and tell that sly fox I said, 'Behold, today and tomorrow I'll exorcise demons and heal the sick and then perfect my work on the third day' – but I must continue my journey these next days, because no prophet may perish outside Jerusalem. Yet Jerusalem, Jerusalem! You who have killed the prophets and stoned to death those sent to you, how many times have I wished to gather your children as a hen gathers chicks under her wing – but you refused. And now your house is left to you barren because you will not see me again until the day comes when you say, Blessed is he who comes in the name of the Lord."[43]

14

On another Sabbath day Jesus was invited to eat at the home of one of the leading Pharisees – and the whole group watched him carefully to see how he would handle himself. Sure enough, a man came in suffering from abnormal accumulations of fluid between his skin and bodily cavities. Jesus asked some of the experts in the Law and other Pharisees whether it was lawful to heal on the Sabbath or not. But when they stayed silent Jesus simply took hold of the man, healed him and sent him on his way.

"Listen, what would *you* do if one of your children or even one of your animals fell into a watery ditch on the Sabbath? Wouldn't you drop everything and rush to haul him out, Sabbath or no Sabbath?" Yet again they had nothing to say.

Jesus then noticed that the Pharisees had taken for themselves the best seats in the house so he said to them, "Here's some advice – the next

43   *Psalms* 118:26.

time someone invites you to a wedding don't grab a seat at the head table because someone worthier than you might happen to be in the room. If that's the case then your host is liable to say, 'Sorry pal, but you're in someone else's seat. You need to get up and make room for him.' Then you'll find yourself slinking down to the lower end of the table. Instead just take the lowest seat first and who knows, maybe you'll be invited to move on up? If that happens you'll find honor in everyone's eyes. Here's the moral of the story: everyone who exalts himself will be brought down while those who humble themselves will be exalted."

Jesus then had a word for his host.

"The next time you throw a lunch or dinner party don't invite your friends and your brothers and your cousins and all your rich neighbors – they'll just invite you back in the future and bingo, that's your reward. But try inviting the poor, the crippled, the lame, the blind. If you do *that* you'll be blessed indeed because they have no way to repay you – instead you'll receive your reward at the resurrection of the just."

Someone at the dinner table then said, "Blessed are those who will dine in the kingdom of God!"

Jesus responded with this parable.

"A certain man prepared a big-deal banquet, inviting a large number of people. When the banquet day arrived he sent his servant to each of those he had invited announcing, 'The feast is ready to start and my master hasn't gotten your RSVP, but do come and dine!' But they all had some excuse why they couldn't be there. The first said, 'I just bought some land and I've got to go inspect it. Can you send my regrets for me?' Another said, 'I've just bought five pairs of oxen and have to try them out in the field. Can you let me off the hook?' And yet another said, 'I just got married and that's why I can't be there.'

"So the servant returned and reported all this. But when his master heard the excuses he went purple with rage and directed his servant to 'Go right out now into the highways and byways of the city and invite the poor and the crippled, the blind and the lame and bring them here.' The servant obeyed and then told his master, 'I've done as you ordered but there's still plenty of room at the table.' The householder commanded him next to go out to the countryside and 'Beat the bushes! Anyone you find, make him show up at the banquet, because I intend my house to be filled. And I promise you, none of those I first invited will taste of my dinner.'"

As Jesus travelled on, a large crowd went with him. He turned to them and spoke these words.

"Anyone who follows after me cannot love his father and mother and wife and children and brothers and sisters or even his own life more than me. If he does he's not able to be my disciple. The cost of discipleship is therefore taking up one's own cross – and following me. If you want to build a building don't you first sit down to budget the cost to see if you'll have enough money to finish it? Otherwise you might only get as far as laying the foundation stone or putting up a few walls and then have to stop because you've run out of cash. If that happens everyone who comes by will mock you saying, 'This schlemiel started to build and was too weak to finish.' Or what king would press on in battle against another king without first deciding whether his 10,000 men are able to take on the other side's 20,000? No, once he sees what he's up against he may well decide to send an ambassador to try to negotiate a peace while his enemy is still a long way off.

"So it is that unless you're willing to renounce all that you have you cannot be my disciples. Salt is a good thing – but if salt becomes tasteless what use is it for seasoning?[44] It's really no good for anything except to be thrown in the garbage. Anyone who grasps what I'm saying had better act accordingly."

15

As Jesus continued on the way he was surrounded by every kind of miscreant, taxmen included. But this led to grumbling among the Pharisees, who said, "Look at the sort of person he is, letting sinners into his presence and breaking bread with them everywhere he goes!"

In response Jesus shared some more parables.

"Suppose you had 100 sheep and one of them wandered off someplace.[45] Is there any one of you who wouldn't drop everything, leaving the 99 behind to search the wilds for the one until you'd found it? And once you had wouldn't you hoist it on your shoulders with glee and carry it back home, calling for all your friends and relations to say,

---

44   *See Job 6:6.*
45   *Isaiah 53:6.*

'Come rejoice with me – I found the lost sheep!' Well that's exactly the way it is in Heaven, where there is more joy over one wicked man who repents than over 99 good who don't need to repent.

"Or what about this – suppose your wife had ten gold rings but lost one. Do you think she wouldn't grab a flashlight and pierce every nook and cranny, scouring the house until she'd found it? And once she had, wouldn't she collar everyone in sight and shout, 'Look! I've found the lost ring, come sing with me!' So too I tell you there is joy before the angels of God when one sinner repents.

"And then there was the man who had two sons, the younger of whom said, 'Father, I would like my 1/3 share of your estate now while you're still alive.'[46] His father acceded, apportioning out his goods to each of the sons. But the youngster took his share and went out West, where he threw it away on fast women. After his money was gone the boy came on hard times, unprepared for famine when the rains failed and crops in the field died. Pretty soon he was headed for starvation so he scrambled for a living, sooner or later falling in with the Gentiles, reduced to a job feeding pigs. But even then no one gave him any food of his own, leaving him to eat the same slop he fed to the hogs.

"Finally he came to his senses and said to himself, 'What a loser I am! Even my dad's servants back home have plenty of good food to eat but I've dug myself into this grave's end, half-starving to death! I'm going to get out of here, head back to my father and confess that I've sinned against Heaven and him. I'll beg him to take me on as one of his hired hands, because I'm no longer worthy to be counted as his son.'

"Thus he journeyed all the way back home. But while he was still barely on the horizon his father spied him from afar and ran toward him, overcome with pangs of mercy, throwing his arms around the boy and filling him with kisses. But his son said, 'I've sinned against God and against you – I don't deserve to be called your child!' Yet his father commanded the servants quickly to 'Fetch the best white robe and clothe my son. Bring too a signet ring for his finger and fresh sandals for his feet. Then slaughter the fatted calf and let us feast – because this my son was dead but now is sprung to life, was lost but now is found!'[47] And so the celebration began.

"But the older brother was out in the field while all this was happen-

---

46   *Deuteronomy* 21:17; *cf.* Herodotus, *The Histories*, 4.115.1.
47   *1 Kings* 8:47-50; *Jeremiah* 3:12.

ing and as he neared home on the way back from work he heard a symphony of joy and dancing. He asked one of the lads what was going on and he said, 'Your brother's come home! Your father has slain the fatted calf in joy to have him back safe and sound.'

"Yet the older brother went into a fury and refused to even walk through the door, forcing his father to come out and plead with him to join in. But he rebuffed him, 'Look how many years I've spent toiling for you – but I never got a dinner. Have I broken any of your rules? No. Did you give me so much as a baby goat to serve to my friends? Not once. And now this wastrel son of yours who's spent your money on hookers comes back and you serve up the best we have? *Are you kidding me*?!'

But the father answered, 'My son, you are and always will be with me and everything I have is yours. But now you must rejoice because this your brother was dead and now he lives, was lost but now is found.'"

16

Speaking further to his disciples Jesus said this.

"A certain wealthy woman began getting accusations that her Chief Financial Officer was running things poorly. She called him to her office and said, 'What's all this I'm hearing about you mismanaging the business? I need an accounting from you right now so I can find out the facts for myself and decide whether to keep you or fire you.' The executive left the meeting and said to himself, 'Now I'm in a pickle. If the boss fires me how am I supposed to get another job? I'm not fit to plow a field and I'm too proud to beg. But I'll think up a way to curry people's favor so that *someone* will take me in if I'm thrown out on the street.'

"He therefore called in each customer who had bought something but hadn't yet paid. He asked the first one, 'How much do you think you owe us?'

'The market price for 100 barrels of oil.'

'Take a 50% discount and pay that much.'

And to the next he said, 'How much do you owe?'

'Whatever 100 bales of wheat now go for.'

'Knock half off and pay that much.'

"When his boss saw the discounts written on the invoices she had to compliment her crooked employee on his shrewdness. This is an example of how the children of this age take care of themselves better than do the children of light. And what's the moral of the story? Make good use of the riches of this unjust world, giving aid to those who cannot repay – and when the whole system collapses they'll receive you into heavenly mansions.

"If you can trust someone with a small job you can trust him with a big one but if he cheats about a little money he'll cheat about a lot. And if you can't handle the passing wealth of this world properly how can you be trusted with God's true riches? Or if you aren't faithful with someone else's money who will give you your own? No servant can serve two masters – either he will hate the one and love the other or he will hold to the one and despise the other. You cannot serve God and Mammon."

When the Pharisees heard Jesus say this they jeered – but that's only because they were greedy people themselves.

"You present yourselves to others as righteous men but God knows what's in your hearts, and the things you hold dear are abominable to him. The Law and the Prophets held sway until John. Since then the kingdom of God is preached and everyone crowds into it. But I tell you it would be easier for Heaven and Earth to pass away than for one dot of the Law to perish. Know then that anyone who divorces his wife and marries another commits adultery; and it's the same with any divorced woman who marries another man.

"But hear now another parable. A certain rich man clothed in purple and fine linen dined in splendor every day. A poor man named Lazarus lay miserably at his doorstep, covered with wounds, craving what food might fall from the rich man's table. All the while dogs walked by, licking at his sores. In time the poor man died and was carried off by angels to Abraham's Bosom. The rich man died too and was buried. Tormented in the midst of death's dark pit he lifted his eyes and saw Abraham afar off and Lazarus resting on his chest. He cried out thence, 'Father Abraham! Have mercy on me! Send Lazarus to dip his finger in some water and cool my tongue, because I'm tortured by this flame!'

"But Abraham replied, 'My son, think on this – while alive you were filled with your good things while Lazarus was filled with his suffering. Now he is comforted but you are in pain. But if that isn't clear enough you need to know there is a great gulf fixed between us – even if someone *wanted* to cross to you from here he couldn't, nor can anyone cross from there to us.'

'Then I beg you, Father, send someone to my father's house, where I still have five brothers. He can give them a solemn warning lest they too come to this place of torment.'

'They have Moses and the Prophets. Let them hear them.'

'No Father Abraham, but if someone should go to them from the house of the dead they will turn from their ways!'

'If they do not hear Moses and the Prophets they will not believe, not even if one should rise from the dead.'"

17

Jesus continued, now speaking just to his followers.

"People are going to be offended by the things I'm saying and doing – there's no way around it. But I fear for someone who is not only offended by me but persecutes those who do believe. It would be far better for that person to have a millstone hung around his neck and be cast with that weight into the sea than to terrorize the littlest of my disciples. So keep a watch on yourselves – if one of your brothers harms you, let him know about it, and if he turns from his ways forgive him! Even if he does you wrong seven times a day and turns around each time and says he's sorry, forgive him still."

"Lord, we need more faith!"

"If you had faith but as small as a mustard seed you could've spoken to a mulberry tree and said, 'Uproot yourself and be planted in the sea!' – and it would have obeyed.

"Suppose you had a servant who'd been out in the field plowing or tending sheep. When he comes back at the end of the day would you say, 'Pour yourself a drink, put your feet up, take it easy this evening?' No, you'd say, 'It's getting on toward dinner time so put on an apron, get my food ready and when I'm finished eating and drinking then you can have yours.' My point is that you don't give special thanks to a servant who simply does what he's supposed to do. Well it's the same for you – when you've done what you're commanded you ought to say, 'We're nothing special, we've only done what was expected of us.'"

As Jesus ventured on toward Jerusalem he walked the boundary between Samaria and Galilee. When he entered one of the villages, ten lepers came out to meet him crying, "Jesus! Master! Have mercy on us!"

"Go now, show yourselves to the priests." And as they went away all were fully cleansed. But one of them, seeing he had been healed, turned and ran back shouting out the greatness of God and falling prostrate before Jesus, filled with gratitude. Now this man was a Samaritan and Jesus said, "Didn't I see ten people here and weren't they all cleansed of their leprosy? So where are the other nine? Couldn't they have come back to give thanks to God, not just this Goy? But you, rise up – your faith has saved your soul."

Answering a question from the Pharisees as to when the kingdom of God would come Jesus explained, "You don't have to be a detective to find the kingdom of God – the kingdom of God is present among you. So don't go listening to people who say, 'It's here!' or 'It's there!' The days are coming when you'll long to see just one of the days of the Son of Man but will not. Yet even then you should turn your backs on those who rush hither and yon saying the kingdom is here or there because the Day of the Son of Man will come as a lightening flash from one end of the sky to the other. But first he must suffer many things and be rejected by this generation. Yet as it was in the days of Noah so it will be in the days of the Son of Man – they were eating, drinking, marrying, giving in marriage, all up to the moment Noah entered the ark. And then came the cataclysm, sweeping them all away. It was just the same in the days of Lot – eating, drinking, buying, selling, planting, building – right up to the moment Lot left Sodom. And then it rained fire and brimstone from Heaven destroying them all.

"This is how it will be in the Day the Son of Man is revealed – if someone finds himself up on the roof with his goods down inside the house he'd better not try to fetch them. And if someone is out in the field he shouldn't turn back home. Remember Lot's wife! Anyone who tries to preserve his life will lose it but whoever loses his life will keep it. That night two will sleep together but one will be taken while the other is left behind. Two women will be grinding at the mill, one taken, the other not. Two men in the field, one gone, one not."

When the disciples heard this they asked, "But where, Lord?"

"Vultures will gather wherever there's meat."[48]

18

Then he told them a parable to encourage them to always pray and not grow faint.

"There once was a judge in a certain city who neither feared God nor cared what people thought of him. A local widow approached and begged him, 'Defend me against my enemy!' He didn't give her the time of day but she kept after him, pestering him day after day. Finally he said to himself, 'I don't care about God and I don't care about people, but this woman won't let up. It's not worth the aggravation of having to listen to her all the time so I'm going to give her what she seeks just to get her off my back.' Do you get my point about the unjust judge? If he was willing to heed the widow's petition don't you think God will avenge his chosen ones, those who cry out to him day and night? Do you think he'll put them off forever? No, he will shortly do them justice. And yet when the Son of Man comes will he find them standing firm in their faith?"

Then he told the people a story about those who think of themselves as righteous men and scorn everyone else.

"Two men went up to the Temple to pray, one a Pharisee and the other a tax-skimming publican. The first stood praying within himself, 'Dear God, I thank you that I'm not like the rest of mankind - thieves, evildoers, adulterers - people like that lackey of a taxman over there. I

---

48 *Job* 39:30; *Hosea* 8:1; *Habakkuk* 1:8.

fast twice a week (even though I don't have to) and I give away a tenth of everything I earn.' But the tax collector stayed far off to the side, not daring so much as to raise his eyes toward Heaven. Instead he beat his breast and prayed, 'Lord, have mercy on me, a sinner.' I promise you this man went home made righteous in the sight of God while the first did not – because everyone who exalts himself will be brought low and whoever humbles himself will be lifted up."

People now started bringing babes in arms for Jesus to touch. When his disciples saw this happening they tried to stop it but Jesus said, "Don't prevent them, for of such is the kingdom of God – anyone who can't receive the kingdom of God as would a child will never get in."

One of the synagogue rulers asked him, "Good Teacher, what should I do to inherit life that endures?"

"Why are you calling me good? Don't you know that God alone is good? But you know the commandments – don't commit adultery, don't murder, don't lie in court, honor your father and mother."[49]

"I've followed all those ever since I was a child!"

"Well in that case you've just got one more thing to do – sell everything you own and give the money to the poor. Don't worry, you'll have treasure in Heaven. And come, follow me." When he heard that, the man was overcome with grief because he was exceedingly rich. Seeing his sadness Jesus exclaimed, "How hard it is for those laden with goods to enter the kingdom of God! It's easier to thread a rope through a needle than for the wealthy to enter the kingdom of God."

The listeners cried, "What?! Who then can possibly be saved?"

"Things impossible for men are possible with God."

Peter interjected, "Look here, we've left everything behind just to follow you!"

"There's no one who's left his home or his wife or his brothers or cousins or even his children for the sake of the kingdom of God who won't receive multiples back in this lifetime and in the world to come, ageless life."

Then he brought the Twelve in close and told them, "We're going up now to Jerusalem and all things written in the Prophets about the

---

49   *Exodus* 20:12-16.

Son of Man will be brought to completion. He'll be handed over to the Gentiles, mocked, abused, spat on, whipped and killed ... but the third day he will be raised from the dead." Yet none of them understood a thing he said – the meaning was hidden to them, ungraspable.

As Jesus neared Jericho a blind man sat begging near the side of the road. Hearing a commotion he asked those around him what was happening. They told him, "Jesus of Nazareth is coming by."

Then he started to holler, "Jesus! Son of David! Be merciful to me!"

The people standing in front of him told him to shut up and stop yelling. But that only made him shout all the more, "Son of David, have mercy!"

Jesus heard him, stood still and called for the man to be brought over.

"What is it you ask of me?"

"Lord, that I might see again."

"Then receive back your sight! It's your faith that's made you whole."

Instantly his sight was restored and he followed after Jesus, praising God as he went – and the crowd, seeing this, gave all the glory to God.

19

Jesus continued walking right through Jericho. A local hedge fund manager, a guy named Zacchaeus, wanted desperately to put eyes on Jesus for himself, but he couldn't see over other people's heads – the crowd was that big and he was that small. So he ran behind the crowd and ahead on the road until he found a sycamore tree. He climbed up and perched on a branch, watching for Jesus to come. When Jesus got there he stopped, looked up and said, "Hey Zacchaeus! Come on down out of that tree and quickly get things ready for me at your house, because that's where I plan to stay tonight."

Zacchaeus fairly jumped down for joy and rushed to do as the Lord had bidden. But the grumblers who saw this murmured, "Can you believe he's going to lodge under the roof of that greedy man??"

Yet once Jesus had gotten to his home Zacchaeus stood before all and said, "Behold, Lord, I'm giving half of everything I own to the poor and if anyone says I've stolen his money by fraud or extortion I'll pay him four times what he claims."

Jesus assured him, "Zacchaeus, today salvation has come to you and your household." And turning to the grumblers he said, "This man too is a child of Abraham – and the Son of Man has come to seek and to save those who are lost." Then he added the following parable because at this point he was fewer than 20 miles from Jerusalem and everyone thought the kingdom of God was about to be revealed.

"Once upon a time there was an Asian king who travelled to Rome to get the Senate's consent before assuming his rule.[50] Before leaving he gathered ten of his chief servants and evenly distributed ten silver coins, each worth around $100. He charged them, 'Take this money and see what you can do with it while I'm away.' But after he'd left a number of the locals sent word ahead to the Senate saying, 'We hate this guy. We're not having him back to rule over us.' But the king obtained Rome's authority despite their opposition. When he returned home he summoned those he had given the silver, in order to learn of their business deals.

The first said, 'Lord, your one coin is now ten.'

'Well done, my good man. Because you've been faithful in handling this small matter I'm putting you in charge of ten of my cities.'

The second said, 'Master, I've earned five coins by investing your one.'

'And you too, my friend, you've done well. Now take charge of five cities.'

But the third said, 'Here's your coin back. At least you can say I kept it safe for you, nicely folded in this napkin. The truth is, I was afraid of you because I know how harsh you can be, collecting interest on money you haven't loaned, reaping crops you haven't sown.'

'Then be judged by your own words, you wicked servant. You say you

---

50   *1 Maccabees* 7:13.

marked me as harsh, extracting interest on loans I don't make or harvesting from someone else's field. Well if that was truly your thought why didn't you cut a deal with the loan sharks and let me take my share of any interest that accrued?'

And to the rest of them he said, 'Take the one coin from this man and give it to the one who earned me ten.'

'But Master, he's already got ten!'

'Yes, but more will go to those who have and those who have little will lose what little they have. And bring now those enemies who rejected my rule and slaughter them in front of me.'"

Once he had finished that story, Jesus moved on toward Jerusalem, coming near to Bethpage and Bethany, two villages backed up against the side of Mount Olive. He directed two of his disciples, "Go into the town opposite and just as you enter you'll find a colt tied to a post. He'll be a bit wild because no one has sat on him, but untie him anyway and bring him to me. If anyone asks you what you're up to just say, 'The Lord needs him.'"

So they went and found things just as Jesus had said. And when they started to untie the animal the owners confronted them and asked, "Just what do you think you're doing?" They replied, "The Lord needs him," and led the colt away. Then some of them cast their own cloaks over the animal, helped seat Jesus on him and strew more garments on the road before him as he went.

As Jesus started on the downslope of Mount Olive riding toward the city, the gathering crowd of his followers began to praise God, shouting in loud joy for the glorious miracles they'd seen and singing,

> Blessed is the king
>> who comes in the name of the Lord![51]
> Peace be in Heaven and
>> glory in the highest!

But some of the Pharisees in the crowd called out to Jesus – "Master! Make your people stop!"

---

51   *Psalms* 118:26.

"If they fell silent the stones would call out."[52]

As he drew closer, gazing on the city Jesus wept over it.

"If only you knew this day the peace that could be yours, but now it's veiled from your eyes. And so the days are coming when your enemies will lay siege to you, encircling you with earthworks, pressing you on all sides, dashing you and yours to the ground, leaving not one stone on top of another, all because you failed to welcome the day of God's visitation."[53]

Once he had entered the Temple precincts Jesus laid waste to the stalls of all those hawking their wares, saying "This is my house, a house of prayer,[54] but you've made it a den of thieves."

20

He spent the next days teaching openly in the Temple. The chief priests and experts in the Law looked for a way to kill him, as did other rulers of the people, yet they couldn't find an opening because the people themselves hung on Jesus' every word. But one day while he was there sharing the good news they approached him and asked, "Tell us by what authority you do these things, or rather, just who is it gave you this right?"

"Let me answer your question with a question – did Johan baptize by the authority of God or of man?" Reasoning among themselves they debated how to respond. They found themselves in a quandary: "If we say 'Johan's authority came from Heaven' then he'll ask why we didn't believe him. But if we say 'his authority was merely human' then the people are liable to stone us because they hold him to be a prophet." So they just said, "We don't know where he got his authority from."

"In that case neither can I tell you where I get the authority to do these things."

Then he shared this parable with the people.

"A certain man planted a vineyard and rented it out to some farmers. He went off on a long trip but around harvest time he sent one of his ser-

52   *Habakkuk* 2:11.
53   *Isaiah* 29:2-4.
54   *Isaiah* 56.7; *Jeremiah* 7:11.

vants to the tenants to collect his share of the proceeds. But the farmers beat the man and tossed him out empty-handed. The owner sent another of his servants but they pummeled him worse than the first and sent him away with nothing as well. Then a third servant was dispatched and he too was beaten to a pulp. Finally the master of the vineyard said to himself, 'What am I to do with these people? This time I will send my son, my most beloved. Surely he will shame them by his presence.'

"But when the farmers saw the son they schemed among themselves, 'This boy is the heir. Shouldn't we just kill him and keep his inheritance for ourselves?' And that's exactly what they did, throwing his body outside the vineyard. Now what do you think the owner will do to them? Won't he come in fury and take the vineyard away and give it to others?"

"God forbid!"

Staring right at them Jesus said, "But indeed, isn't that exactly what the Scriptures say will happen, that the stone the builders rejected is now become the head of the corner?[55] Everyone who falls on that stone will be broken in pieces but whomever it falls upon will be crushed to powder."

The scribes and chief priests wanted to grab Jesus then and there, knowing he had spoken this parable against them, but they couldn't do so because they were afraid of the people. At the same time they kept a close eye on him. They even sent some people they had paid off who, pretending to be truth seekers, tried to catch Jesus in his words so they could frame charges against him before the governing Roman authorities. One of things they asked him was, "Master, we know you speak and teach what is right, favoring no one over another but showing all the true path to God. Tell us then, does the Law permit us to pay taxes to Caesar?"

Jesus saw through their ruse and said, "Show me a silver coin."

They gave him one.

"Whose face is on it? Whose name is written above?"

"Caesar's."

"Well then it's easy – give back to Caesar the things that are his and give back to God the things that are God's."

His logic was irresistible and no one could refute him in front of the people. The fact is they were overpowered, silenced by his words. Even so,

---

55   *Psalms* 118:22.

some of the Sadducees decided to take a shot at him. The Sadducees deny there's life after death and therefore posed this question, "Teacher, Moses wrote to us that if someone's brother dies and leaves behind a wife but no children he should marry the widow and thereby restore his brother's sperm to life.[56] But here's what happened. There were seven brothers and the first died leaving behind a wife but no children. Therefore the second took her to wife. But he died the same way, then the third, fourth, fifth, sixth and seventh. In time the woman died as well. So whose wife is she in the resurrection since she was married to all of them?"

"The children of this world marry and are given in marriage. But those who are deemed worthy of the resurrection of the dead neither marry nor are given in marriage nor can ever die, but in that respect are like the angels. More than that they are God's children, born of the resurrection. Didn't Moses himself confirm that the dead are raised when he wrote of the burning bush, calling the Lord the God of Abraham and the God of Isaac and the God of Jacob?[57] He is therefore not the God of the dead but of the living, because all are alive in him."

Then one of the scribes confessed, "Teacher, you have spoken well."

And after that no one had the nerve to question him again.

But Jesus asked them, "Why is it said that Messiah is David's son? After all, this is what David himself says in the Book of Psalms –

> The Lord said to my Lord:
>> Sit at my right hand
> until I set your enemies as a footstool
>> beneath your feet.[58]

So if David calls him Lord how then can he be his son?"

With all the people listening intently Jesus continued on.

"Be wary of the teachers of the Law. They enjoy strolling about in long robes and love it when they are hailed in the marketplace, given the best seats in the synagogue and set in places of honor at a banquet. But they devour widows' estates and make a show of long prayers. Therefore they

56   *Genesis* 38:8; *Deuteronomy* 25:5.
57   *Exodus* 3:6, 15, 16.
58   *Psalms* 110:1.

will bear the harsher judgment."

21

Jesus looked past the crowd and saw the rich casting their gifts into the Temple treasury. He also saw an impoverished widow toss in two cents among all those gifts. He turned back to the people and said, "Truly this poor widow gave more than everyone because the rest shared out of abundance but she in her poverty gave all that she had, even what she needed to live on."

Then Jesus overheard some in the group marveling at the Temple, how it was covered with precious stones and other ornaments. But he said, "Do you see all this? The days are coming when stone won't be left on stone, all being toppled."

"Teacher, when will all this happen and what will the sign be that these things are about to occur?"

"Watch - and don't be fooled. Many will come in my name saying, 'I'm the One' or 'the End is near.' Don't run after them. And when you hear of wars and chaos don't be startled! That has to happen first but it's not the end. Nation will rise up against nation, kingdom against kingdom. You'll see major earthquakes and famines everywhere, plagues, horrors, great signs from above. And before all that people will persecute and arrest you, handing you over to congregations and prisons, haling you before kings and governors on account of my name. Yet it will turn to your favor as a testimony. Don't feel you have to plan out ahead of time how you'll defend yourself - I will give you a voice and wisdom that none of your adversaries can withstand or oppose. Know that you will be betrayed by your parents and siblings, your kin and your friends. Some of you will be killed and you'll all be hated by everyone for my name's sake. Yet not one hair on your head will be lost from my sight and by patience you'll preserve your souls.

"When you see Jerusalem surrounded by armies you will know her desolation is near. Those in Judea must run for the hills, those in her midst depart, those in the countryside never return – because these are the days of judgment when all that is written will be fulfilled. And woe to those who are pregnant or nurse babes in those days because there will be great distress on the Earth and wrath poured out on this people. They will fall by the edge of the sword and as captives be dispersed abroad. And Jerusalem will be trodden down by the nations until the times of the Gentiles be fulfilled.

"There will be signs in the sun and moon and stars, perplexity among the nations, despair at the roar and fury of the sea, men's hearts failing for fear and dread of all that will come upon the world. The very framework of Heaven will be shaken – but *then* they will see the Son of Man coming in a cloud[59] with power and great glory. And when these things begin to come to pass, lift your heads and look up, because your redemption draws nigh."

Then he shared this parable.

"Take a look at the fig tree. Or any tree for that matter. When they start to show new leaves you know on your own the hot season is near. Therefore when you see these things starting to happen you'll know the kingdom of God can't be far away. And this same generation will not pass until all things have been fulfilled – Heaven and Earth may well disappear but my words will not perish.

"But watch out for yourselves that you don't let your passions get out of hand, staggering like drunks or weighed down by the cares of life, missing the signs of the times, caught in that day like a rat in a trap – because it will spring of a sudden across Earth's face. That's why I urge you to stand watch, praying for the strength to withstand the things that will come and, having withstood, to stand before the Son of Man."

Jesus continued his teachings daily in the Temple, making his camp at night on Mount Olive. Then the people showed up again at the next crack of dawn to hear whatever it was he had to say.

22

---

59 *Daniel* 7:13.

The Feast of Unleavened Bread, also called Passover, was upon them. The chief priests and scribes continued to look for ways to kill Jesus, yet they remained in fear of the mob. But now the Devil took possession of Judas, that man from Kerioth and one of the Twelve, and Judas plotted with the chief priests and Temple officers how he might hand Jesus over to them. They were, of course, thrilled to do business with the traitor. It then became a simple matter of agreeing on a price and, once they did, Judas watched for the chance to catch him someplace far from the madding crowd.

The days arrived to sweep the house clean of leavened bread and slay the paschal lamb. So Jesus charged Peter and John to "make all things ready for the Passover meal."

"Where were you thinking of having it?"

"When you get to town you'll be met by a man carrying a jar of water. Follow him to the house he's heading to, go inside and ask for the homeowner. Say to him, 'The Master asks whether you have a room where he can eat the Passover meal with his disciples.' He'll offer you a large room up the stairs. Take that one and make all the preparations."

Out they went, found things just as Jesus had told them and spread the feast accordingly. When the time came Jesus reclined at the table, the disciples with him.

"I've deeply desired to share this Passover feast with you before my suffering – and I won't eat it again until its fulfillment in the kingdom of God."

Then taking a cup he gave thanks and said, "Take this and share it among you. I tell you I won't drink of the fruit of the vine until the kingdom of God is come."

Taking bread he broke it and gave to them saying, "This is my body, which is given for you. Do this in remembrance of me." Likewise taking the cup after supper he said, "This cup is the new covenant in my blood, which is poured out for you. But look – the hand of the one who betrays me is here with mine at the table! The Son of Man goes as has been ordained but alas for that man who betrays him."

Then they all began to squabble among themselves who it was who might betray him and after that they fought about which of them would be the greatest. But Jesus made them stop, explaining that "the kings of the Gentiles lord it over their people and their power-mongers pretend to be philanthropists. That's not the way things will be with you – the great among you shall be as the youngest and your leaders as those who serve. Who's greater, after all, the master of the house or his servant? It's the master of course – and yet I've been among you as one who serves. You've borne with me through my trials. Therefore I will appoint you kingdoms, just as my Father has appointed a kingdom to me, so that you may eat and drink at the table in my kingdom and sit on thrones judging the twelve Tribes of Israel."

Turning to Peter he said, "Simon, Simon, Satan would sift all of you as so much wheat in a sieve[60] – but I've prayed for you, that your faith not wholly fail. When you turn and repent be sure to strengthen your brothers."

"But Lord! I'm ready to follow you not just to prison but to death, if that's what it takes!"

"I don't think so. The truth is, before the rooster crows you'll deny three times you know me. Yet listen, when I sent you out on the road without so much as a backpack or a wallet or even a pair of sandals, did you lack anything?"

"Not a thing."

"But now I want anyone who has a backpack to grab it along with whatever cash he can carry – and if you don't have a sword sell your coat and buy one. I'm telling you that what's been written about me in the Scriptures must now be fulfilled, even that I be counted as a criminal.[61] And all things concerning me are poised for completion."

"Look Lord – we've got two swords!"

"That's plenty."

Then as was his custom Jesus left with them for Mount Olive. Once they got there he said, "Pray that you enter not into temptation." Then he withdrew a stone's throw from them and fell to his knees and prayed, "Father, if thou be willing, take this cup from me. Yet not my will, but thine be done." At that an angel from Heaven appeared by his side,

---

60 *Amos* 9:9.
61 *Isaiah* 53:12.

strengthening him. But being in agony he prayed with more fervor, his sweat tinged with blood falling in drops to the ground.[62]

Once he had finished praying Jesus returned to his disciples but found them asleep, worn down by their sorrow. "You're sleeping? Get up! And pray that you don't fall into temptation."

Even as he spoke a crowd of men showed up led by Judas, one of the Twelve, who approached to greet Jesus.

"But Judas - betrayest thou the Son of Man with a kiss?"

Then seeing what was about to happen his disciples said, "Lord, should we strike now with our swords?" But before Jesus could answer one of them attacked and sliced off the right ear of the High Priest's top servant.

Yet Jesus said, "Hold back!" Then he touched the man's ear and healed it. Turning to the chief priests along with the Temple guards and elders he said, "What's the point of your coming after me now with swords and clubs, as if I were a thief? Wasn't I with you daily at the Temple? You never tried to seize me then. But now you are swept up by the Dark One's might and you march to his tune."

So they arrested Jesus and brought him bound to the High Priest's own home, while Peter followed at some distance. Once the arresting officers had kindled a fire in the courtyard Peter moved closer and sat down among them. But a servant girl who was also there stared at Peter, his face being caught by the light of the fire, and shouted, "I know you, you're one of them!"

But Peter viciously denied it, "Shut up girl, I don't know him at all!"

Yet a little while later someone else insisted, "You're lying, you *are* part of his group."

"Listen you, I have nothing to do with him!"

But around an hour later another person said aloud to all, "This guy is for sure one of them - look, he's a Galilean like the rest."

"I'm telling you I don't know who you're talking about!"

No sooner were these words out when the rooster crowed. Jesus turned where he stood and looked right at Peter, who remembered what Jesus had said - "before the rooster crows you'll deny three times

---

62   Aristotle, *Historia Animalium*, iii.19.

you know me" – and ran out weeping bitter tears.

Then the men holding Jesus mocked and beat him, covering him with a hood and saying, "Prophesy! Who's hitting you now?" And more than that, they cursed his name.

Once dawn came the elders, chief priests and scribes brought Jesus before the Council and challenged him.

"If you are the Anointed One, tell us now."

"Even if I were to tell you, you still won't believe. And if I ask anything of you, you won't answer. Yet henceforth you'll see the Son of Man seated enthroned at the right hand of God Almighty."[63]

"So you're the Son of God now?"

"Let that be your witness."

"Well that's all the witness we need because we've now heard the blasphemy ourselves!"

23

With that the whole group adjourned and led Jesus to Pilate, where they accused him and alleged, "We've found this man subverting our whole nation, trying to prevent them from paying taxes to Caesar and telling everyone he's God's Anointed King."

Pilate asked Jesus, "Are you really the King of the Jews?"

"Do you say so?"

Faced with that Pilate told the rulers, "This man's done nothing wrong that I can tell."

But the rulers pressed harder, saying to Pilate, "Don't you see? He's riled up everyone from Galilee to Judea!"

When Pilate heard that Jesus was from Galilee, Herod's jurisdiction, and knowing that Herod happened to be visiting Jerusalem at the moment, he sent Jesus over to him to give Herod the chance to deal with the matter. Now this is that same Herod Antipas who had Johan the Baptist beheaded and he was now quite thrilled at the opportunity to meet Jesus

---

63   *Psalms* 110:1.

because he'd been hearing about him for some time, to the point where he even hoped to see some miracles for himself. But when he tried cross-examining him at length he got nowhere, Jesus answering him not a word.

At the same time the chief priests and experts in the Law continued rabidly with their accusations, prompting Herod himself, as well as his soldiers, to mock Jesus, treating him with contempt and ultimately casting a gleaming white robe around him as he was led once more back to Pilate. The whole episode had the effect of healing a rift between Pilate and Herod that had gone on for a number of years and the upshot of it was they now became best friends.

But with the problem now back in his court Pilate summoned the chief priests along with the synagogue rulers and their supporters and told them, "Look, you brought this man to me claiming he's been stirring up the people but when I asked you for evidence you came up with nothing. I gave you another chance to make your case, this time before Herod. But he found nothing wrong, certainly nothing worthy of death, and now he's sent him back to me. I'll rough him up a bit but then I intend to release him at the feast" – because he was obliged as a matter of custom to free one prisoner on that occasion at the people's demand.

Yet they shouted out virtually as one, "Not this man! Free Barabbas instead!" Now this Barabbas was being held in prison as a terrorist. Unwilling to let *him* go Pilate urged their consent to release Jesus.

But the mob became frenzied and cried, "Crucify him! Crucify him!"

So a third time Pilate challenged them, "What in the world has he done wrong? I'm telling you he's committed no capital crime. I'll have him whipped but that's it – then he's a free man."

Nevertheless the people overwhelmed Pilate with continual shouting and turmoil, demanding Jesus' crucifixion and refusing to be silenced until he gave in. At last Pilate yielded to their demands, releasing the murderer but condemning Jesus just as his enemies willed.

As the soldiers led Jesus out of the city, they grabbed hold of Cyrus of Cyrene, who happened to be on his way into town from the countryside, and forced him to carry Jesus' cross for him. A whole slew of people followed behind, including numbers of women who wept and mourned for him. But Jesus turned to them and said, "Don't cry for me, daughters of Jerusalem. Weep for yourselves and your children because the days are coming in which they will say, 'Blessed are the barren, the wombs that never bore, the breasts that gave no milk.' Then they will begin to call to the mountains, 'Fall upon us!' and to the hills, 'Hide us!'[64] - because if they do these things when the trees are green what will happen when the wood is dry?"[65]

The soldiers also brought along two other criminals to be killed at the same time. When they had all gotten to the place called Skull they crucified Jesus and the two evildoers, the one set on his right and the other on his left. And as they did so Jesus prayed, "Father, forgive them, for they know not what they do."

The people stood by and watched, while the soldiers rolled dice to see who would get his garment.

Then the rulers began to taunt him - "He saved others. If he's truly God's chosen, the Anointed One, let him save himself."

The soldiers laughed him to scorn as well, offering him vinegar to drink as they chimed in, "Save yourself, King of the Jews!" And above him a sign was written in Greek and Latin as well as Hebrew, "This man is the King of the Jews."

One of the criminals hanging there with him cursed at Jesus, "If you're the Messiah save us as well as yourself!"

But the other criminal said, "What's the matter with you? Don't you fear God? We're under the same death sentence he is - and we're only getting our just deserts, dying for the wicked things we did, but he's done nothing wrong!" Then looking to Jesus he said, "Lord, remember me when you come into your kingdom." And Jesus assured him, "I promise you, this day you will be with me in Paradise."

By then it was high noon and darkness fell across the whole land until three p.m., with the sun in full eclipse. Then the veil separating the Holiest of Holies within the Temple was split down the middle just as Jesus cried loudly, "Father! I entrust my spirit to your hands!"[66] And he breathed his last.

---

64   *Isaiah* 2:19; *Hosea* 10:8.
65   *Ezekiel* 20:47.
66   *Psalms* 31:5.

When the centurion who stood guard saw this he glorified God and said, "Truly this was a righteous man!" But the mob that had gathered to witness the event dispersed, beating their breasts as they returned to the city. Meanwhile Jesus' own circle stood at a distance, while the women who had followed him from Galilee watched it all unfold.

Now a man named Joseph was there as well. He was from Arimathea, a Judean city, and a good man, just in his deeds, someone who looked for the coming of the kingdom of God. And though he was a member of the council that sought Jesus' death he himself had stood in opposition. But once Jesus was dead Joseph went before Pilate and begged leave to take the body down for burial - which he did, wrapping the corpse in fine linen and placing it in a virgin tomb cut into the hillside. As the light waned the day for Sabbath preparations began. Mary from Magdala, Joanna, Jacob's mother Mary and the other women who had followed Jesus from Galilee saw how his body was laid in a cave and returned to the city to prepare burial ointments and spices.

And when the Sabbath came they rested according to the commandment.

24

But when rosy-fingered dawn appeared the first day of the week these same women came to the tomb, bearing the spices they had prepared. Yet they were perplexed to find the stone had been rolled away from the cave's entrance and, more than that, when they went inside Jesus' body wasn't there! As they stood not knowing what to do or think two men garbed in lightning white appeared by their side. In fear the women fell face to the ground but the men said, "Why are you looking for the living among the dead? He's not here, he is risen! Don't you remember what he said to you when you were still in Galilee, that 'the Son of Man must be betrayed into the hands of wicked men and be crucified and the third day rise from the dead?'" Then they did indeed remember his words.

Leaving the tomb they returned to spread the news to the eleven apostles and the rest - but it all sounded crazy and they were dismissed as babblers. Even so, Peter wanted to see for himself and ran off to the site of the tomb where, peeking in, he saw the grave clothes placed to one side. But then he left, confused and uncertain in his own mind as to what had happened.

Later that same day Kleopas and another of Jesus' followers were walking on the road to Emmaus, a little village some seven or eight miles from Jerusalem. While the two of them were busy discussing and debating all the things that had happened, Jesus himself came up alongside and started to walk with them - but their eyes were veiled to prevent them from recognizing him.

"What are you two tossing back and forth as you go?"

Kleopas turned grimly to Jesus and asked, "Have you been in outer space the past week? Don't you know what's been going on in Jerusalem?"

"No, what?"

"I'm talking about Jesus Nazarene, who was a prophet in word and deed before God and the whole nation. Yet the chief priests and our rulers handed him over to the Romans to be killed, and they crucified him - but we thought he was the one who would ransom Israel. On top of this it's been three days since he died yet some of the women from our group came and told us something unbelievable, that they had gone to the tomb first thing this morning and not only couldn't find his body but saw a vision of angels telling them he's alive. Then a couple of us went to the tomb ourselves and found it just as the women said, but we didn't see Jesus."

"Are you really that dull of heart and slow to believe all that the prophets have written? Wasn't it necessary for Messiah to suffer these things and so to enter his glory?" Then, beginning with Moses and tracing through the Prophets, he interpreted for them everything that had been written about himself in the Scriptures. As they neared the village they'd been heading to he acted as though he would continue on past. But they pressed him not to and said, "It's nearly vesper, stop here and stay with us." So he did. And as they sat to dine he took bread, broke it and shared it with them. At that their eyes were opened and they knew it was Jesus - but just then he vanished from their sight.

"Didn't our hearts burn within us as he spoke to us along the road, explaining the Scriptures?" So right away they turned back toward Jerusalem, where they found the Eleven and the others with them already saying, "The Lord is risen – he's appeared to Simon!" Then they told their own story how Jesus met them on the road to Emmaus and made himself known in the breaking of bread.

Even as they relayed what had happened, Jesus stood in their midst and said, "Peace be with you." But they were so startled and scared they thought they saw a ghost.

"Why are you so stirred up, with doubts rising in your hearts? Can't you see from my hands and my feet that it's me? Touch me if you're not sure – ghosts don't have flesh and bone the way I do!"

Then he showed them his hands and feet. Yet they were so undone with joy they could still scarce believe him.

He asked, "Have you got any food here?"

They grabbed a piece of grilled fish and he took and ate it right in front of them.

"Listen to me, all this is just as I told you while I was yet with you, how everything written about me by Moses and the Prophets and in the Psalms would have to be fulfilled."

Then he opened their minds to understand the Scriptures.

"It was written that the Anointed One would suffer and rise from the dead on the third day and that repentance would be preached in his name to all nations, beginning in Jerusalem, where you have been witnesses of all these things. I will send you the promise of my Father[67] – but stay now in the city until you've been clothed with power from on high."

Then Jesus led them out as far as Bethany, where he lifted his hands and blessed them. But even as he spoke this blessing he was parted from them and caught up into Heaven. And so they worshipped him, returning now to Jerusalem overwhelmed with joy, remaining in the Temple as they praised God continually.

---

67   *Isaiah* 44:3; *Ezekiel* 36:26-27; *Joel* 2:28-29.

ACCORDING TO JOHN

1

The Word existed before all Time, timelessly present with God and himself true God. He was with God at the outset. All that ever came into being did so through the Word - nothing has come to be that he did not bring into being. In him was Life and the Life was the Light of mankind. The Light shines in the Darkness and the Darkness cannot overcome it.

A man named John was sent by God to be a witness testifying about the Light so that all might believe in him. He wasn't the Light itself - just a witness to it - this being the true Light that came into the world and gives light to all mankind. He was in the world, yet even though the world came into being through him the world did not perceive him. He came to his own people but they did not welcome him in. However, he gave the power to become children of God to as many as did receive him - that is, to as many as believed in his Name, those who were born neither of blood nor flesh nor mortal will but from God.

Thus it was that the Word took on man's nature and for a time pitched his tent among us. All of us gazed upon his Glory, Glory as that of the Father's Only Begotten, full of Grace and Truth. John gave faithful testimony concerning him, calling out to all, "This is the One I told you about when I said, 'He who comes after me is superior to me because he was before me.'"

We all have received of his Fullness, Grace upon Grace, because while the Law was given by Moses, Grace and Truth came through the Anointed Jesus. No one has ever seen God. But the Only Begotten Son, who dwells in the heart of the Father, he has made him known.

This was John's testimony when the Jewish leaders sent priests and Levites from Jerusalem to find out more about him.

He told them straight out, "I am *not* the Messiah!"

"Okay then, but who are you? Elijah?"[1]

"No."

"Well, are you the Prophet spoken of by Moses?"[2]

"No."

"But who then – because we've got to give an answer to the people who sent us! What can you tell us about yourself?"

"I am a voice crying in the wilderness, 'Make straight the way of the Lord,'[3] just as Isaiah the prophet spoke."

Now, the people who had been sent to him were from among the sect of the Pharisees and they asked, "Why then are you baptizing people if you're neither the Anointed One nor Elijah nor that Prophet?"

"I'm baptizing in water but someone has taken his place in your midst who you don't even know – he's the one whose advent follows mine and I'm not so much as worthy to unlace his sandals."

All this took place in Bethany just across the Jordan River, which is where John was baptizing people.

The next day John saw Jesus walking toward him and said, "Behold the Lamb of God, who bears the sin of the world.[4] This is the person I was talking about when I said, 'A man comes after me who holds rank above me, because he was before me.' I didn't know who he was, only that I should go about baptizing in order that he be revealed to Israel. But I can also tell you this – I saw the Spirit descending as a dove from Heaven, alighting and remaining on him. That's how I knew who he was because the one who commissioned me to baptize also told me, 'The one on whom you see the Spirit descend and remain is the one who immerses people in

---

1   *Malachi* 4:5.
2   *Deuteronomy* 18:15, 18.
3   *Isaiah* 40:3.
4   *Isaiah* 53:7, 11-12; *see Leviticus* 10:17.

the Holy Spirit.' And I have seen and testified that this man is the Son of God!"

The following day John was with two of his acolytes when he saw Jesus passing by again. Once more he exclaimed, "Behold the Lamb of God!" When these two heard *that* they began to follow Jesus; but when Jesus saw them heading in his direction he challenged them, "What are you looking for?"

"Rabbi,[5] we'd like to know where you're staying."

"Come along then, see for yourself."

It was by then around 4 p.m. One of the two was Andrew. He found his brother Simon Peter and brought him to Jesus' lodging as well, telling him, "We've found the Messiah!"[6]

When Jesus saw Peter he said, "Your given name is Simon, son of Jonah, but I name you Cephas."[7]

The next day Jesus headed out toward Galilee. Finding Philip along the way he said, "Follow me!" Now Philip was from Bethsaida, the same town as Andrew and Peter, and he in turn went to find another local named Nathaniel and told him, "We've found the one whom Moses and the Prophets wrote about - it's Jesus ben Joseph, from Nazareth!"

"You can't be serious - nothing good comes from Nazareth."

"Come, see for yourself."

When Jesus saw Nathaniel walking toward him he said, "Look indeed, a true child of Israel, someone in whom guile does not exist!"

"How do you know who I am?"

"Oh, I saw you sitting under the fig tree before Philip called out to you."

"Rabbi! You are the Son of God, the King of Israel!"

"You believe in me just because I said I'd seen you beneath the fig tree? You'll witness a lot more than that - indeed, all of you will see Heaven opened and God's angels ascending and descending on the Son of Man."

---

5   Which means "Teacher" in English.
6   The "Anointed One," in English.
7   The Aramaic word for stone, the transliterated Greek for which would be "petros," hence the name Peter in English.

2

Three days later there was a wedding in the town of Qana in Upper Galilee. Jesus' mother was an invited guest and so were Jesus and his followers. His mother saw they were running out of wine and told Jesus about
it. But he said, "Ma'am, why is that any of my concern? It's not yet my
appointed time." She then turned to the servants and told them to follow
whatever instructions Jesus might give.

There were six stone jars on hand, normally used for ritual washing and
each able to hold around 20 or 30 gallons of water. Jesus said, "Fill them up
to the top." Once the servants had done so he said, "Draw some off and bring
it to the banquet master." The water had in fact now become wine and once
the banquet master tasted it – having no idea of course where it had come
from, although the servants who had drawn the water knew – he called the
groom over and said to him, "People always serve finer wines first and then,
once people are pretty well drunk, they pour them something second rate.
But you've held the best wine back till now!"

Jesus performed this wonder at Qana of Galilee as the beginning of his
signs, thus manifesting his glory – and his disciples put their faith in him.
After the wedding he, his mother, his brothers and his disciples all went
down to Capernaum, where he remained for a number of days.

It was getting near the time for the Passover Feast and Jesus therefore
went up to Jerusalem. But he found people changing money and selling
oxen, sheep and doves in the Temple precincts – so he picked up some of
the bull rushes where the cattle were bedded down, tied them together
like a whip and drove the animals out. Then he knocked over the moneychangers' stands, scattering their coins on the ground. And he scolded
the bird dealers, "Get this stuff out of here – don't turn my Father's house
into a marketplace!"

Seeing this his disciples called to mind a passage from Scripture –
Passion for your house will consume me.[8]

But the Jewish rulers confronted him about it and asked, "What gives
you the right to do these things?"

"Destroy this temple and in three days I'll raise it back up."

"This Temple took 46 years to build and you'll rebuild it in three days?!"

---

8   *Psalms 69;9; see also Malachi 3:1.*

However, Jesus was speaking about the temple that was his body. It was only after he was raised from the dead that his disciples recalled what he'd said and realized what he'd meant – and then they believed the Scripture[9] and Jesus' word.

Now, many people saw the signs Jesus performed while he was in Jerusalem for the Passover Feast and trusted in his Name. Even so Jesus didn't entrust himself to them because he knew how people are and he didn't need anyone to teach him about human nature, knowing full well what evil lurks in the hearts of man.

3

It happened not long afterwards that a leading member of the Pharisaical sect, Nicodemus by name, came to see Jesus under the cloak of nighttime.

"Rabbi," he said, "we know you are a teacher come from God because no one could have the power to work the miracles you do were God not with him."

"In that case let me tell you this – unless someone is born freshly from above he cannot perceive the kingdom of God."

"But how can an old man like me be born yet again? Am I supposed to go back into my mother's womb and be born a second time?!"

"What I'm saying is that unless someone is born of water and the Spirit he cannot enter the kingdom of God. What's born of mortal flesh is mortal flesh, what's born of the Spirit is spirit. Don't be amazed that I've said to all of you, 'You must be born again.' The wind whistles where it will and you hear a rustling sound but don't know where it comes from – it's the same with everyone who is born of the Holy Spirit."

"But how can these things be?"

"You're a teacher of Israel yourself and don't know about this? But *we* know what we're talking about and give witness to what we've seen – yet you've rejected our testimony. Just think: if I've told you about earthly things and you don't believe then how will you believe if I tell you of the heavenly?[10] No one has ascended to Heaven other than he who descended

---

9   *See, e.g., Hosea* 6:2.
10   *Wisdom of Solomon* 9:16.

from Heaven, the Son of Man.[11] And just as Moses lifted up the serpent in the wilderness so too must the Son of Man be lifted up in order that all who believe in him may have ageless life. For God so loved the world that he gave his only begotten Son that whosoever believeth in him should not perish, but have everlasting life. For God sent not his Son into the world to condemn the world, but that the world through him might be saved. Whoever believes in him will not fall under judgment; but whoever does not believe has been condemned already because he has not believed on the Name of the only begotten Son of God. And this is the judgment – that the Light is come into the world and people loved the darkness rather than the Light because their deeds were evil. Everyone who revels in base deeds hates the Light and refuses to come to the Light lest his deeds be exposed. But whoever does what is true comes to the Light so that all may see that the things he does are done in God."

Later on Jesus and his followers travelled out to the rural districts of Judea. Jesus remained with them for a period of time and his disciples began to baptize people there. Now John had not yet been thrown into prison and was still baptizing people as well, in this case in Aenon near Salim, where there were a number of ready sources of water in the area and penitents aplenty. One of the Jews then sparked a controversy among John's disciples about these purification rites such that they went to John and said, "Rabbi, the person you testified about over on the other side of Jordan now has everyone running after him, while his disciples are even baptizing people!"

"Don't let that trouble you – no one can receive anything other than what God grants him. Remember that I myself told you, 'I am not the Messiah but was simply sent out ahead of him.' It's the groom who weds the bride, while the groom's friend stands by his side and rejoices at the sound of his voice. That's why my joy is now complete – he must increase but I must decrease. He who comes from above is above all while he who is of the Earth speaks earthly things. He testifies to the things he's seen and heard but people aren't accepting his testimony – yet anyone who does receive the things he says sets his seal that God is true because the one whom God has sent speaks the words of God and God has given him the Spirit without limit. The Father loves the Son and has placed all things in his hands. Whoever believes in the Son has life without end

---

11   *Proverbs* 30:4; *cf. Deuteronomy* 30:12.

while whoever disbelieves the Son will not see life, the wrath of God remaining upon him."

4

Once Jesus learned that the Pharisees had heard he was baptizing more people than John – that his disciples were, at any rate - he picked up stakes and moved on from Judea toward Galilee. Now, in order to get to Galilee from where he was he had to cross through Samaria. On the way he came to a town called Sychem, close by the plot of land that Jacob had given to his son Joseph.[12] It was by then around noon and Jesus was plumb worn out from walking the long and rocky road. Chancing on Jacob's Well he sat on it to rest. Shortly thereafter a local Samaritan woman came by to fetch water.

"Draw me some water to drink," he said.

"What's with you, asking me a Samaritan woman to pour you some water? You Jews are supposed to keep away from us!"

"If you had perceived the gift of God and known who asked you for a drink you would've asked of *him* and he would've given you living water."[13]

"But, my Lord, this well is deep and you don't even have a bucket – where are you getting this 'living water' from? Are you greater than our father Jacob who gave us this well, from which he drank and his sons and also his flocks?"

"Anyone who drinks of this water will get thirsty again. But whoever drinks of the water I give him will never thirst, not for all eternity - because the water I will give him will become a well of water springing up in him to imperishable life."

"Lord, give me this water that I may never thirst or come daily here to draw!"

"Go fetch your husband and tell him about this."

"But I'm not married!"

"That's true as far as it goes - but I know you've been to the altar and back five times before. Still, you aren't married to your current partner

---

12   *Genesis* 33:19; *Joshua* 24:32.
13   *Ezekiel* 36:25; *Jeremiah* 2:13; *Zechariah* 13:1.

so you do get credit for your honesty."

"Well sir, you're clearly a seer! But help me understand something – our fathers worshipped on this mountain yet you people say Jerusalem is where one must worship."

"Lady, believe me – the time is coming when people will worship the Father neither on this mountain nor in Jerusalem. The fact is, you don't even know what you worship but *we* know, because salvation comes from the Jews.[14] Even so, the time is now upon us when the true worshippers will worship the Father in spirit and in truth, because the Father seeks such people to be his worshippers. God is spirit and those who worship him must worship him in spirit and in truth."

"I know Messiah is coming, the Anointed One, and that when he comes he will proclaim to us all things."

"I who now speak to you am he."

Just at that moment his disciples showed up and were agape to see him speaking alone with a woman. Still, no one dared ask what she was up to let alone challenge Jesus for speaking to her. But at their arrival the woman abandoned her water jar and ran off to the town, telling everyone, "Come with me and see a man who told me all there is to know about me – doesn't he *have* to be the Anointed One??" So the villagers all headed to the well to see what this was about.

In the meantime his disciples urged him, "Rabbi, have something to eat."

"I have meat you don't know anything about."

The disciples questioned one another, "Did anyone bring him some food?"

"My meat is to do the will of the one who sent me and to complete his task. You say, 'It's still four months until the harvest' – but I say, lift up your eyes and look at the fields because they are ripe for the harvest and those who are harvesting are already earning wages, gathering fruit toward everlasting life so that the sower and the reaper may rejoice together. It's an apt saying that goes, 'One sows but another reaps.' I've sent you to harvest in places you hadn't toiled – others sweated and you've reaped the benefits of their labor."

Many of the Samaritans in that city came to believe in Jesus based just on the word of the woman who said he had known and told her everything

---

14   *Isaiah* 2:2-3.

about her life; and they asked him to stay with them. He remained two days and during that time many more came to have faith in him because of his own word. And so they said to the woman, "Now we believe in him not just because of what you've said but because we've now heard him with our own ears and know this man is indeed the Savior of the world!"

After that Jesus left and went into Galilee. He himself had declared that a prophet is honored everywhere but in his own country and so when he came to Galilee the Galileans welcomed him, having been at the feast in Jerusalem and seen the wonders he performed there.

During this time Jesus visited Qana again, the city where he turned the water into wine. A certain court official in Capernaum heard that Jesus had left Judea for Galilee and so he travelled there seeking help for his son, who lay deathly ill at home. He begged Jesus to come down to Capernaum to heal him. But Jesus responded, "It seems that unless you people see miracles and wonders you won't believe."

"Lord, you must come before my son dies!"

"Go safely back – your son will live."

He took Jesus at his word and left for Capernaum. The man's servants met him as he was still on the road with the news that his son had fully recovered. He asked them what time he began to recover. The servants answered, "His fever broke yesterday at 1 p.m." The boy's father knew this was the very same time Jesus had said to him, "Your son will live" – and so he and his whole household believed. This was the second miracle Jesus performed as he came from Judea into Galilee.

5

Sometime after this Jesus went up to Jerusalem in observance of one of the annual Jewish festivals. Now, there is a pool there not far from the Sheep Gate called בֵּית חֶסְדָּא in Aramaic, which in English means "House of Mercy." It has five arched porticos surrounding it where many of the sick, blind, lame and paralytic lay, including a man who'd been a cripple for 38 years. All those were there waiting for the waters to roil – the story goes that at unpredictable moments an angel of the Lord would descend and stir the waters and whoever was first immersed would be fully healed. So as Jesus passed by he saw the man and, knowing he'd been there for quite some time, said, "Do you want to be healed?"

"Lord, I don't have anyone to let me down into the pool when the water starts to move and whenever I try to crawl there on my own someone else gets in before me."

"Then get up now, start walking and take your stretcher with you!"

Instantly the man was healed and, picking up his cot, began to walk.

But it was the Sabbath day. When some of the Jewish rulers saw this they scolded the man who had just been healed - "It's the Sabbath! You're not permitted to carry anything around!"[15]

"The guy who healed me told me to."

"Who was it you say told you to pick up that stretcher?"

But the man didn't know who let alone where Jesus was because he'd already passed on through the gathered crowd unobserved.

Later on however Jesus found the man in the Temple precincts and told him, "Look, you've been healed - but don't sin again or something worse may happen to you."

The man then reported to the rulers that it was Jesus who had healed him. On account of that they berated Jesus for doing such things on the Sabbath day. But Jesus said, "My Father's at work today and therefore so am I." Then they sought all the more to kill him - not only because he had broken the Sabbath rules but because he called God his own father, thereby making himself equal to God.

"Listen carefully," Jesus continued, "the Son can't do anything on his own but only what he sees the Father doing, because it's in his very nature to do likewise. The Father loves the Son and shows him everything that he himself does - and indeed will show him greater works than these, such as to make you marvel, because just as the Father raises the dead and makes them live again so too the Son gives life to whomever he wishes. The Father condemns no one but has handed over all judgment to the Son to the end that all might honor the Son just as they honor the Father. Whoever does not honor the Son does not honor the Father who sent him.

"I tell you truly that whoever hears my word and believes in the one who sent me has enduring life and enters not into judgment, but has passed from death into life. The time is now upon us when the dead will hear the voice of the Son of God and those who hear shall live. Just as the Father has life in

---

15   *Jeremiah* 17:21-22.

himself so too has he granted the Son to have life in himself and moreover has given him authority to render judgment, because he is the Son of Man.

"Don't be shocked at this, because the time is coming when all entombed shall hear his voice and come forth, those who've done good to the resurrection of life and those who've practiced evil to the resurrection of judgment.

"I cannot do anything on my own – as I hear, so I judge and my judgment is just because I seek not my own will but the will of him who sent me. If I testify to myself my testimony is not true. But there is another who testifies concerning me and I know that the testimony he gives about me is true.

"You sent after John and he testified to the truth – it isn't that I need to receive testimony from mankind, but I'm telling you these things so that you might be saved. He was a lamp burning bright and you were willing for a season to rejoice in his light. But I have a greater testimony than that of John because the works the Father has given me to complete, the very works you see me doing, testify of me that the Father has sent me. And the Father who sent me has himself borne witness about me. You've never heard his voice or ever seen him. And his Word doesn't dwell within you because you do not believe the one he has sent. Search the Scriptures! You suppose you hold unending life in them – well, they are they which testify of me. And yet you will not come to me that you might have life.

"I don't accept honor from men – but I know you, that you do not have God's love within you. I have come in the Name of my Father and you have not received me. If another comes in his own name you'll take him in. How can you believe when you accept praise from one another while never seeking the glory that comes from the only God? And don't have it in your minds that I will accuse you before the Father. It is Moses who accuses you, in whom you place your hope – if you believed Moses you would believe me, because he wrote of me. But if you don't believe his writings, how will you believe the things I say?"

6

Jesus then crossed over the Sea of Galilee to the Tiberian region. An immense crowd followed after him, having seen the miracles he performed for the sick. Jesus went up the slope of one of the seaside hills along with

his disciples and, as was his custom, sat to teach. But looking out over the multitude as the people approached he said to Philip, "Is there someplace nearby we can buy some bread for them to eat?"[16]

"We've got around $200 to spend but that won't be enough to get even a little bit for everyone."

Simon Peter's brother Andrew interjected, "There's a kid here that's got five barley loaves and two fish – but what good is that for so many people?"

"Tell everyone to sit down on the grass."

So they did, all five thousand of them, not counting women and children.

Jesus then took the bread and giving thanks distributed to all. The same with the fish, as much as anyone wanted. When their stomachs were filled he said to the disciples, "Gather whatever fragments remain, that none may be lost." They did so and found they had twelve baskets filled with the surplus of the five barley loaves. When the people saw the miracle that had occurred they said, "Is this not the Prophet that should come into the world?" But perceiving that the people were about to seize him to crown him king Jesus slipped away by himself further up the mountain.

It soon turned dark as evening fell but Jesus had not yet showed up at the boat. His disciples decided to sail on ahead without him and therefore took ship across the sea to Capernaum. But around three or four miles out they got hit with a fierce squall. They were rowing against the roiling seas when suddenly they saw Jesus walking toward them on the waves. They panicked as he neared the boat. But he calmed them saying, "It is I – be not afraid." They were more than happy to bring him on board and once they had done so came instantly to their destined port.

The next day the crowd that still remained on the coast knew that Jesus' disciples had left in their one boat. But they also saw he was no longer on their side of the sea even though he had not gotten on board with his men. When a number of other boats on their way from Tiberias approached the place where Jesus had given thanks and fed the people with bread, as many as could embarked with them and sailed for Capernaum, seeking Jesus. When they found him on the far shore they said, "Rabbi, how and when did you get here?"

"You came looking for me not because you saw miracles but because

---

16   Jesus just said that to test him, because he already knew what he was going to do.

you were satisfied by the bread you were given. Don't strive after food that perishes but that which remains to life imperishable, food the Son of Man will give you – because he's the one on whom the Father has set his seal."

"What shall we do in order to work the works of God?"

"This is the work of God, that you should believe on him whom he sent."

"What miracle will you perform for us that we may see and believe you? Just what is *your* work? Our fathers ate manna in the Wilderness and so it is written, He gave them bread from Heaven to eat."[17]

"It wasn't Moses who gave you the bread from Heaven. But my Father now gives you the true bread from Heaven – because the bread of God is that which descends from Heaven and gives life to the world."

"Lord, give us this bread now and always!"

"I am the Bread of Life. Whoever comes to me will not hunger and whoever believes in me will never thirst. I've said to you that you've seen me and yet do not believe – but all that the Father gives me will come to me. I will not reject any who come to me because I descended from Heaven not to do my own will but the will of him who sent me. And it is his will that I lose none of all that he has given me but instead raise it up on the Last Day. This is the will of my Father, that each person who sees the Son and believes in him may have eternal life – and I will raise him up in the Last Day!"

But the rulers of the people continued murmuring about him because he said that he was the bread that came down from Heaven.

"Isn't this Joseph's son Jesus, whose father and mother we know? How can he now say, 'I descended from Heaven?'"

"Stop all this arguing among yourselves! No one can come to me unless the Father who sent me draws him; and I will raise him up at the Last Day. It is written in the Prophets, They will all be taught of God.[18] All who have listened to the Father and learned come to me – not that anyone has seen the Father other than the one who is from God, he alone has seen him. I tell you that whoever believes has ageless life. I am the Bread of Life. Your fathers ate manna in the Wilderness and died. This is the Bread of Heaven that has descended in order that anyone who eats of it

---

17　*Psalms* 78:24.
18　*Isaiah* 54:13.

might not die. I am the Living Bread come down from Heaven. If anyone eats of this bread he will live for all ages and the bread I shall give is my body for the life of the world."

Then they fought among themselves all the more.

"How can this man give us his body to eat?!"

"If you do not eat the flesh of the Son of Man and drink his blood you have no life within you. Whoever feeds on my body and drinks of my blood has life without end and I will raise him up on the Last Day. My flesh is meat indeed and my blood true drink. Whoever eats my flesh and drinks my blood dwells in me and I in him. Just as the living Father sent me and I live through him so too whoever feeds on me will live through me. This is the bread that came down from Heaven, not as your fathers ate and died - whoever eats this bread will live unendingly."

Jesus spoke these things as he taught in the synagogue in Capernaum.

On hearing this a number of those who had been following him said, "This is a hard saying! Who can take it in?!"

Knowing within himself that his disciples were whispering together about this Jesus challenged them.

"Are you shocked at what I said? What will happen if you see the Son of Man ascending back to where he was at the first? It's the Spirit that gives life - the flesh accomplishes nothing. The words I've spoken to you are spirit and life. And yet there are some among you who will not believe.[19] That's why I told you that no one can come to me unless it is given him by the Father."

At that point a number of his disciples turned their backs on him and walked away. Jesus asked the Twelve, "Do you wish to leave as well?"

Peter answered, "Lord, to whom would we go? You have the words of life without end and we have believed and known that you are the Holy One of God."

"Haven't I chosen you Twelve? And yet one of you is in the Serpent's camp."[20]

---

19 Jesus knew from the outset those who would not believe, and even who would betray him.

20 He was speaking of Judas, the man from Kerioth, the one who was soon to hand him over despite being one of the Twelve.

7

Jesus remained in Galilee after this, not daring to go yet to Judea because the authorities aimed to kill him. However the Festival of Tabernacles, or Booths, was coming around on the annual religious calendar[21] and Jesus' brothers took the occasion to say to him, "You should go up from here to Jerusalem so your followers there can also see the miracles you're performing. No one who seeks to be known openly should work in secret – if you are doing such deeds reveal them to the world!"[22]

"You're free to do whatever you want anytime you want but it isn't my time yet. The world can't hate you but it hates me because I testify that its deeds are evil. You should go up to the festival now if you wish. I'll go when the time is ripe for me, but that's not quite yet."

They had this exchange while Jesus was still in Galilee. His brothers did then go ahead of him to the feast. Jesus went up later on his own, but quietly and without making a show, since the Jewish rulers were still searching for him, asking around where he was. All of this led to a good deal of murmuring and speculation about him among the people. Some said, "He's the essence of Good," while others demurred, "Not so! He's misleading the crowd." But no one spoke what they thought openly because they all feared the rulers.

Midway through the festival Jesus appeared at the Temple and began to teach, causing the Jewish rulers to marvel, "Where did he get all this knowledge and learning? He's not even been to school!"

"My teaching is not my own but his who sent me. If anyone wills to do *his* will he'll know whether the doctrine originates with God or whether I speak on my own initiative. Anyone who speaks on his own authority seeks his own honor but whoever seeks glory for the one who sent him is truthful with nothing insincere about him. Hasn't Moses given you the Law? Yet none of you keeps the Law. And why are you looking for a way to kill me?"

"You must be possessed! Who's trying to kill you?!"

"I performed one miracle and you were all astounded. Listen, Moses

---

21   *Leviticus* 23:39-43; *Deuteronomy* 16:13-17.
22   The truth is, his brothers said this because they didn't have faith in him. *See Psalms* 69:8.

required circumcision of you, following the rule of the fathers, and you circumcise a child on the Sabbath day in order to conform to that rule. So why are you galled at me because I healed someone's entire body on the Sabbath day? Stop judging on the mere face of things, but judge righteous judgment."

Some of the Jerusalemites therefore said, "Is *this* the guy they want to kill? Don't they see he's speaking out in the open and none of them has anything to say against him? But do people think he's really the Messiah? After all, we know where he's from but whenever the Messiah comes no one will know where he comes from."

But then Jesus called out to them sharply as he taught in the Temple – "You both know me and know where I am from and that I haven't spoken of myself but that the one who sent me is true, whom you do not know. I know him because I come from his presence and he sent me."

At that they tried to lay hold of him but no one could because it wasn't yet his time. Many among the people believed in him and said, "When the Messiah comes will he perform more miracles than this man has?"

When the Pharisees heard the crowd muttering like this they and the chief priests sent Temple officers to arrest him.

"I will be with you but a short while longer and then I go to the one who sent me. You will look for me but not find me and where I am you are unable to go."

"Where is he going that we won't be able to find him? Does he mean to go to the lands where our people are scattered? Will he teach the heathen? What's he talking about when he says, 'You will seek me but not find me and where I am you cannot go?'"

At the water pouring ceremony on the great and last day of the feast Jesus stood and cried out, "If anyone thirsts let him come to me! And anyone who believes in me let him come and drink! Then as the Scriptures say, From his innermost being shall flow rivers of living water."[23]

He spoke this concerning the Spirit, which all those who believed in him would receive – you see, the Spirit had not yet been given because Jesus had not yet been glorified.

When some in the crowd heard these words they said, "Surely this is the Prophet!" or "This is the Messiah!" But others said, "Where is it you see the

---

23   *See Isaiah 12:3; Ezekiel 47:1-12; Zechariah 14:8.*

Messiah coming from Galilee? Isn't it written that the Anointed One is of David's descent and will come from Bethlehem, David's own village?"

Therefore the people were split about him and some even wanted him locked up – but as yet no one tried to lay hands on him.

When the Temple officers reported back to the Pharisees they said, "Why haven't you brought him with you?"

"We've never heard anyone speak the way he does!"

"So he's got you fooled as well? Has he roped in any of us Pharisees? or any of the other authorities? But as far as the *hoi polloi*, what do they know about the Law anyway – they're already on the Highway to Hell."

Yet Nicodemus cautioned them, being himself a Pharisee and the one who had earlier visited with Jesus, "Does our Law judge someone before first hearing his defense or finding out what he's actually doing?"[24]

"Oh, so are you from Galilee too? You'd better take another look at the Scriptures – you'll see no prophet arising from there."

Then they all went off to their homes.

8

Early the next morning he went again to the Temple, where the people thronged about as he sat to teach them. And as he was teaching some of the scribes and Pharisees, they dragged in a woman caught in the act of adultery and stood her in full view before him.

"Teacher," they said, "this woman was seized *in flagrante delicto*. Now Moses commanded us in the Law to stone such a woman,[25] but what do you say?" They asked this tempting him, hoping to find some way to denounce him. But Jesus stooped down and traced with his finger in the dust.

They kept badgering him with questions so he straightened up and said, "Let he that is without sin among you cast the first stone."[26] Then he bent down and continued to write.

On hearing this the accusers all began to slink away, starting with the eldest on down to the youngest. By the time they were gone from the pla-

---

24   *Exodus 23:1-2; Deuteronomy 1:16-17.*
25   *Leviticus 20:10; Deuteronomy 22:22-24.*
26   *Deuteronomy 17:7.*

za the woman was there on her own before Jesus and the watching crowd. Standing again and seeing them gone he asked her, "Woman, where are those who accused you? Is anyone left here to judge you?"

"No one, Lord."

"Neither do I condemn you. Go – but from now on sin no more."[27]

He then resumed his teaching.

"I am the Light of the World. Whoever follows after me will never walk in Darkness but will have the Light of Life."

Some of the Pharisees challenged him on this.

"You're validating yourself! Your testimony therefore can't be trusted."

"Even if I were to testify on my own behalf my testimony would be true because I know where I come from and where I am going. But you don't know where I come from or where I'm going. You judge on human standards but I judge no one – though even if I were to judge my judgment would be true because it is not I alone who judge but the Father who sent me. As is written in your Law, the testimony of two persons is true. I am the one who testifies about myself and the Father who sent me likewise testifies on my behalf."

"Where is your father?"

"You neither know me nor my Father. If you had known me you would have known my Father."

He spoke these things as he taught near the Temple alms basin. But no one prevented him because his hour had not yet come. And again he addressed them.

"I will depart and you will seek me, yet you will die in your sins. Where I go you cannot come."

Then they puzzled amongst themselves, "Will he commit suicide, because now he's saying 'where I go you cannot come?'"

"You are from below but I am from above. You are of this world but I am not of this world. That's why I said to you that you'll die in your sins – because if you do not believe that I am he you will die in your sins."

"Who are you?"

"The same as I told you from the outset. I have many things to say and to judge about you but the one who sent me is true and I speak to the world the things I have heard from him."

---

27   Translator's note: certain manuscripts omit the foregoing incident.

But they didn't understand that he had been speaking to them about the Father. And so Jesus continued.

"Once you have lifted up the Son of Man you will know that I am he and that I do nothing on my own but speak just as the Father taught me. And the one who sent me is with me. He has not abandoned me because I always do that which is pleasing to him."

As he spoke these things many put their trust him. Directing his words to those who now professed to believe he said, "If you stay faithful to my word then you are truly my disciples. You will know the truth and the truth shall set you free."

Yet some responded, "We are sprung from Abraham's loins and have never been anyone's slaves! What do you mean when you say, 'you will be set free?'"

"Anyone who commits sin is the slave of sin. The bondservant does not always remain in the household but the son abides forever.[28] Therefore if the Son sets you free you shall be free indeed! I know you are of Abraham's seed and yet you seek to kill me because my word has no place in you. I speak what I have seen in the presence of my Father. You, by the same token, do the things you have heard from your father."

"Abraham is our father."

"If you were Abraham's children you would be doing Abraham's works. But now you seek to kill me, a man who has spoken to you the truth he's heard from his Father – that's not what Abraham did. And thus you perform the deeds of your father."

"We weren't born out of wedlock! And we have but one Father, God himself."

"If God were your Father you would love me because I came from God and now am present among you. And it isn't as though I came on my own but rather he sent me. Why is it you can't understand what I'm saying? It's because you can't stand to hear my word. You spring from your father the Devil and his desires are your desires. He was a murderer from the beginning and takes no part in the truth because there is no truth in him. Whenever he lies he's just keeping in character – he's not just a liar himself but the father of liars – and so the reason you don't believe *me* is that I speak the truth. Can a single one of you charge me with sin? Yet if I'm speaking the truth why don't you believe me? Whoever is of God

---

28 *Genesis* 21:10.

hears the teachings of God. That's why you don't hear me, because you're not of God."

"Aren't we right to call you a Samaritan – and possessed of a demon at that?"

"You dishonor me – I have no demon – but I honor my Father. I don't seek to glorify myself. Yet there is one who will have me honored and he judges all. But let me tell you plainly, if anyone keeps my word he will never see death."

"Now we know for sure you're demon-possessed! Abraham died and the prophets as well, yet you say, 'If anyone keeps my word he'll never taste death.' Are you greater than our father Abraham, who died? Or the prophets, since they died too? Just who do you make yourself out to be??"

"If I credit myself my glory is nothing. It is my Father who glorifies me, he whom you say is your God. You have not known him but I know him. If I were to say I didn't know him I would be a liar, the likes of you. But I do know him and I keep his word. Indeed, your father Abraham rejoiced that he would see my day – and he did see it, and rejoiced."

"Ha! You're not even 50 years old and you've seen Abraham?!"

"Before Abraham was, I am."

Then they grabbed for stones to throw at him but Jesus concealed himself and slipped unseen from the Temple.

9

Sometime later as Jesus passed along he saw sitting by the side of road a man born blind. His disciples inquired of him, "Rabbi, who sinned that this man should be born blind? Was it this man? Or maybe something his parents did?"[29]

"Neither. Instead he came into the world blind so that the mighty works of God should be manifested in him. I must work the works of him who sent me while it is still day. No one can work in the coming night but as long as I am in the world I am the Light of the World."

When he had said that he spit on the ground, mixed spittle with dust, anointed the man's eyes with some of the slime and commanded

---

29 Exodus 20:5.

him, "Go, wash it off in the Pool of Siloam!"[30]

So he went, washed and walked away seeing.

His neighbors and everyone who had known him beforehand said, "Isn't this the blind man who used to sit and beg?"

Some said, "That's the man!"

Others said, "Well, he *looks* like him but it can't be the same person."

But he said, "I am he!"

So they asked, "How is it your eyes were opened?"

"The man named Jesus anointed my eyes with some mud and told me, 'Go, wash in the Pool of Siloam.' I did what he said and received my sight!"

"Where is he?"

"No idea."

Then they brought the man who had been blind to the Pharisees. But it was the Sabbath day when Jesus picked up clay and placed it on the man's eyes. The Pharisees asked the man again how he had come to obtain his sight.

"He put some mud on my eyes and when I washed it off, I saw."

Some of the Pharisees said, "This man cannot be from God - he doesn't keep the Sabbath."

Others said, "But how would a sinful man be able to perform such a miracle?"

And thus there was a deep split among them. They asked the blind man again, "What do you say about him now that he's opened your eyes?"

"He's a prophet!"

Regardless, the Jewish rulers didn't believe him when he said he had once been blind and now saw. Instead, they brought his parents in so they could hear the facts from them, inquiring, "Is this your son? You say he was born blind but how come he now sees?"

"He's definitely our son and yes, he was born completely blind. But we have no idea how he regained his sight let alone who helped him do so. Why don't you ask him? He's a grown man and can speak for himself."[31]

---

30   A name interpreted to mean, "Sent."

31   His parents only said this because they were afraid of the rulers, who had already decided that anyone who claimed Jesus is the Messiah would be thrown out of the synagogue. That's why they simply said, "He's a grown man, ask him."

The rulers summoned the formerly blind man yet again and this time charged him, "Give the glory to God – we know this man is a sinner!"

"I don't know whether he's a sinner or not. All I know is I once was blind but now I see."

"What did he do to you? How did he open your eyes?"

"I've already told you but you wouldn't listen. Why do you want to hear it again? Do you also want to become his disciples?"

With that they railed at him, "*You* go be his follower but we follow Moses because we know that God has spoken to Moses. But as for this fellow, we have no idea where he comes from."

"That's pretty incredible – he opened my eyes and yet you don't know the source of his power? God doesn't listen to sinners – we all know that – but if anyone worships God and does his will, he'll listen to him. Now, ever since the world began no one's ever heard of someone giving sight to the blind. If this man weren't from God he couldn't do anything like this."

"You were born in rankest sin and now dare teach us?!"

So they threw him out to the street.

When Jesus heard they had cast him out he found the man and said, "Do you believe in the Son of Man?"

"Who is he, Lord, that I might believe in him?"

"You've both seen him and he speaks with you now."

"Lord, I believe!" And he fell prostrate before Jesus.

"I've come into this world for judgment, that those who see not may see and those who see may see not."

Some of the Pharisees were nearby. When they heard what Jesus said they asked, "Are we blind as well?"

"If you were blind you would have no sin. But you say, 'We see,' and thus your sin remains."

10

He explained further.

"I tell you for certain, whoever doesn't enter the sheepfold through the gate but climbs in some other way is a thief and a robber; but whoever enters through the gate is the shepherd of the sheep. The gatekeeper opens for him and the sheep hear the sound of his voice. He calls his own sheep by name and leads them out. Once he has led them out he walks ahead of them and the sheep all follow him because they know his voice. They won't follow after a stranger but will flee from him because they don't know the voice of strangers."

But even though he illustrated his thought metaphorically they still didn't understand. So he tried again.

"Listen – I am the Gateway of the Sheep. All those who climbed into the sheepfold before me are thieves and robbers, but the sheep didn't listen to them. I am the Gateway. If anyone enters through me he will be saved and will move freely, finding pasture.[32] The thief comes only to steal, slay and lay waste. But I have come that they may have life and have it to overflowing.[33] I am the Good Shepherd. The Good Shepherd offers his own life for the sheep. A hired hand is not a shepherd – the sheep aren't his own – so when he sees a wolf coming he flees, abandoning the sheep for the wolf to snatch and scatter. Why? Because they aren't his sheep and he doesn't care what happens to them.

"But I am the Good Shepherd. I know my own and my own know me, just as the Father knows me and I know the Father. I lay down my life for the sheep. And I have other sheep that are not of this fold. It's necessary that I gather them in as well. They will hear my voice and there will be one flock and one shepherd.[34] The Father loves me because I offer my very life that I might take it up again. No one takes it from me. I lay it down of my own volition because the Father has granted me power to lay it down and power to take it up again."

Once more the Jewish rulers clashed over his words. Many of them said, "He's demon-possessed, utterly mad – why listen to him?" But others said, "These aren't the words of a madman. And since when does Satan give sight to the blind?"

A couple of months later Jesus came to Jerusalem again, this time to observe the wintertime Festival of Lights. As he walked along Solomon's Portico in the Temple precincts some of the Jewish rulers approached him.

---

32   *Numbers* 27:16-17.
33   *Ezekiel* 34:11-16.
34   *Ezekiel* 34:23, 37:24; *Isaiah* 40:11.

"How much longer will you keep our minds in suspense? Are you the Anointed One or not?"

"I've told you but you refused to believe. Yet the works I do in the name of the Father, don't these testify who I am? Even so you don't believe because you are not sheep of my flock. My sheep hear my voice. I know them and they follow me. I give them life unending – they will never perish neither will anyone snatch them from my hand. My Father, who has given them to me, is omnipotent and no one is able to snatch them from his hand. I and the Father are one."

At that some of the Judeans reached for stones, ready to kill him.

"I've demonstrated to you many good works that come from the Father – for which of these am I now worthy of death?"

"We aren't going to stone you to death for your good works but for your heresy, making yourself into God!"

"But isn't it written in your Law, I said, 'You are gods'?[35] If those to whom the word of God came could in any sense be called gods – and the Scripture cannot be contravened – then how can you say that I, whom the Father has consecrated and sent into the world, blaspheme when I say, 'I am the Son of God?' If I don't perform the deeds of my Father then you ought not believe. But if I do them then even if you don't believe me believe the acts, so that you may perceive and understand that the Father is in me and I am in the Father."

Again they tried to catch him but he escaped their hands and crossed the Jordan to the site where John had first begun to baptize. While he remained there numbers of people came to him, saying among themselves, "John didn't perform any miracles but everything he said about this man was true." And so more and more people came to believe in him there.

11

Jesus had a close friend named Lazarus from the village of Bethany. He was brother to Martha and Mary, that same Mary who anointed the Lord with myrrh and washed his feet with her tears. Now Lazarus had fallen deathly ill and his sisters sent word to Jesus letting him know that his

---

35 *Psalms* 82:6.

friend was in dire straits. When Jesus heard that he said, "This sickness isn't meant to end in death. He's fallen sick for the glory of God, that is to say, in order that the Son of God may be glorified through his illness."

Jesus cared deeply for Lazarus, Martha and her sister - yet when he heard that Lazarus was gravely ill he didn't leave at once but lingered where he was for another couple of days and only after that said to his disciples, "Let's head back to Judea again."

"But Rabbi, the rulers are aiming to stone you to death and now you want to go back there?"

"Aren't there twelve hours in the day? If anyone walks during the daytime he won't trip and fall, because he has the light of this world. But if he wanders around at night he'll stumble because he has no light within himself."

He let that sink in and then said, "Our friend Lazarus has fallen asleep - let's go and rouse him!"

"Lord, if he's asleep he'll get up on his own."

They mistakenly thought Jesus was talking about bedtime whereas he meant the sleep of death. So he said, "Lazarus has died and for your sakes I'm glad I wasn't there, so that you'll have faith."

Thomas, one of the twins, said to his fellow disciples, "Let's go then, that we may die with the Master!"

By the time Jesus approached Bethany Lazarus had been dead for four days and was already entombed. The village itself was around two miles outside of Jerusalem and streams of Jews had gone there to sit shiva with Martha and Mary, consoling them over the loss of their brother. When Martha heard that Jesus was coming she raced out of the house to meet him, leaving Mary back inside.

"Lord, if you had been here my brother wouldn't have died! Yet even so I know that God will grant you anything you request."

"Your brother will rise again."

"Yes, I know - but that's in the resurrection at the Last Day."

"I am the Resurrection and the Life! Whoever believes in me though he's died yet shall he live. And everyone who lives and believes in me shall never die. Do you believe this, Martha?"

"Yes, Lord, I truly believe you're the Messiah, the Son of God who is to come into the world."

Martha then returned to the house and spoke quietly to her sister,

"The Master is here and he summons you."

Mary left the house and quickly headed in Jesus' direction, as he had not yet made it to the village but was still out where Martha had met up with him. A number of Mary's fellow Jews, those who had come to mourn with her, saw her leave in haste and followed after her assuming she was going to Lazarus' tomb to weep. Now when Mary reached Jesus she knelt before him and said, "Lord, if only you had been here my brother would not have died."

Beholding her tears and the women mourning with her Jesus shuddered as he sighed, groaning deep in his spirit even as he asked, "Where have you laid him?"

"Come and see."

Jesus wept.

The Jews with Mary said, "Look how much he loved him!"

But some wondered, "Couldn't the one who opened the eyes of the blind have done something to prevent this man's death?"

Jesus stood at the tomb with torn heart but then commanded, "Take away the stone!"

"Lord no!" - interjected the dead man's sister - "He's already been there four days and the smell will kill us all!"

"Martha, didn't I tell you that if you believed you would see the glory of God?"

And so they rolled the stone away.

Jesus then raised his eyes Heavenward and said, "Father, I thank you for hearing my prayer. I know you always listen but I say this for the sake of those now here with me, that they may believe you have sent me."

Then with a mighty shout he called to the dead, "LAZARUS!! Come out!"

The dead man arose and walked from the cave still wrapped hand and foot with linen, his face draped with a cloth.

Jesus commanded again, "Loose his bonds!"

On seeing this miracle many of the Jews who accompanied Mary believed, and on their return later to Jerusalem some of them reported to the Pharisees what had taken place. The chief priests and the Pharisees gathered the Sanhedrin and said, "Well *now* what are we supposed to do? This man is clearly a miracle worker but if we let him continue pretty soon all our people will believe in him and the Romans will swoop in and wipe out our nation."

But Caiaphas, who was High Priest that year, silenced them.

"You don't know what you're talking about. Don't you see that it's better for you that one man should die for the sake of the people rather than the whole nation perish?"[36]

From that day they took counsel how they might have Jesus killed. He therefore didn't show himself openly among the Jews but from Bethany went instead to Ephraim, a town out near the Wilderness, remaining there with his disciples.

Before long Passover approached and people flowed into Jerusalem from throughout the countryside to be ritually cleansed some days in advance. Meanwhile, the Jewish rulers continued to search for Jesus, speculating about him as they gathered in the Temple precincts.

"What's your view," they asked one another, "do you think he'll show his face at the festival?" And at the same time the chief priests and the Pharisees issued orders that anyone who knew where Jesus kept himself was obligated to detain him.

12

Jesus returned to Bethany six days before the feast. Lazarus – whom he had raised from the dead – and his sisters hosted a banquet for him. Lazarus reclined at the table with Jesus while Martha busied herself organizing and serving the meal. Mary, for her part, brought nearly a pound of purest spikenard, costly in the extreme, anointed the feet of Jesus and then wiped them dry with her own hair. And the house was filled with the perfumed scent.

Yet Judas, the disciple from Kerioth who was shortly to betray Jesus, scolded her, "Why didn't you sell this ointment you had? That's a year's wages we could have given to the poor!" But he didn't give a damn about the poor – he only said this because he had charge of the group wallet and, being a thief, stole from it whenever he wished. Then Jesus rebuked him.

---

36   He didn't speak these words of his own counsel, but rather as High Priest he prophesied that Jesus would die to save all Israel – and not Israel only but that he should gather up into one all of God's people scattered around the globe.

"Leave her alone! She performed this rite as for the day of my em-
balming – the poor you always have with you but me you have not always."

No one could keep secret that Jesus was there and so a large crowd of
the Jews went to Bethany to see him – and not just to see Jesus but also
Lazarus whom he had raised from the dead. But those who opposed Jesus,
including the chief priests, took the occasion to plot against Lazarus, hoping to have him put to death as well because it was now because of him
that many of their fellow Jews were going off to follow Jesus.

The next day the masses who were at Jerusalem for the feast heard
that Jesus was on his way and rushed out to meet him, carrying palm
fronds with them and shouting,

> Save us!
> Blessed is he who comes in the name of the Lord,[37]
> the king of Israel!

Jesus found a small donkey for himself to sit on, in accordance with
the Scripture where it is written,

> Don't be afraid, daughter of Zion –
> Just look! Your king is coming,
> seated on the colt of an ass.[38]

The people who were with Jesus when he called Lazarus out from
the tomb and raised him from the dead continued to testify what they
heard and saw. That's why this larger crowd ran out to hail him. As they
watched the Pharisees said to themselves, "See? We're getting nowhere –
the whole world is siding with him!"

There were also some Gentile proselytes in Jerusalem who had gone
up to worship at the festival. They approached Philip, who was from Bethsaida on the shore of the Sea of Galilee, and asked, "Sir, will you bring us
to see Jesus?" Philip passed it along to his landsman Andrew and then the
two of them told Jesus.

On hearing their request Jesus said, "The time has come for the Son of

---

37   *Psalms* 118:25-26.
38   *Zechariah* 9:9. I should add that Jesus' disciples didn't understand any of what was
       happening at the time, but when he was glorified they remembered these things and
       that all that was written of him had been done to him.

Man to be glorified. Listen carefully – unless a grain of wheat falls to the soil and dies it remains by itself, but if it dies it yields much fruit. Whoever loves his life will lose it and whoever hates his life in this world will keep it to life eternal. If anyone would be my servant let him follow me and where I am there shall my servant be also. And if anyone serves me the Father will honor him. Now troubles threaten my life and therefore I say, 'Father, deliver me!'[39] Yet it's for this very reason I have come to this moment. And Father, glorify your Name!"

Then a voice from Heaven spoke, "I have glorified it and will yet once more glorify it!"

When the people that stood there heard the voice some said it sounded like thunder but others said, "An angel has spoken to him!"

"This voice came not for my sake but for yours. It is now judgment time for this world. The ruler of this world will be cast out and I, if I be lifted up from the earth, will draw all people to myself."[40]

"We've heard from the Law that when the Anointed One comes he will abide forever.[41] How is it then you say the Son of Man must be lifted up? Who is this Son of Man anyway?"

"You only have the Light among you a little while longer. Walk while you have the Light, lest darkness overtake you. Whoever walks in the darkness has no idea where he's going. Therefore while you have the Light believe in the Light that you may become sons of Light."

Having said that Jesus cloaked himself and left. Yet though he had performed so many miracles in their presence the people as a whole did not believe in him, thus fulfilling Isaiah's prophecy where he said,

> Lord, who has believed our report?
> And to whom has the arm of the Lord
> been revealed?[42]

They were unable to believe, as Isaiah explained again,

> He has blinded their eyes and dulled their heart,
> lest they see with their eyes,

---

39   *Psalms* 6:3-4, 25:17, 40:12-13 and 69:1.
40   He said this signifying the kind of death he would die.
41   *Psalms* 89:36 and 110:4; *Daniel* 7:13-14.
42   *Isaiah* 53:1.

understand in their heart, and be turned from their ways,
so that I would heal them.[43]

Isaiah spoke these words because he saw the Savior's glory and therefore prophesied of him. Now, many of the Jewish rulers *did* believe in him
but wouldn't admit it because they feared excommunication, prizing the
praise of men more than the honor that comes from God.

Then Jesus called out to the people again.

"Whoever believes in me believes not in me so much as the one who
sent me and whoever sees me sees the one who sent me. I have come as
light into the world so that every person who believes in me may no longer dwell in darkness. I am not the judge of those who hear my teaching
but don't keep it. I didn't come into the world to judge the world but that
I might save the world. Yet whoever rejects me, not receiving my word,
does have a judge – the word that I have spoken will judge him at the Last
Day because I haven't spoken on my own authority but rather the Father
who sent me commanded me what to say and what to speak. And I know
that his commandment is life unending. I therefore speak just as the Father has spoken to me."

13

The Paschal Feast was upon them and Jesus knew it was now his time to
pass from this world to the Father. Having loved his own who were in the
world he loved them to the end. By then the Devil had persuaded Judas,
Simon's son from Kerioth, to betray him. But Jesus knew the Father had
placed all things into his hands and that he had both come from God and
would return back to God. He therefore rose from the table once supper
had been laid, divested himself of his outer garments, took a towel, tied it
around himself, poured water into a basin and began to wash the feet of
his disciples, drying them with the towel girt around him.

But Simon Peter questioned him, "Lord, what's this with you washing
my feet?"

"You don't understand what I'm doing now but you will later."

---

43   *Isaiah* 6:10.

"But you shouldn't be washing my feet!"

"If I don't you'll have no part in me."

"Well in that case don't just wash my feet, wash my hands and my head as well!"

"No need to go that far. Those who've been washed need do no more than have their feet washed to stay clean. And you've all been cleansed – all but one of you, that is."[44]

Once he had finished washing their feet he clothed himself again and returned to the table.

"Do you at all grasp what I've just done for you? You call me 'Master' and 'Lord' and well you do for so I am. If I therefore both Lord and Master have washed your feet so should you wash one another's feet. I've done this as a paradigm of how you ought to treat one another. A servant can be no greater than his master nor one who is sent greater than the one who sent him. If you know these things happy are you if you do them. And I'm not speaking about all of you – I know whom I have chosen but the Scripture must be fulfilled, It's the one who ate my bread who rose up against me.[45] I'm telling you all this before it happens so that when it happens you'll believe that I am he. And count on this – whoever receives someone I send receives me. And whoever receives me receives the one who sent me."

Having said that Jesus was stirred within his spirit and testified, "It's true – one of you will betray me."

The disciples gaped at one another, at a loss to know whom he was talking about. One of them – whom Jesus loved – reclined at his side. Beckoning to him Simon Peter asked if he knew who Jesus was talking about. He didn't, but leaning close to Jesus he asked him who it was.

"It's the one I give this bit of bread to after I dip it."

When Jesus had dipped the morsel he gave it to Simon's son Judas, the man from Kerioth. Judas took the bread and once he ate it the Devil had him. So Jesus told him, "What you do, do quickly."

None of the others understood why Jesus had said that to him. Some of them thought because Judas was the treasurer that Jesus was telling him something like, "Go buy whatever we need for the feast," or maybe that he should give alms to the poor. Either way, once Judas had accepted

---

44   Jesus said it this way because he knew who the traitor was.
45   *Psalms* 41:9.

the morsel of bread he left right away. And by then it was night.

After he was gone Jesus said, "Now the Son of Man is glorified and God is glorified in him. If God is glorified in him God will also glorify him in himself and will quickly glorify him. Little children, I am with you but a little while longer. You'll look for me and I say the same to you that I said to the Jewish rulers, 'Where I go you cannot come.' But I also give you a new commandment – that you love one another. Just as I have loved you so you are to love one another. By this all the world will know that you are my disciples, if you have love for one another."

Simon Peter asked him, "Lord, where are you going?"

"Where I go you cannot now follow but you will later."

"Why can't I follow you now? I would give my own life for you!"

"Would you, Peter? Believe me when I tell you that before the rooster crows you'll have denied me three times."

14

Yet Jesus comforted them with this.

"Let not your hearts be troubled. You believe in God, believe also in me. In my Father's house there are many dwelling places. If that weren't so would I have told you I'm going to prepare a place for you? And because I go to prepare a place for you I will come again and bring you to myself so that where I am you may be also. And you know the road to the place I'm going."

But Thomas said, "We don't even know where you're going! How can we know the way there?"

"I am the Way, the Truth and the Life. No one comes to the Father except through me. If you've known me you've known the Father and from here on you both know and have seen him."

Yet Philip said, "Lord, show us the Father and we'll be satisfied."

"I've been with you all this time and you don't know me, Philip? Whoever has seen me has seen the Father – so how can you say, 'Show us the Father?' Don't you believe that I am in the Father and the Father is in me? I don't speak the words I speak at my own instance. And the Father who dwells in me does his works. Believe me when I say that I am in the Father and the Father is in me – or at least believe on account of the works themselves.

"Whoever believes in me will do the works I've done and indeed will do greater works than these because I go to the Father. Whatever you may ask in my Name that will I do in order that the Father may be glorified in the Son. And this is my promise, that I myself will do what you ask.

"If you love me you will keep my commandments. I will petition the Father and he will give you another Intercessor, the Spirit of Truth, whom the world cannot receive because it neither recognizes nor knows him. But you know him because he dwells with you and will be in you. I will not leave you orphans – I will come to you. In a little while the world will no longer see me, but you will see me and in that day you will understand fully that I am in the Father, you are in me and I am in you. Whoever holds onto my commandments and keeps them, that's the one who loves me. And whoever loves me will be loved by my Father and I will love him and reveal myself to him."

Then the other Judas said to him, "Lord, how will you be able to show yourself to us but not to the world?"

"If anyone loves me he will keep my word and my Father will love him and we will come to him and make our dwelling by his side. Whoever does not love me does not keep my word, and the word you hear is not mine but that of the Father who sent me.

"I've spoken all this to you while I am still with you. But the Comforter, the Holy Spirit, whom the Father will send in my Name – he will teach you all things and remind you of all that I've said to you. I leave my peace with you – my peace I give to you, not as the world gives do I give to you. So let not your hearts be troubled neither be afraid. You heard me say to you, 'I go and will come for you.' If you loved me you would have rejoiced that I go to the Father because the Father is greater than I. But now I've told you all this before it takes place so that when it does happen you may believe. I won't be able to speak with you a whole lot longer because the ruler of this world is on his way. It's not that he has any power over me, but I do as I have been commanded by the Father so the world may know that I love the Father.

"Now, let's get up from the table and find another place to gather."

15

Jesus then continued with these words of assurance.

"I am the True Vine and my Father the vinedresser. He removes every branch that does not bear fruit in me and prunes every branch that does in order that it bear more fruit. You've been purified through the word I have spoken to you – take care that you remain in me, as I in you. A branch cannot bear fruit on its own without remaining part of the vine and therefore neither can you unless you remain in me. I am the vine, you are the branches. Whoever remains in me and I in him bears much fruit. But separated from me you can do nothing. If anyone does not remain in me he will fall like a broken branch, wither and die only to be gathered up, thrown to the fire and burned. But if you abide in me and my words abide in you then ask what you will and it shall be done for you. My Father is glorified in this – that you bear much fruit and thus become my disciples.

"As the Father has loved me so have I loved you. Abide in my love. If you keep my commandments you will remain in my love just as I have kept my Father's commandments and abide in his love.

"I have spoken these things to you that my joy may be in you and your joy may be full. This is my commandment, that you love one another as I have loved you. Greater love hath no man than this, that a man lay down his life for his friends. You are my friends if you do whatever I have commanded you. And I no longer call you servants because the servant doesn't know what his master does. But I have called you friends because I have revealed to you all I have heard from my Father. You haven't chosen me, I have chosen you and laid a path before you to bear fruit and for your fruit to remain, so that anything you ask the Father in my name he will give to you.. I command these things to you so that you will love one another.

"If the world hates you know this – it hated me before you. If you belonged to the world the world would love its own. But because you do not belong to the world and I have chosen you out from the world the world hates you. Recall the words I spoke to you, 'The servant is not greater than his master.' If they've persecuted me they will persecute you. If they've kept my word they will heed yours. But whatever they do to you they will do on account of my name because they don't know the one who sent me. If I hadn't come and spoken to them they wouldn't bear guilt. But now they have no excuse for their sin. Whoever hates me also hates my Father. If I hadn't done among them the deeds no other had performed they would still be guiltless. But now they've seen and hated both me and my Father. Yet all this has happened in order that the word written in their Law be fulfilled – They hated me for no reason.[46]

"When the Advocate comes (whom I shall send to you from the Father, the Spirit of Truth who proceeds from the Father) he will testify concerning me. And you will bear witness as well because you've been with me from the beginning."

16

"I've told you all these things so you don't get tripped up when they throw you out of the synagogues. Indeed, before long people who put you to death will think they are doing service to God. But they will do such things because they've known neither me nor the Father. You therefore need to know this ahead of time so you can call my words to mind when it happens.

"I didn't say all this before because I was there with you. But now I go to the one who sent me and none of you asks me anymore, 'Where are you going?' I can see that your hearts are filled with grief at what you're hearing – but believe me it's to your good that I depart. If I don't you won't receive the Comforter. But if I go I will send him to you and when he comes he will expose the sins of the world and convict it as to righteousness and judgment – as to sin because they do not believe in me, as to righteousness because I go to the Father and you will see me no more and as to judgment because the ruler of this world is condemned.

"I have a lot more to say to you but it would be too much for you to bear right now. Yet when the Spirit of Truth comes he will guide you into all truth. He will not testify of himself but whatever he hears he will say and will reveal to you all that the future holds. He will glorify me, taking what is mine and proclaiming it to you. All that the Father has is mine – and that's the basis for my telling you he will take what is mine and declare it to you.

---

46   *Psalms* 35:19 and 69:4.

"In a little while you will see me no more, yet again a little while and you will perceive me."

Some of the disciples said to one another, "What does he mean when he says, 'In a little while you will see me no more, yet again a little while and you will perceive me?' and again, 'because I go to the Father?'" And, "What does this mean, 'a little while?' We can't understand what he's saying."

Jesus knew what they wanted to ask him without their having done so.

"I know you're puzzling over this phrase, 'In a little while you will see me no more, yet again a little while and you will perceive me.' Let me say this to you – you will weep and lament while the world rejoices. Yes, you will grieve, but your sorry will turn to joy. Compare it to a woman giving birth. She suffers grief when the time comes but once she has given birth she forgets her anguish for joy that a child in born into the world. And so now you sorrow but I will see you again. Then your hearts will rejoice and no one will take your joy from you. You won't ask me anything in that day. Truly I tell you that if you ask anything of the Father in my name he will give it you. Up to now you've asked nothing in my name. Ask and you shall receive, that your joy may be full.

"Before this I've spoken to you in figures of speech but soon I will leave off speaking in parables and proverbs and will tell you plainly about the Father. In that day you will ask in my name and I will not need to ask the Father on your behalf – because the Father himself loves you because you have loved me and believed I have come from God. I have come from the Father into the world and now I depart the world and go to the Father."

His disciples said, "You've spoken clearly – we do understand and believe that you've come from God!"

"You've believed up to now but the time is upon us when you will be scattered, each to his own people, abandoning me. And yet I am not alone because the Father is with me. I tell you all this that you may have peace in me. In the world you shall have tribulation – but be of good cheer, I have overcome the world."

17

Then Jesus lifted his eyes Heavenward and said,

"Father, the hour has come: glorify your Son that your Son may glorify you, just as you have given him authority over all mankind that he may give eternal life to all you have given him. And this is life imperishable, that they know you, the only true God, and the Anointed One, Jesus, whom you have sent. Having completed the tasks you gave me I glorified you on the Earth. Now, Father, glorify me at your side with the glory I had in your presence before the foundation of the world.

"I revealed you as the Father to the people you gave me out from the world. They were yours and you gave them to me and they have kept your word. Now they have known that everything you've given me is from you alone because I have given them the words you gave me and they received them.[47] So it is that they understood it to be true that I came from your presence and they believed that you have sent me. I am pleading for them, not for the world, but for those you have given me – because they are yours. All that are mine are yours and yours are mine and I am glorified in them. I am no longer among them in the world but they remain in the world, while I come to you. Holy Father, preserve by your name those whom you have given me that they may be one as we are one. When I was with them I kept them in your name and not a single one was lost – save the Son of Perdition, in order that the Scripture be fulfilled.

"And now I come to you and speak these things in the world that they may have my joy fulfilled in themselves. I have given them your word and the world hated them because they do not belong to the world just as I do not belong to the world. I don't ask that you take them out of the world but that you safeguard them from the Evil One. They are not of the world just as I am not of the world. Sanctify them in the truth – your word is truth. And just as you sent me into the world so I send them into the world. I set myself apart for their sake so that they too may be sanctified in truth.

"And I pray these things not for them alone but for all those who will come to believe in me through their word – in order that they all may be one just as you, Father, are in me and I in you, that they all may be one in us and that the world may believe you sent me. I have given them the glory you have

---

47   *Deuteronomy* 18:18-19.

given me in order that they may be one as we are one - I in them and you in me, that they may be made perfect in one, that the world may know that you sent me and loved them just as you loved me.

"Father, I would that those whom you have given me be with me where I am in order that they behold my glory, the glory you have given me because you loved me before the foundation of the world. Righteous Father, the world has not known you but I have known you and these have known that you have sent me. I revealed your name to them and will yet reveal it, in order that the love with which you loved me may be in them and I in them."

18

Thereafter Jesus left with his disciples and crossed over the Kedron Valley to a garden place. It was one they frequented and was thus well known to his betrayer Judas. He therefore gathered up a cohort of Temple soldiers and officers provided by the chief priests and Pharisees and went with them as they carried torches and pitchforks to go after Jesus. But Jesus, knowing all that would happen to him, stepped forward and addressed them directly.

"Who are you looking for?"

"Jesus Nazarene."

"I am he."

But at the sound of his word they were swept to the ground. So he asked them again, "Whom do you seek?"

"Jesus, the man from Nazareth."

"I told you I'm the one - so if you're looking for me, let the rest of these go."

He said this in order to fulfill the words he himself had spoken, "I lost none of those you gave me."

But Simon Peter had a sword with him, drew it and attacked Malcus, the High Priest's servant, cutting off his right ear. Yet Jesus halted him from going further and said, "Sheath your sword! Am I not to drink the cup the Father has given me?"

At that the Temple soldiers, led by their captain and other officers, seized and bound Jesus. They led him off first to Annas, who next sent

him still bound to his son-in-law Caiphas, who was then High Priest. And this is that same Caiphas who had prophesied that it was best for the Jewish nation that one man should die for all.

Simon Peter followed Jesus as did another disciple, one who was known to the High Priest and therefore able to continue on with Jesus into the High Priest's courtyard while Peter was left outside the gate. This other disciple (the one known, as I said, to the High Priest) spoke to the servant girl who kept watch at the gate and had her let Peter inside.

But she asked Peter, "Aren't you also one of this man's disciples?"

"Not I!"

So when the Temple servants and officers started up a charcoal fire to warm themselves from the cold Peter joined in with them, also warming his hands by the fire.

In the meantime, the High Priest began to question Jesus about his disciples and his teaching.

"I spoke out in the open, teaching freely in the synagogue and the Temple where all Jews gather and have said nothing in secret. Why are you asking me all this now? Ask those who heard me – they know what I said."

At that one of the nearby officers slapped him in rebuke.

"Is that the way you speak to the High Priest?!"

"If I'm lying say so. But if I speak the truth why strike me?"

As Peter remained in the courtyard keeping warm the others said to him, "You're one of his group, aren't you?"

"I'm not!"

But someone kin to Malchus, whose ear Peter had sliced off, challenged him, "Didn't I see you right there in the garden with him?"

Peter denied Jesus yet again – and then and there a rooster crowed.

It was thus early morning when they next led Jesus from Caiphas' house to the Praetorium. But the Jewish officials wouldn't enter the Governor's office at Roman headquarters lest they be made ritually unclean and unable to eat the Passover. Pilate therefore met them outside and asked, "What are the charges against this man?"

"Why do you ask? If he weren't an evildoer would we have brought him to you?"

"Then take him yourselves – judge him according to your Law."

"But you've prohibited us from putting anyone to death!"[48]

Pilate then summoned Jesus inside.

"So, you're the king of the Jews?"

"Is that your own view or did someone tell you that about me?"

"Ha! You think I'm a Jew? It's your own people, even the chief priests, who've turned you over to me. Tell me then, what is it you've done?"

"My kingdom is not of this world – if it were my servants would've fought to stop them from handing me over. But this isn't the seat of my kingdom."

"So you *are* a king then."

"As you say – and indeed it's for this very reason I was born and came into the world, that I might testify to the truth. All those who are of the truth hear my voice."

"Ah, but what is truth?"

Once he said this Pilate went back out to speak to the Jewish leaders.

"I've found no guilt in him. As it's become a custom for me to release one person to you at the Passover shall I release the king of the Jews?"

"No, not him – Barabbas!"

Now this Barabbas was a rebel and a thief.

19

Pilate therefore sent Jesus out to be scourged. The soldiers plaited a crown of thorns, placed it on his head and draped him in a purple robe. Then they began to chant, "Hail, king of the Jews," as they beat him about the face. When this was done Pilate stepped outside and told the assembled crowd, "I'm offering him back to you having found no fault with him."

Jesus stood before them as well, still wearing the purple robe and bearing the crown of thorns.

---

48   This was said in order to fulfill Jesus' own prophecy signifying that his death would come at the hands of the Romans.

Then Pilate said, "*Ecce homo!*"

But when they saw him the chief priests and their entourage cried out, "Crucify him, crucify him!"

"*You* take and crucify him. I find him guiltless."

"But under our Law he deserves to die because he made himself out to be the Son of God."

When Pilate heard these words he feared all the more and returning inside the Praetorium he asked Jesus, "Just where have you come from?"

Silence.

"Won't you answer me? Don't you realize I have the power to free you as well as crucify you?"

"You'd have no power at all if it hadn't been granted you from above. That's why the one who handed me over to you bears the greater sin."

After that Pilate looked for some way to release him but the Jewish rulers harangued him saying, "If you free this man you are no friend of Caesar because anyone who sets himself as king is Caesar's enemy."

On hearing those words Pilate led Jesus outside and took his judgment seat, which was set in an open space known in Aramaic as Gabbatha.[49] This all took place on the Paschal day of preparation. Around noon Pilate again addressed the rulers and said, "Behold your king!"

"Take him away! Crucify him and let him be gone!"

"Am I to crucify your king?"

"We have no king but Caesar."

And thus Pilate yielded him up to be crucified.

Jesus was led out bearing his own cross to a spot called in Hebrew Golgotha.[50] There he was crucified with two others, one on each side. Pilate himself wrote out an inscription to be placed on the cross reading, "Jesus of Nazareth, King of the Jews." As the place where he was crucified was near the city many there saw and read it and, indeed, it was written in the three common languages, Hebrew, Latin and Greek.

But when they saw the sign the chief priests went back to Pilate and complained, "Don't write 'the King of the Jews' but only, 'This man said, "I am the King of the Jews.""

---

49   Which in English means the "Stone Pavement."
50   Which in English means "Place of the Skull."

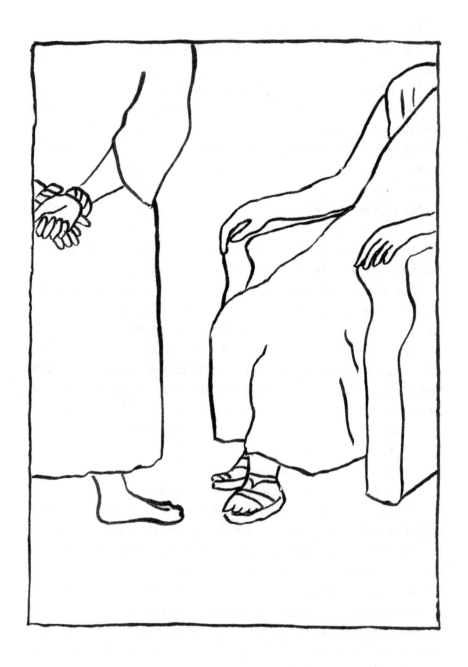

"What I have written, I have written."

When the soldiers had crucified Jesus they divided his garments among the four of them. But Jesus also had a tunic and it was seamless, the whole being woven in one piece top to bottom. So they said, "Let's not tear it up but draw lots to see who gets it." The soldiers did these things in order that the Scripture be fulfilled,

> They divided my clothes amongst themselves,
> gambling for my garments.[51]

While this was happening Jesus' mother and his aunt, Mary the wife of Klopas, stood by the cross, as did Mary from Magdala. When Jesus saw his mother there, along with the disciple whom he loved, he said to his mother, "Woman, behold your son" and to the disciple, "Behold your mother." From that time on the disciple took Jesus' mother into his care as one of his own.

Jesus, knowing that everything had now been accomplished and in fulfillment of the Scriptures said, "I thirst."[52] There was a pitcher full of soured wine at hand and the soldiers took a sponge, wrapped it around a hyssop branch, dipped it in the wine and lifted it to Jesus' mouth. When he had tasted the wine Jesus said, "It is finished."

Having then bowed his head he yielded his spirit to God.

Because it was still the day of preparation the Jews went to Pilate asking that the Romans break the legs of the crucified, thus speeding their deaths, and then take the bodies down so they would not remain on the crosses during the Sabbath – that particular Sabbath being a great and festal day. The soldiers went to break the legs of the first of the crucified, then the second, but when they came to Jesus they saw he was dead already and therefore didn't break his bones. Instead, one of the soldiers took a lance and pierced his side just to be sure he was dead and immediately out flowed blood and water.

The one who saw this bore witness to it. His testimony can be relied on and he bears true witness in order that you may believe, because all

---

51 *Psalms* 22:18.
52 *Psalms* 69:21.

these things occurred in order to fulfill the Scriptures,

> They shall not bruise his bones.[53]

And again,

> They will gaze on him whom they have pierced.[54]

Thereafter, Joseph of Arimathea, one of Jesus' followers (though a secret one out of fear of the rulers) approached Pilate seeking permission to take Jesus' body down from the cross. Pilate gave him leave. He then retrieved the body for burial. Nicodemus (the one who had come to Jesus at night) came along as well, bringing with him a mixture of myrrh and aloe, about 75 pounds in weight. Then they wrapped the body in linen and spice for burial in accordance with Jewish custom. There was a garden tomb near the place where Jesus was crucified where no one had yet been laid and they entombed him there, it still being the day of preparation.

20

It was early gloom on the first of the Sabbaths when Mary Magdalene came mourning to the tomb – but there she saw the sealing stone rolled away. Mary ran back for Simon Peter and the other disciple, the one whom Jesus loved, and blurted, "They've taken the Lord from the tomb and we don't know where they've laid him!"

Peter and the other disciple then rushed to the grave as well, but though they ran together the other disciple was faster than Peter and got there first. He bent down to look inside and glimpsed the linen cloths lying there but didn't go any further. When Peter arrived he did enter and saw the covering that had been on Jesus' face folded and set off to the side, separate from the other burial wrappings. Then the other disciple,

---

53   *Exodus* 12:46; *Numbers* 9:12; *Psalms* 34:20.
54   *Zechariah* 12:10.

the one who had gotten there first, also entered the tomb - and he saw it too and believed. Even so, they still didn't understand the Scripture that Jesus must rise from the dead and so went back again to their lodgings.

But Mary stayed outside grieving by the grave. As she cried she too looked inside the tomb and there saw two angels garbed in white sitting one at the head and one at the feet of where Jesus' body had lain.

"Woman, why this weeping?"

"They've taken my Lord and I don't know where they've put him."

She then turned around and saw Jesus standing - except she didn't know it was Jesus - and he said, "Woman, what are you crying about? Who are you looking for?"

Thinking he was the gardener she said, "Sir, if you've spirited him away someplace tell me where so I can bring him back."

"Mary."

"Rabboni!"[55]

"Touch me not, because I have not yet ascended to the Father. But go to my disciples and tell them I said, 'I ascend to my Father and your Father, to my God and your God.'"

Mary Magdalene then raced to tell the disciples, "I've seen the Lord!" And she relayed what he'd said to her.

Later that day, in the evening of the first of the Sabbaths, the disciples were gathered together behind closed doors, locked for fear of the Jews. Yet Jesus appeared, stood in their midst and said, "Peace be with you." Then he showed them his hands and his side - and the disciples were taken with joy at the sight of the Lord.

"Be at peace. As the Father sent me so now I send you."

Then he breathed upon them[56] and said, "Receive the Holy Ghost! Any sins you remit will be forgiven but any sins retained will remain."

One of the Twelve, the twin named Thomas, wasn't with the other disciples when Jesus appeared to them. When they saw him later they told him - repeatedly - "We've seen the Lord!"

"Unless I myself see where the nails pierced his hands, push my finger into the holes and thrust my hand into his side, I will *not* believe."

---

55   Which means "my master" in Aramaic.

56   *Cf. Genesis* 2:7.

About a week later the disciples were again indoors together and this time Thomas was with them. Even though the doors had been locked tight Jesus entered and stood before them.

"Peace be with you all. And Thomas, come here and see my hands. Take your finger, if you will, and thrust it into my side – and be not faithless but believing."

"My Lord and my God!"

"Because you have seen me you have believed. Blessed are those who have not seen and yet believed."

Jesus performed many other miracles in the presence of his disciples but they haven't been written down in this book. These have been written, however, that you may believe that Jesus is the Messiah, the Son of God, and that believing you might have life in his name.

21

Afterwards Jesus manifested himself again to the disciples by the Sea of Tiberias, where a group of them were together – Simon Peter, Thomas the twin, Nathaniel from Qana in Galilee, the two sons of Zebedee and a couple of others. Simon Peter said, "I'm going fishing."

"We're coming with you."

So they got into a boat and fished all through the night but came up with nothing. At daybreak Jesus stood at the shore – except they didn't know it was Jesus – and said, "Children, have you got anything to eat?"

"Not a thing."

"Well, cast the net to starboard – that's where the fish are!"

They did as he said and caught so many fish they couldn't haul the net up. The disciple whom Jesus loved then said to Peter, "It's the Lord!"

When Simon Peter heard the Lord was there he quickly tied a cloak around himself, since he was otherwise stripped for work, and dove into the sea to swim ashore. The other disciples came in the boat – which wasn't that far off the land anyway, only a hundred yards or so – dragging the full net with them. Once they disembarked they saw a fire had already

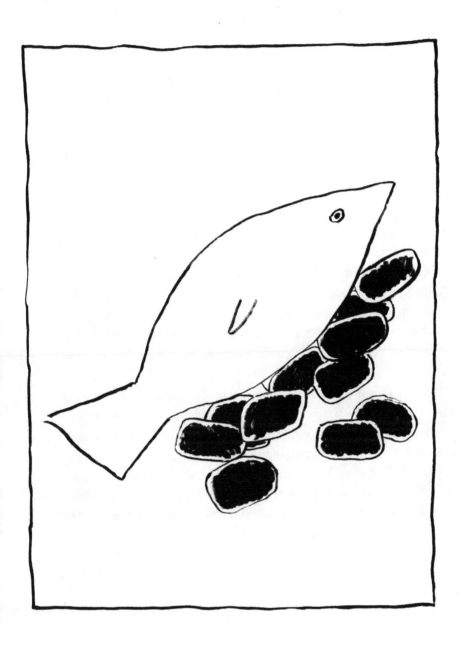

been prepared for the fish to be laid on the hot coals, with bread on hand to accompany the meal.

Jesus said, "Bring some of the fish you've caught."

Simon Peter went over to the boat to help the others haul in the net, as it was filled with a number of large fish, 153 in fact – yet the net didn't break. Then Jesus took some of the fish, cooked the meal and said, "Come and dine!"

None of the disciples dared ask him, "Who are you?" – because they knew it was the Lord. Jesus then took bread, gave it to them and did likewise with the fish. This was now Jesus' third appearance to the disciples after he was risen from the dead.

When they had finished eating Jesus said to Simon Peter, "Simon, son of Jonas, do you love me more than you love those with you?"

"Lord, you know you're my best friend!"

"Then feed my lambs. But Simon, do you *love* me?"

"Lord, you know that I care!"

"Then shepherd my sheep. Yet Simon, am I truly your friend?"

Peter was grieved that Jesus asked him this third time whether they were that close and so he said, "Lord, you know all things. You know my love for you!"

"Then feed my flock. When you were young you wore what you wanted and went where you wished but when you grow old you will stretch out your hands and another will gird you, carrying you where you would not." Jesus said this as a way of signifying the manner of death by which Peter would glorify God – and having told him that he said, "Follow me!"

Peter looked back over his shoulder and saw the disciple whom Jesus loved following them (this is the disciple who leaned against Jesus' chest at dinner and asked who was to betray him) and asked, "Lord, what about this man?"

"Suppose I want him to stay here until my return, how is that any of your business? But you, follow me."

The saying then went around among the brethren that this disciple would never die. But Jesus didn't say he wouldn't die, just that "If I wish him to remain until I come, what's that to you?" This is that same disciple who has here testified and written concerning all these things and we know his witness is true.

There are of course many more things that Jesus did, but if each were written down I doubt the world itself would have room for all the books.

ACTS OF THE APOSTLES

1

Dear friend of God, this is Part Two of the work I've composed concerning the things Jesus began to do and teach from the start of his ministry right up to the day he was taken up to Heaven. He stayed with the messengers he had chosen for the 40 days before his ascension, giving them instructions through the Holy Spirit as to their continuing tasks. He was fully alive and visible to many people, confirmed his presence with irrefutable proofs and explained to them the nature of the kingdom of God. Thereafter, having first gathered his people together to break bread, he ordered them not to leave Jerusalem but rather to "Wait there for the promise of the Father that you have heard about from me. John indeed baptized with water but before many days are out you will be baptized in the Holy Spirit."

"Lord, is it now that the kingdom will be restored to Israel?"

"It's not for you to know the times or the seasons, things the Father has reserved for the exercise of his own authority. But at the same time, you will receive power when the Holy Spirit has come upon you – and you will be my witnesses in Jerusalem and through all Judea and Samaria and as far as the very ends of the Earth."

Even as he spoke these things, even as they watched, Jesus was lifted up and taken out of their sight, supported by a cloud. While the disciples stood there watching, gaping as he ascended to Heaven, two men garbed in luminous white appeared suddenly beside them and said, "You Galilean men, what are you doing standing here staring at the sky? This Jesus you've seen taken up to Heaven will return just the same way you saw him going."

Then they turned back to Jerusalem from Mount Olive (which is near Jerusalem, about as far as it was lawful to walk on a Sabbath day). After entering the city they went to the upstairs room of the house where they usually met. The core group that gathered there included Peter, John, James, Andrew, Philip, Thomas, Bartholomew, Matthew, Jacob the son of Alphaeus, Simon the Zealot and Judas the son of Jacob along with Jesus' siblings, his mother Mary, and the several other women who followed Jesus. They were wholly united in their thoughts, faithfully devoting themselves to prayer, waiting on the next steps.

During this period Peter stood up in the midst of the brethren - and by then there were around 120 of them in the whole assembly - and said, "Men and brothers, the Scriptures written by King David had to be fulfilled where he prophesied concerning Judas. That man was one of our number and had even taken a share in the work the Lord appointed us. Yet he became the guiding hand to those who arrested Jesus. As you well know he took the wages earned by his evil deed and bought a parcel of land. But he plunged headfirst into it from the heights, cracking his head open and spilling his brains all over.[1] But this is just what David foresaw in the Book of Psalms -

> May his homestead become a wasteland
> and no one dwell therein;[2]

and

> Let his bishopric be given to another.[3]

We therefore need to pick someone out to take his place and be a witness with us of Jesus' resurrection, someone who's been with us from the beginning, starting from the time of John's baptism through the Lord Jesus' comings and goings right up to the day he was taken up from us."

They settled on two possibilities: Joseph, surnamed Justus but

---

1   And so this spot is now known in the local dialect to all Jerusalem's inhabitants as חֲקֵל דְּמָא - which in English means, "Field of Blood."
2   Psalms 69:25.
3   Psalms 109:8.

nicknamed Barsabbas, and Matthias. Then they prayed, "Lord, you know the hearts of all - show us clearly which one of these two you have chosen to take the share of this ministry and apostolate that Judas cast aside, having gone to his appointed place among the damned." They put the two names into a hat and drew out Matthias' - and so he was added in with the eleven.

2

As the Day of Pentecost approached they were all together, seated in one place. Suddenly a noise came from Heaven sounding like a violent wind and it filled the whole building. Cloven tongues as of fire appeared, suspended over each of them. Then they were all filled with the Holy Spirit and began to speak in various languages, as the Spirit enabled them.

Now at that time there were devout Jews visiting Jerusalem from all nations under the heavens. When they heard the noise of the rushing wind the surrounding multitude gathered together - but they were confused because each one heard the disciples' words in his own native language. Being totally at a loss they wondered, "Aren't all of these who are speaking Galileans? How is it that each of us hears them in his own dialect - Parthians and Medes and Elamites, those of us who live in Mesopotamia and Judea, Cappadocia, Pontus and the province of Asia, Phrygia, Pamphylia, Egypt and even the parts of Libya around Cyrene, Jews as well as converts visiting from Rome, Cretans and Arabs? Just how is it possible that we all hear them speaking our own languages, telling out God's mighty deeds?!"

Honestly, they were so bewildered they didn't know what to think. Some said to one another, "What does all this mean?" Yet others simply mocked the disciples saying, "They've had too much sweet wine to drink!"

But Peter and the other eleven stood before the crowd and Peter addressed them with boldness in his voice -

"Men of Judea and all you who dwell here in Jerusalem, listen to me and understand what I say. Don't think for a minute these people are drunk, and not just because it's only nine in the morning! On the contrary, what's happening is what God foretold through Joel the prophet concerning the last days –

> I will pour out of my Spirit on all mankind
>> and your sons and your daughters will prophesy–
> young men will see visions,
>> older men will dream dreams.
> In truth in those days I will pour out of my Spirit
>> upon all my servants, both men and women.
> And I will show marvels in the sky above
>> and miracles on the Earth below –
> blood and fire and cloud of smoke –
>> the sun will turn to darkness, the moon to blood
> on the cusp of the great and glorious day of the Lord.
>> And it shall come to pass that everyone
> who calls upon the name of the Lord will be saved.[4]

"Men of Israel, heed these words! You yourselves know that Jesus Nazarene was a man confirmed to you by God through the signs and wonders and miracles God performed through him in your midst. Yet you delivered him up and killed him, nailing him to the cross by the hands of lawless men. Even so, all this happened in accordance with God's foreknowledge and determinate will because God raised him up again, freeing him from the snares of death,[5] it being impossible for death to hold him fast. Thus as David speaks concerning him –

> I have seen the Lord agelessly before me,
>> because he sits at my right hand
> that I be not shaken.
>> Therefore my heart rejoiced
> and my tongue was glad;
>> more than that, my mortal self will live in hope –
> because you will not leave my soul behind
>> in the land of the dead

---

4   *Joel* 2:28-32.
5   *Psalms* 18:5.

neither let your Holy One see corruption.
You have made known to me the ways of life;
you will fill me with joy in your presence.[6]

"My brothers, it's for certain that the Patriarch David is dead and buried, lying in his tomb in our midst to this very day.[7] But because he was a prophet and knew God had sworn an oath to him that one descended from his loins would sit upon the throne,[8] he spoke foretelling the resurrection of the Messiah: that he would neither be left in the land of the dead nor would his body see corruption.[9] God raised this same Jesus from the dead – and of this all we are witnesses. Having thus been exalted by the right hand of God[10] and receiving from the Father the promise of the Holy Spirit he has now poured out this that you see and hear. David has not risen up to Heaven (as he would have if the prophecy had applied to him), but he himself says,

The Lord said to my Lord, 'Sit at my right hand
until I make your enemies
a footstool beneath your feet.'[11]

Let the whole House of Israel therefore know beyond any doubt that God has made this same Jesus whom you crucified Lord and Savior."
When they heard this they were cut to the heart and called on Peter and the rest of the apostles, "Our brothers, what shall we do?!"
"Turn from your ways, confessing the name of Jesus the Christ and be baptized every one of you for the forgiveness of sins. Then you too shall receive the gift of the Holy Spirit – because the promise is for you and your children and all those who are far off, as many as may call upon the Lord our God."
And with many other words he testified to them and urged, "Be saved from this wicked generation!"[12] Those who welcomed his word

6   Psalms 16:8-11.
7   1 Kings 2:10; Nehemiah 3:16.
8   Psalms 132:11; 2 Samuel 7:12-13.
9   Psalms 16:10.
10   Exodus 15:6, 12; Psalms 60:5
11   Psalms 110:1; see Matthew 22:44 and Mark 12:36.
12   Deuteronomy 32:5.

were baptized such that around 3000 souls were added to their number that same day, devoting themselves to the teaching of the apostles and the fellowship of the brethren, sharing in the breaking of bread and in prayers.

Every soul was in awe as the apostles performed a multitude of signs and miracles. Those who believed spent their days together and held their goods in common, selling their own lands and other possessions and distributing the profits in accordance with anyone's particular needs. They went daily with one mind and accord to the Temple, breaking bread together in their homes, receiving their food with great joy and simplicity of heart. They praised God continually, finding favor among the whole people. And the Lord added daily to their company as many as were being saved.

3

It happened that one day, at the time of the evening sacrifice, Peter and John went up to the Temple to pray. A certain man crippled from birth was just then being carried to one of the gates of the Temple, the one called Ὡραῖα – which in English means "ripe for harvest." He was brought there every day to seek a handout from those coming in or going out. When he saw Peter and John about to enter the Temple he therefore begged for alms. Fixing his eyes on the man Peter said, "Look at us."

Turning to them the man looked up, expecting to receive some money. But Peter said, "I don't have any silver let alone gold, but I'll give you what I *do* have – in the name of Jesus the Anointed One from Nazareth, stand up and walk!" Then taking hold of the man's right hand he gave him a leg up. Instantly the soles of his feet and his ankles were strengthened and springing right up he entered the Temple with them, walking and leaping and praising God. Everyone who saw him walking and praising God knew him to be the very same man who was always at the Temple gate begging for money – and they were not just awestruck but also bubbling with glee at what had been done for him.

Even as the man continued to cling to Peter and John the whole crowd came running toward them in astonishment, reaching them at the part of the Temple precincts known as Solomon's Court. But when Peter saw them massing about he spoke out –

"Why are you so surprised at this and why are you gaping at us, as though we made this man walk through some power or holiness of our own? Know that the God of our fathers, the God of Abraham, Isaac and Jacob[13] has glorified his Servant,[14] this Jesus whom you handed over and denied in the presence of Pilate when he condemned him to death. And you not only rejected that holy and righteous man but petitioned Pilate to pardon you a murderer. Yet although you had the Prince of Life killed, God raised him from the dead – of that we are witnesses. And it is by the power of his name and through faith in his name that this man – whom you've seen and know – has been given his strength and been brought to perfect health in your presence.

"But now, brothers, I know you acted in ignorance, as did your rulers, because God had foretold through the mouths of all his prophets that Messiah was to suffer and thus has he brought it to fulfillment. Turn back therefore and repent so that your sins be blotted out and the times of cool refreshing may come from the presence of God. Indeed it was to this end he appointed Jesus to be Savior! And Heaven must now receive him until the time all things shall be restored, of which day God has spoken from the beginning through the mouth of his holy prophets. As Moses for his part told our fathers –

> The Lord our God will raise up for you a prophet like me from
> among your brothers. Be prepared to obey him
> in all that he says[15] – because anyone who rejects that
> prophet will be utterly destroyed and plucked
> from among the people.[16]

"All the prophets from Samuel on have spoken of these days. You are the children of the prophets and the covenant that God made with your fathers when he said to Abraham, In your offspring shall all the families of

---

13   *Exodus* 3:6, 15.
14   *Isaiah* 40-60, *passim*.
15   *Deuteronomy* 18:15-16.
16   *Deuteronomy* 18:19; *Leviticus* 23:29.

the world be blessed.[17] And so God having raised up his Servant sent him first to you, blessing you in turning each one from your wicked ways."

4

But the priests, the prefect of the Temple police and the Sadducees were also present while the apostles were speaking. The Sadducees became especially agitated as they listened to the apostles' teaching because they proclaimed in Jesus the resurrection of the dead. So they laid hold of Peter and John and, as it was now evening, kept them in their custody overnight. Yet many of those who had heard the word believed and around 5000 people were added to their number that day.

The next morning the rulers and elders and scribes met in Jerusalem, including the High Priest Annas along with Caiphas, John and Alexander, members of the high-priestly caste. Having brought Peter and John to their midst they inquired of them,

"By what kind of power and in what sort of name have you done this act?"

Peter responded in the fullness of the Holy Spirit,

"You rulers and elders of the people, if we are being called to account today for the good deed done for this crippled man and to explain how he was cured from his weakness, then let it be known to each of you and to all Israel that he stands now before you having been healed in the name of Jesus Nazarene, the Anointed One whom you crucified but God raised from the dead. This same Jesus is the stone you builders rejected, yet he is now become the chief cornerstone.[18] There can be no salvation through anyone else because there is no other name under Heaven given among mankind whereby we are to be saved."

The priests and rulers were astonished when they saw how confidently Peter and John spoke, realizing that these companions of Jesus were untaught and untrained men. But with the former cripple fully

---

17   *Genesis* 22:18, 26:4.
18   *Psalms* 118:22.

healed and standing right in front of them they had nothing to say. So they ordered Peter and John to step outside the Council Chambers while they conferred with one another.

"What are we going to do with these men? Everyone in Jerusalem has seen this miracle and there is no way we can deny it. But we've got to nip this in the bud lest it spread further among the people. Let's therefore warn them now not to speak further in this name to anyone."

They recalled Peter and John and commanded them never again to speak or teach in Jesus' name or authority. But Peter and John replied,

"Decide for yourselves whether it's right in God's eyes for us to listen to him or to you. But there's no way we'll stop speaking about the things we've seen and heard."

They continued to threaten them, but on the other hand there was nothing they could do to stop or punish them because the man who had been healed was over 40 years old and all the people were giving glory to God for the miracle he'd experienced. So once Peter and John had been let go they returned to their own people and reported to them all that the High Priest and the elders had said. Those who heard them lifted their voice with one accord to God,

"Lord, you made the sky, the land and the sea and all that is in them and you spoke through the mouth of your servant our father David saying,

> Why are the nations puffed up
>> and the people scheme vain schemes?
> The kings of the Earth arose
>> and its rulers allied themselves
> to stand together against the Lord and his Anointed.[19]

Thus Herod, Pontius Pilate and the Gentiles and even the people of Israel joined themselves together in this city of Jerusalem against your Anointed Servant, accomplishing all you purposed to occur by your hand in accordance with your predetermined will. Now Lord, gaze upon their threats and give your servants full confidence to

---

19   *Psalms* 2:1-2.

speak your word. And stretch forth your hand[20] in healing, granting signs and miracles to be performed in the name of your Holy Servant Jesus."

As they prayed the place where they gathered was shaken.[21] They were filled with the Holy Spirit, such that all of them now began to speak the word with boldness.

The apostles themselves continued in great power, preaching the resurrection of Jesus, while the whole assembly was continually filled with the grace of God, all those who had become believers being of one heart and mind. Moreover, no one counted any of the things he had as his own but rather considered all goods to be held in common. As a result none in the congregation was left poor – those who owned lands and houses sold them and brought the proceeds to the apostles to be distributed among the disciples, as any might have need. To give one example, a Cyprian Levite named Joseph sold his farm, took the money he got and laid it at the feet of the apostles to be shared. The apostles called him Barnabas – בַּר נְבָא – which in English means "son of encouragement."

5

But another man, one Ananias, also sold some property, in this instance land that he and his wife Sapphira owned as joint tenants. However, he held back a portion of the proceeds and then brought what was left to the apostles. Basically he falsified the accounts, first pledging to give the full proceeds of the sale for the common good and then misrepresenting that the gift given was the total received in the sale. Even worse, Sapphira was fully on board with the plan.

When he came with the money Peter therefore said to him, "Ananias, how is it the Tempter has so filled your mind as to lie to the Holy Spirit and hold back some of the money you got from selling your property, even though you had already pledged it to the Lord? Wasn't it yours to do with as you pleased before you sold it? And didn't you have it under your control once you got paid? How could you have schemed in your

---

20   *Exodus* 7:5.
21   *Cf. Ezekiel* 38:19-20.

heart to hide things the way you've done? But know this: you haven't lied to men but to God." The moment Ananias heard these words he dropped dead on the spot and all who saw it were scared out of their wits. Then some of the youths in the assembly came forward, quickly wrapped up the body and carried it off for burial.

About three hours later Sapphira came in, not having heard yet what had happened. Testing her, Peter asked whether she and her husband had gotten such-and-such amount when they sold the property. She said, "Yes, exactly that much." Then Peter said to her, "Is it really possible that you two agreed to tempt the Holy Spirit this way? But look, the feet of those who buried your husband are at the door and they'll carry you out as well." And immediately she too fell down dead at his feet. So when they entered the room the young men saw the second corpse, scooped it up and buried her next to her husband. The whole assembly was overcome with awe and reverence, as were any others who heard about these events.

Numerous other signs and miracles were performed among the people through the hands of the apostles, who spent their days in unity in Solomon's Porch. For fear none of the other rich and landed dared join themselves to the apostles – yet the common people magnified them. And so increasing numbers became believers in the Lord, multitudes both of men and women, to the point that people brought the sick on pallets and cots, placing them in the open roadways in the hope that at least Peter's shadow might fall over them as he passed by.[22] And beyond that, crowds of people living in the Jerusalem suburbs brought their sick as well, even those tormented by unclean spirits, and the apostles healed them all.

But seeing this the High Priest and members of the Sadducean sect with him were filled with jealousy, laid hold of the apostles and had them taken to the city jail. But in the middle of the night angels of the Lord opened the gates of their cell and led them out, telling them, "Go to the Temple and stand openly, preaching to the people all the words of this life." Acting on those instructions they went to the Temple at dawn and taught.

Unaware of what had happened in the prison the High Priest and his retinue arrived at work to start their day, summoning the Sanhedrin and the whole council of elders of the sons of Israel and sending to have

---

22   *Isaiah* 32:2.

the apostles brought to them from the jail. But when the police officers got there they found the apostles missing. They therefore returned to the priests and elders and said, "We found the cell block securely locked and the guards standing at their posts but when we went inside there was no one there!"

When the prefect of the Temple police and the High Priest heard these words they were at a loss to know what to do, nor could they think where this all might end. But just then someone came in and reported, "Look! Those men whom you threw into jail are standing right there in the Temple and teaching the people!" The captain and his officers went to get the apostles - but they led them gently, afraid the crowd might stone them to death for seizing the apostles.

Once brought inside the apostles were presented for questioning by the Sanhedrin. The High Priest said, "Didn't we give you strict instructions *not* to teach in this name? But now look - you've gone and filled all Jerusalem with your doctrine, so it's obvious you're determined to bring this man's blood on us."

"We must obey God rather than men. The God of our fathers raised up Jesus, whom you murdered hanging him on a tree. By the power of his right hand God exalted this man as Prince and Savior and lifted him on high, that he might grant repentance to Israel and forgiveness of sins. And we are witnesses to these declarations and to the Holy Spirit, which God has given to those who obey him." When the rulers heard this they hit the roof and took counsel with the purpose of killing them. Yet a certain man named Gamaliel stood up to speak. He was a Pharisee and a member of the Sanhedrin, a teacher of the Law, prized by all the people. He directed that the apostles step outside for a little while and then said, "Fellow Israelites, take care what you are about to do with these men. Some time ago Theudas arose claiming to be someone to be listened to and around 400 men followed him. But he was killed and all of them scattered so it came to nothing. After that Judas the Galilean appeared on the scene during the time of the census and led a number of people away in revolt. But he was killed as well and his cohorts dispersed to parts unknown. So what's my advice to you now? Stay away from these men and let them go! If this scheme or this work comes from men it will collapse. But if it is purposed by God you cannot suppress it, lest you find yourselves fighting against God."

The rulers were persuaded by him, summoned the apostles and let them go, but only after flogging them and once again ordering them not to speak in the name of Jesus. Yet they emerged from the Sanhedrin rejoicing that they'd been counted worthy to be dishonored for his name's sake and went daily to the Temple and from house to house ceaselessly teaching and spreading the good news that Jesus is the Messiah.

6

Throughout this time the number of disciples kept multiplying. But some of the Greek-speaking Jews started grumbling that the local Hebrew-speaking brethren were shortchanging their widows in the daily distribution of food and other goods. The Twelve therefore convened a meeting of the whole group and said, "We've spread ourselves too thin. It's clear we aren't able properly to oversee or keep good account of the daily needs of the people and still see to the teaching of the word. But we also can't abandon the one in favor of the other. Our brothers, you're closer to this than we've been and so it makes the most sense for you to be in charge of choosing out seven Spirit-filled men, faithful and wise, to be ordained to manage all aspects of the ministry to the people's daily needs while we ourselves focus on the ministries of prayer and the word."

The idea pleased the entire assembly and they selected Stephen, a man filled with faith and the Holy Spirit, Philip, Prochorus, Nicanor, Timon, Parmenas and Nicholas, a convert from Antioch. They brought them before the apostles, who commissioned them by the laying on of hands and with prayer. Thereafter the word of God abounded and the number of disciples in Jerusalem increased yet more, with many of the priests also becoming obedient to the faith.

Now Stephen was filled with grace and power and began performing mighty signs and miracles in the midst of the people. But members of three local synagogues – that of the Freedmen, *i.e.*, Jews who had been expelled from Rome; that of people from Cyrene and Alexandria; and that of people from Cilicia and other parts of the Asian District – undertook to argue and dispute with Stephen.

However they were unable to counter the wisdom and Spirit by which he spoke. Instead they induced a few men to say, "We heard this man speak blasphemies against Moses and against God." They also agitated against him among the people and the elders and the scribes. Finally they seized him suddenly one day and brought him before the Sanhedrin, where they procured false witnesses to say, "This man never ceases to rail against this holy place and the Law. And we have also heard him say that Jesus of Nazareth will destroy this place and abolish the traditions handed down to us by Moses." Yet as all those seated in the Sanhedrin stared intently at Stephen they saw his face radiant, as if it were the face of an angel from Heaven.

7

Then the High Priest demanded that Stephen answer whether these accusations were true. But Stephen spoke as follows –

"My brothers, my fathers, listen attentively to me. The God of Glory[23] appeared to our father Abraham while he was still living in Mesopotamia, before he dwelt in Harran, and said to him 'Leave your land and your kin and come to a land I will show you.'[24] And so he left the land of Chaldea and settled in Harran until the time his father died and from there he migrated to this land where you now dwell. But God gave him no inheritance here, not even a place for a footstool. Instead he promised to give it as a possession to him and his descendants,[25] though at the time Abraham had no child. But thus spoke the Lord to him, Your descendants will be strangers in another land, serving there as slaves, suffering bitterly for 400 years. But I will judge the nation that enslaves them and after that time they will depart from there and serve me in this place.[26] Then God made a covenant with him, sealed by circumcision.[27] And Abraham became father to Isaac, whom he circumcised on the eighth day; and Isaac to Jacob; and Jacob to the twelve patriarchs.

"But Joseph's eleven brothers were filled with envy against him and

---

23   *Exodus* 24:16-17.
24   *Genesis* 12:1.
25   *Genesis* 12:7.
26   *Genesis* 15:13-14.
27   *Genesis* 17:12.

these patriarchs sold him into Egypt.[28] Yet God was with Joseph, raising
him up out of all his sufferings and giving him grace and wisdom in the
sight of Pharaoh, the ruler of Egypt, who made him governor over the land
and his whole household as well.[29] But a famine and great grief fell over all
Egypt and Canaan and our fathers found no way to survive. So when Jacob
heard there was food to be had in Egypt he sent our fathers to first scout
it out. When they returned a second time Joseph revealed himself to his
brothers and made his family known to Pharaoh.[30] Then Joseph summoned
his father Jacob, who came with all his tribe to Egypt, some 75 souls in all.[31]
And Jacob died in Egypt, as did our fathers, and their bodies were brought
back to be buried in Shechem, in the tomb Abraham had purchased for a
certain sum of silver from the sons of Hamor.[32]

"Now the time approached for God to fulfill his promise to Abraham. The number of the people had greatly increased, so much so that
they filled all of Egypt. But a new Pharaoh arose in Egypt who knew
nothing of Joseph.[33] He brought grief and bitterness to our fathers
with a genocidal scheme, forcing them to cast their newborn males
into the Nile with the goal of cutting off all future generations.[34] But
Moses was born in the midst of that era, a child full of grace in God's
sight. Though set adrift in the river after being nursed three months
in his father's home he was rescued from the elements by Pharaoh's
daughter and raised by her as if her own son.[35] And so Moses was
trained in all the wisdom of the Egyptians, becoming a man powerful
in his words and his deeds.

"When he was nearing 40 Moses had it in his heart to visit his true
brothers, the Children of Israel. While with them he saw an Egyptian
treating one harshly, for no just reason. Therefore he avenged his kin,
striking down the Egyptian and killing him. He thought his brothers
would thereby perceive that God had appointed their ultimate rescue
to come at his hands. But they didn't. When he came again the next

---

28 *Genesis* 37.
29 *Genesis* 41.
30 *Genesis* 42-45.
31 *Genesis* 46.
32 *Genesis* 50.
33 *Exodus* 1:7-8.
34 *Exodus* 1:22.
35 *Exodus* 2:11.

day he saw two of his brethren fighting with each other.[36] Seeking to reconcile them in peace he said, "My friends, you are brothers. Why mistreat one another?" But the one who had started the fight with his neighbor rebuffed Moses and charged, Who set you up to be a ruler and judge over us? Or are you going to kill me the way you killed that Egyptian yesterday?[37] When Moses heard that he fled Egypt and lived as a stranger in the land of Midian, where he fathered two sons.[38]

"After another 40 years passed Moses was in the desert near Mount Sinai when a messenger of God appeared to him in the flames of burning brambles.[39] Moses wondered at the vision and approached the brush to see what it was. But then he heard the voice of the Lord saying, I am the God of your fathers, the God of Abraham and Isaac and Jacob. And Moses trembled, not daring to look. But the Lord said to him, 'Loose the sandals from off your feet, for the ground on which you stand is holy ground. I have indeed seen the evils visited upon my people in the land of Egypt and given ear to their groaning. I have descended to set them free. Therefore go now! I am sending you into Egypt.'[40] And so this Moses whom they rejected saying, Who set you up to be a ruler and a judge?[41] – this same man God sent as ruler and redeemer, accompanied by the angel who appeared to him in the thorn bush.

"He led them out, performing signs and wonders in the land of Egypt and at the Red-Weed Sea and in the desert for the space of 40 years. And this is that same Moses who said to the children of Israel, God will raise up a prophet like me for you and your brethren.[42] He was present in the assembly in the wilderness[43] as mediator between our fathers and the angel who spoke to him at Mount Sinai. And he was given Living Oracles of God to share with us.

"But our forefathers did not wish to obey and instead rejected him and turned in their hearts back to Egypt,[44] telling Aaron, Make gods for us who will lead us ahead. But as for this Moses who led us out of the

---

36   *Exodus* 2:13.
37   *Exodus* 2:13-14.
38   *Exodus* 2:17-22, 4:20, 18:3.
39   *Exodus* 3:2-3.
40   *Exodus* 3:4-10.
41   *Exodus* 2:14.
42   *Deuteronomy* 18:15.
43   *Exodus* 19.
44   *Numbers* 14:4.

land of Egypt? We have no idea what's become of him.⁴⁵ So in those days they made a calf and brought sacrifices to the idol, taking pleasure in the works of their hands.⁴⁶ But God turned against them and left them to worship the sun and the moon and the stars in the sky,⁴⁷ just as is written in the scroll of the prophets,

> O House of Israel!
> Didn't you bring me offerings and sacrifices
> during 40 years in the desert?
> Yet now you raise up a tabernacle to Moloch
> and your star-god Rephan,
> worshiping their statues?
> Therefore I will thrust you in exile out beyond Babylon.⁴⁸

"Our forefathers also had the Ark of the Covenant with them in the desert in the Tabernacle made according the instructions God gave to Moses⁴⁹ and they brought it with them when they entered the land with Joshua, God driving out the nations before them. It remained with our forefathers until the time of David, who found grace in God's sight and sought to build a house for the God of Jacob. And though Solomon did build it⁵⁰ yet the Most High does not live in a house made by hands, even as the Lord spoke through his prophet,

> Heaven is my throne and the Earth my footstool –
> so what sort of house can you build for me,
> or what will be my place of rest?
> Has not my hand made everything?⁵¹

"O stiff-necked people, uncircumcised in hearts and ears!⁵² You have always resisted the Holy Spirit, just as your fathers did before you.⁵³ And

---

45   *Exodus* 32:1, 23.
46   *Exodus* 32:4.
47   *2 Kings* 17:16, 21:3-5, 23:4-5; *Jeremiah* 19:13; *Zephaniah* 1:5.
48   *Amos* 5:25-27.
49   *Exodus* 25.
50   *2 Samuel* 7:2-13.
51   *Isaiah* 66:1-2.
52   *Exodus* 33:3, 5; *Ezekiel* 44:7; *Jeremiah* 6:10, 9:26.
53   *Isaiah* 63:10.

which of the prophets did your forefathers not persecute? But no, they killed those who declared beforehand the coming of the Righteous One, whom you have now betrayed, becoming his murderers – you, the very people who received the Law at the direction of angels but kept it not!"

When they heard these words the rulers ground their teeth in anger, their hearts inflamed with rage against Stephen. Yet filled with the Holy Spirit Stephen gazed into Heaven and seeing the Glory of God and Jesus at God's right hand said, "Look up! For I see Heaven opened and the Son of Man standing at the right hand of God!"[54] But crying out in horror they covered their ears and rushed on him all together, haling him outside the city to stone him to death.[55] Taking off their cloaks these men laid them at the feet of a young man named Saul, as a witness of their deed.

As they stoned him Stephen called out, "Lord Jesus, receive my spirit." And falling to his knees he shouted, "Lord, lay not this sin against them!" At that he fell asleep. Then certain devout men took Stephen and buried him, amidst deep lamentation and mourning.

8

So it was that a great persecution began that day against the assembly in Jerusalem. Nearly all the disciples scattered throughout the regions of Judea and Samaria, while the apostles stayed fast in Jerusalem to strengthen those remaining. But Saul – the one who had stood by consenting to Stephen's death – went about wreaking havoc on God's elect, going from house-church to house-church dragging out both men and women to have them thrown into prison.

Even so, those who were dispersed continued proclaiming the good news wherever they went, including Philip, who on arriving in one of the cities of Samaria preached Christ to the inhabitants. The multitude there eagerly took in the words he spoke, one and all listening to him and also seeing the miracles he did – and with shrieks the unclean spirits came out of many people, while numbers of the lame and crippled were also healed, such that the whole city was filled

---

54 *Cf. Zechariah* 3:1.
55 *Leviticus* 24:14-16.

with joy.

A certain man named Simon had been practicing magic in the city, wowing the Samaritans and promoting himself as a great someone with everyone from least to most giving him heed and saying, "This man is the Great Power of God." They were devoted to him for all that time because of the amazing sorcerer's tricks he performed. But when they heard Philip preaching the kingdom of God and the name of Jesus they believed and were baptized, both men and women. And indeed Simon himself believed and was baptized, latching onto Philip, astonished when he saw great signs and wonders taking place.

When the apostles in Jerusalem heard that Samaria had received the word of God they sent Peter and John to visit. On arriving they prayed for the new disciples that they might also receive the Holy Spirit because it had not yet fallen on any of them – that is, they had so far only been baptized in the name of the Lord Jesus – and when Peter and John laid hands on them they too received the Holy Spirit. But when Simon saw that one could get the Holy Spirit by the apostles' laying on of hands he offered them money and said, "Give me this power as well! That way if I lay hands on anyone they'll receive the Holy Spirit."

Peter abjured him, "Your silver perish with you for thinking that the free gift of God can be gotten with money. You have no part in the ministry of this word – God knows that your heart is not upright. Turn from this evil path and entreat the Lord, if perhaps he may forgive the thought of your heart, because I perceive you are eaten up with bitterness and bound in the prison of wickedness."

"Pray for me then to the Lord that none of these evils you've spoken may fall upon me."

After testifying further and speaking the word of the Lord, Peter and John returned to Jerusalem, spreading the good news as they passed through the many villages of Samaria.

Following these events an angel of the Lord spoke to Philip, "Rise up and go at noontime along the road that leads from Jerusalem through the desert and on to Gaza. And when he did he came upon an Ethiopian eunuch, Queen Candace's trusted chamberlain and the overseer of her entire wealth, who was on his way back home after making his prayers in Jerusalem. And as he went, borne on a chariot, he read aloud from a scroll of the prophet Isaiah. Then the Holy Spirit told Philip to follow close after the chariot where, running alongside, he heard the man reading from Isaiah. Calling out he said, "Can you understand what you're reading?"

"To be honest, no – but how can I with no one to guide me?" So he urged Philip to come up and sit beside him. And the passage he was reading was this –

> He was led as a sheep to the slaughter
> > and as a lamb is silent before its shearer
> so he too opened not his mouth.
> > Humiliated, he was deprived of justice –
> who can describe his descendants?
> > For his earthly life was taken away.[56]

Then the Queen's chamberlain asked Philip, "Can you explain to me who the prophet is speaking about? I'm not sure whether he is talking about himself or someone else." And beginning with these verses and coursing through the Scriptures Philip related to him the gospel of Jesus Christ.

As they continued along they came to an oasis and the Ethiopian said, "Look! There's a spot of water – does anything prevent me from being baptized?"

"Nothing at all, if you believe in your heart that Jesus is the Son of God."

"I do believe!"

Having ordered the chariot driver to stop, both the Ethiopian and Philip went down to the pool of water, where Philip baptized him. But when they came up out of the pool the Spirit of the Lord snatched Philip away. The Ethiopian never saw him again, but filled with glee he joyfully went on his own way home while Philip, for his part, was found to be in Azotus. And so, evangelizing all the cities in that region he travelled on to the coastal city of Caesarea.

---

56 *Isaiah* 53:7-8.

9

In the meantime Saul's every breath was threat and death to the disciples of the Lord. In his pursuit of God's people he obtained letters from the High Priest authorizing him to go to the synagogues in Damascus, where he hoped to find some more men and women following the Way in order to bring them back to Jerusalem in chains. He headed off to Damascus with that goal but as he neared the city a light from Heaven flashed suddenly around him and, falling to the ground, Saul heard a voice saying, "Saul, Saul, why are you persecuting me?"

"But who are you, Lord?"

"I am Jesus, whom you persecute. Now get up off the ground and go into the city. Once there you will be told what you must do."

The men traveling with him were struck dumb, hearing a sound but seeing no one. Then Saul got up from the dirt. Yet when he opened his eyes he saw nothing. So the men led him by the hand and together they entered Damascus. For the next three days Saul went sightless, nor did he drink or eat a thing.

Now there was a certain disciple in Damascus named Ananias and the Lord called out to him in a vision saying, "Ananias!"

"Behold your servant, Lord."

"Rise up now and go to Judas' house in the narrow road called 'Straight Lane' and ask for Saul of Tarsus, who in his prayers has seen a man come and lay his lands on him that his sight be restored."

"But Lord, I have heard about this man from many people, how he has devastated your own saints in Jerusalem! And more than that he's now gotten authority from the High Priest to arrest all those here who call on your name."

"Go, I said – because this man is my chosen instrument to bear my name to the Gentiles and their kings, as well as to the children of Israel. And I will show him what things he must endure for my name's sake."

Ananias therefore left and came to the house as the Lord directed. Having first laid his hands on Saul he said, "Brother, the Lord Jesus, he whom you saw on the road as you came here, has sent me that you may receive back your sight and be filled with the Holy Spirit." And instantly there fell something like scales from off Saul's eyes and his sight was fully restored. Then rising up he was baptized and, taking nourishment, began to regain his strength.

Saul spent the next few days with the disciples in Damascus and soon went into the synagogues preaching Jesus, declaring him to be the Son of God. But all who heard him were shocked and said, "Isn't this the same person who raised Cain against those in Jerusalem who called on the name of the Lord? And hadn't he come to arrest the followers here and carry them off to the High Priest?" Yet Saul increased all the more in power and confounded the Jews in Damascus, reasoning with them and demonstrating that Jesus was the very Messiah.

After some time, however, the Jews who remained in opposition conspired to kill him. But Saul learned of the plot and was aware that the conspirators constantly watched the gates of the city hoping to find and attack him. His fellow disciples therefore snuck him out by night, lowering him down the city wall as he lay huddled in a hamper.

Saul went straight on from there to Jerusalem, where he tried to meet in fellowship with the disciples. Yet they were all afraid of him, not believing he had truly converted. Barnabas stepped in however and took charge of Saul, bringing him to the apostles and relating how Saul had seen the Lord on the road to Damascus, how the Lord had spoken to him and how he had been preaching in the name of Jesus in Damascus with all boldness. And so he joined their assembly, continuing to speak boldly in the name of the Lord, coming and going freely with them in Jerusalem. When he got into a series of disputes with the Hellenized Jews they too set their hands to find a way to kill him. But again the plot was found out in time and various of the brethren led Saul away to Caesarea, sending him thence by sea to his hometown of Tarsus.

Thereafter the whole assembly had a moment of peace throughout Judea and Galilee and Samaria as it was being built up, with the believers multiplying their numbers as they walked in the fear of the Lord and with the comfort of the Holy Spirit.

Now at the time Peter also happened to be traveling through these regions, arriving in Lydda to visit the local believers. When he got there he came upon a certain man named Aeneas who had for eight years lain on a cot, paralyzed. He said to him, "Aeneas, Jesus Christ heals you! Stand on your own two feet and pick up this pallet" – and he stood up right away. When everyone in Lydda and throughout the nearby Plain of Sharon saw this they turned to the Lord.

The city of Joppa was also nearby and a certain disciple lived there named Tabitha – in Aramaic טָבְיְתָא, which in English means "Gazelle" – who overflowed with good works and charity. But during those days she fell gravely ill and died. After ritually washing her body the local brethren laid her in an upper room for the mourning period. However, once these disciples heard that Peter was in the next town they sent two men to him with this urgent message – "Hurry now and come to us." So Peter arose and went with the men and when they arrived in Joppa they took him upstairs.

The upper room was filled with the widows of the town, who wept and mourned and also made a point of showing Peter the cloaks and other garments they wore, all woven for them by Tabitha while she was still with them. But Peter sent them outside, knelt down and prayed. Then turning to the corpse he said, "Tabitha, wake up!" Immediately she opened her eyes and on seeing Peter sat fully upright. Taking her hand Peter lifted her to her feet. Having called for the widows and the rest of the saints he presented her alive and well. This miracle became known throughout all Joppa and brought many to believe in the Lord. Peter therefore remained in Joppa for a number of days, staying at the house of Simon, a tanner.

10

During this same period there was a Roman army officer named Cornelius stationed in Palestinian Caesarea, commanding the sixth part of a cohort of an Italian regiment – in other words, a squad of soldiers equal to half a maniple. He was a devout man and reverent toward God, as was his whole household, and he was generous in his almsgiving and faithful in his daily prayers. One mid-afternoon as he prayed he saw in a clear vision an angel of the Lord approaching and calling out, "Cornelius!"

Frightened, he simply stared at the angel, but then said, "What, Lord?"

"Your prayers and alms have come before God to be a memorial to your faithfulness. Send men now to Joppa to bring back a certain Simon, also known as Peter. He is the guest of Simon the tanner, whose house is by the sea." As soon as the angel had departed, Cornelius summoned two of his servants along with one of his soldiers – this latter being a man who stood out for his piety from among those attached to his regiment. He then described everything he had seen and heard and sent the three of them off to Joppa.

The next day around noon and just as the travelers were nearing the city, Peter went up to the rooftop to pray. It happened that he was famished and more than ready to eat. But as he waited in prayer for lunch to be served he became ecstatically rapt and saw in a vision Heaven opened and something like a large sheet being lowered from Heaven to Earth by ropes bound to its four corners. In it he saw every type of creature – tetrapods and creeping things and birds that course the sky. Then he heard a loud voice telling him, "Get up, Peter, slit their throats and eat."

"No Lord, God forbid! I've never broken the food laws, never eaten profane or unclean foods."

But the voice spoke to him a second time – "What God has cleansed don't you call unclean." This happened three times[57] and the sheet was then taken back up to Heaven.

But Peter was at a loss to know what the vision might mean. Just then the men sent from Cornelius found Simon's house and stood at the door, calling out to see if anyone named Simon Peter was a guest inside. And as Peter continued pondering the vision the Spirit said to him, "Behold, three men are looking for you. I have sent them. Therefore descend and go with them, doubting nothing."

So Peter went downstairs and said, "I am the man you seek – but why?'"

"A holy angel gave divine command to our master Cornelius to send for you at this house so that he might hear God's message from you. He is a Roman centurion, a just man, one who fears God and is held in high regard by the whole nation of the Jews."

Peter welcomed them in as guests and the next day departed with them for Joppa. He brought along some of the local brethren as well and arrived in Caesarea the next day following. Cornelius, of course, was waiting expectantly for them and had in fact gathered his close

---

57   *Cf. Genesis* 41:32.

friends and relatives to be ready to greet Peter. And the moment Peter arrived Cornelius rushed forward and fell prostrate before him, doing obeisance to Peter. But Peter reached out, helped him to his feet and said, "Stand! I'm a man just like you."

As they began to share thoughts with one another the people gathered. Once they were assembled Peter stated –

"As you surely know, it is forbidden for a Jew to associate or mix with any other race of men. But God has shown me I ought not reject anyone whom God has made clean. Therefore I came to you when summoned, and without objection. But now, Cornelius, I need to hear directly from you why you've sent for me."

So Cornelius related –

"It was just four days ago right at this same time of day that I was fasting and praying in my house when a man stood before me clothed in radiance and said, 'Cornelius, your prayers have been listened to and have come up for a memorial before God. Therefore send now to Joppa and seek out Simon, also called Peter, a guest in the house of Simon, a tanner living by the sea.' So I sent for you at once and it is good that you have come. But now we sit in the presence of God to hear all the Lord has commanded you."

Then Peter declared –

"Now and for the first time I fully understand this truth, that God does not favor one person over another but in every race and nation anyone who fears him and acts justly is welcomed by him. This is the message he sent to the Children of Israel preaching the good news of peace through Jesus the Messiah and declaring that he is indeed the Lord of all mankind. And you yourselves know what was spoken – for the message was spread throughout all Judea – how Jesus started off in Nazareth of Galilee and after his baptism by John was anointed by God with the Holy Spirit and power to perform good works and heal all those who had been under the thumb of the Devil, God being present with him. Indeed, we are witnesses to all that he did throughout the land of Judea and in Jerusalem. And though they killed him, hanging him on a tree, yet God raised him on the third day. Moreover, God allowed that he make himself visible – not to everyone but to those chosen by God to be witnesses, to us, that is, who ate and drank with him after he was risen from the dead. And he commanded us to preach to the people and to testify that God has appointed him to judge the living and the dead. All the prophets testified to this very thing: that there is forgiveness of sins in Jesus' name to all who put their trust in him."

Even as Peter spoke these words the Holy Spirit fell on all those listening. And as they heard them speak in other languages magnifying and praising God, those who had come with Peter - all of them Jews by birth - were beside themselves with awe and wonder that the gift of the Holy Spirit was being poured out on Gentiles. And so Peter said, "Can anyone hold back the water of baptism from these people, who have been gifted with the Holy Spirit just the same as we?" Hence he instructed them to be baptized in the name of Jesus Christ. And they prevailed on him to stay there for a number of days.

11

The apostles and other brethren in Judea soon heard that the Gentiles had also received the word of God. But when Peter came back to Jerusalem some of his fellow Jews took issue with him and asked, "How is it that you not only met with uncircumcised men but even ate with them?" So Peter walked them through what had occurred at each step of the way.

"I was in the city of Joppa in the midst of praying when I fell into an ecstatic state and had a vision in which I saw something like an immense sheet lowered down to me from Heaven by its four corners. I stared inside the thing and saw the different kinds of four-footed animals that walk the Earth, wild beasts included, along with all sorts of reptiles and even the birds of the air.

"And then I heard a voice speak to me, 'Rise up, Peter, kill and eat.' But I said, 'Lord, no! I've never let unclean foods so much as touch my lips!' Yet the voice came a second time from Heaven and this time said, 'Whatever God has cleansed cannot be unclean to you.' And all this happened three times, at which point the sheet was taken back up into Heaven. Then just that moment three men arrived at the door of the house where I stayed, having been sent to me from Caesarea. And the Spirit told me to go with them without harboring doubts.

"So I went, taking with me six of the brethren. When we arrived we entered the house of the man who had sent for me. Then he recounted for us how he had seen a messenger of God in his own home standing before him and saying, 'Send to Joppa to summon Simon, also known as Peter, who will declare to you true words and teaching by which you and your whole household may be saved.' And even as I began to speak the Holy Spirit fell on them just as it had on us at the beginning. It was then I recalled the word of the Lord when he said to us, 'John baptized you with water but you will be baptized in the Holy Spirit.' If God therefore has given the same gift to them as to us who have believed in the Lord Jesus Christ, who was I to resist the power of God?"

When they heard these things they were at peace and, moreover, glorified God – "For God indeed has granted the Gentiles repentance, that they too may turn to life."

Now, some of those who had been scattered because of the persecution that arose on account of Stephen went as far as Phoenicia, Cyprus and Antioch. But they were only preaching the word to other Jews. But then some of the Cyprians and Cyrenians who had also come to Antioch began to spread the good news about Jesus to the Greeks. And the hand of the Lord was with them, with a great number believing and turning to the Lord. Word of this came to the assembly in Jerusalem, so they sent Barnabas out to Antioch. He was a good man, faithful and filled with the Holy Spirit. When he arrived there he saw the grace that was upon the congregation and rejoiced with them, urging them all to stand fast in the Lord with all the resolve their hearts could muster. From there he went to Tarsus, seeking out Saul. Once he found him he brought him back to Antioch. They stayed with the local congregation for the whole next year, teaching a great many people. And it was there in Antioch that believers were first called Christians.

During this same time prophets came from Jerusalem to Antioch. One of them by the name of Agabus stood up in the assembly and signified through the Spirit that a great famine
was about to fall across the whole Empire, which in fact did happen
during Claudius' reign. The disciples therefore determined that each
would send as much help as he could afford to the brothers in Jerusalem, and thus dispatched relief aid to the elders there by the hands
of Saul and Barnabas.

12

It was also during this time that Herod the king set about to destroy
the assembly in Jerusalem. He started with John's brother James,
having him slain by the sword. When he saw that this deed pleased
the Jewish rulers he went on to arrest Peter as well. All this occurred during the Feast of Unleavened Bread. Once he had caught
Peter he threw him in jail, putting a rotating series of four squads
of four soldiers each around him, intending to put him on public
trial after the Passover. But while Peter languished in prison the
assembly prayed unceasingly for him.

The night before Herod was to put him on trial Peter lay asleep.
He was bound in chains with one soldier on his right and one on his
left and two more soldiers standing guard, one at the inner prison
gate and the other at the outer. Then behold! - an angel of the Lord
appeared, its radiant light illumining the cell. Tapping Peter on his
side to waken him the angel said, "Get up quickly!"

Just then the chains fell off Peter's hands and the angel spoke
again, "Get dressed! And don't forget to tie your shoes."

Peter did as he was told and once again the angel spoke,
"You forgot your jacket! Put it on now and follow me."

So Peter left the cell with the angel - but the truth is he thought
he was dreaming, not that he was *really* following an angel. Even so,
they passed through one guard post then another until they came to

the iron gate leading out to the city, which opened to them of its own accord. They exited to an alleyway and as they walked down the lane the angel disappeared from Peter's sight.

It was only then that Peter came out of his daze and said to himself, "Now I know for certain that the Lord sent his angel and rescued me from the hand of Herod and all that the Jewish rulers expected to happen to me."

At that point Peter looked up and realized he had ended up at the home of a certain Mary – this was in fact Mary the mother of a disciple named John who was also called Mark – and a good number of disciples were gathered there in prayer. When Peter knocked at the outer gate a young servant girl named Rhoda came to answer. She recognized Peter's voice and was so excited to hear it that she forgot about opening the door and instead ran back to tell everyone that Peter was standing outside at the gate.

They said, "Don't be silly!"

But she insisted Peter was there.

"It can't be him, it must be his guardian angel."

Peter kept knocking, of course, and when they finally opened the door they were crazed with joy. But Peter shushed them with his hand and told them the whole story of how the Lord had led him out of the prison. Then he told them to inform Jacob and the other brothers and sisters, while he left and went elsewhere.

Well, the next morning there was utter chaos at the prison, the soldiers having no idea what had become of Peter. Herod had them search high and low but he couldn't be found. After interrogating the guards and learning nothing, Herod had them led away to their deaths and then went down from Judea to stay at his palace in Caesarea.

Now Herod had been seriously upset with the people of Tyre and Sidon about something having to do with the food trade. But they sent a united delegation to him, beseeching him in an effort to settle things. They were able to persuade Blastus, the king's chamberlain, to take their side and were thus able to negotiate the peace they needed, being fully dependent on the king's territories for their food supplies.

In celebration of the accord and on a set day Herod clothed himself in royal garments, appeared on a rostrum and delivered an address to the assembled crowd. But when the people heard him they cried out, "This is the voice of a god, not a man!" Yet Herod did not give the glory to God. For that an angel of the Lord struck him down. And so Herod gross by sinning grown died in descent from the dais, all his insides consumed by worms.

But the word of God continued to flourish and multiply.

13

By now Barnabas and Saul had completed their mission at Jerusalem and therefore returned to Antioch, taking John Mark with them. In addition to Barnabas and Saul there were a number of prophets and teachers at the assembly in Antioch, including Simeon (who was also called Niger), Lucius the Cyrenian and Manaen (who had been raised with Herod the tetrarch). While they were ministering to the Lord in fasting, the Holy Spirit spoke through one of these prophets, "Separate out for me Barnabas and Saul for the work to which I have called them." After they fasted and prayed they commissioned them by the laying on of hands.

Having thus been sent by the Holy Spirit and bringing along John Mark as an aide-de-camp, Paul and Barnabas arrived at Seleucia and from there sailed to Barnabas' homeland of Cyprus. Landing at the port of Salamis they began to preach the good news in the synagogues of the Jews and continued across the whole island until they reached Paphos on the western coast. There they came across a certain Jewish sorcerer named "Son of Joshua" who had attached himself to Sergius Paulus, the provincial governor. Now this Sergius Paulus was an intelligent man and sent for Barnabas and Saul, seeking to hear the word of God from them.

But the magician – whose name in the local language was Elymas, meaning "wise" – opposed them, aiming to block the governor from the faith. However, Saul (by now known as Paul) fixed his eyes on him and being filled with the Holy Spirit said, "O you son of Satan, mired in all wickedness and deceit, enemy of all that is just, will you not cease from twisting the straight paths of the Lord? But now watch! The hand of the Lord is against you and you will be blinded, not seeing the light of the sun for a season." Instantly the seer was clouded with a mist of darkness and wandered about searching for someone to guide him by the hand. When the governor witnessed what had happened he was astounded by the power and teaching of the Lord and he himself believed.

Thereafter Paul and his companions put out to sea from Paphos and soon arrived at Perga in Pamphylia, on the southern coast of what is now Turkey. But John Mark left them at this point and headed back to Jerusalem. From Perga they travelled inland, arriving at a town near Pisidia that also had the name Antioch. As it was the Sabbath they entered the synagogue to worship with the congregation. Following the readings from the Law and the Prophets the presiding member of the synagogue turned to them and said, "My brothers, if any of you has a word of encouragement or exhortation to share with the people, speak out!"

Sweeping with orator's hand across the room thus Paul began –

"Fellow Israelites and all you who fear God, listen closely. The God of the nation Israel chose our forefathers and sustained them during their exile in Egypt, leading them out of that land with uplifted arm, nourishing them for 40 years in the wilderness. Having destroyed the seven nations of Canaan he then settled them in that land as their inheritance, some 450 years having passed from the time of exile to their return. He set judges in their midst until the time of the prophet Samuel. But they begged of him a king and so God gave them Saul, the son of Kish, a 40 year old from the tribe of Benjamin. But after deposing him God raised up David to be their king, testifying of him I have found David, the son of Jesse, a man after my own heart,[58] and he will carry out all my desires.[59]

"God has now fulfilled his promise to Israel and brought a Savior

---

58   *I Samuel* 13:14; *Psalms* 89:20.
59   *See Isaiah* 44:28.

from the descendants of David, Jesus, of whose coming John prophesied
when he proclaimed repentance in baptism to the whole people of Israel.
And indeed as John was ending his ministry he asked the people, 'Who
do you suppose I am? Because I myself am not the One. And yet watch!
He *does* come after me and I am not worthy so much as to loose the sandals from off his feet.'

"My brothers, children of Abraham's family and those among you
who fear God, this word of salvation is now sent to you. The inhabitants
of Jerusalem and their rulers did not recognize the Messiah even though
the words of the prophets are read to them every Sabbath. But having
judged him they brought those prophesies to fulfillment, urging Pilate
to put him to death though no just cause was found. And when all that
had been written about him had been accomplished they took him down
from the cross and placed him in a tomb. But God raised Jesus from
among the dead and he was seen over the course of many days by those
who had been with him from Galilee to Jerusalem – they are his living
witnesses to the people.

"We therefore bring you the good news that God has fulfilled the
promise he made to our forefathers by raising up Jesus for us, their
children, even as is written in the first Psalm, You are my Son – this
day have I begotten you.[60] As to his resurrection from the dead, never
to turn to dust, the Psalmist said, I will give you the sure and holy
promises I made to David.[61] And elsewhere he says, You will not allow
your Holy One to see corruption.[62]

"Now David died having served out God's will in his own generation and was laid to rest with his fathers, his body turning to dust.
But he whom God raised did *not* decay. Let it therefore be known to
you, my brothers, that through Jesus forgiveness of sins is now proclaimed to you. And the Lord will justify you in his sight as you turn
in faith to him, granting you the righteousness that the Law of Moses
was unable to accomplish in you. Take heed therefore that what the
prophets spoke does not fall upon you –

---

60   *Psalms* 2:7.
61   *Isaiah* 55:3.
62   *Psalms* 16:10.

> Look now, you who despise, be dumbstruck and perish,
>> for I will work a work in your days,
> a work you will not believe
>> though it be fully declared to you."[63]

The people left the synagogue amazed, clamoring for Paul and Barnabas to bring more of this teaching at the next Sabbath. And having left the gathering many of the Jews along with devout proselytes followed after Paul and Barnabas, who continued speaking to them, urging them to remain faithful to the grace of God. Then on the following Sabbath practically the whole town came to hear the word of the Lord. But some of the rulers of the Jews became jealous when they saw how the crowd filled the place. They began to speak against Paul and Barnabas, alleging that the things they spoke were blasphemies.

Yet Paul and Barnabas grew even bolder and said, "It was right that the word of God be first spoken to you. But since you reject it and judge yourselves unworthy of endless life, then watch as we turn to the Gentiles. For thus the Lord commanded,

> I have set you as a light to the Gentiles,
>> that you may bring salvation to the
> ends of the Earth."[64]

When the Gentiles heard this they rejoiced and glorified God and as many as had been set in the way of eternal life believed, such that the word of God spread throughout the whole region. But the Jews incited some of the prominent and devout women as well as the leaders of the city and roused up some people to persecute Paul and Barnabas, running them out of the whole territory. So they shook the dust from off their feet as a testimony against them and went on into Iconium. And the disciples were filled with joy and the Holy Spirit.

---

63   *Habakkuk* 1:5.
64   *Isaiah* 49:6.

14

As was their custom, Paul and Barnabas entered the synagogue of the Jews there and spoke about Jesus. A great number believed, both Jews and God-fearing Gentiles. Therefore they remained there for some time testifying with boldness as to his word and his grace, the Lord confirming their preaching with signs and miracles. But the chief rulers of the synagogue rejected the good news and stirred the people up, poisoning the minds of the Gentiles against the brethren to the point where the city was divided into two camps – one supporting the rulers of the synagogue and the other the apostles. The rulers went so far as to scheme together with Gentiles to attack Paul and Barnabas, planning to stone them to death. But the plot was discovered and Paul and Barnabas were able to flee the city in time, moving on to the nearby Lycaonian cities of Lystra and Derbe, evangelizing there and in the surrounding region.

Now there was a certain man in Lystra who had been born severely lame. He had never walked in his whole life but had to stay seated, curled around his own feet. Paul was speaking to the people at one point when he noticed the man listening intently to him. Paul fixed his sight upon him and perceived that the man had faith to be healed. So Paul raised his voice and said, "Stand up straight on your feet!" Immediately the man jumped up and began to walk about.

When the crowd saw what Paul had done they exalted his name, shouting, "The gods have come down to us in the form of men!" They called Barnabas "Zeus" and Paul "Hermes" (since he was the one who spoke God's word). But they spoke all this in their own Lycaonian language, such that the apostles didn't understand what they were saying. Yet when Zeus' local temple priest heard the people's acclamation he went ahead and brought oxen wreathed in garlands to the city gates for the people to offer sacrifices to Barnabas and Paul, since he too supposed them to be gods.

But as soon as Paul and Barnabas saw this and realized what was happening they were horrified, tore their clothes and rushed out yelling to the crowd – "Stop!! What do you think you're doing? We're not gods, just ordinary men, same as you! But we're bringing you the good news about Jesus so that you'll turn away from your worthless idols and superstitions to the living God, he who made the sky and the land and the sea and all that is in them. Yes, in days gone by he allowed you Goyim to go your own ways. But even then he gave you witnesses to himself – in kindness sending rain from Heaven for your crops, assuring that they yield their fruits at the appointed seasons, nourishing you with food, filling your hearts with cheer." But even with his strenuous efforts to deter them Paul was only barely able to stop the people from offering sacrifices to him and Barnabas.

While they were still in Lystra certain Jews came from Antioch and Iconium and persuaded some of the people to go after Paul, stoning him. And having done so they dragged his body outside the city, certain he was dead. But even as the disciples gathered mournfully around him in a circle Paul rose up and went back into the city. Setting out the next day with Barnabas he headed to Derbe. Once they had spread the good news to that city, making disciples of numbers of its people, they began retracing their steps back toward Lystra, then on to Iconium and then to Pisidian Antioch. They strengthened the souls of the disciples all along the way, encouraging them to stay firm in the faith, explaining that only through much suffering would we enter the kingdom of God. They also appointed elders in each assembly, selecting those whom the believers themselves chose by a show of hands, commending them with prayer and fasting to the service of the Lord.

Passing on next through the rest of Pisidia they came to the district of Pamphylia where, after preaching in Perga, they went a bit further down along the coast to Attalia. There they caught a ship sailing eastward back toward Antioch (from which, of course, they had originally been commissioned by God's grace to their now completed task). Once they had landed they gathered the assembly together to tell them all the things that God had accomplished on their mission – and especially how widely he had opened the door of faith to the Gentiles. And so they remained with the disciples in Antioch for quite a good while.

15

At that time some of the Jewish believers came to Antioch from Jerusalem and taught the brothers, "Unless you are circumcised in accordance with the Law of Moses, you cannot be saved." That gave rise to no small controversy and debate between them on the one hand and Paul and Barnabas on the other. They all therefore decided that Paul and Barnabas, taking along some others of the local brethren, should go up to Jerusalem to address the issue with the apostles and elders there. Having been commissioned for this purpose by the assembly they passed through Phoenicia and Samaria along the way, telling the local congregations about the conversion of the Gentiles, something that brought great joy to all the brethren they met.

Once they arrived in Jerusalem they were received warmly by the assembly, the apostles and the elders as they related all God's dealings with them on their mission trip into the Asian province. But some of those who had been members of the Pharisaical sect stood up in the congregation and insisted that new Gentile believers be told they must not only be circumcised but also generally keep the Law of Moses.

The apostles and elders therefore conferred on the question and after considerable discussion and debate, Peter gave his views –

"My brothers, you know that some time ago God revealed through me that he had appointed the Gentiles as well as us Jews to hear the word of the gospel and to believe. And God – who knows our hearts – confirmed his will in this regard by giving them the Holy Spirit just as he had to us, making no distinction between us and them, cleansing their hearts by faith in just the same way. Now therefore why would we tempt God by placing a yoke on their necks that neither we nor our fathers had strength to bear? We trust instead that we will be saved by faith and they the same."

At that the whole assembly grew silent and listened carefully to Barnabas and Paul as they detailed the signs and miracles that God had performed through them among the Gentiles. When they had finished giving their account, Jacob spoke –

"My brothers, give heed to me. Simon has previously explained how God in his oversight has taken a people for his name from among the Gentiles. God's works are known to him from before all time and indeed what has happened fully accords with Scripture as written in the words of the prophets –

> After this time I will return again
>   and rebuild the fallen House of David
> and whatever things have been torn down,
>   those will I rebuild and restore –
> that Earth's remnant may seek the Lord,
>   even the Gentiles who are called by my name.
> Thus says the Lord, who accomplishes these things.[65]

"For this reason I myself judge that we should stop causing grief to the Gentiles who are turning to God but rather command them only this: that they keep themselves from things offered to idols and from the polluted meat of strangled animals, since it still contains the blood. And as for general knowledge of the Law of Moses, it has been read and taught in the synagogues of every city from ancient times and so continues each Sabbath day."

Then the apostles and elders, with the agreement of the whole assembly, decided to send some of their most trusted men to accompany Paul and Barnabas back to Antioch carrying a letter written by the apostles to the believers. They chose Judas, also called Barsabbas, and Silas, and wrote as follows –

"From your brothers, the apostles and elders in Jerusalem, to our Gentile brothers in Antioch, Syria and Cilicea – greetings! We have heard that some people visiting you from our midst have troubled your souls, undermining the foundations of your faith, saying you must be circumcised and otherwise keep the Law of Moses. But we didn't authorize them to go on this mission or address these questions. We therefore with unanimity of mind decided to send you Judas and Silas, who will confirm verbally what we now write and who for this purpose accompa-

---

65   *Amos* 9:11-12.

ny our beloved brothers Paul and Barnabas, men who have yielded over their own lives for the sake of the Lord's name. Our message is that it seemed right to the Holy Spirit and to us to lay no greater burden on you than certain necessary obligations, which you will do well to observe: that you stay away from the pollutions of idolatrous offerings and from the meat of strangled animals, the blood still remaining in it. Be strong and of good cheer!"

Having been thus dispatched Paul and Barnabas went straight to Antioch, where they gathered the congregation together and delivered the epistle. The people read and received the letter with joy, taking it as a great consolation. Moreover Judas and Silas, themselves being prophets, added their own words of encouragement and comfort. After staying for some days they were sent off in peace to return back to Jerusalem while Paul and Barnabas stayed on in Antioch, where they and many others shared in the teaching and ministry of the word of the Lord.

Thereafter Paul said to Barnabas, "We should go visit all the brethren in each of the cities where we preached the word of the Lord, to see how they're getting on and to exercise whatever care for them we may." Barnabas agreed but also wanted to have John Mark accompany them. However Paul didn't want to bring John Mark along, taking the view that he might not be up to the task since he had already left them once (that was early, you'll recall, on the first missionary journey, when John Mark returned back home from Pamphylia rather than continuing on in the work). The contention between Paul and Barnabas was so sharp that they actually broke from one another, with Barnabas sailing off to Cyprus with John Mark while Paul chose Silas as his new co-worker. After being commissioned for this next journey in the grace of the Lord by the brethren Paul left Antioch and passed through Syria and Cilicia, strengthening the assemblies as he went.

16

In due course Paul arrived at Derbe and then Lystra, where he met up with a disciple by the name of Timothy, child of a mixed marriage between a believing Jewess and a Greek. Now this Timothy was well regarded by the brethren both in Lystra and Iconium and Paul wished to bring him along with them on their further journeys. First, however, he circumcised Timothy in consideration of the Jews in those parts, all of whom knew that his father was a Gentile and that Timothy had therefore never been circumcised. Thereafter passing from city to city Paul delivered to the local assemblies the doctrines as determined by the apostles and elders in Jerusalem, so that they too could adhere to them. And these assemblies grew stronger, their numbers multiplying day by day.

But they were prevented by the Holy Spirit from speaking the word further south in the Roman province of Asia and therefore travelled through Phrygia and Galatia instead. Turning now toward Mysia they attempted to enter Bithynia but the Lord's Spirit deflected them from there as well. Being thus guided on their way they passed through Mysia and continued on to Troas, where Paul had a night vision in which he saw and heard a certain Macedonian call out, "Cross over into Macedonia and come to our aid!"

Heeding Paul's dream we immediately aimed toward Macedonia, being fully persuaded that God was calling us to preach the good news to the people there. The next day we therefore set sail, running before the wind to the Isle of Samothrace and continuing the following day to Neapolis. From there we went by foot a few miles inland to the Roman colony of Philippi, a leading city in the district of Macedonia, remaining there several days.

The next Sabbath we left through the Philippi city gates and went down by the riverside, which we understood to be a local place of prayer. Once seated we spoke to a group of women gathered there. Among them was a certain Thyatiran woman named Lydia who ran a successful business trading purple-dyed cloths. She herself was reverent and pious and God opened her heart to receive Paul's teaching. She was baptized accordingly, she and her whole household in fact. She then urged us, "If you have judged me faithful to the Lord, abide in my house." Now Lydia was someone not used to taking no for an answer and so she prevailed on us to remain with her during our time in Philippi.

As we walked to prayer one day a young slave girl came up opposite us. She was a palm-reader of sorts and had made her owners rich charging people for her fortune telling. She then began to follow along after Paul and the rest of us crying out, "These men are the servants of God Most High and are declaring to you the way of salvation." She continued like this for a number of days, causing grief to Paul. So finally he turned around and spoke to the spirit and said, "In the name of Jesus Christ I command you to leave this woman!" And the spirit left her that moment.

But when her masters saw their profits disappear they seized Paul and Silas and haled them to the town square to face the local authorities, petitioning the magistrates and charging, "These Jews are causing an uproar in our city, teaching customs that are unlawful for us as Romans to receive or observe." Then a mob gathered to join in the attack and the magistrates, tearing their own cloaks in rage, ordered Paul and Silas beaten with rods. Having lashed them numerous times they took them to the prison and directed the warden to hold them in secure custody. Thus commanded, the jailer brought them to the innermost cell and clasped their feet in wooden stocks.

But 'round about midnight Paul and Silas prayed, singing hymns to God, while the rest of the prisoners listened. Then of a

sudden the ground shook violently, the earth shuddering the prison's foundations to the point that the gates of the cells came off their hinges and the prisoners' chains broke open. The warden was rousted from his sleep by the quake and when he saw the gates of the prison open and the chains loosed he drew his sword to kill himself, assuming all had escaped.

But Paul shouted to him, "Don't harm yourself! We're all here inside!"

Grabbing a torch the jailer rushed inside trembling with fear and when he saw Paul and Silas fell prostrate before them.

"My masters, what must I do to be saved?!"

"Believe in the Lord Jesus and you will be saved, you and your household with you."

The jailer then led them outside to his own home and he himself washed the blood from their wounds. Paul shared the word of the Lord with him and his whole house, all of whom were baptized straight away. The jailer then had a meal set out before them, rejoicing that he and his household had been brought to faith in God.

The next day the magistrates sent for the police and said, "You can tell the jailer to let those men go now."

The jailer relayed this to Paul, telling him the magistrates had sent word they should be freed.

"Therefore go now, leave in peace."

But Paul responded, "We are Roman citizens yet they beat us in public without any hearing or trial and threw us into prison, and now they think they can just push us away quietly with no one noticing? Not a chance! Let them come get us themselves."

The warden passed *that* message along to the police and thence to the magistrates. But when the authorities realized they had broken Roman law by mistreating two of its citizens they were seriously afraid and raced to the prison begging Paul and Silas to leave the city. And so they left, after stopping first at Lydia's house to encourage as well as comfort the brethren.

17

Departing from Philippi and continuing southwest along the Via Egnatia they walked through Amphipolis and Apollonia and thus came to Thessalonica, where there was a Jewish synagogue. As was his custom Paul attended and for three Sabbaths in a row discussed the Scriptures with them, expounding and explaining that the Messiah had first to suffer and then be raised from the dead. And he declared, "This Jesus whom I preach to you, this very man is the Messiah."

Some of those in the congregation believed and joined in with Paul and Silas as did many God-fearing Greeks and a number of upper-class women. But others of the Jews were filled with envy and sought out some roughneck good-for-nothings, getting them to put a vigilante mob together to look for Paul and Silas at the house of one of the local brethren named Jason in order to hale them before the people's assembly.

But they didn't find them there and so they grabbed Jason and some of the other brethren instead, dragging them to the city magistrates, where they cried out, "The people who've been roiling the whole Empire have now come to our city and this man Jason has taken them in. They've set themselves against Caesar's decrees and say there is another king, one Jesus." When the officials and the crowd heard this they were greatly upset. After first securing bail money from Jason and the others they released them pending trial.

But the brothers spirited Paul and Silas away in the night, sending them to Berea. Once they arrived there they went into the Jewish synagogue. The Jews in Berea were more open and fair-minded than those in Thessalonica and received the word with all zeal, examining the Scriptures daily to see whether the things Paul spoke were true. Many of them in fact believed as did a number of the town's most influential Greek men and women. But when the Jews of Thessalonica heard what was going on – that Paul was now preaching the word of God in Berea as well – they came down from their own city to stir up trouble, inciting the people.

At that the brothers quickly took Paul from Berea to a nearby seaport while Silas and Timothy remained behind. They embarked from there, these brethren accompanying Paul as far as Athens and bringing a message from Paul back to Berea urging Silas and Timothy to meet him in Athens as soon as they were able.

While Paul waited for them in Athens he became enraged when he saw how the city was laced throughout with idols. He therefore spent the days arguing the subject in the Jewish synagogues and in the Agora with whomever happened to be around. Some of the philosophers of the Epicurean and Stoic schools of thought also conversed with him, a number of them saying, "What scrap of knowledge has this seed-gathering bird picked up?" And others, "He seems to be talking about some sort of foreign gods" (this was because Paul was proclaiming Jesus and his resurrection).

After he had been there a few days they brought him up to a place opposite the Acropolis named Ἄρειος Πάγος - which in English means "Ares' Rock" - and said, "Explain to us more about this new teaching of yours because what we're hearing from you are strange notions, unknown to us, and we therefore want to know just what it's all about." The Athenians, you see, as well as people who visit there, are always itching to learn something new and are happy to spend their time hearing or talking about any sort of novelty.

Paul therefore stood up in the midst of this forum and said, "You men of Athens, I see from your temples and statues how you are more than ordinarily devout because as I passed through the city, examining your shrines and temples, I found one on which it had been written, 'To an Unknown God.' So while you may be worshiping him without knowing any more than that I am here to reveal him to you: this God is the one who made the world and all that is in it, the Lord of Heaven and Earth. But he doesn't live in a temple like these, all built by men's hands, as though he had need of care or shelter or anything else that could come from mankind. No, he it is who gives life itself and breath to all creatures.

"And from one man he created every nation in order that mankind should spread across the face of the Earth. He set fixed seasons for their lives and boundaries for their habitations, all so they might reach out for God in the hope of finding him. In fact, however, he is not far from each one of us because in him we live and move and exist. And it's just as some of your own poets have said: 'We are God's family.'[66] Therefore being God's children we shouldn't think the Deity to be a mere thing conceived by man and fashioned into gold or silver or stone. But God has looked past the times of your ignorance, now calling on people everywhere to turn from their ways because the day is coming in which he will judge the world in righteousness by the man he appointed, giving proof in that he raised him from the dead."

Yet when they heard about a resurrection of the dead some laughed at him and others said, "Maybe we can hear more about this ... some other time." So Paul left off from them. But a few people joined with Paul, believing the word, among whom were Dionysus the Areopagite and a woman named Damaris, plus a few others with them.

18

Following his time in Athens Paul travelled to Corinth. There he met a certain Pontian Jew named Aquila along with Priscilla his wife. They were newly arrived from Rome, having left under compulsion of the Emperor Claudius' decree ejecting all Jews from Rome. Paul's initial contact with them was based on the fact that they were skilled in the same craft – tentmakers like him. Paul labored at his job during the weekdays and then went to the local synagogue each Sabbath to reason with the congregation, trying to persuade both Jews and Greeks of the things he said.

Once Silas and Timothy had come down to the Corinthian coast from Macedonia to assist him they found Paul deeply absorbed in preaching the word, testifying to the Jews that Jesus was the very Messiah. But the rulers and some of the people remained opposed, going so far as to blaspheme God. Paul therefore shook out his cloak before

---

66   Aratus, *Phaenomena*, 5; Kleanthes, *Hymn to Zeus*, 4.

them and declared, "Let your blood be on your own heads! I am pure of conscience in this matter[67] and therefore turn now to the Gentiles alone."

So he left them and moved his meeting place over to the house of a man named Titius Justus, a worshipper of God who happened to live right next door to the synagogue. And despite the opposition of many others, the synagogue president himself, one Crispus, came to believe in the Lord and was baptized along with his whole household.

Then the Lord spoke to Paul in another night vision and said, "Neither fear nor keep silent but continue speaking as you have, for I am with you. No one will rise up to mistreat you – and in truth I have many people in this city." Paul therefore settled in for a year and a half, teaching the word of God among them. But thereafter the Jews gathered together as one and attacked Paul, dragging him before the judgment seat, where Seneca's brother Junius Gallio then presided as provincial governor of Achaia. They accused Paul of inciting people to worship God in a manner contrary to what the Law prescribed.

Paul was just opening his mouth to respond when Gallio cut in and said to the Jews, "I'd be willing to bear with you and your accusations if this had to do with some sort of crime or evil doing, but if you are starting in now about a bunch of words or names or laws of yours then it's your problem not mine because I'm not going to issue rulings on such things." So he threw them out of court. Then the crowd turned against the Jews, grabbing Sosthenes, the new synagogue leader, and beat him right in front of the judgment seat – but at that point Gallio couldn't have cared less what happened to any of them.

Having continued on in Corinth for a number of days Paul took his leave of the brethren, sailing next to Syria along with Priscilla and Aquila, shaving his head in Cenchreae because of a vow he had made. When they arrived in Ephesus Paul left Aquila and Priscilla behind while he went to the synagogue and reasoned with the Jews. They tried to persuade him to stay with them longer but he could not. However as he bid farewell he promised them, "I will return back to you, God willing." He then sailed on from Ephesus, landing at Caesarea, where he greeted the assembly

---

67   *Ezekiel* 3:17-21; 33:4.

and then moved on to Antioch. After spending some time there he journeyed throughout Galatia and then Phrygia, strengthening the disciples along the way.

Now about this time a certain Alexandrian Jew named Apollos arrived in Ephesus. He was highly learned and wielded the Scriptures with power, having been well instructed in his own country in the ways of God. He spoke fervently in the Spirit, teaching with clarity whatever facts he knew about Jesus - even though he had otherwise known only the baptism of John - and began speaking boldly in the synagogue. When Priscilla and Aquila heard him they took him aside and explained to him more exactly the doctrines of the Lord. He then desired to go to Achaia to share the good news. The brethren encouraged him in his wishes, writing on ahead to the Achaian disciples that they should take him into their fellowship. Once he got there Apollos contributed greatly to the congregation by helping to build up the faith of those who had through grace already believed. Moreover he publicly refuted the Jews, vigorously demonstrating from the Scriptures that Jesus is the Messiah.

19

While Apollos was in Corinth, Paul travelled through the upcountry and came back to Ephesus. He found some dozen or so disciples there and asked them, "Did you receive the Holy Spirit when you became believers?"

"No one's even told us there *is* a Holy Spirit!"

"Well, what sort of baptism have you had?"

"John's baptism."

"When John baptized people for the forgiveness of sins he told them to watch for someone coming after him and believe in him. That person was Jesus."

When they heard that they were baptized in the name of the Lord Jesus. Then Paul laid hands on them and when the Holy Spirit came upon them they spoke in other languages and prophesied.

Paul spent the next three months reasoning and discussing the Scriptures in the local synagogue, speaking with all boldness and persuading people of the kingdom of God. But some remained stubborn and hard of heart, refusing to believe and even speaking ill to the rest of the congregation about what was now being called the Way. Paul therefore withdrew from their midst, taking a number of disciples with him. Over the next two years he held forth daily at the School of Tyrannus from late morning to late afternoon – the word of the Lord thus being heard by Jews and Gentiles from throughout the whole of the Asian pvrovince.

God worked some one-of-a-kind miracles through Paul during this period, such that if people took aprons or handkerchiefs that had come into contact with Paul's skin and laid them on those who were sick they got well, and if they were oppressed by evil spirits the demons departed. When some itinerant Jewish exorcists saw this they also sought to cast out demons, shouting, "I command you in the name of Jesus whom Paul preaches."

A couple of those who tried that were sons of a chief priest named Sceva. But when they spoke these words to a man who was demon-possessed the evil spirit shot back, "I know who Jesus is and I also know Paul but who the Hell are you?!" And at that the possessed man leapt onto the two of them and with overwhelming strength tore off their clothes and beat them to a pulp to the point they scarcely got away from that house alive, fleeing naked away. This incident quickly became known to the whole Jewish and Gentile community in Ephesus, and fear and awe fell upon them – while the name of the Lord Jesus was magnified in their sight.

Many of those who came to believe had previously been involved in the dark arts and now confessed and renounced their practices. Numbers of them brought their spell books and divination manuals and burned them in open public. When they reckoned up the value of all those books, moreover, they were worth some 50,000 silver coins of the realm. And so the word of the Lord grew strong and spread.

Having seen this much fulfilled Paul set his mind to pass through Macedonia and Achaia again and then head on to Jerusalem. "After that," he said, "I must see Rome." To that end he sent his right-hand men Timothy and Erastus ahead into Macedonia while he continued on for a bit in the Asian province. But in the meantime a good deal of trouble was brewing over the Way because a certain silversmith named Demetrius – whose specialty was making silver statues of Diana the Hunter – had rounded up his fellow craftsmen and others of like sort and said, "Men, you know that all our fortunes are staked on our idol-making but now you've seen how this man Paul has gone around not just here in Ephesus but all throughout the Asian province turning people away from us, persuading people there's no such thing as a god made with hands. And it's not just that our own business is being ruined, but more important is the threat to the glory and majesty of the temple and dwelling of our great goddess Diana, who is worshipped not only in our own province but throughout the whole Empire."

When they heard that the other craftsmen went berserk, shouting, "Great is Diana of Ephesus!" And soon enough the whole city was in an uproar with mobs of people single-mindedly rushing into the local stadium, dragging two of Paul's Macedonian aides, Gaius and Aristarchus, along the way. Paul was intent on entering the stadium as well so he could speak to the gathered assembly but the other

disciples prevented him. Some of the Asiarchs (a class of local government officials) who were loyal to Paul also sent word telling him
to stay away. Meanwhile the stadium itself was a mass of confusion
with some people shouting one thing and some another and a lot of
the people not really knowing why they were there in the first place,
having simply run inside after everyone else.

One group tried to get Alexander to speak to the people so he
motioned with his hand calling for silence in order to mount some explanation of what was going on. But when the crowd realized he was a
Jew they started chanting in unison, "Great is Diana of Ephesus," and
went on shouting the same thing for some two hours.

Finally the town clerk calmed the crowd down and addressed
them –

"Men of Ephesus, is there anyone out there who *doesn't* know that
our fair city is verger for the holy temple of Diana and that her statue
came down to us from Zeus himself? No one can gainsay this. But
that being the case I urge you not to take some reckless action now,
because you've dragged in these men who aren't temple robbers nor
have they spoken evil of the goddess. If Demetrius and the other
craftsmen believe they have been wronged and want to file charges
against them on some grounds then the courts are open and pro-con-
suls are available to judge the matter. Let them bring a lawsuit there
if they wish and have it resolved the normal way. But this uproar
might well be mistaken for insurrection, putting us all at risk of being
charged with incitement to riot for what's happened today, having no
excuse for all this tumult."

And so saying he dismissed the assembly.

20

Once things had settled back down Paul summoned the disciples
and, after encouraging them, departed for Macedonia. As he passed
through that region he likewise built up the disciples he visited along

the way, sharing often by way of teaching and instruction. Before long he arrived in Greece, where he spent three months. But when he was about to sail next for Syria they discovered a plot against him by some of the Jewish rulers. Having been thus forewarned he decided instead to go by land back through Macedonia. On this leg of the journey he was accompanied by Sopater the Berean, son of Pyrrhus, the Thessalonicans Aristarchus and Secundus, Gaius of Derbe, Timothy, and the Asians Tychicus and Trophimos. These had all gone ahead of Paul and were waiting for us to arrive in Troas. But we first spent the Feast of Unleavened Bread at Philippi and when it was completed sailed off to Troas, reaching there five days later and then staying a week.

We gathered on the first day of the week to break bread, with Paul intending to depart the next day. He therefore extended his teaching and instruction on through the day, even as far as midnight. There were a number of window seats in the upper room where we were gathered and a boy by the name of Eutychus was perched in one of them, listening. Yet as Paul wore on he just couldn't keep his eyes open any longer. Overcome with sleep he lost his grip, rolled backwards out the window and plummeted three stories to the ground outside. When the people rushed down to find him they took him for dead. But Paul pressed in close, embraced the boy and cried out, "Stop all this mourning, for his life is yet in him!" And so the people lifted the lad up alive and well, rejoicing. Paul went back upstairs and when he had broken bread and eaten he resumed talking to the brethren straight through till dawn, at which point he left the city.

We went ahead of him by ship and sailed as far as Assos, the plan being to pick Paul up there since he'd wanted to travel by land. Once he arrived in Assos he joined with us, sailing thence due south to Mitylene. From there the next day's sail took us opposite Chios. Thereafter we put in at Samos and the following day at nearby Trogyllian, where we tarried a few days. And from there we crossed on to Miletus.

That route had us sailing past Ephesus but we didn't plan a stop there because it was Paul's earnest wish to spend no more time in the Asian province than was necessary so that, if possible, he could get to Jerusalem in time for Pentecost. Instead of stopping at Ephesus Paul therefore sent word to the elders of the congregation to journey south to Miletus to meet him. He then shared these parting thoughts –

"You know how from the very first day I arrived in the Asian province I was with you serving the Lord in all humility and through tears and testings brought on by the plots of the Jewish rulers, how I held back nothing needful from you, steadfastly teaching and preaching publicly to the Jews and the Gentiles and from house-church to house-church, testifying of repentance to God and faith in the Lord Jesus. But now I am bound in my spirit to go to Jerusalem, not knowing what things may happen to me when I get there – other than that the Holy Spirit has been warning me from city to city in prophecies as I go that chains and suffering await me. Yet I consider nothing to be of value in my own life other than to finish the race and complete the ministry I've received from the Lord Jesus: that I testify to the good news of the grace of God.

"I've gathered you here now, you to whom I have preached the kingdom of God, because I know this is the last time we will see each other face to face. I can testify to you that to this day I am guiltless of the blood of any man because I have not held back from declaring the whole counsel of God to you.[68] Keep a close watch on yourselves and the whole flock the Holy Spirit entrusted to you because he has set you as overseers to shepherd the Lord's chosen people, those whom he purchased with his own blood.

"I also know that once I've left ruthless wolves will slip in among you, not sparing the flock, and even from your own midst men will rise up distorting the truth and seeking to steal away the disciples. Therefore be vigilant – remembering that day and night for the space of three years I never ceased to warn and instruct you, even with tears in my eyes. But now I place you in God's hands and the word of his grace, in whose power it is to build you up and grant you an inheritance among all those he has sanctified.

"Keep in mind that I've never gone after anyone's silver or gold or so much as a cloak. Instead with my own two hands I labored at my trade to support not only myself but also those who accompanied me. I did all this to demonstrate to you that through our own toils

---

68 *Ezekiel* 3:17-21.

we must help those who are poor and in need, remembering what the Lord Jesus himself said, 'It is more blessed to give than to receive.'"

Then Paul knelt and prayed in their midst even as they clung to him, weeping and kissing his neck, deep in grief above all at his telling them they would see his face no more. Thus we parted as they saw us safely on board ship saying final farewells as we put out to sea.

21

Setting a course due south we sailed before the wind from Miletus to Cos, the next day bearing east to Rhodes and thence to Patara. We found a merchant ship bound for Phoenicia and embarking with them we sailed due east. Cyprus came into view above the horizon and, leaving it behind to port, we held our course for Syria, putting in at Tyre where the ship was to unload its cargo. We sought out the disciples there and stayed with them for seven days. But they spoke to Paul by the Spirit urging that he not go up to Jerusalem. However, once our time there was over they helped us along in our way, accompanying us to the shore where, together with their wives and children, they knelt with us and prayed as we bid farewell to one another. And so we went aboard ship while they returned to their own homes.

From Tyre our voyage took us farther down the coast to Ptolemais, where we greeted some of the disciples and stayed with them for a day. Leaving on the morrow we sailed to Caesarea and when we arrived there we stayed at the house of Philip the Evangelist, one of the original seven deacons. Now Philip had four unmarried daughters, all of whom prophesied. We had been there for several days when a certain prophet named Agabus came down from Judea. He approached us and took Paul's belt from him, binding his own hands and feet with it and saying, "So shall the Jews in Jerusalem bind the man whose belt this is and hand him over to the Gentiles."

When we heard this we and the local brethren begged Paul not to go up to Jerusalem. But Paul responded, "Why all this wailing? Why crush my heart? But cease! I am ready not only to suffer bonds but even to die in Jerusalem for the sake of the Lord Jesus' name." Being unable to dissuade him we held our peace, saying only, "The Lord's will be done."

Our time there coming to an end we prepared for the last leg of our journey, heading up to Jerusalem. A number of the Caesarean brethren accompanied us, leading us to the home of an elderly disciple named Mnason, with whom we stayed overnight.

On arrival in Jerusalem the brethren received us gladly and after we got settled in Paul went on the following day to see Jesus' brother Jacob, with all the elders also present. Having greeted them Paul rehearsed one by one the works God had performed through his ministry among the Gentiles. When they had heard all this they gave glory to God and said to Paul, "You can see, brother, how many thousands of the Jews have now come to believe. But they are all zealous for the Law and have heard from some that you teach heresy, telling the Jews who live among the Gentiles that they are free from Moses with no need to circumcise their children or otherwise follow the traditions of the fathers. They will certainly be aware by now that you've arrived. We'd therefore like you to consider a thought we have about how to deal with this situation. It happens that there are four men with us who at their own initiative have taken on a Nazarite vow of purification.[69] We suggest you join with them, purify yourself and also cover the expenses when it comes time for them to shave their heads. When everyone sees this they will realize that there is nothing to what they've been told about you but rather that you yourself live uprightly, observing the Law. As far as the Gentiles go, we've already sent them a letter instructing them to keep away from food that has been sacrificed to idols and from the meat of animals that have been strangled, the blood still being in the carcass."

Paul therefore purified himself in accordance with the Law and, bringing these four men along with him, went into the Temple to declare that their vows would last seven days, at which point they were to present their sacrificial offerings. But when they came to the Temple at the end of the seven days to fulfill their vows some of the Jews from the Asian province saw him there and stirred up the crowd, laying hold of

---

69 Numbers 6:1-21.

him with their hands and shouting, "You Israelites, come help us! This is the very man who's been spreading teachings against our nation and against the Law everywhere he goes and now has even gone so far as to bring Gentiles into the Temple, defiling this holy place!" They said this because they had seen the Ephesian Trophimos in the city with Paul and assumed that Paul had brought him into the Temple.

The whole city was then thrown into an uproar, with the people forming a mob and dragging Paul outside the Temple, at which point the Temple officials quickly barred the doors.

The crowd began to pummel Paul and was bent on lynching him. However, word came to the local Roman tribune that all Jerusalem was breaking out in riots. He therefore immediately sent out soldiers from his cohort under the command of centurions to take to the streets and quell things. As soon as the mob saw the soldiers they stopped beating Paul. When the tribune himself came on the scene he ordered Paul arrested and bound in chains between two soldiers. He then demanded of the crowd an explanation of what was going on. Some shouted one thing and some another, such that he couldn't find out what the rioting was all about. He ordered Paul brought to headquarters but the mob was still so unruly that it was only by carrying Paul on their shoulders that the soldiers brought him safely up the staircase leading to the guardhouse. Yet the crowd followed along crying out, "Do away with him!"

As they were about to enter the barracks Paul turned to the tribune and said, "May I speak to you, sir?"

"You speak Greek? But I thought you were that Egyptian revolutionary who led a band of 4000 armed terrorists out into the desert some time ago."

"I'm a Jew from Tarsus, citizen of a city of no mean importance in Cilicia. I pray of you let me speak to these people."

So the tribune gave him leave. Paul, standing at the head of the stairs, motioned downward with his hand and called for silence. Once the people gave heed he spoke to them in their native Aramaic dialect as follows.

22

"My brothers, my fathers, give ear now to my defense" - and when they heard him addressing them in Aramaic, they kept quiet all the more - "I myself am a Jew, born in Cilician Tarsus but raised in this city, educated at the feet of Gamaliel, trained with strictest precision in the Law of our fathers, as zealous toward God as any of you are to this day. And I persecuted the followers of this Way, binding both men and women and handing them over to be executed. The High Priest and all the elders of that time can testify this fact to you because they issued letters for me to show to the Jewish brethren in Damascus, authorizing me to arrest such people and bring them to Jerusalem for punishment.

"But it happened that as I neared Damascus at midday a brilliant light from Heaven flashed around me and, falling to the ground, I heard a voice say to me, 'Saul, Saul, why are you persecuting me.' I answered, 'Who are you, Lord?' He said to me, 'I am Jesus Nazarene, whom you persecute.' Those who were with me saw the light but didn't hear the voice that spoke to me. I then said, 'Lord, what shall I do?' And the Lord told me, 'Rise up and go on to Damascus. There you will learn all that has been appointed for you to do.' But I could no longer see because the glory of that light blinded me. So with my companions leading me by the hand I entered Damascus.

"Now a certain man named Ananias - a pious man, observant of the Law, held in all regard by the Jews of that city - came and stood over me saying, 'Brother Saul, see again!' And immediately my sight returned to me. Then he said, 'The God of our fathers has appointed you to know his will, to see the Just One and to hear the voice spoken by his mouth, to the end that you be a witness to every race of mankind of the things you have seen and heard. And now why delay? Rise up! Be baptized and wash your sins away, calling on his name!'

"When I returned thereafter to Jerusalem I went to pray at the Temple and fell into an ecstatic trance, where I saw the Lord say to me, 'Hurry, leave Jerusalem quickly, because they will not accept your

testimony about me.' And I said, 'Lord, they know I went from synagogue to synagogue beating and imprisoning those who had believed
on you and that when they shed the blood of your martyr Stephen I
myself stood by in full agreement, guarding the cloaks of those who
struck him down.' And he said to me, 'Go – I will send you far off to
the lands of the Gentiles.'"

They had listened to Paul thus far but when they heard that last
pronouncement about the Gentiles they shouted, "Rid the Earth of
this man because such a one is not fit to live," screaming at him, shaking their garments and throwing dust into the air. Seeing this the
tribune ordered that Paul be brought inside the barracks to be interrogated by whips until he admitted why they were so enraged at him.
As the soldiers prepared the leather straps to flog him he turned to
the centurion in charge and said, "Since when do you think it's lawful
to whip an innocent Roman citizen?"

As soon as he heard that the centurion went to his commanding
officer and said, "Do you know what you're about to do? This man is
a Roman citizen!"

The tribune then came up to Paul and asked, "Is that true? Are
you a citizen of Rome?"

"Indeed, I am."

"It cost me dearly to buy that citizenship."

"But I am a citizen by birth."

The inquisitors backed off immediately and the tribune took fear,
realizing he had chained up a Roman. But he still wanted to find out
what the accusations were against Paul and so the next day, having
released him, he ordered the High Priest to convene the Sanhedrin
and brought Paul before them.

23

Then Paul began to address the elders, his eyes piercing each of them.

"My brothers, I stand before you with a clear conscience, having lived uprightly before God to this very day."

But when he said that the High Priest, one Ananias, ordered his aides to strike Paul's mouth.

"So will God strike you, you white-washed wall! You pretend to judge me according to the Law and yet command me beaten, contrary to the Law?"

From Ananias' side they demanded, "Who are you who dares revile God's High Priest?!"

"But, my brothers, I hadn't considered him to *be* the High Priest, it being written in the Scriptures, Do not speak wickedly of a ruler of your people."[70]

At that point Paul perceived that the Council was composed of both Sadducees and Pharisees. He therefore cried out, "Men and brothers I am a Pharisee and the son of a Pharisee and am today being called to account for my hope in the resurrection of the dead!"

At that the Sanhedrin was thrown into turmoil, the Pharisees and Sadducees being torn apart from one another on this question because the Sadducees hold there is no life after death, no such thing as angels, no such thing as spirits, while the Pharisees hold the opposite. They all began shouting at one another and some of the scholars of the Pharisaical sect stood up and said, "We find nothing evil in this man. What if the Spirit of God or one of his messengers has spoken to him?" But the chaos was so great that the tribune was afraid the two sides might literally tear Paul apart. He therefore ordered his soldiers to grab Paul out from their midst and bring him back to the headquarters.

Once night had fallen the Lord stood by Paul and said, "Take heart, for just as you have testified to me in Jerusalem so too must you witness to me in Rome."

While all this was happening, around 40 men gathered together to scheme against Paul, binding themselves to one another with a grievous oath, swearing they would neither eat nor drink until they had killed him. Then they approached the chief priests and the elders to let them in on the plot.

---

70   *Exodus* 22:28.

"We've conspired together, swearing a curse on ourselves that we would neither eat nor drink until we've done Paul in. We therefore need you to tell the tribune you want him to bring Paul back before the Sanhedrin in order to examine more carefully the things said by and about him. We for our part will lie in wait to ambush and kill him as he draws near."

But Paul's nephew happened to be in the wings, overheard their scheme and ran quickly to the jail cell to tell Paul. Paul then called one of the centurions over and said, "This boy has a message for the tribune. You need to take him to see him." The centurion led the boy to the tribune and said, "The prisoner Paul asked me to bring this young man to you to deliver a personal message." The tribune took the boy by the hand, led him privately to one side and asked him what this was all about. "The Jews plan to ask you to bring Paul back to the Council tomorrow in order to examine him more closely about the things he says. Don't believe them! Some 40 of their men have sworn a curse on themselves not to eat or drink until they kill Paul and they lie ready to pounce once you order him brought there." The tribune saw the boy out, warning him not to tell anyone that he had told him this.

Summoning two of his centurions he instructed them, "Assemble 200 soldiers, 70 horsemen and 200 spear-bearers to take Paul to Caesarea. Provide a mount for him as well. Leave here in the middle of the night and deliver him safely to Felix the Governor."

The tribune also wrote the following letter for them to hand-deliver, sealing it with his signet –

"Claudius Lysias to the Most Excellent Governor Felix: Greetings! This man was seized by the Jews. They were about to kill him but I rescued him from their hands as soon as I learned he's a Roman citizen. Wishing to know the nature of their accusations against him I brought him before the Sanhedrin, where I determined that this all involved disputes about their own laws. I myself found nothing in him worthy of imprisonment let alone death. But I was then informed of a murderous plot against him and have therefore sent him immediately to you. I have likewise directed his accusers to explain to you just what their issue is with him."

The soldiers escorted Paul as they had been instructed, first conducting him to Antipatris in the night. The next day the foot soldiers were allowed to return to Jerusalem while the cavalry continued on with him to Caesarea, delivering Paul to Felix along with the tribune's letter. Once Felix had read the letter he asked Paul what district he was from. Learning that he was from Cilicia Felix said, "I will hold a hearing on this matter as soon as your accusers get here." In the meantime he kept Paul under guard in Herod's palace complex.

24

Five days later the High Priest Ananias and a number of the elders arrived accompanied by a professional orator named Tertullus, who outlined the charges against Paul.

"O Most Noble Felix, we who always and in all places have enjoyed fullness of peace at your hands are grateful for your liberal and providential rule over our nation. We do not wish to overburden you with this matter and are therefore happy to state the issue in brief. This man is a pestilence, a rabble-rouser, a ring-leader of the Nazarene sect who has been stirring up Jews all over the Empire. And he has now dared to desecrate the Temple, over which we ourselves rule. We sought to judge him for this blasphemy in accordance with our own laws but Claudius the tribune snatched him from us by force and ordered us to present our charges before you. You may therefore now examine him yourself and learn the truth of our cause against him."

Once the others with him had also affirmed this to be the case the Governor motioned to Paul to stand for his defense, and thus he began.

"I know that for many years now you have been the judge over this people and so I take good heart in responding before you to these charges. In the first instance you can easily determine that it was only twelve days ago I went up to Jerusalem to worship and spent none of that time arguing with people in the Temple or the synagogues, let alone inciting crowds of people anywhere in the city. They've certainly given you no proof to the contrary nor provided any other support for their accusations against me. But this I do confess: I worship the God of my fathers, believing the Law and all that the prophets have written. And I hope in God for the same resurrection of the dead that these men themselves profess – a resurrection of both the just and unjust. And although they now call this Way of belief heresy I follow it with a clear conscience before God, always striving to avoid giving offense to anyone.

"So it is that now after many years I have come back to Jerusalem, bringing alms and offerings for my people. While there certain Asiatic Jews found me in the Temple fulfilling a vow of purification. Even though I was surrounded by no crowd and raised no ruckus they stirred everyone up. But if they had any real complaint against me they should've brought it right to you. Nevertheless they haled me before the Sanhedrin and these same men who now stand before you from Jerusalem can say whether they found any fault or injustice in me, unless it's this one thing I said to them, that 'I stand here today before you to be judged concerning the resurrection of the dead.'"

As it turned out Felix was quite well informed on the subject of the Way. He therefore adjourned the hearing and said, "When Lysias the tribune comes down I will inquire more particularly concerning these things." He then ordered one of the centurions to protect Paul, giving him liberty and further allowing any of his friends to visit and aid him. And after several days Felix, along with his wife Drusilla, herself a Jew, sent again for Paul to hear more about this faith in Jesus the Messiah. Paul discussed with him in detail matters of righteousness, right behavior and the future judgment on all mankind – to the point that Felix grew fearful and trembled. But he said to Paul, "*Cras credemus, hodie nihil.*"

But the truth was, he hoped Paul would pay him off to be let go and therefore sent for him quite frequently. After two years of this, Portius Festus took over as successor Governor. Yet Felix left office with Paul still under house arrest, as a favor to the Jews.

25

Three days after Festus arrived in the province to take up the gover-norship he went up to Jerusalem from Caesarea. The chief priests and leaders among the Jews took the opportunity of his presence to explain to him their grievances against Paul and asked him to indulge them by sending Paul back to Jerusalem to stand trial – but their true purpose was to kill him by organizing an ambush along the road. Festus, however, said that Paul was already in Caesarea and he him-self was soon heading back there. "Let those who hold power among your people therefore come along with us to Caesarea. If you believe he has done anything wrong you can press your charges against him once we get there."

After spending another eight or ten days in Jerusalem Festus went back to Caesarea and convened his court, summoning Paul to be brought before him. The Jews who had also come from Jerusalem gathered around Paul and laid out multiple accusations of grievous wrongs but presented no evidence to support the charges.

Paul then stood for his defense and said simply, "I have committed no sin against the Law or against the Temple or against Caesar."

But Festus, still wishing to indulge the Jewish leaders, asked Paul, "Are you willing to respond to these charges back in Jerusalem?"

"I stand here in Caesar's court and that is where I must be judged. You know perfectly well I have done nothing wrong to the Jewish people. If I have committed any crime under Roman law, even one punishable by death, I am prepared to be tried and suffer just punishment. But if the charges brought now by the Jewish rulers are false then no one has the power to hand me over to them and certainly not as a way to curry their favor. I therefore call upon Caesar as my judge."

After taking counsel with his advisers Festus said, "Since you appeal to Caesar off to Caesar you go."

Several days later King Agrippa and his wife Bernice were in Caesar-ea and came by to pay their respects to Festus, remaining as his guest for some period of time. Festus took the occasion to describe the whole business to the king.

"I've got a certain man on my hands named Paul whom Felix left behind for me under house imprisonment at the instance of the Jews. When I was recently in Jerusalem their chief priests and elders presented me with their indictments against him, alleging various wrongdoings and asking that he be brought to Jerusalem to be judged. But he's a Roman citizen and I explained to them that due process forbids us to condemn anyone absent a hearing where he can face his accusers, hear their charges and present his defense. I therefore promptly convened a trial and had both his accusers and the man himself brought in before me.

"Yet as far as I could tell from anything they had to say he's done nothing wrong, let alone anything worthy of the death penalty. Instead the whole thing appears to be some dispute about matters of the Jewish religion and in particular some dead man named Jesus who Paul says is still alive. So how in the world am I supposed to decide that kind of controversy? I asked Paul if he were willing to go to Jerusalem to have it all thrashed out. But Paul insisted his case be carried over to the Emperor's docket. I've therefore ordered him held here until I could send him on to Caesar."

So Agrippa said, "I'd like to hear from this man myself."

Accordingly – and with much pomp and circumstance – Agrippa and Bernice ascended to the Great Hall of the Palace together with their retinue of military officers and local notables, at which point Paul entered as well, having been summoned by Festus. Festus then presented the matter.

"King Agrippa and all you gathered here today – *ecce homo*! For this is the man about whom the Jews have petitioned, crying out to me both here and in Jerusalem that he is unfit to live a day longer. But I have scrutinized the matter and found him to have done nothing worthy of death. Yet he has now appealed to the Emperor to resolve the matter in final fashion and to that end I have resolved to send him to His Imperial Majesty. But in truth I am not sure how best to specify the issues for Caesar. I have brought him before you all now, especially before you, King Agrippa, in order that I may have something intelligible to write following further investigation, because it would be wrong to send a prisoner off to Rome with no clear statement of the charges against him."

26

Agrippa then turned to Paul, granting him leave to give account of himself. And with a sweep of his hand Paul opened his speech.

"I consider myself fortunate today that I am able to defend myself before you, King Agrippa, against the accusations brought by these men, because I know you to be well acquainted with Jewish customs and controversies. I therefore ask you to listen with patience to what I have to say about this matter. My life is an open book and the Jews standing here, if they wished, could tell you themselves how from my youth in my own country and then in Jerusalem I lived as a Pharisee in accordance with the strictest rules of our manner of worship. But now, Your Majesty, I am brought up on charges for the very hope in God's promise given to our forefathers. And indeed the Twelve Tribes of Israel, worshiping night and day, seek to attain this same hope.

"So I ask all of you here – if God chooses to raise the dead, who are we to refuse to believe it? Yet I admit I myself rejected this work of God at one time, going far as to take every action possible against those who believed on the name of Jesus of Nazareth, imprisoning them not just in Jerusalem but anywhere I could find them. Indeed, I had been given authority to do so by the chief priests. And I cast my vote in favor of their execution, going from synagogue to synagogue in my efforts to persecute them, forcing as many of them as I could to deny their faith, so maniacal in my zeal that I pursued them even when they fled outside the cities.

"*But* – as I went on the road to Damascus with the authority and commission of the chief priests to continue this course of action I saw at midday shine down from Heaven, O King, a light more brilliant the sun. This light surrounded me and my companions and we all fell straight to the ground. Then I heard a voice speak to me in Aramaic saying 'Saul, Saul, why are you persecuting me? It must be hard on you, kicking against the pricks of your conscience just like an ox to its master's goad!'[71] I answered, 'Who are you, Lord?' And the Lord said, 'It is I, Jesus, whom you persecute. But rise up now and stand on your feet. I have appeared to you now to appoint you my servant and witness of the things you've seen of me and things I will yet show you. I will deliver you from the hands of your own people and send you out to the Gentiles to open their eyes – that they may turn from darkness to light, from the thrall of the Devil to God, receiving forgiveness of sins and inheritance with the holy ones through faith in me.'

"King Agrippa, I did not disobey this Heaven-sent vision. Going first to Damascus, then to Jerusalem and the whole Judean territory and thence to the Gentile nations I have preached that people should repent of their sins and turn toward God, doing good works as proof of their changed lives. And for this some of the Jews seized me in the Temple, aiming to kill me. Yet God has been my help from then until now, allowing me to testify to both the lowly and the mighty, declaring nothing other than what Moses and the prophets said would happen – that the Messiah would suffer but be the first one resurrected from the dead, a light to lighten the Gentiles and the glory of his people Israel."

But as he was giving this defense Festus interjected – "Paul, you've gone nuts! Have those books you read now made you mad?"

"O noble Festus, I'm far from crazy. What I'm telling you is the true Word of God and I speak it with all seriousness and sobriety and confidence. And I might venture to say that none of the things of which I've spoken has escaped the King's notice either, as they weren't done in secret."

Then turning to Agrippa he said, "And you do believe the prophets, King Agrippa, don't you? Indeed, I know you believe them."

"Paul, I think you'd just as soon turn me into a Christian!"

"Would to God that sooner or later not only you but everyone present might become such as I am – except for these chains of course!"

---

71   Pindar, *Pythian* 2.173; Aeschylus, *Agamemnon* 1624; Euripides, *Bacchae* 794-95; Terence, *Phormio* 1.2.27.

King Agrippa then arose and with him his wife Bernice, the Governor and all who had accompanied them. Once they had left they said to one another, "This man has done nothing worthy of prison, let alone death."

And Agrippa told Festus, "If he hadn't appealed to Caesar he could've been set free."

27

It was thus determined that we should sail to Italy and Caesar's court. Paul was therefore handed over along with various other prisoners to the custody of a centurion named Julius, commander of a cohort of the Imperial Legion. We went onboard a ship out of Adramyttium bound for her home port on the eastern shore of the Aegean Sea, opposite Lesbos, thus sailing along the coast of the Asian province. Aristarchus, a Macedonian from Thessalonica, came along with us. The next day a fair wind brought us to Sidon where Julius, showing kindness to Paul, allowed him to visit his friends in the area, who could thus care for his needs. Launching out from there we had to sail under the lee side of Cyprus, *i.e.*, to its north, the winds being against us. Crossing through the open sea we passed by Cilicia and Pamphylia and harbored next at Myra, a Lycian port, where we disembarked.

The centurion then located a ship in that harbor on its way from Alexandria and *en route* to Italy with a cargo of wheat, so he put us on board. But with the wind out of the northwest we were required to tack multiple times once underway and thus had slow going, having a hard time reaching Cnidus. From there we bore south by southwest, sailing past Cape Salmone and thence along the southern coast of Crete. But with the same northwest wind against us we were hard pressed to make it much farther along that coast, arriving only with difficulty to a certain port named Fair Havens, not far from the city of Lasea.

We spent a good deal of time there because, with late Fall upon us, navigation remained dangerous. Paul took the occasion to warn the crew – "Men, I perceive that if we continue on now the ship will be lost along with its cargo with the same risk to the lives of all onboard." But the centurion ignored Paul's warning and deferred instead to the ship's owner and his helmsman, who advised him to push on. It was their view that Fair Havens was a poor place to winter given its exposure to most winds of the upcoming season. They therefore determined to make headway as far as Phoenix, a Cretan harbor some further distance on, considering Phoenix a safer place to winter because the harbor was better protected from storms, open to the east but sheltered by a small island at its mouth, thus leaving entrances looking to both the northeast and southeast.

Soon a gentle southern wind came up and the sailors judged this to be the moment they were waiting for. So we weighed anchor and sailed west from Fair Havens, hewing to the coastline. But as we approached the Paximades Islands not far along past Cape Matala we were caught in typhonic winds sweeping down from Crete through the Gulf of Messara. The ship was unable to turn into the wind and we were forced to yield to the gale. We were thus driven southwest, running before the wind to the leeward of a small island named Clauda. There we managed with a good deal of effort to haul onboard the landing skiff we had in tow, which the waves would otherwise have smashed into the hull.

We then ran thick ropes crosswise underneath the ship to brace and undergird her in the hope of protecting ourselves, lest being blown further off course we should run aground on the sinking Syrtis Sands off the coast of Libya. And in a further effort to avoid that happening we lowered the mainsail yard, set storm sails and hove-to on a starboard tack. We were still being battered and storm-driven the next day and therefore began to lighten the ship, tossing some of the cargo overboard. When this continued yet a third day we heaved the mainsail yard into the sea with our own hands. Yet we saw neither sun nor stars for many days as the storm lay hard upon us, to the point we lost all hope of survival.

But with the food stores now mostly gone and everyone malnourished, Paul stood up in the midst and said, "I *told* you not to set out from Crete but no, you wouldn't listen to me, and now you're suffering this damage and loss. Yet cheer up – the ship will be lost but no one will die. For this night a messenger of the God I serve stood by me and said, 'Fear not, Paul, you will yet appear before Caesar and as a show of his grace God will preserve not only you but all those with you.' Therefore keep up your courage, men, because I am confident that it will turn out just as the angel told me. But first we must run aground on some island."

At midnight of the 14th night of our voyage and still being driven about in the Sea of Adria the sailors heard breakers ahead and suspected we might be nearing some land. Using a lead line to take soundings they measured the depth at 20 fathoms. Going on a little further they measured the depth at 15 fathoms. Fearing we might be swept leeward onto the rocky places they dropped four anchors through hawseholes off the stern of the ship and wished for the daylight to come. At the same time, the sailors were of a mind to abandon the ship and as a pretext even let down the skiff, saying they were going to carry out anchors from the bow. But Paul told the centurion and his soldiers, "Unless these men stay onboard the ship none of you will be saved." So before the sailors could get into the skiff the soldiers cut the lines and let it drift away.

While they waited for daybreak Paul called on everyone to take something to eat. "It's been two weeks that we've abstained from food and I'm urging you now to eat, because you'll need the strength. And don't worry, I promise you that not a hair on any of your heads will be lost." Having said that he took bread, gave thanks to God, broke it and ate, encouraging them to do likewise. Those onboard were 276 in total and once everyone was fully sated they took to lightening the ship yet more, throwing the rest of its provisions into the sea.

When morning came the sailors did not recognize the coastline from any past voyages. But they did spy a bay ahead with a creek opening to a sandy shore and thus decided to try to beach the ship there. Cutting the cables they left the anchors in the sea. Then they loosed the leather thongs that tied the port and starboard rudders and hoisted the foresail in order to catch the wind and drive onto the shore. But before reaching the inside of the bay the ship ran aground at a point where two seas meet and the bow stuck fast on the clay bottom. The force of the sea began to break the ship apart at the stern, which would've allowed the prisoners to escape. The soldiers proposed to kill them all rather than let any swim to freedom. But the centurion

prevented them, if only because he wished to save Paul. He then ordered anyone who knew how to swim to jump overboard and get to the land first, with the others to follow holding onto planks or whatever else they could salvage from the wreckage of the ship. And so, just as Paul had said, they all made it safe to shore.

28

Once we were gathered we came upon some of the local inhabitants, who treated us with great kindness and informed us we had landed on the island called Malta. They kindled a fire to warm us from the cold and the rain then falling. Paul set to gathering some more brushwood but as he was adding it to the fire the heat drove a viper out of the bundle and it clasped its fangs on Paul's hand. When the natives saw the viper hanging from Paul's hand they said to one another, "This man was a murderer! For though he was rescued from the sea goddess Justice has not suffered him to live." But Paul simply shook the snake off into the fire and seemed none the worse for its venom. Yet everyone stared at him, expecting him to swell up with burning fever any minute or just drop down dead. After a long time passed with nothing bad happening they changed their minds and said he was a god.

The chief ruler of the people in that place was named Publius and he welcomed us in with great hospitality, making us his guests for three days. But his father lay grievously ill with fever, suffering from dysentery, wracked with pain. Paul visited him and, having prayed, laid his hands on him - and the man was cured on the spot. When that happened all the rest on the island who were sick came forward and were healed, after which they heaped gifts and honors on us. All told we spent three months on Malta while winter passed, at which point the centurion found an Alexandrian ship marked with the sign of the Gemini, the patron saints of sailors risking shipwreck. It had taken shelter in another harbor during the period and was now able to carry us onward. As we prepared to embark, the islanders gave us full provisions for the rest of the journey, all and more than we needed.

From Malta we sailed to Syracuse, where we remained for three days. We zig-zagged thence against a westerly wind to Rhegium on the Italian mainland. But the next day a southern wind came up and in two days brought us to Puteoli, where we found certain brethren who had gotten news of our coming. We were able to stay with them for a week and then went on by land toward Rome. Some brethren from there who had also heard of our travels came out to meet us at the market square in Appius and then others joined us at the Three Taverns, an inn along the way. When Paul saw these brethren he was filled with courage and cheer, giving thanks to God. Once we entered Rome itself the rest of the prisoners were handed over to the local captain but Paul was given leave to stay in his own dwelling place, though with a guard posted for security.

After three days Paul asked the local Jewish leaders to gather and once they were all together addressed them.

"Although I have done nothing contrary to the Law or the customs of our fathers I was taken as a prisoner from Jerusalem and put into the hands of the Romans. They would have released me, having interrogated me and found me guilty of nothing meriting death. But the Jewish authorities there spoke against my release, forcing me to appeal to Caesar even though I have no accusation to bring against my own people. So it is because of these charges that I wanted to speak with you because I am only here in chains on account of the Hope of Israel."

"We've received nothing in writing about you from our brothers in Jerusalem nor has anyone come here speaking evil about you. We therefore do want to listen to what you have to say because the one thing we *have* heard is that your sect is spoken against all over."

They appointed a set day for a larger group to come to Paul's lodgings to listen to him. He reasoned with them from early morning until late at night, testifying to the kingdom of God and persuading them about Jesus from the Law of Moses and from the Prophets. Now, some believed but others didn't, remaining in discord after Paul told them this –

"The Holy Spirit spoke truly to your fathers through Isaiah the prophet when he told him to go to this people and say,

You will hear with the ear but not understand
    and see with the eyes but not comprehend.
For the caul has fattened around this people's heart,
    their ears grown heavy of hearing,
their eyes shut to sight –
    lest they see with their eyes
and hear with their ears
    and understand in their heart
and turn to me and be healed.[72]

Know therefore that this message of God's salvation has now been sent to the Gentiles – and they will listen."

Paul remained in his own rented house for the next two years, paying the expenses himself. And he continued unhindered in his preaching of the kingdom of God, teaching openly and with boldness all things concerning the Lord Jesus Christ.

---

72   *Isaiah* 6:9-10.

LETTERS

TO THE ROMANS

1

I Paul write to you as a servant of Jesus Christ. I was called to be an apostle, dedicated to that work for the sake of God's good news. I'm speaking here of the message promised through God's prophets long ago in their holy writings, the story of God's own Son coming to us in bodily form through King David's bloodline. And this man, our Lord Jesus Christ, was in fact determinately marked as the Son of God by the power of the Spirit of Holiness that raised him out from among the dead. It's through Jesus that we apostles have received grace and authority to bring all nations to faith's obedience for his name's sake, among whom you in Rome are also now called to be Jesus Christ's. And so I am writing to you, beloved of God and called to be holy ones, sending grace and peace from God our Father and from the Lord Jesus Christ.

But first let me give thanks to my God through Jesus Christ for all of you, because your faith is proclaimed throughout the whole world. God is my witness - he whom I serve with my spirit in the gospel of his Son - how unceasingly I remember you always in my prayers, seeking if somehow sometime in God's will a clear path may be opened to visit you. It's my heart's desire to see you and share some spiritual gift to strengthen you. And I myself also hope to be encouraged and strengthened with you on account of the faith we share with one another. My brothers and sisters, even though I've been hindered from visiting you so far, I promise you it's often on my mind to find a way to do so. The truth is, it's been my goal to gather some fruit from you, just as I have from among the other Gentiles. I'm a debtor in that regard to the Greeks and those of other nations, to the wise and the foolish, and am therefore likewise eager to share the good news with you in Rome.

I'm not ashamed of the gospel.[1] On the contrary, it's the effective power of God bringing salvation to all who believe - with priority to the Jew but also for the Gentile - because God reveals his saving grace through the good news of Jesus, a state of righteousness attained through faith and faith alone. That's why Habakkuk wrote that whoever is made righteous by faith shall live.[2]

And God has also revealed his wrath from Heaven against both the impious and the unjust, those who suppress the truth with wrongdoing. He hasn't kept who he is a secret either. On the contrary, he's disclosed what he's like to all people. From the beginning of God's creation even things otherwise unseen have been clearly discerned – I'm referring to his unending power and divine nature – such that no one has any defense to make before the bar of his justice. Nevertheless, despite knowing who God is some people don't give him the glory or worship him. Instead, they clothe their thoughts with foolishness and darken their innermost feelings. Claiming sagacity they instead became morons,[3] building themselves idols in the form of men, birds, four-footed animals and snakes[4] – as if the glory of the incorruptible and changeless God could be found in the likeness of things that crumble and decay![5]

People like this reverse God's truths, worshiping and serving created things rather than the Creator, he who is blessed forever.[6] And because they put themselves in the thrall of idolatry God left them to the wild passions of their cultic orgies, dishonoring their own bodies

1   *Isaiah* 50:7-8.
2   *Habbakuk* 2:4.
3   *Isaiah* 19:11.
4   *Psalm* 106:19-20.
5   *Wisdom* 13-15.
6   See *Psalms* 106:19-20.

with impurity – their women trading sexual relations natural to them for those that were not, the men as well forsaking natural relations with women, burning in their desires, abusing one another, suffering within themselves the penalty due to those who stray.

And because they considered it worthless to hold God in their minds God left them to mind worthless things. Evil acts followed their evil thoughts and they were filled with every kind of injustice, wickedness, greediness, cowardice – fraught with envy, strife, deceit and malice. They became whispering gossips, slanderers, God-haters, hubristically proud, arrogant, braggarts, snare-crafters, dishonoring their parents, witless, treacherous, baby-killers, merciless.[7] Such people know that by God's command those who practice such things are worthy of death – yet they not only continue doing evil themselves but look kindly on others who do the same.

2

But what about you, going around judging other people? The fact is you have no excuse for your own behavior because you're doing the same things as those you criticize. So you're really just judging yourself. But God's judgment is true against all those who do such things. Think about this, you hypocrite: you're judging someone else for doing the same things you do – do you think you can escape God's condemnation? Will you scorn the wealth of God's kindness, his truce with mankind, his forbearance? Will you ignore the mercy he shows as he seeks to turn you from your ways? Yet with a hard and unrepentant heart you store up for yourself wrath in the day of wrath, the day God will reward each according to his deeds[8] – everlasting life to those who with patience in good works seek glory and honor and immortality, but fury and rage to those reject the truth, absorbed with themselves, won over by injustice. Dark and tightening anguish is the lot of those who revel in evil, for the Jew first[9] yet also for the Gentile. But glory and honor and peace will

---

7   Cf. Plato, Gorgias 525a.
8   Psalms 24:12, 61:13; Proverbs 24:12
9   Deuteronomy 28:53, 55, 57; Isaiah 8:22.

light on all who do good, the Jew first but also the Gentile – because God does not play favorites.[10]

What I'm saying is that people who do wrong without having the benefit of the Law of Moses will face the consequences of their sins measured against what they knew to be right and wrong, while people who know the standards laid down by Moses but do wrong anyway will be judged by the terms of God's Law. The point is that just because you hear what God says in the Law doesn't mean you're righteous in God's eyes – far from it – it's the people who *do* what God commands, whether they know the written Law or not, who will be justified.

The Goyim, who didn't receive the Law of Moses, are wild by nature. But does that mean that they aren't able to do the right thing? Of course it doesn't. And when they act in harmony with the commandments they are a Law unto themselves – in a good sense! In other words, they demonstrate that the Law's commands are in fact written on their hearts.[11] Such people know right from wrong and they face the same internal struggles as do their Jewish brothers, mediating the conflicting demands of their desires on the one hand and their consciences on the other. All of this will be revealed, even the things people *think* they have hidden, on the day God brings everyone to judgment in accordance with the gospel of Jesus Christ that I preach.

Yet here you are, surnamed a Child of Israel. You rest your hopes in the Law and have your exultation in God. You know the divine will and discern the transcendent, being well instructed from the Law. You are confident you are a guide to the blind, a light in the darkness, a teacher of those who don't know any better (whether fools or children). And you are to all outward appearance one filled with the knowledge and truth of the Law. How then do you teach others but can't teach yourself – stealing when you're telling others not to steal, committing adultery while condemning others for the same sin, robbing pagan temples[12] while saying how much you detest idols? But you dishonor the Law, breaking it at the same time you make it

---

10   *2 Chronicles* 19:7; *Ecclesiasticus* 35:12.
11   *Jeremiah* 31:33.
12   *See* Josephus, *Antiquities of the Jews* IV.8.10.

your boast – and so it is written, the Gentiles curse the name of God because of you.[13] If you keep the Law then of course you benefit from the covenant evidenced by your circumcision. But if you transgress the Law then being circumcised won't help you – you might as well be a Gentile.

By the same token, if a Gentile – otherwise outside the covenant, uncircumcised, treyf – if he observes the commandments, won't God look on him as a member of the tribe? The truth is God will condemn you because even though that Gentile may be lawless by nature he observes the commandments, while you who are circumcised and have God's written word, sin against it. God doesn't look at things the way people do. We see the outward appearance but he sees the inner heart. It therefore isn't just your outward appearance that makes you a Jew, nor circumcision alone. No, a Jew in the fullest sense is also cleansed in his heart,[14] his share in the covenant vouchsafed by the Spirit not the written letter – and he has his praise from God, not men.

3

If that's the case, what's the point of being circumcised? And what's so great about being Jewish? Plenty in every way! In the first instance, the Jews have been entrusted with God's precepts. And what about those Jews who failed in that trust? Did their unfaithfulness cancel out God's own faithfulness? Of course not! God is true no matter how many people are liars, just as it is written,

> Let your righteousness, O Lord, be seen in your words
> and by them defeat those who judge you.[15]

But suppose our injustice throws God's justice into relief? Can someone then argue that God is wrong to judge us? Never! How else is God to judge the world? But still someone might ask, "Why should I

---

13   *Isaiah 52:5; Ezekiel 36:20.*
14   *Isaiah 51:7; Jeremiah 31:33.*
15   *Psalms 51:4.*

be judged a sinner if my unfaithfulness ends up redounding to his glory? Shouldn't we therefore do evil since good comes from it?" And if you can believe it, some people even allege that we're antinomians! They should be condemned for such slander.

What we are saying is much simpler – none of us is better than any other and all of us have sinned, both Jews and Gentiles. The fact is, what I'm preaching is found throughout the whole Bible –

> There's not a single righteous person,
> no one who understands,
> no one who seeks God.
> They've all gone off the track, all turned aside –
> not a one has the milk of human kindness.[16]
> Their throat is an open grave, their
> tongues a snare,[17]
> their lips a viper's sting,[18]
> their mouths all curses and gall,[19]
> their feet on the run to shed blood,
> their pathways strewn
> with doom and destruction.
> They hate peace[20]
> and have lost the fear of God.[21]

We know that whatever things are said in the Law are spoken to those who possess the Law, in order that every contrary voice be silenced and the whole world stand under the judgment of God. And there is simply no way anyone can earn righteousness or be justified in God's eyes by ritual observances.[22] Instead, the Law itself brings our sins out to the open, showing precisely what's right and what's wrong.

It is now plain in the Law and the Prophets that God justifies

---

16 *Psalms* 14:1-3, 53:1-3; *Ecclesiastes* 7:20; W. Shakespeare, *Macbeth* 1.5.18.
17 *Psalms* 5:9.
18 *Psalms* 140:3.
19 *Psalms* 107.
20 *Isaiah* 59:7-8; *Proverbs* 1:16.
21 *Psalms* 36:1.
22 *Psalms* 143:2.

us in his sight *apart* from the Law's requirements,[23] God's righteousness being imputed to us through faith in the Anointed Jesus. This is God's gift given freely to all who believe, without distinction between Jews and Gentiles. Why? Because *all* have sinned and fallen short of the glory of God. Our only source of justification, our only means of redemption from sin, comes as a gift through Jesus. God in his timeless purpose provided Jesus as a propitiatory offering at the place of atonement, made effective through faith in his blood. How is that? Because God accepted Jesus' death in remission of past sins passed over in his forbearance, showing his justice now at the appointed time in justifying those who trust in Jesus.

What is there left to brag about on our part? Nothing, boasting is excluded. But by what sort of law? That of ritual observances? No, by the law of faith. In other words, we recognize that no one is found righteous before God by observing the Law's obligations but only by faith. And this rule applies to everyone since there isn't one God for the Jews and another for the Gentiles: there is but one God and he acquits both the circumcised and the uncircumcised through faith. Do you think we're destroying the Law by saying this? Not in the least. In fact, we're upholding it.

4

Let me explain what I mean, using our ancestral forefather Abraham as the example. He was considered righteous in God's eyes. If that was on account of the good deeds he did he would've had reason to boast about it (to men, anyway, if not to God). But that's not what we're told. On the contrary the passage of Scripture says that Abraham believed God and God counted his faith as righteousness.[24] It's clear that when someone earns a salary by working, the money paid to him is paid as a debt by the one he works for – it's not a gift. It follows that the righteousness God attributes to those who do not strive to earn it by the things they do comes *not* as a debt God

---

23   *E.g., Genesis* 15:6; *Habakkuk* 2:4.
24   *Genesis* 15:6.

owes them but as his gift to those who believe in him, the acquitter of the ungodly.

This is also what King David says of the blessing that comes to the man God deems righteous *apart* from his actions,

> Blessed are they whose transgressions are forgiven,
>   whose sins are covered over,
>   and blessed is the man whose sin
>   the Lord will not count against him.[25]

Is this blessing available just to the circumcised or is it also to the uncircumcised? We say, after all, that Abraham's faith was accounted to him as righteousness.[26] But when did that come about? Before or after he was circumcised? It must have been when he still had his foreskin, because its removal was just an outward sign confirming the righteousness God credited to him *before* he was circumcised.[27] Thus Abraham became the father to all who believe, those who are likewise deemed righteous whether circumcised or not - in other words, to all who follow in Abraham's footsteps, trusting God by faith as he did before his own circumcision.

That's why I said we aren't destroying the Law but upholding it: God's promise to Abraham and his descendants - that they would inherit the Earth - didn't come by means of the Law but through the righteousness God attributed to Abraham when he believed that promise. Again, faith would be useless and God's promise meaningless if the only ones who could receive that inheritance were those who depend on the Law. Why? Because the Law brings wrath, revealing sin not grace. That's the whole reason the promise comes by faith - it's God's gift by grace. That way it is guaranteed to everyone who trusts God as did Abraham, not just those who are his natural offspring and also received the Law. In this sense, Abraham is father to all of us. That's why it is written, I have made you the father of many nations[28] - meaning that in God's sight we are all children of Abraham, those of us who've trusted God.

---

25   *Psalms* 32:1-2.
26   *Genesis* 15:6.
27   *Genesis* 17:11.
28   *Genesis* 17:5.

This is the same God who gives life to the dead, calling into existence things that do not exist. Abraham, you see, trusted God even when it seemed hopeless that he would in fact become the father of many nations. After all, God had told him that these nations would spring from his own sperm cells[29] – but he was pushing 100, his body was as good as dead and Sarah's womb wasn't in any better shape. Yet Abraham was strengthened in his faith. Neither did he harbor unbelief, doubting God's promise, but continued to give glory to God, fully convinced that God was able to do everything he promised.

So that's why we say his faith was counted in his favor as righteousness.[30] Most importantly, it wasn't just written for Abraham's sake that his faith was counted to him as righteousness. It was written down for us as well, to whom righteousness will likewise be imputed because we trust in him who raised Jesus our Lord from the dead – Jesus, who was betrayed because of our sins but raised for our acquittal.

5

Having been made righteous by faith we are therefore now at peace with God through our Lord Jesus Christ, through whom we may also approach God thanks to the grace in which we abide, rejoicing in confident hope of the glory of God. Not only that but we even glory in our sufferings – not because we're masochists, of course, but because we know that distress builds patience, patience builds character and character builds hope. And we will never be ashamed if we have hope, because God's love is poured out in our hearts by the Holy Spirit given to us. God gave proof of his love for us by sending the Savior at the appointed time and in our greatest weakness to die for us ungodly people. It's scarce to find someone ready to trade his life to save the upright – though some will hazard themselves for the kind. But God proves his love in that the Savior died for us though we were still mired in our sins. Much more than that, having now been rescued from our sins through his blood we will be spared God's just anger.

---

29 *Genesis* 15:5.
30 *Genesis* 15:6.

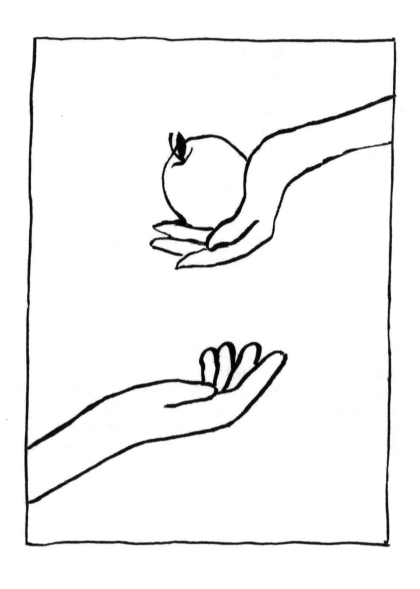

Let me say it again – we were reconciled to God by the death of his Son even though we had been his enemies. And now being brought into friendship with God we shall be saved through his life. And now that we've been received into God's favor we can honestly glory in him through our Lord Jesus Christ, who reconciled us to him.

Some background might help. The way all this came about is that sin first entered the world through one man, and through sin, death. Moreover death came to everyone because all sinned by virtue of Adam. Sin was therefore present and active in the world before the Law was given. Now, sin was not charged against people in the absence of the Law, but death as sin's consequence *did* rule men's lives from the time of Adam to Moses. This was the case even as to those who didn't trespass in the same way Adam did – Adam being a prefiguring, or type, of the one who was to come.

Yet the gift of God's grace is different in measure from the original violation. Because of Adam's transgression many died. But the grace of God overflowed to the many through the gift given in grace by the one man, the Anointed Jesus. And the results of God's gift are also unlike those of one man's sin: the guilty verdict brought death because of one man's sin but the acquittal was God's free gift despite the sins of many. So if one man's misstep gave death the power to rule, much more shall those who receive abounding grace and God's gift of righteousness rule in endless life through one man, Jesus Christ. In other words, in God's economy one trespass led to judgment against all; but one righteous act meant the acquittal of all, resulting in life everlasting. Therefore as through the one man's disobedience many were made sinners, now through the one man's obedience the many will be made righteous.

The Law was added to intensify sin, throwing it into relief. But where sin increased grace increased beyond measure so that where sin had ruled with death its outcome now grace might rule through righteousness, with *its* outcome life beyond time through our Lord and Savior Jesus.

6

How are we to respond to all this? Should we dig ourselves deeper into sin assuming that grace will increase that much more? God forbid! How can we think of living in sin now that it's been put to death in us? Surely you know that when we were baptized into Jesus Christ we were baptized into his death. We were buried with him that just as he was raised from the dead by the glorious power of the Father we too should conduct ourselves in a new way of life.

Now, if we were joined together in the likeness of his death so shall we also share in the likeness of his resurrection. Our former selves were crucified with him to destroy sin's power working in our bodies. Thus were we freed from bondage to it – since anyone who's died is released from bondage. If we've died with Christ we are therefore confident we shall also live with him. The Savior, after all, cannot die again but is raised from the dead – death has no hold on him. And the death he died was a death to sin once, finally and for all time, while the life he lives he lives unendingly to God. In the same way account yourselves dead to sin but alive to God in Christ Jesus.

Don't let sin control your mortal selves – which is what happens when you submit to corrupted desires. And don't let your bodies become weapons of injustice on sin's behalf. Instead, give your bodies and souls over to God as his instruments of righteousness, as those who live having once been dead. So get this straight – sin doesn't run your lives anymore. You're not under the condemnation of the Law but are rather the objects of his unmerited grace.

Now does that mean we might as well keep sinning since we're not subject to the condemnation of the Law but live under grace? Once again I say, God forbid! You've got to serve somebody: if you serve sin your reward will be death; but if God, his righteousness. So thank God that even though you were once sin's servants you were delivered to a sound form of teaching and took it to heart obeying it. Thus you became servants of righteousness, freed from the tyranny of evil. Let me try to put it in more human terms, given the weakness of your understanding: just as you once indentured your bodies to the mastery of wickedness and iniquity leading to lawlessness, so now present them as servants of righteousness leading to sanctification.

When you served sin you were free, in one sense, from justice. But what good did it do you? Nothing. And I know you're ashamed of your past because it was leading you to death. But what a contrast now! Having been freed from sin's dominion you've become bondsmen to God with the fruit of your servitude holiness and *its* fruit life without end. For the wages of sin is death; but the gift of God is eternal life through Jesus Christ our Lord.

7

Let me speak to you, my Roman brothers, as people familiar with legalities. You know, don't you, that laws only govern during life? For example, the law binds a woman to her living husband but if he dies she's free of that tie. That's why if she runs off with another man while her husband's still alive people will call her an adulteress – but once he dies she's no adulteress if she's joined another, being free of the former legal constraints. The spiritual comparison here is that you were crucified to the Law through Christ's body, free to be wed to another, even to him who was raised from the dead, all in order that we now might bear fruit to God. Before we died to the Law we were always subject to our natural passions and desires. These were energized by the Law and worked through our bodies and minds to make us unproductive to God. But now we've been loosed from those bonds, dead to the Law's condemnation, freed to serve God in the new life of the Holy Spirit rather than in subjection to written commands.

What's the upshot of all this? Does it mean that the Law itself is sin? Of course not. The point I'm making is that apart from the Law I wouldn't have fully perceived the import of sin working in me. For example, while I desired things that belonged to other people I didn't recognize my covetousness as a direct transgression of God's will until the 10th commandment said, Thou shalt not covet.[31] Sin thus found means through the commandment to energize all *kinds* of rebellious desires within me, because without the letter of the Law sin cannot spring into action. I was alive before the Law hit home – but once it did, sin flourished in me and I died, finding the commandments to be deadly for me

---

31   *Exodus* 20:17; *Deuteronomy* 5:21; *cf. Genesis* 3.

even though God's Word itself is life. In other words, sin took occasion through the commandment to deceive me and by it slew me.

Now the Law itself is holy and the commandments holy, just and good. So am I saying that something good became death to me? Not at all. My point is that sin – in order that it be revealed for what it is – wrought death by means of that which was good, becoming exceedingly sinful as it worked in me to *resist* the commandments. We all know that the Law is spiritual but I'm just fleshly and under sin's thumb. I have a wish to do what's right but lacking the strength to resist I end up doing things I know in my heart to be wrong. But this also shows that I recognize the Law's truths even though I don't obey them, because the Law *also* disapproves of the things I know to be wrong.

With sin's power overpowering my will it's clear that nothing good dwells in me (in my flesh, that is). That's why when I find something good I'd like to do I can't always carry it out – even worse, I not only don't do the good thing I'd like to do but then I go and do something I'd rather *not* have done. And if I'm doing things I know I shouldn't be doing it's plain that there's a defect in my will. What I find is that my wish to do good is subject to a stronger force pressing me to do evil. My innermost soul embraces God's Law – but I perceive a different kind of law at war within me, battling against the Law my mind delights in and holding me captive to the rule of sin and death that is in my members. What a miserable state of affairs is this! And so I ask myself, "Who will rescue me from the body of this death?" For in the depths of my soul I serve the Law of God but my carnal nature remains slave to sin's rule.

8

Yet thanks be to God there is no more condemnation to those who are in Christ Jesus. Why? Because in the Anointed Jesus I've been set free to live according to the rule of the life-giving Spirit, no longer sold as a slave and bound to follow the desires of my carnal nature, no longer subject to the rule of sin and death. The Law was unable to defeat sin's power because it had to act through the weakness of my corrupted self. God therefore sent his own Son, who assumed the

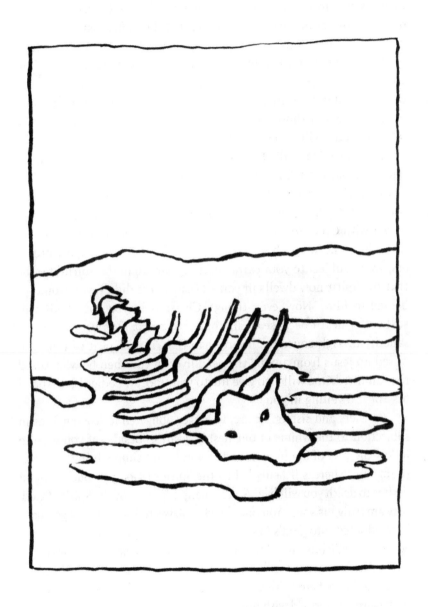

likeness of sinful flesh in order to put away sin. And Jesus triumphed over sin's power in the flesh to the end that the righteousness requirements of the Law might be fully accomplished in us – we who live lives led by the Spirit, not lending our minds and bodies to the law of sin and death. It's plain that those who live their lives in subjection to their natural desires are always focused on whatever their minds and bodies crave; but those who subject themselves to the Spirit are free to mind God's will as revealed by his Spirit.

It follows from all that I've said that death is the payoff for a purely carnal life while peace and life unending are the gift of God to those who live according to the Spirit. I say it again – if you put your mind to the service of your natural desires you'll find yourself at war with God. You won't be subject to God and on your own you won't have the strength or ability to please him. But you, my brothers, aren't subject to your carnal natures but are in the Spirit, if so be that the Spirit now dwells in you – because if it didn't, you wouldn't belong to him. Now, even though Christ is in you your body will still suffer death because of sin, but your spirit lives because of his sanctifying righteousness. More than that, if the Spirit of him who raised up Jesus from among the dead lives in you then he who raised the Anointed One will also give life to your mortal bodies by virtue of his Spirit dwelling in you.

Brothers and sisters, we are no longer obligated to live our lives in subjection to the whims of our fleshly desires. Besides, if you were to follow the rule of sin in your bodies you would simply bring death on yourselves, whereas if being led by the Spirit of God you put wrongful desires to death you will live. And as many as are led by the Spirit of God, they are truly his sons. You once lived as slaves to fear but now you have been adopted into God's family, enabled by the Spirit to call out אַבָּא – which in English means, "my Father." And the Spirit itself confirms to our spirit that we are God's children and if children also heirs, heirs of God and fellow heirs with Christ – seeing that we suffer as he suffered, so may we be glorified with him.

Yet as far as I'm concerned the sufferings of this present time aren't worth comparing to the glory that will be revealed in us. Indeed, the natural world itself eagerly awaits this revelation, this unveiling of the sons of God. What do I mean by that? I'm saying that God's creation – the

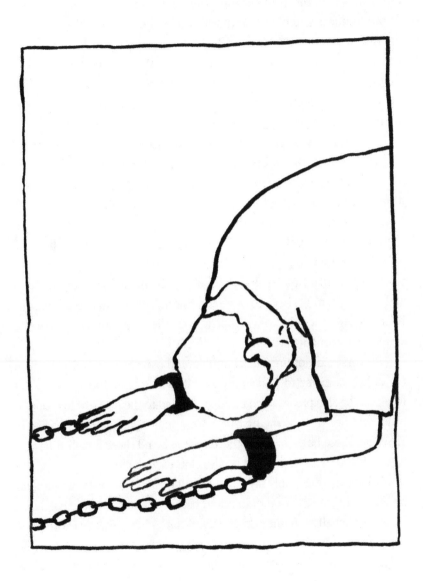

physical world, the animals and other creatures in it - was subjected to randomness and corruption not as its willed purpose but in hope, because creation *itself* will be set free from this law of decay into the freedom of the glory of God's children.[32] We can see for ourselves that the land mourns and the grass withers, the whole creation groaning in agony together from the beginning to now - and not only the creation but we, having the first fruits of the Holy Spirit, sigh within ourselves eagerly awaiting the final redemption of our body in full manifestation of our adoption.

We've been saved with this hope in our hearts. If we were already able to see the object of our hope, why bother hoping for it? Instead, because we hope for something we cannot yet see we wait for it with patience. And though we are weak the Spirit comes to our aid: because we don't really know what we should pray for or even how to pray for it, the Spirit itself pleads before God on our behalf, interceding with sighs and yearnings beyond our expression. The one who searches our hearts knows the mind of the Spirit, that the Spirit intercedes for the saints in accordance with his will.

Rest assured, nothing can triumph over those who love God, those who are called according to God's purpose. Why? Because those whom God foreknew he also preordained to be conformed to the image of his Son[33] in order that he might be the first-born, preeminent among many brethren. Therefore those he preordained he also called; and those he called he also justified; and those he justified he also clothed with glory.

What can we possibly say in light of all this! If God be for us who can be against us? And if God didn't hold back his only Son but handed him up on our behalf, won't he also give us all things freely together with him? Who will accuse God's own elect? It is God who acquits them. Or who judges them? It is the Savior Jesus who died, after all - indeed, it is the Savior who was raised and is at the right hand of God interceding for us.[34] Can anyone or anything separate us from the love of Christ - pain? suffering? persecution? famine? destitution? danger? the sword? Just as it is written,

---

32   *Isaiah* 11:6-9, 65:17; *Hebrews* 12:27; 2 *Peter* 2:13; *Revelation* 21.
33   1 *Corinthians* 15:49.
34   *Isaiah* 50:7-8.

> For your sake we are killed all the day long,
> We are counted as sheep for the slaughter.[35]

But no, in all these things we are more than conquerors through him who loved us. For I am persuaded that neither death nor life, angels or archangels, things present or things to come, not the highest height or the deepest depth, not any powers, not any other creature – none of them will be able to separate us from the love of God which is in Christ Jesus our Lord.

9

But let me tell you the truth, speaking deep from within my spirit, I'm in constant grief and sorrow over my kinsmen, my flesh and blood, my brother Israelites, so much that if it were possible for me to trade my own place in Heaven for their salvation, I would do so. They're the ones whom God adopted. To them belong the Law and the covenants and theirs are God's promises and his rituals. They are the very children of the Patriarchs. And it is from their blood that Jesus came into the world, the Anointed One who is over all, God blessed forever, age without end.

Yet don't think for a minute that God's purposed will has failed – it has always been the case that not everyone born into Israel belongs to Israel. For example it was told Abraham that only those born of Isaac's seed shall bear your name,[36] as opposed to all whose bloodline is traceable to him. The children of God are therefore not just those derived from one man's sperm cells. Instead, God's children are reckoned according to God's promises. Such was his promised word to Abraham – I will come at this time next year and Sarah will bear a son.[37]

This was not only the case where Abraham had sex with two women and each bore a child but also when Rebecca bore two children

---

35   *Psalms* 44:22.
36   *Genesis* 21:12.
37   *Genesis* 18:10, 14.

from one sexual act. In that instance God told Isaac even before the twins were born, before they could do anything good or anything bad, that the older shall serve the younger.[38] It is thereby established that God's purposed plan is one of election and calling and is not based on anyone's deeds – as it was said, I chose Jacob and rejected Esau.[39]

How should we react to that? Does it seem that God is being unfair? No, not at all. It's the same as he said to Moses – I will have mercy on whom I have mercy, compassion on whom I have compassion.[40] That way God's kindness doesn't depend on our will or our striving but only on his mercy. And as God told Pharaoh, the only reason I lifted you to kingship was as a means to demonstrate my saving power, in order that my name be proclaimed throughout the whole Earth.[41] So he is kind to whomever he wishes and hardens whomever he chooses.

I know you want to say to me, "If that's how things are, how can he blame anyone for what they do? Who's resisting his will?" But you, mere man, who are you to answer back to God? Can the molded image say to the sculptor, "Why did you make me like this?" Or doesn't the potter have the power to fashion from clay whatever kind of vessels he wishes, one to be honored or another to be scorned?[42] And what if God, wishing both to demonstrate his anger and make known his saving power, endured with great patience vessels fit for destruction as objects of his anger in order to reveal the riches of his splendor toward vessels preassigned to glory as objects of his mercy? We being of the latter sort, he called us not only from among the Jews but also from the Gentiles, just as he spoke through Hosea,

> I will name as my people those who are not my people
> and call beloved she whom I did not love.[43]
> And where it was said to them,
> "You are not my people,"

---

38 *Genesis* 25:23.
39 *Malachi* 1:2-3.
40 *Exodus* 33:19; *cf. Exodus* 3:14.
41 *Exodus* 9:16.
42 *Jeremiah* 18:3-6; *Job* 9:12, 10:8-9; *Isaiah* 29:16, 45:9, 64:8; *Ecclesiasticus* 33:13.
43 *Hosea* 2:23.

now they will be called sons of the living God.[44]

Isaiah also cried out for Israel's sake,

> Even though the number of the children of Israel
> be as the sand of the sea
> a remnant shall be saved,
> for the Lord will accomplish his word on
> the earth, soon bringing it to a just completion.[45]

And as Isaiah foretold,

> If God Almighty had not left us a seed
> we would be just like Sodom,
> just like Gomorrah.[46]

What then should we say? That the Goyim though not pursuing God's righteousness have nevertheless laid hold of it, the very righteousness which comes of faith – while Israel though pursuing the law of righteousness fell short even of the Law that was given them. How can this be? It's because Israel sought justification from God not as a matter of faith but by ritual observance, tripping over the stumbling stone laid before them as had been written,

> Behold! I am placing a stumbling stone in Zion,
> a rock of offense,
> and whoever puts his faith in it will not be ashamed.[47]

---

44   *Hosea* 1:10.
45   *Isaiah* 10:22-23.
46   *Isaiah* 1:9.
47   *Isaiah* 8:14, 28:16.

10

Brothers and sisters, the deepest desire of my heart and my prayer for Israel is their salvation. It's certain they act with great zeal for God but not with accurate knowledge. Instead, ignoring God's justice they seek to establish their own, failing to be subject to God's righteousness. But the goal of the Law is Messiah, who brings upright status to all who believe.

Moses describes the form of righteousness that comes by way of the Law: The one who performs the deeds of the Law will find his life in them.[48] But the righteousness that comes by way of faith speaks this way: Do not say in your heart, "Who will ascend into Heaven?" or "Who will descend into the Pit?" - which being interpreted means, "Who will lead Christ down to save us?" or "Who will bring Christ back from among the dead?" Rather, faith says, the Word is in your mouth to confess, in your heart to believe[49] - this being the very word of faith we preach.

So in sum, if you confess with your mouth the Lord Jesus and believe in your heart that God raised him from the dead you will be saved. It is with the heart one believes and finds God's righteousness accomplished in him and it is with the mouth one confesses and lays hold of salvation. Indeed as the prophet wrote, everyone who believes in him will never be put to shame.[50] Simply stated, there is no difference in God's eyes between Jew and Gentile. The same Lord is Lord of all, showering riches on all who call upon him - because *everyone* who calls upon the name of the Lord will be saved.[51]

But how can people who haven't believed in him call on him? Or how can they believe in someone they've never heard of? Or how can they hear about him unless someone preaches to them? Or how can someone preach unless he's been sent out? As it is written,

---

48 *Leviticus* 18:5.
49 *Deuteronomy* 9:4, 30:12-14; *Job* 28:12-14; *Baruch* 3:29; *see Proverbs* 30:4.
50 *Isaiah* 28:16.
51 *Joel* 2:32 (emphasis added).

how beautiful upon the mountains are the feet of him that bringeth good tidings, that publisheth peace.[52]

Yet the truth is, not everyone has responded to the good news they've heard. Thus Isaiah says, Lord, who hath believed our report?[53] Even so, faith comes from hearing and hearing through the Savior's voice. So I ask, "Haven't they heard?" Indeed they have, because their voice has gone out to the world at large and their message to the ends of inhabited land.[54] But I say, "Didn't Israel know?" In the first instance Moses says, I will make you jealous of a nothing people, angry on account of a foolish nation.[55] And then Isaiah dares to say, I was found by those who weren't even looking for me, revealed to those who weren't asking for me.[56] But with regard to Israel he says, all day long I have reached out my hands to a faithless and contrary people.[57]

11

Do you think that God has pushed aside his chosen people? That could never be! Indeed I myself am an Israelite, a direct descendant of Abraham through his son Isaac and Isaac's son Jacob and Jacob's son Benjamin - therefore God has not cast off his people,[58] having foreknown them. Recall what the Scriptures say in telling the history of Elijah, how he pleaded with God against Israel saying, Lord, they've killed your prophets, torn down your altars, and now I'm the only one left and they're coming after me![59] But what was the divine response to him? You're *not* the only one left. I've kept for myself 7,000 men who have not bowed down to the demon god Ba'al.[60]

---

52 *Isaiah* 52:7; *Nahum* 1:15.
53 *Isaiah* 53:1.
54 *Psalms* 19:4.
55 *Deuteronomy* 32:21.
56 *Isaiah* 65:1.
57 *Isaiah* 65:2.
58 *Psalms* 94:14; *1 Samuel* 12:20-23.
59 *1 Kings* 19:10, 14.
60 *1 Kings* 19:18.

Same now: there is at present a remnant according to God's gracious election. If the election is according to grace then it's not a question of anyone's actions – otherwise what would be the point of grace? What then? Israel itself did not find what it searched for. Instead the elect obtained it while the hearts of the rest were hardened just as is written,

> He gave them a spirit of deep sleep,
> > their eyes not seeing,
> their ears not hearing,
> > even until today.[61]

So too says David,

> Let the feast they spread become a snare and a net,
> > a hindrance to them, their recompense.
> Let their eyes be darkened lest they see,
> > their backs continually stooped down.[62]

But have they stumbled that they should fall? God forbid! Rather through their trespass salvation has come to the nations in order to provoke Israel to jealousy. And if Israel's transgression occasioned riches to the world and their loss wealth to the Gentiles, how much greater will their restoration be!

I'm speaking now to you Gentiles. I honor my ministry as apostle to the uncircumcised by hoping I may somehow provoke my own flesh and blood to be jealous of what's now been given to you and thereby save some among them. And if their rejection means the reconciliation of the world what will it mean when they are received back but the resurrection of the dead?

If the offering baked from the first fruits of the wheat harvest is holy so is the rest of the dough[63] and if the root of the tree is holy so are the branches. Now be sure you don't lord it over the branches just

---

61 *Deuteronomy* 29:4; *Isaiah* 29:10.
62 *Psalms* 69:22-23, 35:8.
63 *Leviticus* 23:9-14; *Numbers* 15:18-21.

because some of them were broken off and you – born of a wild olive tree – were grafted in among the rest of the branches and now share together in the root, which is the richness of the good olive tree. Remember, you don't bear up the root – it's the root that bears you. But you've been saying, "Branches were broken off so *I* could be grafted in." That's true as far as it goes in that they were broken off for lack of faith and you were grafted in, standing firm in faith. Yet don't be so high and mighty about this but rather be afraid – because if God was willing to let go some of the natural branches do you really think you're any more secure?

Herein lies both the mercy and severity of God: severity toward those who have fallen but God's mercy toward you (if you abide in kindness, that is, lest you too be cut off). But the Children of Israel as well, if they do not remain in unbelief, will be grafted in because God is more than able to graft them in again. Just think about it: if you were cut from the wild olive tree to which you belong by nature and grafted into the cultivated olive tree then how much more will the native stock flourish when grafted back to their own olive tree?[64]

Listen carefully my brothers and sisters. I don't want you to be ignorant of what was once hidden but is now revealed lest you be wise in your own conceits: a partial hardening has fallen on Israel until the full measure of Gentiles shall have come in. Thus all Israel will be saved as is written,

> A Deliverer will come out of Zion,
> > turning godlessness from Jacob.
> And this will be my covenant with them,
> > when I take away their sins.[65]

So as far as the gospel is concerned they are at enmity for your benefit but with regard to the election they are beloved by reason of the Patriarchs – because God's gifts and calling are irrevocable. And just as you were at one time disobedient to God but have now

---

64   Cf. *Odyssey* V.476-77.
65   *Isaiah* 59:20-21.

been granted mercy through their disobedience, so too they have now disbelieved in order that through God's mercy to you they may also receive mercy. And thus God enclosed all in unbelief that he might have mercy on all.

O the depth of the riches and wisdom and knowledge of God, how unfathomable his judgments, how unknowable his ways!

> For who has known the mind of the Lord?
> Or who was his counselor?[66]
> Who gave anything to him?
> Whom does he need to repay?[67]

Nay, all things are from him and through him and for him – and to God be the glory for all ages, amen.

12

Brothers and sisters for all these reasons I exhort you through the mercies of God to present your whole selves in service to God, living sacrificially and in a manner holy and well pleasing to him. Don't look to whatever the current mode of thinking is as a blueprint for your own behavior but be continually transformed by the renewing of your mind. That way you'll be able to recognize for yourselves what God's will is for you – that which is good, perfect and well pleasing to him.

Let me say to all of you by virtue of the grace given me: don't think more highly of yourselves than you should but rather make a good estimate of yourselves, giving heed to the measure of faith God apportioned to you. Consider our bodies for a moment. We have one body with many parts to it but not all parts function the same way. So too we many are one body in Christ and each of us members of the others, each having a different skill gifted us as a matter of grace. If we prophesy, let us do so in proportion to our

---

66 *Isaiah* 40:13.
67 *Job* 41:3.

faith; if we assist in the practical needs of the congregation let us do so in service to one another; if we teach let us be attentive to our manner of instruction; if we are called to encourage someone let us do so in a comforting way. Whoever is in charge of distributing money, food, clothing and the like must do so with simplicity and generosity; whoever administers the affairs of the church must be diligent in its business; and whoever cares for the sick and the aged, let them do so with good cheer.

Let your love be sincere. Reject that which is evil. Cling to what is good. Love one another with brotherly love, in honor preferring one another over your own selves. Don't be lazy but jump up to do good, bubbling over with the Spirit, serving the Lord. Rejoice in hope. Endure any suffering. Devote yourselves to prayer. Take care of the needs of those in the church but also be graciously hospitable to strangers. Bless those who would persecute you – bless them, do not curse. Rejoice with those who rejoice, weep with those who weep. Let your minds be in harmony with one another.

Don't look up to the powerful but link arms with the downtrodden. And again, be sure not to think too highly of yourselves. Don't repay evil with evil. Think ahead of time what will be just and right in the sight of all. Be at peace with everyone if it's at all possible to do so. Don't worry about taking revenge, beloved ones, but give a wide berth to anger. The Lord has said, I will exact justice, I will repay.[68] So instead,

> If your enemy is hungry, feed him;
>   if he is thirsty, give him something to drink;
> for by doing so it is as if you were heaping burning coals
>   upon his head.[69]

Don't let evil overcome you but overcome evil with good.

---

68   *Deuteronomy* 32:35.
69   *Proverbs* 25:21, 22.

13

Keep yourselves in orderly submission to the authorities. From time to time they're in charge of things but the only power they have comes from God and he establishes limits to their rule. So don't stand in opposition to rightful authorities lest you find yourself resisting God's own ordinance and just end up bringing judgment on yourselves. Good rulers, after all, shouldn't cause fear to those who do good only to those who work ill. Therefore if you wish to be free from fear of those in power, do the right thing. Who knows, you might even earn praise from them, being God's servants for your good.

But if you break the law, watch out! They don't carry weapons for nothing. Rather, they're God's servants to punish evil, executing wrath against those who do wrong. That's why it's necessary that we submit ourselves to them not only on account of their wrath but much more as a matter of good conscience. And that's another reason you need to pay your taxes - government officials are also God's servants to provide for the common good. Basically, pay what you owe - taxes to the taxman; duties to the customs officer; fear to whom fear is due; and honor to whom honor.

Owe nothing to anyone (other than to love one another, of course) because in doing so you fulfill the whole Law. Commandments such as don't commit adultery, don't murder, don't steal, don't covet[70] - and all the other commandments for that matter - are summed up in love your neighbor as yourself.[71] Love works no ill toward one's neighbor. Therefore love is the Law's full measure.

Knowing where we are in the sweep of history, it's high time for you to wake up because our salvation is nearer now than when we first believed. Night is on the wane and dawn approaches. Let's therefore lay aside the hidden deeds of darkness and clothe ourselves with the armor of light, walking about soberly in the daytime - not in Bacchic revels or excess drinking, not sleeping around or going to

---

70   *Exodus* 20:13-15, 17; *Deuteronomy* 5:17-19, 21.
71   *Leviticus* 19:18.

orgies. Avoid all strife and jealousy. And don't spend your time planning how to satisfy your fleshly desires but clothe yourselves instead with the Lord Jesus Christ.

14

Accept to your fold those who may be weak in confidence about their faith but don't get involved in trivial disputes with them. For example, one person might have confidence now that he's a Christian that he's permitted to eat any kind of food while another, lacking that confidence, thinks he should only eat vegetables. But whoever feels he can eat any kind of food at all must not look down on the one who doesn't. Neither should the one who abstains judge the one who eats. God has accepted her so who are you to judge someone else's servant? She stands or falls to the same master as you. And they *will* stand, because God is able to make them stand.

Again, some people believe they should treat one day as more special than another as far as their worship of God is concerned. Others think all days are the same in God's eyes. Let each be fully convinced in her own mind. That way whoever observes a given day as holy can be confident she does so for the Lord. Same with food - whoever eats meat eats in reverence to the Lord because he gives grace to God, while whoever abstains from meat abstains in reverence to the Lord because he too gives him thanks.

No one lives for himself alone and no one dies for himself alone - if we live we live unto the Lord and if we die we die unto the Lord. Therefore whether we live or die we are the Lord's. Indeed for this very reason Christ died and lived again, that he might be Lord of the living and the dead.

So I ask, what's up with you, judging your brothers and sisters? Or how is it that you look down on them? We will all stand before God's judgment seat as is written,

> As I live, saith the Lord,
>> every knee shall bow to me
> and every tongue shall confess to God.[72]

Therefore we all must give account of ourselves to God.

Let's stop judging one another. Decide this instead: that none of you puts a stumbling block or temptation in your brother's or sister's path. I know and am persuaded in the Lord Jesus that nothing in creation is ritually unclean in itself – but if someone considers something to be so then it is unclean for him. Therefore if you cause grief to your brother over food you're hardly walking in love. Don't destroy your brother, for whom Christ died, over a matter of ritual practice.

Don't let God's good news be evil-spoken of. The kingdom of God is not meat and drink but justice, peace and joy in the Holy Spirit. If you serve God in *these* things you'll be pleasing to God and respected by others. Follow after things that are peaceful, things that will build one another up. But please don't tear down God's work for the sake of food! All things are clean except to the one who eats while giving offense to his brother. It would be good neither to eat meat nor drink wine nor do anything else that causes your brother to stumble.

Do you have faith? Have it to yourself before God. Blessed is she who doesn't judge herself as to the things of which she approves. But whoever wavers in what she eats is judged because she does not eat in faith. So it's just plain sinful to act without the confidence that faith provides.

15

We who are strong shouldn't worry about looking after ourselves but should carry the burdens of those who are weaker. And we should take care to encourage our neighbors, building them up, providing for

---

72 *Isaiah* 45:23; 49:18.

their good. The Savior, as you know, did not look to please himself; but as it is written, I bore the hatred of those who hated you.[73]

Whatever things were written beforehand were written for our instruction so that through the Scriptures we might have hope and patience. May the God of patience and hope give you the same mind toward one another as was in Christ Jesus, that being of one mind together you may with one mouth glorify God and the Father of our Lord Jesus Christ.

That's why you must accept one another, just as Christ accepted you for the glory of God: the Anointed One became a servant of the Hebrew people for the truth of God in order to confirm the promises made to the Patriarchs and to the further end that the Gentiles might glorify God for his mercy, as it is written,

> Therefore I will confess you among the nations
> and sing your praise with my mouth.[74]

And again he says,

> Rejoice, you Gentiles, together with his people.[75]

And,

> Praise the Lord, all you nations,
> and let all the peoples praise him.[76]

And Isaiah says,

> There shall be a shoot springing up from Jesse,
> rising up to rule over the nations,
> and the Gentiles will rest their hopes in him.[77]

---

73   *Psalms* 69:9.
74   *Psalms* 18:49.
75   *Deuteronomy* 32:43.
76   *Psalms* 117:1.
77   *Isaiah* 11:10.

So too may God, the source of hope, fill you with all joy and peace in believing, that you may overflow with hope by the power of the Holy Spirit.

My brothers and sisters, I myself am persuaded that you are in your own right full of generosity and goodness, filled with all knowledge, able to instruct one another. And I know I've written to remind you of certain matters in a style perhaps bolder than what you're used to. But I do so by virtue of the grace given me by God to be Jesus Christ's minister to the Gentiles, serving the gospel of God in holiness to the end that the offering of the Gentiles may be found acceptable to God, sanctified by the Holy Spirit. This boasting I have in my service to Christ Jesus is pride in God alone. I wouldn't dare speak about anything other than what Christ has accomplished through me to bring the Gentiles into obedience – in word and in deed, in the power of signs and wonders, in the power of the Spirit. The result is that from Jerusalem and its surrounds to the Province of Illyricum I have fully preached the gospel of Christ, taking it as a point of honor to preach where the Savior is not known so as not to build on some other man's foundation but rather as is written,

> Those who have not been told about him will see; and
> those who have not heard about
> him will understand.[78]

And that's why I've been diverted from coming to you these many times. But no longer having any matters to attend to in these regions it's my deep desire to visit you after so many years. My hope is to pass through Rome to see you as I journey on toward Spain, being helped by you on my way after spending some time together. I must first leave for Jerusalem to minister to the saints there because the churches in Macedonia and Achaia were pleased to make a distribution in common to aid their brothers and sisters in Jerusalem, who are now impoverished. That is as it should be because the Gentiles

---

78 *Isaiah* 52:15.

are their debtors – that is to say, given that the Goyim share in the spiritual blessings of their Hebrew brethren it's also their duty to assist them in their physical needs. But once I've taken care of this and confirmed the gift to them, I will head in your direction *en route* to Spain. And I know I will be coming to you with the fullness of the blessing of Christ.

Brothers and sisters I ask you through our Lord Jesus Christ and through the love of the Spirit to strive together with me in your prayers to God for me, that I be delivered from those in Judea who are disobedient; that my service in Jerusalem be welcomed by the saints there; and that I come to you in joy, able to take some rest with you, all in accordance with the will of God.

May the God of peace be with you all, amen.

16

By this letter I also want to commend our sister Phoebe to you. She is a deacon of the church in the Corinthian port of Cenchrae. I ask that you welcome her in the Lord in a manner worthy of the saints. Extend help in whatever matters may concern her because she's been a stalwart help to many, including me.

Greet Prisca and Aquila for me, my co-workers in Christ Jesus, who put their own necks on the line to guard my life, to whom not only I but all the Gentile churches are grateful as well as those in their own house-church. And greet my beloved Epaenetus, who is Asia's first fruit in Christ. Say hello as well to Marian, who has worked hard for your sakes. Andronicus and his wife Junia – be sure to give them my best – they're not only from my hometown but have also been my fellow prisoners. These two are outstanding among the apostles and were born into Christ before I was.

And Ampliatus, greet him too, well-loved of me in the Lord. Don't forget to give my greetings to Urbanus, another of our co-laborers in Christ, and also to Stachys, whom I love. Then there's Apelles, tried and true in Christ – please greet her as well. And do embrace the family of the late Aristobulus.

Bear with me a little more – I also need to give a shout-out to my cousin Herodion. And of course similar greetings to everyone in Narcissus' house, at least those who are in the Lord. I've also got the twin sisters Tryphaena and Tryphosa on my prayer list so don't forget to pass my goodwill on to them – they've nearly worn themselves out in their service to the Lord – and the same goes for my beloved Persis, as she too has toiled to the point of weariness.

Warm greetings to Rufus – elect in the Lord – and also to his mother, who's been like a mother to me. Please add to this list Asyncritus, Phlegon, Hermes, Patrobas, Hermas and all the brothers with them. Then there's Philogus and his wife Julia, their son Nereus and his sister Olympas, and all the saints who gather with them. Greet one another with a holy kiss. And finally, all the churches of Christ send their greetings to you.

I urge you, brothers, watch out for those who stir up conflict and lay down traps, spreading teachings contrary to those you've been given. Keep out of their way! People like that don't serve our Lord Christ but are just in it for themselves – and it's by smooth talking and flattery that they manage to trick the hearts of the innocent. But your own obedience is known to all and so I rejoice in you. I wish you to be wise as to what is good and innocent as to what is evil. The God of peace will soon crush Satan under your feet. May the grace of our Lord Jesus be with you.

My co-worker Timothy greets you as do my kinsmen Lucius, Jason and Sosipater. Gaius also says hello – he is my host and indeed not mine alone but extends his hospitality to the whole church. Erastus the city treasurer also sends greetings, as does brother Quartus.

And finally I, Tertius, greet you in the Lord – I'm the one who drafted this letter to you as Paul's amanuensis.

Now to the one who is able to strengthen you in accordance with my gospel – the saving message of Jesus Christ, God's revelation of the mystery which though silent for ages has now been openly proclaimed, confirmed through prophetic writings and made known to all nations by command of the everlasting God to the end that all might be brought into obedience by faith – to God alone wise be glory through Jesus Christ forever and ever, amen.

FIRST LETTER TO THE CORINTHIANS

1

To the assembly of God gathered in Corinth, to all you who are being purified in Christ Jesus and bear the name "saints" – indeed, to all those everywhere who call on the name of the Lord – I Paul send grace and peace from God our Father and the Lord Jesus Christ.

I write this letter by the hand of our brother Sosthenes, sending it by authority of my own calling as one of Jesus' apostles according to God's will. I want you to know that I am always grateful to God for the gifts he has given you, enriching you in doctrine and knowledge, confirming the testimony of Christ among you. Indeed, you have no shortage of charismatic gifts while you await Jesus' coming Apocalypse – because he will strengthen you to the very end, to the Day of the Lord itself.

But you do have a problem. It's been made clear to me by some of the people in Chloe's house-church that you are riddled with strife, some of you saying, "I'm a member of Paul's denomination," others "I'm with Apollos," others "I'm siding with Cephas," and still others "I belong to Jesus." Now I'm begging you in Jesus' name – stop it! You need to agree with one another. Be of one mind. Speak with one voice. End your schisms.

Do you think the Savior is divided? Do you think I was crucified for you? Or were you baptized in my name, not his? The way you're acting

I'm glad I didn't baptize any of you – except for Crispus and Gaius and the servants in Stephanus' home – so no one can say he was baptized in my name. The real point is that I wasn't sent by Jesus to baptize people but to spread the good news.

And I haven't preached with words of worldly wisdom, lest the cross of Christ be emptied of its power. The very idea of the cross is absurd to those who are perishing but to us who are being saved it is the power of God. And so it is written,

> I will destroy the wisdom of the wise
> and set aside the learning of the learned.[1]

Tell me, where do you find the wise man? the scholar? the silver-tongued orator of the day? Hasn't God turned the world's wisdom into sophistry? It's part of God's own wisdom that we don't come to him by means of our own thoughts and perception but, rather, God saves those who come to faith through the foolishness of gospel preaching. So while the Jews seek signs and the Greeks crave intellect we preach a crucified Savior – an utter scandal to the Jews and nonsense to the Gentiles, but to those who are called, both Jews and Greeks, Christ the very power and wisdom of God. The truth is that in the case of God what seems foolish is wiser than men and what seems weak is stronger.

My brothers and sisters, just look around you at those who are called. You don't see a lot of people the world considers clever, not a lot of power brokers, not many from the 1%. No, God chose for himself the world's fools to shame the wise, the weak to confound the mighty. And he chose the wretched of the Earth, the off-scourings, even things that are not – all to bring down things that are to the end that no one can stand and boast in his presence. Yet thanks to him you are now joined to the Anointed Jesus, who being sent from God became for us wisdom, righteousness, holiness and redemption – so as it's written, Whoever glories let him glory in the Lord.[2]

---

1   *Isaiah* 29:14; *cf.* Aristotle, *Nicomachean Ethics* VI.7, 10.

2   *Jeremiah* 9:24.

2

That's why when I came to you I gave God's testimony plainly, without overwrought speech or intricate words. I put my mind to nothing else when among you other than the knowledge of the Jesus Christ and him crucified. And I spent my time among you in weakness, in fear, in much trembling. Nor did I preach with rhetorical twists but simply relied on the demonstrated power of the Spirit, all toward the goal that your faith be grounded not in the wisdom of men but the power of God.

However, we *do* speak wisdom among those who are full-grown in the faith. I don't mean what counts for wisdom in worldly terms, nor even what's known to the spiritual powers who now rule the world (and whose rule will one day cease). I mean God's wisdom, marked out for our glory before time began. And this mystery was hidden to the fallen spirits - because if they had perceived it they never would have crucified the Lord of Glory. But as it is written, Eye hath not seen, nor ear heard,[3] neither have entered into the heart of man, the things which God hath prepared for them that love him.

Yet God has revealed them through the Spirit to us who believe because the Spirit searches all things, even the deep things of God. The only one who really knows what's on a person's mind is that person himself. So too no one discerns the mind of God but his Spirit. We haven't received the spirit of the world but the Spirit that comes from God, in order to grasp the things God has freely given us. That's also why we don't speak academically but rather in spiritual terms, interpreting spiritual things in spiritual ways. A worldly person rejects the things that come from God's Spirit because they are foolish to him: he has no way to understand them, because they must be spiritually discerned. And so the spiritual person examines all things, while she herself is weighed by no one, save the Lord. No one has known the mind of the Lord, so as to instruct him[4] - but now through the Spirit we have the mind of Christ.

---

3   *Isaiah* 64:4, 65:16-17; *cf. 1 Clement to the Corinthians* 34:8.
4   *Isaiah* 40:13.

3

Even so, my brothers and sisters, I've been unable to speak to you as spiritual people but as those who are carnal, still babes in Christ. I've been giving you milk to drink because you lacked the strength to eat solid food – and you're still not able to do so. Why? Because as long as you are jealous of one another, as long as you harbor strife, aren't you just as bound to your corrupted nature as if you'd never been saved? And whenever one of you says, "I'm of Paul" or "I'm of Apollos," aren't you still carnal?

Who do you think Apollos is, or who Paul? We're no more than servants of the Lord through whom you came to believe, each of us given a task to that end. I planted the seed, Apollos watered the plant, but the Lord saw to its increase. The one who plants and the one who tends therefore work toward one goal. And each will be rewarded according to his labors. We may be God's field hands, but the field and its crops are the Lord's.

Let me use another illustration. I laid out the foundation using the gifts God gave me as a skilled architect,[5] but someone else built on it. Each person needs to take care how she builds, because there is only one proper foundation – the foundation of the Savior Jesus. Now, if anyone builds something on *that* foundation the Day of the Lord will reveal what sort of work it is - regardless of whether it's built of costly materials like gold, silver or precious stones, or perishable as wood, hay or stubble. Thus each person's deeds will be tested by fire.[6] If the work survives testing the builder will be rewarded. But if it's burned up she will suffer loss - although not the loss of her salvation, just as a building may be lost in a fire but its owner saved.

Aren't you aware that you're gathered as the temple of God and the Holy Spirit therefore dwells among you? If anyone corrupts the assembly of God, God shall destroy him - because you are his temple, sanctified for him. And don't deceive yourselves. If any of you thinks himself to be learned and wise let him become foolish in order that he learn true wisdom, because the wisdom of this world is foolishness to God. As it is written,

---

5   *Cf. Exodus* 31:3-5; Aristotle, *Nicomachean Ethics* VI.7.1.
6   *See Malachi* 3:2-3.

He snares the wise in their own conceits.[7]

And again,

The Lord knows the inner thoughts of the wise: t
hat they are empty.[8]

None of you should exalt mere people, because all things are yours, whether Paul or Apollos or Cephas or the world or life or death or things present or things to come. It all belongs to you – but you belong to Christ and Christ proceeds from God.

4

Think of us as the Savior's servants, stewards of God's revealed treasures. Now, people expect stewards to be faithful. But to be honest I'm not all that worried about you or anyone else calling me to account for my faithfulness. The truth is, I don't waste time focusing on how I'm doing.[9] So let's not judge anything before the Lord comes, because he will reveal the hidden things of darkness and bring to light the true counsels of the heart. And then will each person have her praise from God.

I'm using myself and Apollos as examples so that you'll learn from us not to think too highly of yourselves, let alone form separate groups in opposition to one other. What distinguishes you from anyone else after all? What have you got that you didn't get from someone else? So why are you boasting as if you've gotten where you are on your own? Oh, but you think you're all set, wealthy, sitting in the catbird's seat. If only that were true! If only you *did* reign as kings – because we'd love to reign with you.

But I've pretty much come to the conclusion that God has put us apostles in last place. We're under a death sentence. We're like clowns in a theater on public display, laid bare to be mocked, a spectacle even

---

7   *Job* 5:13.
8   *Psalms* 94:11.
9   Now, I can't for the life of me think of any way I've *failed* to be a faithful steward of these mysteries. Even so, I'm not vindicated by any self-assessment; it's God who is my judge.

before God's angels. We're taken to be fools on account of Jesus. But you, you're wise. We're weak, you're strong. You're honored, we're despised. And right now, even as I write, we're famished, parched, ragged, punched, homeless, dead-tired working our fingers to the bone. But when people curse at us, we bless them. Persecuted, we tough it out. Slandered, we speak gently. Yes, to this very day we're considered little more than scum, scapegoats for all the world's ills.

You think I'm writing this to embarrass you? I'm not. I'm just writing as I would to my own beloved children – to warn you. You've got count-less people guiding and teaching you about the Messiah, but not many fathers. The truth is I've begotten you in the Anointed Jesus through the gospel. That's why I'm calling on you to follow my footsteps and do what I do. That's also why I'm sending Timothy to you. He is my beloved son and faithful to the Lord. He'll remind you of the things I teach in every congregation everywhere concerning the Lord.

Some of you have gotten quite self-important, assuming I'll be too in-timidated by you to visit. But I will get there, and quickly, if the Lord wills. And I'll find out whether those of you who've taken charge are all hat and no cattle – because the kingdom of God is not in word but in power. What's your preference? That I come to you with the rod of correction or in love with a spirit of meekness?

5

And here's another mess. I gather there's incest in your midst that even the heathen wouldn't put up with – someone is openly having an affair with his stepmother![10] But that doesn't seem to bother you at all. On the contrary, you act as though your fellowship is healthy when you ought to be in mourning, separating yourselves from this man. For my part, how-ever, I'm present with you in the Spirit even though I'm not there in per-son. I have already passed judgment on this matter in the Lord's name: when you are gathered together, my spirit and the power of the Lord Jesus also being present, it's my direction that you yield such a person over to the Accuser that though he suffer in the body he may be saved in the Day

---

10   Cf. Cicero, *Pro Cluentio*, V.14.

of the Lord.

Your self-satisfaction is not good, my brothers and sisters. Don't you know that a little yeast causes the whole lump of dough to rise? Purge the old yeast from your midst[11] in order that you truly be new and unleavened bread – because Christ our Passover is sacrificed for us.[12] Therefore let us keep the feast not with the old leaven, which is malice and wickedness, but with the unleavened bread of sincerity and truth.

I've already written to you in a prior letter not to get mixed up with people living a flagrantly immoral life. But you apparently misunderstood me. I wasn't talking about cutting yourselves off from the rest of the world with its revels and orgies, its robber barons, its idolaters. No, you'd have to live in the desert to do that! What I meant was – stay away from people who *say* they are Christians but don't act like it. I'm telling you that if someone calls himself a brother yet goes about in riotous sex, craves wealth, worships idols, speaks nothing but filth, walks around drunk or steals from the poor – well, don't even sit down to eat with him. Do you think I bother to judge people outside the pale? That's God's task, not mine. But as for you, purge the evil from your midst.[13]

6

Here's another problem. Some of you have sued one another in the local courts. Why do you seek justice from the unjustified rather than your fellow saints? Don't you know that we who are justified will one day judge the world?[14] If you are to judge the world don't you think you can handle petty lawsuits? We will judge angels – yet you can't handle everyday matters?! Or maybe you should appoint judges from among those who otherwise don't count for much in the church.[15] Isn't *any* of you competent to judge disputes among the brethren? But one brother sues another – and that before the unbelievers!

Look, it's a failing on your part to even *have* fights like this, no matter

---

11   *See Exodus* 12:15, 13:7.
12   *Matthew* 26:17; *Mark* 14:12; *Luke* 22:7, 11, 15.
13   *Deuteronomy* 17:7, 19:19, 22:21, 22:24, 24:7.
14   *Daniel* 7:22.
15   I speak this to shame you.

who's judging them. Why don't you simply suffer injustice and let yourselves be cheated? But you, on the contrary, do wrong and defraud, and that your brothers and sisters. Or don't you know that the unjust will not inherit the kingdom of God? Don't kid yourselves: libertines, idolaters, adulterers, pederasts, pedophiles, thieves, greed mongers, lushes, slanderers, swindlers – none of them will inherit the kingdom of God. And that's what some of you were. But you washed those things off, you've been sanctified, you've been justified in the name of the Anointed Lord Jesus and by the Holy Spirit of God.

"I'm not subject to the Law," you say. True, but irrelevant – it's still the case that not everything is good for you. "I'm not a slave to rules," you say again – and yet you allow yourself to be mastered by desire. "But food is there for me to eat and my stomach craves it." Just so – and one day God will destroy both food and the belly.

And as far as sex is concerned? Well, the body is God's creation – so don't dishonor God's creation by misusing it, because God raised up Jesus by his power and will raise our bodies as well. Or are you unaware that your bodies are members of the Body of Christ? Shall I take a member of the Body of Christ and join it to a whore? God forbid! Don't you know when you have sex with a prostitute you become one body with her? For the two shall be one flesh, he said.[16] Yet he who is joined to the Lord is one spirit with him. Flee illicit sex! Every other sin that a person might commit involves things outside the body – but with wrongful sex you're sinning *against* your body. Don't you know that your body is the temple of the Holy Spirit who is in you, whom you've received from God? Because you were bought with a price you're simply not your own anymore: therefore glorify God in your body.

7

Let me address some other things you've written to me about, many of them variations on the same theme.

It sounds as though some of you are compulsive skirt chasers. You might do better to stay away from women altogether! But if you marry be sure you're faithful to your wives. And you women as well – be faithful to your husbands, because you owe each other that. Think of it this way: a man's

---

16   *Genesis* 2:24; *Matthew* 19:5.

body belongs to his wife and a woman's body to her husband. So don't deprive one another of sex. I'm speaking generally – it's fine, of course, if the two of you mutually agree to have some time apart for a prayer retreat or the like. Just be sure to resume your normal sex life thereafter and don't give the Tempter a chance to capitalize on your tendency to self-indulge.

I'm saying all this given your weaknesses rather than making any general command about marriage. But then again not everybody can be like me, obviously. Instead, we must each discern our own gifts from God – some to marry, some not. That's why I say both to those who remain single and those who are widows – you do well to remain as you are, just as I have done. Still, it's far better to marry than to sleep around, burning with uncontrollable desires.

With respect to divorce it's my instruction (and the Lord's as well) to those who are married that a wife should not part from her husband. But if she does she should either remain unmarried or be reconciled to her husband. And the same goes for a husband with respect to his wife.

For the other things you asked about I don't have any instructions from the Lord, but my own views are these. If a brother has a non-believer for a wife and she is pleased to live with him he shouldn't divorce her; and the same goes for a sister with a non-believing husband. Why? Because the non-believing husband is sanctified by his union with his wife, marriage being ordained by God from creation. And the same goes for a non-believing wife by union with her husband. If that weren't so your children would be unsanctified – but now they've been dedicated to the Lord. Yet if any non-believing spouses wish to separate themselves, let them depart. A sister or brother is not bound in such circumstances. But God has called us to peace – and how do you know, wife, whether you just might end up saving your husband; or you, husband, your wife?

The bottom line is that it's to each as the Lord has apportioned. My teaching in all the churches is therefore that people should live the best lives they can in whatever state they find themselves. For example, if anyone is called having been circumcised he shouldn't try to mask it.[17] And if uncircumcised he need hardly be circumcised. Honestly, circumcision doesn't mean anything and neither does uncircumcision – what counts is keeping the commandments of God.

Again, it's not wrong for a person to remain in the status she held

---

17   *See 1 Maccabees* 1:15.

when she was called by God. So if you came to faith while a slave don't be heartsick about that. But at the same time, if you're able to get free then certainly do so! The underlying truth is that although called as a slave you are still free in the Lord's sight and though called as free you are a slave to Christ. You were bought with a price – don't become slaves to others. In short, in whatever state you find yourselves when called, stay there side-by-side with God.

Now, you've also asked about problems you're encountering among those who have been married but are now single, and with those who've never married but are still virgins. I admit I have no commandment from the Lord. I'm therefore only giving you my best judgment as someone graced by the Lord to be faithful. In dealing with the current distress your people are experiencing I'd advise them all to hold steady, at least for now – there's nothing inherently wrong with remaining single, after all. But you men, keep this in mind – if you're joined in matrimony don't start looking for a way out. And if you've already been divorced don't rush out and marry the first girl you see. Even so, if you do remarry you haven't sinned. And likewise if a virgin marries she hasn't sinned. After all, marriage is an honorable estate, though not by any to be entered into unadvisedly or lightly; but reverently, discreetly, advisedly, soberly, and in the fear of God. Yet marriage isn't a cakewalk either, especially in times of persecution, where you will face suffering, even an early death. So all else being equal, I would spare you that.

My counsel is therefore to keep your hearts loosed from cares: though married as if unmarried; though weeping as if joyful; though joyful as if weeping; though buying as if owning nothing. And for those of you who are engaged in commerce I advise you to deal with goods most fleeting-ly – for Earth's revels shall be ended and the cloud-capp'd towers, the gorgeous palaces, the solemn temples, even the great globe itself shall dissolve.[18]

I would therefore have you free from cares. Whoever is unmarried cares for the things of the Lord, to please him. But one who is married cares for the things his wife needs, to support her – and so he finds himself with divided interests. And in the same way a woman once married but now single, as well as one who is still a virgin, will put her focus on the things of the Lord, how she may be holy in body and spirit. In contrast

---

18   W. Shakespeare, *The Tempest*, 4.1.152-54.

she who is married will be anxious over worldly things, wishing to care for her husband. I'm saying all this in an effort to help you find some sensible ways out of the present confusion. I'm in no way trying to put you in a straitjacket but rather to look for ways you can serve the Lord without distraction.

Notwithstanding, if any of you who are engaged find the waiting period intolerable, your desires starting to overtake, then by all means tie the knot! That's no sin, as I've said. Yet for those of you who are firm in your resolve, your passions not compelling - you do well to let your engagement run its natural course. So if you marry your betrothed you do well and if you let your engagement run for a while, even better.

And finally, remember that a woman is bound to her husband till death do them part. If he dies, she's free to remarry, yet within the faith. However, it's my own view that she'd be happier as a widow - and I think I've got the Lord on my side on this one.

8

Next let's talk about food that's been sacrificed to idols. You're all very knowledgeable people, I'm sure, but knowledge can make you conceited, while love builds others up. And I've found that people who think they know something often don't understand things the way they should, while if anyone knows God, God knows him as well. So as far as food that's been offered to idols goes, we know that idols are worthless objects and not one of them is a god. It's true that there are all sorts of things *called* gods and lords in Heaven and on Earth, but as far as we're concerned there's only one God, the Father, from whom all things come and we are in him - just as there is but one Lord Jesus Christ by whom are all things and we in him.

However, not everyone understands this. For example, some people who used to be in the habit of worshiping idols feel that when they eat food that had first been sacrificed to an idol they are somehow tainted by that object. They still have sensitive consciences and it would grieve them to eat such food. Of course, *we* know there's nothing to all this and God doesn't care what food we eat - eating one thing or another doesn't make us better or worse as far as he's concerned.

But here's why I said earlier that knowledge can make you conceited – you don't want to harm someone just because *you* know there's no such thing as the "wrong" kind of food. And yet here's the problem you seem to be having: when someone with a weak conscience sees you go to the marketplace outside a pagan temple to buy food that had been sacrificed to idols, he thinks it's ok for him to do so as well – but then when he does he feels guilty and condemns himself. Do you think it's right that your weak brother should come to grief just because you are stronger in your own mind? Jesus died for him just as much as you, so if you sin against your weak brother, wounding his conscience, you're really sinning against Christ. As for me, if meat shocks my brother's conscience then I won't eat meat from now till Kingdom Come.

9

Don't you think I'm free? Don't you know I'm an apostle? Haven't I seen the Lord Jesus? Aren't you my work in the Lord? Even if I'm not other people's apostle it's a sure thing I'm yours, because you yourselves are the sign of my apostolate in the Lord.

That's why I when I hear that some of your people judge the way I live I want to ask them whether they really think I couldn't eat or drink anything I feel like and send you the bill? Or that if I wanted to I couldn't get one of the sisters to marry me – just as Peter and the rest of the apostles and even Jesus' own brothers have done – and then bring her along on my missionary journeys at your expense? Or whether it's just Barnabas and I who have to work for a living and can't live off our preaching?

Let me elaborate a bit on this last point. No general leads an army to war yet has to buy all the provisions himself. And no one who goes to the trouble of planting a vineyard fails to eat of its grapes, just as no one tends sheep but doesn't drink their milk. I'm using ordinary human examples but the Scriptures say the same thing – as it's written in the Law of Moses, Don't put a muzzle on the ox while he's trampling out the grain.19 Do you think God is worried about oxen and not us too? No, it's

---

19   *Deuteronomy* 25:4.

for us as well, because those of us who plow and thresh do so in the hope of sharing in the harvest.

If we have sown spiritual things among you, would it be asking a lot for you to share material goods with us? You give shares to others - how much more should *we* be entitled! Even so, we haven't taken advantage of the rights we have over you. Instead, we bear our own burdens rather put any obstacles in the way of the gospel of the Savior.

Again, don't you know that those who serve in the Temple also get their food there, that those who minister at the sacrificial altar take their share of the burnt carcasses? In just the same way the Lord has directed that those who proclaim the good news should earn their keep by their preaching. Even so, I haven't asked you for a dime in the past and I'm not asking now either. Better for me to *die* than let anyone deprive me of this one little boast. What I mean is, I don't deserve any credit just because I preach the gospel. I can't even say I have much choice in the matter because, the way I see it, I'm in serious trouble if I *don't* preach the gospel.

As you've no doubt heard, it's not exactly as though I undertook my ministry voluntarily - in which case I might be entitled to some sort of re-ward - but rather by force of the Lord's own appearance to me. It's therefore my bounden duty to be faithful to his trust. Since that's the way things are, what is my reward and my boast? Just that even though I have the right to be supported in my preaching I make the gospel free to everyone.

I am free from everyone, yet I've made myself a servant to all to win over as many as I can. I became a Jew to the Jews to win the Jews - *i.e.*, to those subject to the Law as if I myself were subject to the Law (which I'm not) to win those who are subject to the Law. And I even became as one outside the Law[20] to win those who are outside the Law. I became weak to the weak to gain the weak. Indeed, I've become all things to all people that by all means I might save some and thereby share with them in salvation's blessings.

Take another analogy. Runners fill the track at the start of a race but only one of them gains the laurels. Each of you should therefore run as for a crown. And while Olympic athletes train strenuously it's all to gain a perishable wreath - but we an imperishable. So when I race I don't run in circles and when I box I don't punch the air. No, I try to keep my body

---

20 I don't mean lawlessly but rather subject to the Savior - because to live outside the Law you must be honest.

under disciplined control lest having preached to others I myself am left in the dust.

10

Take note that our fathers dwelt under the cloud that covered them in their journeys from Egypt, passed together through the Red-Weed Sea and were baptized unto Moses in the cloud and the sea. They all were nourished with the same spiritual food given them daily by God and drank of his Spirit's drink from the spiritual rock that followed them[21] – and that rock was the Anointed One. But God was displeased with most of them and so their bodies were strewn about the Wilderness.

Yet these events serve as figural examples[22] to us not to crave evil things, as some of them did: Don't become idolaters – as it is written, The people sat down to feast and rose for devilish orgies.[23] Don't go whoring after foreign gods – 23,000 of them perishing in a single day.[24] Don't tempt the Lord – one after the other succumbing to serpents' fangs.[25] And don't grumble – those who did who were destroyed by the Destroyer.[26]

But the things that befell them typologically were written down as admonition for us, we who have reached the Latter Days. Therefore whoever thinks she stands should be careful not to fall. Please understand that none of the temptations facing you is out of the ordinary. Moreover, God is faithful and will not allow you to be tempted beyond what you can endure, but will in every case provide a way out of the temptation, lest you be overcome.

The sum of this, beloved, is that you must flee all forms of idolatry. I speak to you as those who are wise in such matters and know what I'm referring to. Isn't the cup we bless our communal share in the blood of Christ? And when we break the bread aren't we participants in the body of Christ? Therefore we many are become one body – because all of us

---

21   *Deuteronomy* 32:4, 15, 18, 30, 31.
22   *See Romans* 5:14; *cf.* G. Herbert, "The Bunch of Grapes" (1633).
23   *Exodus* 32:6.
24   *Numbers* 25:1-9.
25   *Numbers* 21:4-6.
26   *Numbers* 16:41-50.

partake of that one bread.

Look again to the Children of Israel. Don't those who eat of the sacrificed flesh share in the altar? I'm not at all suggesting that food offered to idols has power in itself or that idols are anything but worthless objects. But they sacrifice to demons not to God,[27] and you must steer clear of any fellowship with evil spirits. Let me say it point blank - you can't drink the cup of the Lord and the cup of demons. You can't sit at the Lord's table and that of the demons. Should we provoke the Lord to jealousy?[28] Are we stronger than he?

"All things are lawful to me," you say. Perhaps, but not everything is good for you. "I am permitted all things," you say again. Yes, but some things aren't constructive. Don't look at what's good for you but rather what's good for your brothers and sisters. So here are some practical guidelines. When you go shopping just buy what's offered you without probing where it comes from, for the sake of your conscience. After all, it's plain that the Earth is the Lord's and the fullness thereof.[29] The same principle holds if you're invited to dinner at the home of non-Christians and you decide to go - just eat what's put in front of you without asking questions.

However if someone says to you, "Oh by the way, they offered this meat to idols before you got here," then don't eat it for the sake of *his* conscience. In other words, I'm not worried about your conscience if you eat, but why should my freedom be judged by someone else's standards? Why should I allow someone to go around saying I'm feasting with fiends when in fact I've received the food with gratitude and given thanks to God for it? The point is, whether you eat, drink or do anything else, do all to the glory of God. Don't do anything that will offend the Jews or the Gentiles or your brothers and sisters in God's assembly. That's why I don't spend my time figuring out what's best for me but rather what will benefit most other people. Why? In order that they find salvation.

So just do as I do, because I pattern myself on the Savior.

---

27   *Deuteronomy* 32:17.
28   *Deuteronomy* 32:21.
29   *Psalms* 24:1, 50:12, 89:11.

11

I do have a few positive things to say about you, however, because you've been holding onto various of the church traditions I've given you. As I've emphasized it's important that we display a certain order in the assembly so as not to give offense to those around us.

And as matter of orderliness you should understand that the Anointed One proceeds from God and is the source of every man, while the source of woman is the man. Every man who prays or prophesies with his head draped therefore dishonors his source. And every woman who prays or prophesies having her hair unveiled dishonors hers - it's just as if she had shaved her head. So if a woman is not veiled then let her be shorn. On the other hand, if it's considered shameful for a woman to have her hair cut short or shaved[30] then she should leave it veiled.

A man shouldn't shroud his head, however, being in the image and glory of God. But the woman is the glory of man because in creation man was not taken out of woman but woman out of man - that is, in the beginning man was not created through woman but woman through man.[31] Therefore a woman ought to hold her authority on her head for the sake of the watching angels.[32] In the Lord, of course, woman is not separate from man nor man from woman. And just as the first woman was taken out the man so now man is born through woman. But all things come from God.

Judge for yourself, does it seem right to you that a woman prays to God unveiled? And isn't it in the nature of things that men have shorter hair while long hair is a woman's glory, it being given her as a covering? Look, if anyone wants to fight about this just tell them we have no such custom nor do the assemblies of God.

Back to some more serious issues. I'm afraid I've got a bone to pick with you about your gatherings, where things seem to have gone from bad to worse. From what I hear whenever you meet you split right off into factions - and from everything else that's been going on I pretty much believe that to be true. I'm not speaking now of the doctrinal divisions

30   *See* Tacitus, *Germania* 19; *cf. Numbers* 5:18.
31   *Genesis* 2:21 *ff.*
32   *Revelation* 8:2-4; *Tobit* 12:12-15; *cf. Isaiah* 6:2.

that on occasion must arise in order to reveal who among you is faithful and who is not. What I'm concerned about here is that when you gather together you're not taking advantage of your opportunity to partake of a common meal. Instead of sharing with those in the congregation who aren't as wealthy, many of you richies just go off and have your own private feasts – eating, drinking and (incredibly enough) just plain getting drunk! Can't you eat and drink in your own homes? Do you despise God's assembly so much that you flaunt your wealth, putting the poor in your midst to shame? Do you expect to get any credit for this? Not a chance.

Listen instead to what the Lord has instructed me and I now instruct you concerning how properly to share in his table – for on the night he was betrayed the Lord Jesus took bread and when he had given thanks he brake it and gave to his disciples, saying, "Take, eat. This is my body, which is given for you. Do this in remembrance of me." Likewise after supper he took the cup and when he had given thanks he gave it to them, saying, "Drink ye all of this, for this is my blood of the new covenant, which is shed for you and for many for the remission of sins. Do this, as oft as ye shall drink it, in remembrance of me." So as often as ye eat this bread, and drink this cup, ye do show the Lord's death till he come.

The net result is that whoever eats the bread or drinks the Lord's cup in an unbefitting manner will be bound in guilt of the Lord's body and blood. Each person should therefore examine his conscience before partaking and then let him eat and drink – because whoever eats and drinks unworthily drinks and eats judgment to himself, not perceiving the presence of the body of the Lord. And this is *exactly* why so many of you are sick and weak and, indeed, why some have died. If we would but judge ourselves we'd have no need to be judged by another. But remember that when we are chastised by the Lord we learn from the experience, so as not to be condemned with the world.

Here's the sum of all this, my brothers and sisters: when you gather together don't push ahead of one another, but wait. If you're hungry, eat in your own house so you don't end up poisoning your fellowship when you meet. I'll straighten the rest of this out whenever I get there.

12

You've also asked me some questions about spiritual gifts. I don't want you to be in the dark about them. You know, of course, that when you were ignorant heathen you listened to speechless idols. So heed me on this - no one who is filled with the Spirit of God can ever suggest that "Jesus is cursed," any more than he can confess that "Jesus is the Lord" except by the Holy Spirit.

Now there are all sorts of spiritual gifts but there is only one Spirit who distributes them. Similarly, there are many different ways of providing service to God's people and many different ways of doing good to others, but always the same Lord and God who shows himself distinctly in all of us. It follows that he has apportioned something to each person, whatever gifts and skills will be of the greatest benefit to all. Thus the same Spirit has gifted one person with wise words and another with deep understanding; to someone else great faith and to another gifts of healing; to one the ability to work miracles and to another prophecy; to yet another the power to discern spirits; to one the gift of speaking an angelic language while to another the gift of interpreting what the first has said. Yet it is the same Spirit who works in *all*, distributing gifts to each in accordance with his will.

Think of it this way. A body is a single entity but has many parts, yet together they comprise one body, not many - it's the same with the Body of Christ. We've all been baptized by one Spirit into one body - Jews and Gentiles, slave and free - and we all drink of one Spirit. And the body does not consist of just one part, but many. Let me give a silly example. Suppose a foot could speak and said, "Since I'm not a hand the hand and I must not be part of the same body." Does it thereby cease to be part of one body? Same with an ear - even if it were to say, "I'm not an eye so the eye and I must not be part of the same body," it would still be part of the body. You get what I mean - if a body were all eyes how could it hear? And if it were all ears how could it see? But God has pieced all parts together in the body as he best determined. If all the parts were the same, what kind of body would that be? So there are many members, but one body. And that's why - continuing my example - the eye can't say to the hand, "I don't need you," nor likewise the head to the feet.

What you have to keep in mind is that members of the body we might think the weakest may turn out to be the ones we need the most and members we might think less important are the ones we end up relying on. That's why we ought to clothe with honor the parts of the body some people think to be less valuable or even less attractive - the parts that everyone thinks are valuable and attractive don't need our special attention. God has brought all the parts of the body together and put greater value on parts thought to have less value precisely so the body not be divided, but rather function in harmony. Thus when one member of the body suffers, all suffer; when one is honored, all are honored.

To the point: you are parts of the whole, members of one body, the Body of Christ. God placed some in the assembly first to be apostles, second prophets, third teachers, next miracle workers, healers, ministers, overseers, masters of language. Is everyone an apostle? Everyone a prophet? Everyone a teacher? Everyone a miracle worker? Does everyone have gifts of healing? Does everyone speak other languages? Does everyone know how to interpret other languages? No, but seek after God's best gifts for you.

13

And yet - let me show you a better path.

Even if I speak the languages of men and of angels but don't have love I'm just clashing gongs and cymbals. I might be able to see into the future, perceive all the mysteries of God, possess all the knowledge in the world, have faith so as to move mountains - but all this without love? Useless. And it wouldn't be worth anything to me to sell all that I own to feed the poor if I did so without love. Even if I were to yield my body to be martyred in the flames it would benefit me nothing in God's eyes if done without love.

Understand this - true Christian love is patient, full of mercy, jealousy-free, doesn't jump out in front or try to be number one, isn't arrogant or shameful, doesn't fly off the handle. Love doesn't give place to evil things or rejoice at injustice - it rejoices with all that is true. Love endures all things, trusts all things, hopes all things, holds out to the end.

Love never fails. But prophecy will cease one day, tongues will be still and human understanding will reach its limits – because we know in part and prophesy piecemeal, but when all is fulfilled what is partial will end. When I was a child I spoke like a child, thought like a child, reasoned like a child. Once I became a man I had done with childish things. Up to now we see through a glass darkly, but then face to face. Now I know in part, but then I will know with perfection, even as I am known. Faith, hope and love remain, but the greater of these is love.

14

Strive for love but also seek spiritual gifts, most of all that you are able to prophesy. The reason I say this is that if someone speaks in angelic tongues she's speaking to God, not other people. No one understands her even though in spirit she speaks deep mysteries. But if someone prophesies she is able to share words of consolation and encouragement that build up others. Don't misunderstand – when someone prays angelically he himself is built up spiritually. It's just that when someone prophesies he strengthens the whole assembly. Listen, I'd be quite happy if you all had the gift of glossolalia, but happier still if you would all speak prophetic words. Someone speaking prophetically is therefore more valuable than someone who speaks angelically – unless the person so speaking also interprets what he's saying so that the whole assembly can be edified.

Think about it this way. If I come into your gathering speaking some language you don't understand, what good is it to you if I can't provide you with a revelation or doctrine or prophecy or teaching? It's something like that even with lifeless musical instruments – unless someone plays different notes on a flute or guitar no one can figure out the tune. Or if the pipes pipe confusion how will the regiment mass for battle? Speak the speech trippingly on the tongue or no one will know what you're saying – you might as well be speaking to air. There happens to be a multitude of languages in the world and they're all meaningful. But if I can't speak someone else's language I'm a barbarian to him and he's a babbler to me.

So as far as you're concerned, it's okay to be enthusiastic about spiritual gifts but go for the most useful ones, those that will build up the assembly, and excel in those. Here are some guidelines in that regard. Whoever speaks in an unknown language should also pray that interpretation be given, because if I pray in an unknown tongue my spirit prays but my understanding is lacking. What then? I will pray with my spirit but also with my understanding, sing with my spirit and also with my mind. Otherwise, while you're praising God in spirit the newcomer sitting to you has no idea what you're saying. How then can he add an "Amen?" He can't - he has no idea what you've just said. So it's nice that you've given thanks to God but you haven't helped him any. Again, don't misunderstand me, I'm not against speaking in tongues. On the contrary, I'm grateful to God that I pray angelically more than any of you. However, in the congregation I'd rather speak five words that everyone can understand than thousands in an unknown language.

Brothers and sisters, don't act like children in all this - although of course you're free to be innocent of vice - but have a mature understanding of things. As it is written in the Law,

> I will speak to this people
>   in strange languages
> and with foreign lips,
>   but still they will not heed me, says the Lord.[33]

What this means is that speaking in angelic languages can be confusing to outsiders who come into your assembly and find you all speaking unknown words at the same time - they might even think you're crazy, whether they're believers yet or not! On the other hand, prophetic words intelligibly spoken can be a sign both to those who believe and those who don't. Suppose now an unbeliever enters while you are all prophesying in *his* own language. I tell you that by conviction of the Holy Spirit his conscience will be exposed by all of you in turn, the secrets of his heart laid bare, and he will fall prostrate before you worshiping God, proclaiming him to be in your midst.

---

33   *Isaiah* 28:11-12; *Deuteronomy* 28:49.

So what's the best way to order your worship, my brothers and sisters? When you are gathered together let each one have a psalm, a teaching, a revelation, a message in tongues, an interpretation of the message – all of it with the goal of building yourselves up. If any of you are moved to speak in an unknown language ideally it should be two or maybe three of you at the most, and then someone should give the interpretation. However, if no one is around at the time with the gift of interpretation then hold your tongues and commune in your hearts, speaking only to God. Prophets, same thing – let two or maybe three of you speak in series and then if anyone wishes to expound on what was said she can do so. However, if something is being revealed at a given moment to another person sitting in the group then the first speaker should stop speaking and defer. You'll all get the chance to prophesy one by one so that everyone can learn and everyone be comforted. Keep in mind that the spirits of the prophets are within the prophets' control – God is the author of peace, not chaos.[34]

Do you think the Word of God originated with you or that you're the only ones it came to? If anyone considers himself to be a prophet or a spiritual person let him recognize that what I'm writing has the seal of God's authority. If anyone doesn't understand or disagrees, there's nothing you can do about it other than ignore him. My brothers and sisters, be zealous about prophesying and don't forbid anyone to speak in tongues. Just to be sure that everything is done in a decent and orderly way.

---

34 Translator's note – the following verses appear in certain manuscripts: "Wives should hold their tongues during worship services, because it's not their role to speak there but rather to be subordinate. It is customary in our assemblies (as it also was under the Law) for wives who wish to learn something new to hold their questions for discussion with their husbands at home so as to avoid inappropriate behavior in the congregation." However there is reason to doubt these two verses were originally part of the letter. Not only are they inconsistent with other portions but good textual evidence indicates that the verses first appeared as a scribal gloss in the margin of a particular manuscript and were then mistakenly incorporated into others.

15

Having said all that, I'm afraid I have to lay out for you once again the whole gospel I preached to you - this good news you received and believed, on which your faith is founded, by which you are saved. Hold fast to it! Your faith wasn't in vain. But let's go over it once more - I delivered the key points to you just as I received them:

Jesus died for our sins in accordance with the Scriptures.

He was buried.

He was raised on the third day, also in accordance with the Scriptures.

He was seen by Cephas (you know him as Peter) and then the Twelve.

After that he was seen by more than 500 of the brethren at one time (and most of them are still alive, so feel free to ask them if you don't believe me).

Then he was seen by Jacob and all the apostles.

And last of all I saw him, as someone born beyond the due date.[35]

So if the good news is that Jesus was raised from the dead, what's with some of you saying there's no such thing as a resurrection of the dead? Because if there's no resurrection then Jesus wasn't raised. And if Jesus wasn't raised our preaching is a big joke and your faith is a waste of time. Oh also, that means we're proved to be false witnesses about God because we've testified that God *did* raise up the Savior - who obviously wasn't raised if the dead aren't raised because if the dead aren't raised he wasn't either. What I'm trying to get across to you is that if the Savior wasn't raised then your faith is pointless - you're still in your sins. The same goes for those who've already died believing in Christ - they've perished. Believe me, if our hope in Jesus ends with this life we're the most miserable bunch there is.

But in fact Christ *has* been raised from the dead as the first fruits of God's harvest from the dead. Since death came into the world through man it follows that the resurrection of the dead should also come by way

---

35 What I mean by that is I'm the least of all the apostles and shouldn't even be *called* an apostle, because I persecuted the people of God. Yet by the grace of God I have become who I am. And I should note that God didn't grant me that grace to no end - the fact is I've worked harder than any of them. (Well, it's not really me, but God's grace working in me.) But either way, whether I'm preaching or they're preaching, it's the same good news you've believed.

of man. Just as we all died in Adam so in the Savior will we all be brought to life, yet each in his proper rank – first Jesus then those who are his at his coming. Then all shall be fulfilled and he will deliver up the kingdom to God the Father, having nullified all opposing spiritual rule and authority and power. And he must rule until he has put all enemies under his feet. The last enemy to be abolished is death – for he has put everything under his feet.[36] When all things are in subjection to him then even the Son himself will submit himself to the one who subjected all things to him, so that God alone may be all things in all.

And what about those who are baptized as proxies for the dead? Why do they bother, if the dead aren't raised?

More to the point, why do you think we risk danger every hour? I swear, every day I die a little and I do it all for you, the object of my pride in Christ Jesus. So what was the use of my battling raging beasts in Ephesus, me a mere mortal? Honestly, if the dead aren't raised then let's eat, drink and be merry, for tomorrow we die.[37] But don't kid yourselves – "evil communications corrupt good manners."[38] Therefore sober up and awake to righteousness, because you've fallen into sin spending time with people who are so ignorant about God. I speak all this to your shame.

But someone might ask, "Just exactly *how* are the dead raised back to life? What kind of body do they get?" Those are foolish questions. You know that when you sow seeds the seed first dies before it comes to life. What I mean is that when you sow a seed you don't sow it in the form the plant will ultimately take but just the bare seed, whether it's wheat or something else. God then gives it the bodily form he's determined, to each kind of seed the form appropriate to it, whether plant or animal. And not every member of the animal kingdom has the same kind of body but rather each to its phylum and class, whether mammals, birds or fish; or its order, whether carnivores or primates; and so too with each family, genus and species. Likewise, there are heavenly bodies and earthly bodies, while the glory of the heavenly bodies is of one type and that of the earthly another. And the sun differs in splendor from the moon and the moon

---

36   *Psalms* 8:6. When the Scripture says he has subjected "everything," obviously the one who put all things into subjection is excepted.

37   *Isaiah* 22:13, 56:12.

38   Menander, *Thaïs*, fragment 187.

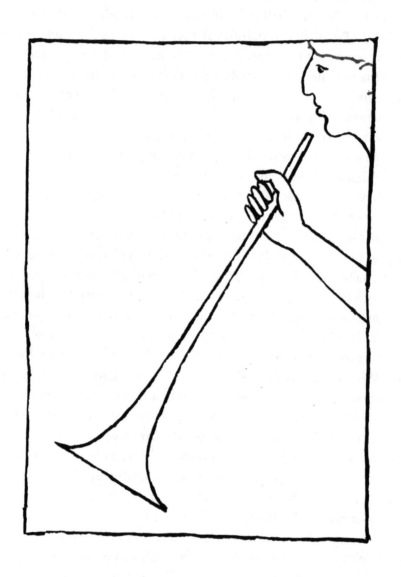

from the stars and even one star from another.

It's the same with the resurrection from the dead. It is sown in corruption but raised incorruptible; sown in dishonor but raised in glory; sown in weakness but raised in power; sown an animate body but raised a spiritual one. If an animate body exists so too does a spiritual. It is written that the first man, Adam, became a living soul[39] – but the last Adam a life-giving spirit. In other words, what came first was not spiritual but ensouled and thereafter what was spiritual. The first man came of Earth's dust but the second man from Heaven. Those born of the Earth are earthly, those born from Heaven heavenly. As we have borne dust's image so we shall bear Heaven's.

What I'm telling you, brothers and sisters, is that flesh and blood are not able to inherit the kingdom of Heaven any more than the perishable succeed to what's imperishable. Listen while I tell you a mystery – not all of us shall die but all of us will be changed: in a flash, in the twinkling of an eye, at the last trumpet. For the trumpet shall sound and the dead shall be raised incorruptible, and we shall be changed. For this corruptible body must be clothed in an incorruptible, this mortal body clothed in immortality. And when the corruptible shall have put on incorruptible – that is, when the mortal shall put on the immortal – then shall this word be fulfilled,

> Death is swallowed up in victory.[40]
> O death, where is thy sting?
> O grave, where is thy victory?[41]

The sting of death is sin and the strength of sin is the Law. But thanks be to God, who gives us the victory through our Lord Jesus Christ.

Therefore, my beloved brothers and sisters, be firm, immoveable, abounding in the work of the Lord, knowing your labor in the Lord is not in vain.

---

39   *Genesis* 2:7.
40   *Isaiah* 25:8.
41   *Hosea* 13:14.

16

Let me turn to some miscellaneous items before I close. First, I'd like to give the same direction to you I've given to the assemblies in Galatia concerning alms for our needier brothers and sisters. On the first day of each week going forward gather up whatever excess funds you have so you don't have to scramble around to take up a collection when I get there. And provide me with letters authorizing whomever you decide should safeguard your gifts en route to Jerusalem. I haven't decided yet whether I will go there myself, but if it seems worth my while to do so then they will go there with me.

My plan is to go next to Macedonia, pass through and then move on to Corinth. If it works out I would just as soon spend the Winter with you. You can help me on my way after that. I don't want to visit you on the fly, in other words, but rather stay for a while, God willing. For now, however, I will remain in Ephesus until Pentecost because the Lord has opened up a large opportunity for me here (although there are also a lot of people lined up against me).

Timothy may also come visit you. If so, see to it he has nothing to fear among you, as he's been as tirelessly zealous in the Lord's work as I. I don't want anyone to look down on him. And if he does visit be sure to send him off in peace on his return trip to me, along with any brothers who may accompany him.

Now about our brother Apollos – I had strongly urged him to go see you as well along with the other brothers, but he didn't feel led to do so at the time. However, he will visit you when he next sees the opportunity.

Keep watch. Be steadfast in the faith. Have courage. Be strong. Let love govern your actions.

Allow me to call on you in another matter, brothers and sisters – you're familiar with Stephanus, he and his household being the first believers in Achaia. They have set themselves fully to the service of their fellow believers. Defer to them as you would to all such persons who labor in service to the Lord and his people. I need to add that I was particularly cheered when Stephanus, Fortunatus and Achaicus came here because they were some consolation for my inability to be with you in person. They graced my spirit, as well as yours. Be sure to honor such people on their return.

All the congregations in the Asian District greet you. Prisca and Aquila send their warmest greetings in the Lord, along with the believers who meet in their house. All the brothers and sisters greet you. Greet one another with a holy kiss.

I close with a greeting in my own handwriting,

Paul

Post scriptum –
If someone doesn't love the Lord, let him be damned.
מָרֵן אֲתָא *(which in English means, "The Lord is coming").*
And may the grace of the Lord Jesus be with you – so too my
love for you all in Christ Jesus.

Amen!

SECOND LETTER TO THE CORINTHIANS

From Paul, by the will of God made an apostle of the Anointed Jesus, and Timothy, a brother, to the Assembly of God gathered in Corinth and all the believers living in the Asian District: *Grace and peace to you from God our Father and the Lord Jesus Christ!*

1

All praise be to the God and Father of our Lord Jesus Christ, the Father of mercies and the God of all consolation, who comforts us in every affliction so that we're able to comfort others in any kind of sorrow they have, drawing as we do on the consolation by which we ourselves are comforted by God. Just as the Savior's own sufferings overflow in us, so much more do we abound in compassion through him. If we are pressed on all sides it is for your encouragement and salvation. If we are comforted it is to share that consolation with you, a solace that works patience in you to endure the same afflictions we suffer. And we stand firm in our hope for you, knowing that as you share the afflictions so too will you share the consolation.

Brothers and sisters, I don't want you to be unaware of the harshness we've endured in the Asian District. I admit that things got so bad, so excessively grim, that with a sentence on our heads we prepared ourselves to die. We cast all our fortunes on God, no longer trusting in ourselves but in him who raised the dead. But in fact he *did* rescue us from that great peril of death and will yet deliver us, as we put our hope of salvation in him. We were also strengthened by you through your faithful petitions to God on our behalf, so that in truth the mercy shown to us came as a gift from many people and is one for which many can give thanks.

If there's anything we can take pride in it's this – that we have lived our lives among you in all holiness and sincerity. We say this with a clear conscience because we have ministered to you not with words of worldly wisdom but abundantly and in accordance with the grace of God.

When we write to you do we write anything other than what you can read or understand? I know for a fact you've fully understood the things we've been saying and I hope you will maintain that understanding right through to the end. And this part you know for sure – that you are our pride. But we trust that you take pride in us as well and indeed will to the Day of the Lord Jesus.

Given such confidence in you I had earlier purposed to come visit your city. My original thought was to provide you with two opportunities to gain a blessing from that round of journeys and therefore planned to stop by you on my way into Macedonia and then visit you again on the way back, at which point you would be able to help me on my continued trip to Judea. Yet just because I've now changed my plans you're acting as though I make them lightly, carelessly, without really meaning what I say.

Do you think I make these decisions on a whim, relying on my own ideas? Or that when I say "yes" it doesn't always mean "yes" but some-times means "no"? On the contrary, God is faithful and our message to you isn't some kind of "yes and no." Far from it. The Son of God, the Anointed Jesus proclaimed by me and Silas and Timothy, did not come to us as "yes, no or maybe" – in him there is nothing but "yes" and "yes" again! Indeed all God's promises are "yes" and "amen" in him and through us, all to the glory of God. It is God who strengthens us with you in Christ, he who has anointed us all, sealed us as his own and given us a down payment on our inheritance, his Spirit in our hearts.

Let God be the witness against my soul if it wasn't to spare you pain that I held off coming to Corinth before now. It isn't that we are the lords of your faith - we aren't - but we are fellow laborers with you to increase your joy, with the goal that you stand strong in the faith.

2

I therefore set it firmly in my mind not to visit you in sorrow, because if *I* were to cause you sadness then who would be left to bring me joy but the same ones I had grieved? I've therefore now written you the reason for my delay in coming - *i.e.*, to spare you distress - so that I might not be saddened by those who should instead bring me joy. I trust that you appreciate the value in this, so that when we do meet our mutual joy may be full. I'm sure you saw from my prior letter how bowed down I was by the weight of inward turmoil, how afflicted in my heart, how tearful with sorrow - and I wrote not to cause you pain but so you would know the abundant love I have for you.

I don't mean to lay any more weight than necessary on the one who caused this sorrow. He didn't grieve *me* so much as all of you. And the punishment you've inflicted on him (the majority   of you anyway) by shunning him seems to have been fully sufficient. But now you ought reach out to him, forgive him and comfort him lest he drown, overwhelmed by regret and remorse. I therefore urge you to affirm your love for him. Indeed, that's why I wrote to you in the first place, to test you in assurance of your obedience in all things. If you forgive someone, so do I. And anyone whom I forgive I forgive for your sakes as a vicar of Christ lest the Accuser steal him out from under us - because we are onto Satan's tricks.

When the Lord granted me an opening I visited Troas to share the good news of salvation. But I had no rest in my spirit because I couldn't locate my brother Titus. I therefore had to leave Troas and head back to Macedonia. Now that I've found him and gotten his report about you I can give thanks to God, who precedes us in triumphal procession, spreading knowledge of the Savior in all places, diffused as the scent of burnt spices offered along the victor's path. And we ourselves are for God the Savior's salve to those being saved and those who are perishing, to the one a savor of life to life but the other of death to death. Who then is up to the task he has set before us? We're not roadside hucksters like those who market the gospel for profit. No, we speak to you as from God, with sincerity in his sight and before his presence in Christ.

3

Do you think we're promoting ourselves? Do you think we need someone to write us a letter of recommendation to you, as some people do? Or do you think we need *you* to write one for *us*? Hardly. You yourselves are our letter of recommendation, written on our hearts, known and read by everyone, an epistle of Christ ministered to you by us in words written by the Savior, penned neither in ink nor graven in stone but inscribed by the Spirit on the heart's living tablets.[42]

We have this confidence in God through the Savior, not that we are up to the task in our own right or consider ourselves sufficient within ourselves but rather that God is our sufficiency. And he has made us able servants of a new covenant,[43] one drawn not from inscription but the Spirit - because the text condemns but the Spirit enlivens.

How much more glorious, indeed, is this ministry of the Spirit than the ministry marked by letters carved in stone! Now *that* ministry was itself glorious, so glorious in fact that the Children of Israel could not gaze on the face of Moses because of the splendor reflected in it.[44] But even that splendor passed away. If the ministration of the Law led to condemnation and yet was glorious, how surpassing in glory is the ministration of righteousness? In this respect that which had been glorified was diminished in radiance by virtue of the exceeding brightness of that which is new. In other words, if that which has ceased was glorious how much more glorious is that which remains!

---

42   *Jeremiah* 31:33; *Ezekiel* 36:26; *cf. Exodus* 31:18.
43   *Jeremiah* 31:31-32.
44   *Exodus* 34:29-30.

Having such a hope we do what we do openly and with boldness. We need keep nothing hidden, as did Moses, who placed a veil on his face to cover its radiance[45] lest the Children of Israel gaze toward the telos of what is passing away.[46] But their thoughts became dulled – even today the selfsame veil hangs over the reading of the former covenant, not revealing that it was made ineffective in the Savior. Whenever Moses is read a veil therefore still lies on Israel's heart. Yet when the heart turns to the Lord the veil is removed[47] – because the Lord is the Spirit and where the Spirit of the Lord is there is liberty. But we all with unveiled face gazing as in a mirror the glory of the Lord are transformed into the same image from glory to glory, even as by the Spirit of the Lord.

4

Seeing that we have this ministry, the Lord having shown us mercy, we show no weakness in our task. We've renounced the kind of shameful behaviors that people hide. We don't go about our work with craft and guile, diluting the Word of God. Instead, openly declaring the truth, we commend ourselves plainly and in the sight of God to the conscience of all mankind. But if our gospel is hidden it's only hidden to those who are perishing. And if they are perishing it's because the god of this age has blinded the minds of those who do not believe, lest the light of the glorious gospel of Christ – who is the image of God – shine in them.

We don't preach ourselves but Christ Jesus the Lord and ourselves your servants for Jesus' sake. The same God who said, Light will shine out of darkness[48] is he who has shone in our hearts that we might shine forth the light of the knowledge of the glory of God in the face of the Anointed Jesus.[49] Yet we hold this treasure in breakable vessels of clay in order that the surpassing power might always be God's, not ours.

We are pressed on every side, yet not constrained; uncertain of our next steps, yet not in despair; persecuted, yet never abandoned; shot

---

45   *Exodus* 34:33.
46   *Romans* 10:4.
47   *Cf. Exodus* 34:34.
48   *Genesis* 1:3-4; *Isaiah* 9:2.
49   *Cf. John* 1:4-9.

down, yet not destroyed. We bear in our own bodies the killing of Jesus so that his life might be revealed in our bodies as well. And those of us who live for him are always being delivered to death for his sake so that his life may be manifested in our mortal selves.

The upshot of this is that death is at work in us but life in you. And because we share the same spirit of faith – as it is written, I believed and therefore spoke[50] – so also we believe and therefore speak. Moreover, we know that he who raised up Jesus will raise us up as well and present us together with you at the Day of his Coming. All of this is to your benefit so that grace overflowing through the ever-increasing thanks given by many may redound to the greater glory of God.

Why don't we quit, you ask? Because even though our outward man perish yet the inward man is renewed day by day. And our light affliction, which is but for a moment, works for us a far more exceeding and unending weight of glory. How, you say? Because we look not at the things which are seen but at the things which are not seen – for the things which are seen are temporal but the things not seen are timeless.

5

We now dwell, as it were, in earthly garb. But even if that tent should collapse or wear away we have a dwelling from God not made with hands, an aeonian home in the heavens. Therefore we do indeed groan inwardly, yearning to be clothed over with our heavenly body that having been stripped of the earthly we will not be found naked. And thus we sigh, we who bear the weight of our earthly bodies, not that we wish to be unclothed but rather clothed so that mortality might be swallowed up by life. It is God himself who prepares us for this transformation, who has also given us his guarantee in the form of the Spirit.

Why do we take heart no matter what? It's because we know that while we are at home in the body we are absent from the Lord – for we walk by faith, not by sight. We are confident, I say, and willing rather to be absent

---

50   *Psalms* 116:10.

from the body and present with the Lord. It is therefore our life's goal that whether present or absent we be accepted of him because we shall all be seen for what we are when we stand before the throne of the Lamb, each of us to receive the wages due for what we have done while in our bodies, whether it was something useful or something worthless.

Why are we so gung-ho to persuade others of our sincerity? It's because we understand the fear of the Lord. And I hope we are seen this way in your consciences as well. Do you think we are out to recommend ourselves to you again? No, our purpose in saying all this is to give *you* something to boast about in response to people who put greater store in outward appearances than in the heart. If we're in a trance, we're in ecstasy to God. If we're sober, then we're stone-cold so for your benefit. It is the very love of the Savior that constrains us to this one end – because we judge that if one died on behalf of all then all died with him. And he died so that all who live should no longer live for themselves but to him who died and rose again for them.

We don't rely on our old natures when we interact with people. Even though in the past we understood Christ in a limited way we don't any longer. No, if anyone is in Christ she is a new creature. Old things are passed away, behold, all things are become new. Now, all things are from God, who reconciled us to himself through the Savior and has given us the ministry of reconciliation. God in the person of Jesus was reconciling the world to himself, not counting people's sins against them. God therefore placed with us his word of reconciliation – think of it this way, that we are the Lord's ambassadors, as if God himself were calling to you through us. And so we urge you: Get right with God!

For he hath made him to be sin for us, who knew no sin; that we might be made the righteousness of God in him.

6

We're your partners in God's work. That's why we beg you not to treat the grace of God lightly, as he says,

> I gave ear to you at the moment of grace;
> I came to your aid in the day of salvation.[51]

And look! This is that favored moment – now indeed is the day of salvation. We ourselves have offended in nothing so that our ministry not cause scandal to the gospel. On the contrary, as faithful servants of God and in everything that comes our way we commend ourselves to all, enduring all manner of sufferings, distress and calamities – in beatings, prison and riots; laboring as we watch through the night for you with fasting; maintaining purity of character in the grace of the Holy Spirit with all our understanding, patience and forbearance; with kindness and love that's not hypocritical; by the word of truth and the power of God; wielding weapons of righteousness in attack and defense; through glory and shame (because sometimes we're slandered and called deceivers and sometimes we're honored, but we always stay true); in obscurity and notoriety; as dying and yet, behold, we live; punished but not killed; sorrowful yet always rejoicing; poor yet making many rich; as those who own nothing yet possess everything.

O Corinthians! We hold back nothing – our very hearts are open wide to you! If your affections are constrained it's because of your own lack, not ours. But as children would for their parents, return our love, open your hearts.

Let me warn you of this – you must not tie yourselves to unbelievers. Can righteousness and lawlessness agree? Or what do light and darkness have in common? Can the Savior be partners with בְּלִיַּעַל (which being interpreted means "the Wicked One")? Or one who believes with one who does not? And how can idols be found in the temple of God? And we are indeed the temple of the living God, just as God has spoken,

> I will dwell and walk among them.
> I will be their God
> and they will be my people.[52]
> Therefore, come out from their midst,
> separate yourselves, says the Lord.
> Do not touch any unclean thing

---

51   *Isaiah* 49:8.
52   *Leviticus* 26:12; *Jeremiah* 32:38; *Ezekiel* 37:27.

and I will welcome you in[53]
    and be a father to you
and you will be my sons and my daughters,[54]
    so says the Lord God, the Almighty One.

7

Seeing that we have such great promises, beloved, let us cleanse ourselves from every stain of soul and spirit, perfecting holiness in the fear of the Lord. Make room for us - we did no one wrong, seduced no one, grabbed no one's money. I'm not saying this to get down on your case - as I've told you before it's in our hearts to stand by you whether that leads to death or to life. I'm simply being up front with you - you're my pride and my boast to all people, filling me with comfort so that my own joy overflows even in all our sorrow and pain.

And I have to tell you again that even when we got to Macedonia we had no rest but our very souls were pressed down with afflictions, external strife, internal fears. Yet God, who comforts the oppressed, encouraged us by Titus' arrival as he, encouraged by you, reported to us how much you longed for us, how you mourned, how zealous you are on my behalf, so that I rejoiced all the more. I know I grieved you by my last letter - but I don't regret it. Yes, I have to admit that before Titus came with his news I had been concerned that my letter might have caused you too much sorrow. And indeed, for a time I know it did pain you. But now I rejoice, not that I caused you any distress but that you grieved in a godly way, suffering no harm from us.

What I mean is that godly sorrow leads to repentance - and that to salvation, which is no cause for grief at all - whereas worldly remorse leads to death. Take this very case: you sorrowed after a godly sort and see what carefulness it wrought in you; what clearing of yourselves; what indignation; what fear; what vehement desire; what fervor; what justice! In all things you have approved yourselves to be clear in

---

53   *Isaiah* 52:11; *Ezekiel* 20:34, 41.
54   *2 Samuel* 7:14; *Isaiah* 43:6; *Jeremiah* 31:9.

this matter.

Therefore when I wrote to you it wasn't so much for the sake of the one who committed incest or even the one he harmed as it was to let you see for yourselves and in the sight of God the depths of your own zeal for us. And thus we have been consoled. But beyond that we rejoiced all the more when we saw Titus' joy, how his spirit was refreshed by all of you. Nor was I embarrassed by any boasting I had made to him about you, because just as all that we've said to you is true so is everything we told him about you. And he abounded in deepest affection for you as he recounted to us your full obedience, how you received him with fear and trembling. Therefore I too rejoice, being thus reassured in my confidence in you.

8

We also want to let you know what the assemblies in Macedonia have done. You've heard of course of the great testing and affliction they've been suffering. Well, despite that and even though they themselves live in abject poverty they felt led to give alms for the impoverished saints in Jerusalem. Moreover, they did so not simply according to their means but well beyond their means. They begged us, in fact, to be allowed to share in the grace of providing this relief. Indeed, far past our expectations, they gave themselves above all to the Lord and to us by the will of God. We therefore urged Titus that as he had begun taking up this thank-offering in Macedonia he should follow it through with you. And just as you abound in all things – in faith, in word, in knowledge, in all zeal and in love that flows from you to us – so too we implore you to excel in this act of grace.

Please understand, I'm not ordering you what to do. I write this because you yourselves led the way when you put this gift in motion a year ago, not only purposing in your hearts to provide the alms but also beginning to organize the collection. So I'm exhorting you to prove all the more the sincerity of your love. For you know the grace of our Lord Jesus Christ, that though he was rich yet for your sakes he became poor that you through his poverty might be rich.

Here's my advice: it's time now to bring the task to completion. And don't focus on the amounts involved. The first step is to have a willing heart and then act accordingly. Your gifts are accepted by God in proportion to what you have not based on what you don't have. It's therefore not my aim to put burdens on you and let others kick back and relax, but simply that there be equality. And consider this – they're in need now and you're in a position to help them, but the tables may be turned one day and they may be in a position to help you in your time of need. As it is written, He who had much did not have too much and he who had little lacked for nothing.[55]

But thanks be to God for putting in Titus' heart the same care and concern for you that I have. He heard and heeded our call in this matter, to be sure, but was already well-set in his mind to head toward you. We've sent along with him the brother who is praised among all the congregations for his service to the gospel. And it's not just that he carries with himself this good reputation but he has also been appointed by show of hands in the assemblies to be our traveling companion, joining us in our passion to perform this ministry to the Lord's own glory. We are sending him along as an extra safeguard given the magnitude of the gift to assure that no one calls into question the manner in which it's being handled.

Our purpose is to maintain what is right and good not only in the sight of God but all mankind. And so, going above and beyond, we've *also* sent as part of the team that brother of ours whose diligence we have proven oft times and in many places. Indeed, he is all the more eager to assist in this task because of his great trust in you. If anyone asks about Titus let them know he is my right hand and co-worker in all things concerning you. And as for our brothers who accompany him – they are apostles, sent to you by the churches as a glory to the Savior. Bring them openly before the assemblies as a sign both of your love to us and our trust in you.

---

55 *Exodus* 16:8; *accord* K. Marx and F. Engels, *The German Ideology* (Amherst: Prometheus Books, 1998), 566.

9

I'm going on at length on the subject of the collection for Jerusalem because, to be honest, I've gone a bit out on a limb for you and don't wish to find my boasting to be in vain in this one matter. The fact is, once I knew you'd started on this project a year or so ago I let everyone in Macedonia know that you in Achaia were all set to go with your gift. That way I used your enthusiasm to provoke a great many others to participate as well. So now you understand why I've sent some of our brethren on ahead to be sure you are *in fact* prepared, because it's possible that some of the Macedonian brothers will come along with me when I visit you and I wouldn't want them to discover that you're not on top of this. Needless to say, that would cause me (not to mention you) shame and embarrassment, my confidence having been so misplaced. Anyway, that was reason enough to send them ahead so that your pledge would be ready in advance as the free gift you promised some time ago, lest it appear when we arrive that we've coveted anything of yours.

It's clear enough, of course, that whoever sows few seeds reaps little in return while whoever sows bountifully reaps bountifully. Let each of you therefore give as you determine in your heart, not because someone is pestering you or because you have to but cheerfully – for God loves a cheerful giver. Nor should you worry about your own needs. God is able to make all grace overflow to you so that in all ways and at all times having all that you need you will overflow with every good work. As it is written,

> He has lavished his wealth
>   and given to the struggling poor:
> his righteousness endures forever.[56]

And so may he who provides seed to the sower and bread for his food multiply your seed and increase the fruit of your righteousness.

There are numerous benefits to a ministry of generosity. For one thing,

---

56 *Psalms* 112:9.

you yourselves will abound in every way, allowing you to be generous in meeting the needs of others, something for which we give thanks to God. In addition, when you provide for the needs of your poorer brethren they will glorify God for your sakes. And your gift itself testifies to your obedience to the trust you placed in the good news of the Savior, as you show generosity in fellowship toward them and to all. And so in their prayers they yearn for you, giving thanks for the exceptional grace of God shown to you.

But thanks be to God for *his* indescribable gift!

10

I'm urging you through the meekness and kindness of the Savior – I, Paul, whom you think of as lowly when he's with you but bold when he's not – don't force me to be stern when I'm with you next time, as I do with those who are under the delusion that we manage our lives in a purely human way. For though we walk in the flesh we don't war in the flesh. On the contrary, the weapons of our warfare are not carnal but mighty in God even to the destruction of strongholds, casting down all sophistries and every proud tower raising itself against the knowledge of God, capturing every purpose of the will and bringing it into obedience to Christ, being ready to pass sentence on all disobedience once your obedience is complete.

Open your eyes! If anyone considers himself to be the Lord's let him take a close look at himself and understand that just as he is Christ's so are we. And I'm not ashamed if I boast a bit more than other people about the authority the Lord has given us. After all, this authority has been given us to build you up, not to knock you down. You seem to think I write these letters just to appear frightening – I gather that some of you say, "His letters sound tough but he's not much to look at in person and can't even speak without mumbling." I'd like those people to understand that we'll be just the same in action when we are with you as we are in our letters when away.

As for us, we're not like those who decide how important they are by comparing themselves to themselves – we don't run with such fools. We don't boast about our ministry more than is just. The truth is we don't measure ourselves by ourselves but only against the limits apportioned us by God. And within that range our ministry certainly stretches as far as you Corinthians. It follows as well that if we *didn't* extend our reach to you with the gospel of Christ we wouldn't be stretching as far as God has asked us to.

By the same token, by staying within our God-ordained limits we don't take credit for some other person's work let alone muscle in on their territory. Instead, we have hope in your faith that as it expands we ourselves will be enlarged with you, overflowing in our ministry in order to be able to evangelize the regions beyond you, not boasting about anything done in someone else's territory but operating within our own proper sphere. Therefore he that boasts, let him boast in the Lord.[57]

In short, whoever awards himself a prize hasn't been awarded anything – it's only God's commendation that counts.

11

Would you mind bearing with me in what might at first seem to you like foolishness? Follow me along in this, because the truth is I'm jealous over you with a godly jealousy. I have espoused you to one husband to present you as a chaste virgin to Christ, but I fear that just as the serpent beguiled Eve with his wiles so too he might corrupt your will, turning it from the simplicity and holiness you now show toward him.

As things now stand it looks to me as though you're willing to tolerate some newcomer preaching a Jesus other than the one I've preached. And you're willing to take on from him a spirit different from the one you'd already received and, worse still, to accept a gospel other than the one you'd accepted before. But do you think I'm in some way lesser than that sort of big-deal apostle? I might not be a professional orator like those guys but *I'm* the one who knows what he's talking about and *we're* the ones who

---

57 *Jeremiah* 9:24.

have made all things manifest to you.

Did I make a mistake when I humbled myself in your presence in order that you might be exalted, taking no gifts from you when I preached the gospel of God? I got my support from other churches - robbing Peter (as it were) to pay Paul. When I was with you and found myself in need I didn't let myself become a burden to you but instead had the brothers come from Macedonia to bring me whatever I needed to keep myself going. The fact is, I've never been nor ever will be a burden to you. Before God and as the Savior's truth is in me, no one in the whole of Achaia will shut down my boasting on this point!

And why, you ask, don't I let you support me? Because I don't love you and don't want to be in your debt? Far from it - God knows I *do* love you. No, I do what I do in order to stop short those who would like to find some excuse to criticize our ministry. I want us to be judged on a fair and equal footing with them as to the boasts they or we may make. And in the clear light of day it will be plain that these people are nothing but pseudo-apostles, tricksters, masquerading as the Lord's apostles. Oh, and don't be so shocked! You know the Adversary masks himself as an angel of light so it's not a big leap to find his servants disguised as ministers of righteousness. But they will reap what they sow.

I hope you don't *really* take me to be senseless in this - but if you do think this is all foolishness then listen closely and I'll say it not the way the Lord might but as would a fool. What I mean is that since they boast about their skills and achievements, I will too. After all, you're so wise in your own eyes that you readily put up with fools in your midst. Surely you won't mind listening to another one. Indeed, as far as I can see you're happy enough not only to let someone tell you what to think but also let him devour your goods, exploit you, take over the show and then kick you around.

What a shame I was too weak to pull any of these stunts when I was with you! Yet if any dare exalt themselves (I speak now as a fool), so do I: Are they Hebrews? So am I. Are they Israelites? I am as well. Are they offspring of Abraham? Me too! Are they servants of Christ? Indulge me - I am, but more so. How? Well, I've worked harder, been in jail more times, suffered worse beatings and been nearer death more often. Let me give you some particulars. The synagogue rulers had me flogged five times, each with 39 lashes. Then I was beaten with rods three times, pelted with stones once, shipwrecked three times and I even spent a night and a day adrift in the sea. I'm always traveling someplace, in danger from rivers and robbers. I'm at risk not just from the Goyim but my own people as well. I'm in peril in the city, in peril in the desert, in peril at sea. Threatened by false brethren. At labor and toil, often at watch in the night, often fasting, often in thirst. Sick. Cold. Naked. And if that weren't enough I'm anxious every day, caring for all the churches. So who is weak and I'm not? Who's tempted to sin and I don't yearn to reassure him?

Yet if I must boast let me take pride in the things that make me weak. And God and the Father of the Lord Jesus - he who is blessed for all ages - knows I'm not making any of this up. Oh and before I forget, let me add that when I was in Damascus the Prefect of the city, Aretas, was on the lookout to grab me. But I was let down in a hamper through an opening in the wall and thereby escaped from his hands.

12

I feel I have to boast some more, although there's normally no real benefit in doing so. But for your present needs let me speak for a minute about visions and revelations from the Lord. And this time I don't want to boast about myself but will tell you about someone I know. Fourteen years ago he was caught up to the Third Heaven - I myself don't know whether he was taken up bodily or just in his spirit, although of course God knows - and when he was in the Garden of Paradise he heard things spoken that he cannot repeat, things inexpressible by man. So I will boast about *that* person, not myself, unless it is to take pride in my weaknesses. And even if I were to boast about myself you still couldn't count me a fool because in fact I'm telling the truth. Even so, I choose not to speak about the abundance of revelations given me by the Lord lest anyone form his views about me based on anything other than what he himself sees and hears.

And because God knows me well, he allowed one of the Tempter's messengers to afflict me with what I'll call a thorn in my flesh, just to prevent my becoming too full of myself. Don't get me wrong, I wanted none of this and begged the Lord three times to rid me of it. But he said, "My grace is sufficient for you, that my power be perfected in your weakness." And that's why I'm now gladly taking pride in my weaknesses in order that the power of Christ may rest upon me. So for the Savior's sake I endure weakness, mistreatment, distress, persecution, anguish – because whenever I am weak, I am strong.

Well, there you have it. You've pretty much forced me to speak in a foolish and boasting way. But the truth is, you're the ones who should've been standing by me, ratifying my ministry among you – because I don't take second place to any of the so-called apostles you've been listening to. On the contrary, the signs of an apostle have been fully wrought by me among you, in all patience, through signs and wonders.

Did I treat you worse than the rest of the congregations? Hardly, unless you want to criticize me for not letting myself become a burden to you. But please, do forgive me that injustice.

I'm getting ready to visit you now for the third time and I won't burden you on this visit any more than the past two – I'm not looking for anything that's yours, just you yourselves. And that's as it should be, since children ought not store up treasure for their parents but parents for their children – and so I would gladly spend and be spent for your souls. Just because I've loved you too much, should I be loved by you less? But some of you might be thinking, "He was crafty and trapped us by refusing to let us support him." What nonsense. I urged Titus to go to you and sent our brother with him – did Titus turn greedy on you? Didn't we live by the same Spirit? Didn't we follow down the same road?

You've probably been thinking for some time that we're being awfully defensive in this letter, as though we were trying to justify ourselves to you. Not so. What we speak we speak before God and all that we say we say to build you up in Christ. But I'm deeply afraid that when I come to you this time I'll find you in a state I don't wish for and then you'll find me compelled to act in a way I'd rather not – I'm worried that I'll find rivalry, jealousy, rage, self-promoting, backbiting, gossip, conceit, disorder and will thus be humiliated by God before you, mourning those among you who have not yet turned from the debaucheries of their Dionysian revels.

13

So as I say, this is the third time I'm coming to see you. In the mouth of two or three witnesses shall every word be established.[58] I told you the second time I was with you and I'll tell you again even though I'm not there yet: I won't hold back in dealing with those who have continued in their sins, or any of the rest of you who might be tempted to follow them. It seems that you're looking for some proof that the Savior is speaking through me – the Savior, I say, who is far from weak but mighty in dealing with you. For though he was crucified through weakness yet he lives by the power of God. So we too are weak in him, yet we shall live with him by the power of God toward you.

Examine yourselves, if you are still in the faith – put *yourselves* to the test, not me! Can it be you don't know that Christ Jesus is in you (unless of course you fail that test)? I hope you don't think we haven't been tested and proved. I don't wish to do you any harm, *quod advertat Deus,* but only wish to assure that you do the right thing – not to make us look good but so that you be proved faithful even if we appear to be of less repute. And we have no power to act against the truth but only for the truth. We are glad when we are weak and you are strong – and this also we wish, even your perfection.

I write all this while I'm away from you so that when I'm with you I'll have no need to act harshly in accordance with the power the Lord gave me for edification, not destruction.

In closing here's the sum of what I want to say, my brothers and sisters: Rejoice! Pull yourselves together. Take comfort. Be of one heart and mind, at peace with one another, and the God of love and peace will be with you. Greet one another with a holy kiss. All the saints greet you.

The grace of the Lord Jesus Christ and the love of God and the fellowship of the Holy Spirit be with you all.

---

58 *Deuteronomy* 19:15.

TO THE CHURCHES OF GALATIA

1

Paul to the assemblies in Galatia:
I and the brethren with me send you grace and peace from our God and Father and from the Lord Jesus Christ, who gave himself as an offering for our sins in order to rescue us from the present evil world in accordance with the will of God our Father – to whom be glory for endless ages, amen.

I don't speak to you as one sent out by other people, nor do I hold my office by human appointment. No, I write in the authority given me as an apostle by the Anointed Jesus and God the Father, who raised him up from among the dead. Speaking as God's vicar I'm therefore shocked to find you're becoming turncoats, quickly deserting to another gospel, abandoning the one who called you into grace! Now, it's not that there's really any such thing as *another* gospel, but what's happened is that some outside agitators have stirred you up, twisting the good news of Christ. So get this straight – if we, or even one who seems to be an angel from Heaven, should proclaim to you any gospel other than what we've already preached, let him be cut off from among you.

Do you think I seek other people's approval rather than God's? No, I don't care what people think of me. If I were worried about pleasing others I wouldn't be of much use to God as a servant. And brethren, you can be sure that the gospel I preach didn't come to me from some other person. I didn't receive it from anyone nor was I taught it. Instead, it came by direct revelation from Christ Jesus.

I know you've heard what I was like while still immersed in ritual observances: I was at the top of my class, ahead of all my peers as far as religious studies were concerned, excelling them in my zeal to keep the traditions handed down by our forefathers. And in pursuit of that goal I even went after the people of God with hammer and tongs, doing my best to destroy his church.

But God set me apart for his own purposes before I was born. And when it pleased him to call me through his grace to reveal his Son in me so that I might spread his evangel among the Gentiles, I didn't stop for a minute to discuss it with anyone. I didn't even go up to Jerusalem to confer with those who were apostles before me. No, I went off instead to the Arabian Desert and afterwards returned to Damascus.

Three years later, though, I did go up to Jerusalem to visit Cephas and stayed with him 15 days. But the fact of the matter is that besides him I didn't meet with any of the other apostles at that time, except for Jesus' brother James. After that I went into the regions of Syria and Cilicia. So I was still basically unknown by sight to the believers in Judea. The only thing they'd heard were reports that the person who used to persecute them was now spreading the good news he'd earlier tried to stamp out. And they glorified God's work in me!

2

Some 14 years later I again went up to Jerusalem by divine revelation, this time traveling with Barnabas and also taking Titus along. There I laid out for them the message of the gospel as I was preaching it among the Gentiles. I did so in a closed meeting with the people in charge of the local assembly, to confirm I hadn't just been spinning my wheels. Yet although I had brought along the Gentile Titus no one forced him to be circumcised.

The situation was that some false brethren had slipped in to spy out the freedom we have in Christ Jesus and even though they wanted to bring us into bondage we didn't give them the time of day, in order that we might safeguard the truth of the gospel among you.

And note: the top people in Jerusalem didn't impose any added burdens on us either, let alone seek to alter the gospel we preach – not that I would have yielded to someone just because he had assumed a leadership role. As I've said, outward appearances mean nothing to me, only the truth. But in fact the leaders there understood that I had been entrusted with the gospel as far as the uncircumcised were concerned, while Peter with those of the circumcision; and that he who was at work in Peter as apostle to the circumcised was at work in me to the uncircumcision. So when Jacob and Cephas and John (who were looked up to as pillars of the church) perceived the grace that God had given me they extended the right hand of fellowship to Barnabas and me, to the end that we should go to the Gentiles and they to the Jews. The only thing they asked was that we be sure to remember the poor – something I was already on top of.

Even so, when Cephas came to Antioch I had to stand him down because he fell into error. What happened was that when he first got there he shared meals with the Gentile believers, as did the rest of us. However, when some people came on a mission from Jacob he made a move to withdraw and separate himself because he was afraid of them. As if that weren't bad enough, the rest of the local Jewish believers went along with his pretense – indeed, even Barnabas was swept into the hypocrisy!

But when I saw they weren't staying true to the straight path of the gospel I challenged Cephas in front of everyone: "If you though a Jew live as a Gentile and not as a Jew, how can you now force the Gentiles to adopt Jewish customs?" My point was that even we who are Jews by birth, not sinners like the Gentiles, know that no one is vindicated in God's sight by observing the Law's obligations, but only through the faith of the Anointed Jesus. We as well as the Gentiles have therefore put our trust in him in order to be deemed righteous by faith in the Savior and not by the Law's observances – because no mortal is made righteous by such observances.[1] But is it Jesus' fault if we fall sinfully back while professing to be justified in him? Hardly! If I rebuild the structure I've already torn down then I've simply reverted to sin.

---

1   *Psalms* 143:2.

Through the Law I died to the Law in order to live unto God. In truth I have been crucified with Christ - it is no longer I who live but Christ in me, such that the life I now lead in this mortal coil I live by faith in the Son of God, who loved me and gave himself for me. God forbid that I should frustrate the grace of God - if we could have become righteous in God's sight by obedience to the Law then Jesus died for no reason.

3

O Galatians, you fools! Who's put a hex on you, before whose eyes Jesus' crucifixion was so graphically presented? Let me ask you this - did you receive the Spirit by observing the Law's rituals, or through the faith you heard proclaimed? And are you so dimwitted that having been initiated in the Spirit you think you'll be perfected through fleshly efforts? What was the point of your suffering? Was it all in vain? Are you empowered through the Law to work miracles and enjoy the fruits of the Spirit - or do these good things come by faith, just as Abraham believed God and it was credited to his account as righteousness?[2]

Be sure you get this: it is people of faith who are the children of Abraham. And so with the foreknowledge that God would make the Gentiles righteous by faith the Scripture proclaimed the good news to Abraham ahead of time saying, In you shall all the nations be blessed.[3] Therefore those who are of faith are blessed with faithful Abraham. But those who rely on the Law's observances fall under a curse, as it is written, Cursed is anyone who fails to persevere in doing the things written in the Book of the Law.[4] Just as it's clear that no one is considered righteous in God's sight by virtue of the Law so too is the contrary clear, The just shall live by faith.[5]

Now, the Law is not grounded in faith, it's a matter of doing. That's why the Scripture says whoever performs these things shall live by them.[6] But the Messiah redeemed us from the curse of the Law, becoming a curse on our be-

---

2   *Genesis* 15:6.
3   *Genesis* 12:3, 22:18.
4   *Deuteronomy* 27:6.
5   *Habakkuk* 2:4; *see also Exodus* 14:31 (and *Mekilta de-Rabbi Ishmael* thereon); *Psalms* 91:2; *Lamentations* 3:24-26.
6   *Leviticus* 18:5.

half[7] – as it is written, Cursed is anyone hanged on a tree[8] – so that in Christ Jesus the blessing promised to Abraham might also come to the Gentiles and all thereby receive the promise of the Spirit[9] through faith.

Brethren, let me try explaining this in more human terms. Think about last wills and testaments. Once they're signed, sealed and delivered no one can cancel them let alone impose new terms and conditions. But here the promises were spoken not just to Abraham but also to his descendant. Note that the Scripture doesn't say "and by your descendants shall all nations be blessed" as if it referred to many, but rather in your seed shall all nations be blessed,[10] referring to a unity, that is, to Messiah.[11] So this is my point: since the covenant with Abraham had previously been ratified by God, the Law, coming into being 430 years later,[12] could not annul it and thereby do away with the promise. If the inheritance is by virtue of the Law it logically cannot be a matter of promise. But Abraham was graced with the inheritance by virtue of God's promise.

So why the Law? It formalized sin as transgressions, revealing sin for what it is[13] until the coming of the seed to whom the promise was made. And the Law was instituted by angels[14] and mediated by the hand of Moses.[15] Now, a mediator does not stand alone but between two parties. Yet God in his promise is One. Is the Law therefore in opposition to God's promise? God forbid! If a quickening law had been given then it follows that obedience to the Law would have made people righteous in God's sight. Instead, the Scripture[16] put all under sin's lock and key that through the faith of the Anointed Jesus the promise might be gifted to those who believe.

Before the advent of this faith we were kept in guardianship under the Law, fenced in until the coming faith should be revealed. The Law was our tutor,[17] guiding us to Messiah in order that we be made righteous by faith. But now that faith has come we are no longer wards. And so you are all the children of God by faith in the Anointed Jesus, because as many of

---

7   *Leviticus* 4:25, 29.
8   *Deuteronomy* 21:23.
9   *Joel* 2:28-29.
10   *Genesis* 22:18.
11   *Hosea* 11:1 and *Genesis* 21:12; *see Matthew* 2:15 and *Romans* 4:18, 9:7.
12   *Exodus* 12:40.
13   *Romans* 5:20, 7:7 *ff.*
14   *Deuteronomy* 33:3.
15   *Exodus* 20:19; *Deuteronomy* 5:5; *cf.* Philo, *Life of Moses (Vol. I)* I (5).
16   *Deuteronomy* 27:26; *Psalms* 143:2.
17   See Plato, *Lysis* 208c.

you as have been baptized into Christ have been robed in Christ. There can be no Jew or Gentile, nor bond or free, no male and female, for you are all one in Christ Jesus. And if you be the Savior's then are you Abraham's seed and heirs according to the promise.

4

Let me explain further. As a legal matter, the heir of the house differs little from one of its servants while he is still a minor. Even though he will come to own everything he remains subject to the authority of guardians and stewards until the time appointed by his father. It's the same with us. As children we were bound to rules governing our behavior and the elements of our worship were likewise mundane. But in the Fulness of Time God sent his Son, taking on human nature and born under law to redeem those under law, in order that we all might be adopted as sons. And it is evident you are sons because God sent forth the Spirit of his Son into our hearts crying "Abba, Father!"[18] Therefore you are no longer a servant but a son and if a son then an heir of God through Christ.

Recall that when ignorant of God you were enslaved to things that by nature are not gods.[19] So now that you recognize God – or I should say, are recognized by God – how in the world can you revert to the weak and worthless elements? What's gotten into you that you once more want to serve them? Yet now I find you're scrupulously observing solemn days, new moons, festal seasons and sabbatical years.[20] I'm worried my efforts for you will prove to have been wasted! I beg you, brothers, become as I am now – for I too was once bound as you are.

You didn't treat me this wrongfully before. On the contrary, when I first arrived you not only didn't despise me but welcomed me with open arms – and that's despite my ill-appearance, the thorn in my own flesh becoming a test for you even as I preached the good news. No, far from rejecting me or gagging at my sight you received me as though I were an angel from God, even the Anointed Jesus himself! What's happened to

---

18   *Mark* 14:36; *Romans* 8:15.
19   . *Cf. 2 Chronicles* 13:9.
20   *See Judith* 8:6; *cf.* Origen, *Against Celsius* 8:21-23.

all that goodness? I swear that if you could've you would've dug out your own eyes and given them to replace mine. So now I'm your enemy just because I'm telling you the truth?

But these people so eagerly currying your favor are only in it for themselves. They want you to join their exclusive group so they can turn you into zealots for them. Don't get me wrong, I'm not against zeal whether I'm there with you or not, but it has to be zeal for something good. As things stand, my little children, I suffer birth pangs for you all over again until Christ is formed among you.[21]

I wish I could be present with you and able to change the tone of my voice, but right now I'm at a loss about your state. So tell me, you who wish to be under the Law, haven't you heard what the Law says? It is written that Abraham fathered two sons, one by a slave girl and one by a free woman. The son of the slave was born in the natural course of things but the son of the free through the power of God's promise. These historical events have allegorical meaning[22] because the two women represent two covenants. The one is from Mount Sinai, giving birth to slavery. That's Hagar, because Mount Sinai is in Arabia[23] but by allegory parallels the earthly Jerusalem, which is in bondage with her children. Yet the heavenly Jerusalem[24] is free and she is *our* mother, as it is written,

> Sing, O barren,
> > thou that didst not bear;
> break forth into singing,
> > and cry aloud,
> thou that didst not travail with child:
> > for more are the children of the desolate
> than the children of the married wife.[25]

And you, brothers and sisters, are children of the promise, as was Isaac. But just as the one born of the slave according to the flesh mocked

---

21   *cf. Ephesians* 4:13.
22   *cf.* Philo, *On Abraham* XX (99); *On Sobriety* II (7-9).
23   See *Genesis* 16:7, 14; 1 *Chronicles* 5:19; *Psalms* 83:6; *Baruch* 3:23.
24   *Revelation* 21:2.
25   *Isaiah* 54:1.

the one born of the free by way of the promise,[26] so it is now. Yet what does the Scripture say?

> Cast out the slave woman and her son –
> for the son of the slave woman
> shall not inherit with the son of the free.[27]

Therefore, my brethren, we are not children of a bondwoman but of the free.

5

Stand fast therefore in the liberty you have as Christians. You've been set free from the Law's yoke of bondage – don't submit to it again. And get it straight in your heads what I, Paul, am telling you: if you persist in practicing circumcision then the Savior is of no use to you! I protest again that if you yield to circumcision you've also taken on the burden of keeping the *whole* Law. You cancel out everything the Messiah did for you in making you righteous in God's sight – in other words, you've fallen from grace if you're seeking vindication through the Law. But we who are in the Spirit eagerly await our hope of perfected righteousness, because in Christ Jesus neither circumcision nor uncircumcision counts for anything, but only faith working through love.

You'd been running a good race up to now – who tripped you up? Someone's kept you from obeying the truth. But if that's now your persuasion it doesn't suit you well. And I can promise you it doesn't come from the one who called you. A little yeast makes the whole loaf rise. But as far as I'm concerned, I'm persuaded you'll come to be of one mind and that whoever's been stirring you up will suffer the penalty. Brethren, if I yet preach circumcision then why am I still being persecuted? I wouldn't be, of course, because if I were to urge circumcision on you I'd be severing

---

26 *Genesis* 19:14.
27 *Genesis* 21:10.

the offense of the cross. As it is, I wish those inciting you would just go castrate themselves!

My brothers, you've been called into freedom. Just don't allow that freedom to be an excuse for carnal living. Instead, serve one another through love, because the entire Law is summarily complete in this one verse – Love your neighbor as yourself.[28] But if you bite and devour one another watch out that you aren't consumed by one another.

What I mean is this: if you walk spiritually you won't placate your carnal desires. Your fallen nature itself is at war with the Spirit and the desires of the Spirit at war with those of the flesh. They are in such enmity that, as I explained to the Romans,[29] you cannot do the good things that in your heart you really want to do. Yet if you are spiritually led you are not under the Law.

I'm sure it's obvious to you what I mean when I refer to "carnal deeds" – I mean wanton sex, uncleanliness, debauchery, idolatry, sorcery, hatred, strife, jealousy, rage, cabals, denominationalism, heresies, envy, murder, drunkenness, orgies ... things like that. And if I've said it once I'll say it again, people who do these things won't inherit the kingdom of God.

But the fruit of the Spirit is love, joy, peace, longsuffering, gentleness, goodness, faith, meekness, temperance: against such there is no law. And they that are Christ's have crucified the flesh with the affections and lusts. If we live in the Spirit let us also walk in the Spirit. Let us not be desirous of vainglory, provoking one another, envying one another.

6

Brothers and sisters, if you see anyone being pulled over the line then those who are spiritual should restore him to his right self. But be sure you do so with empathy and in a spirit of meekness so you don't fall into some form of temptation yourselves. Bear one another's burdens and you will thoroughly fulfill the law of Christ. If anyone thinks he's something

---

28   *Leviticus* 19:18.
29   *Romans* 7.

vspecial he's just kidding himself. Let each of you put your own deeds to the test. That way if you want to take proper pride in what you've done you'll be taking responsibility for your own actions rather than getting credit for that of others.

I have a few more exhortations.

Those of you who are being taught should contribute to the support of those who teach.

Don't be fooled – God is not mocked. The old saying is true, you reap what you sow: if you sow to your lusts you'll just reap corruption, but if you sow to the Spirit you'll reap eternal life.

And let's not lose heart at doing good. We'll harvest at the harvest time, if we hold on. Let's lend a hand wherever we can, but especially to members of the household of faith.

I want you to notice that I'm writing this last section of the letter with my own hand – if you can imagine, my eyesight is even worse than it was before, hence the big letters! I'm not concerned how things look from the outside, unlike those who want to parade your flesh around, forcing you to be circumcised so they don't have to suffer the cross. And the hypocrisy of it all is that the people who are promoting circumcision don't even keep the Law themselves! They only want you to be circumcised so they can boast about your flesh to others holding the same view.

But God forbid that I should boast, save in the cross of our Lord Jesus Christ, by whom the world is crucified to me and I to the world. For in Christ Jesus neither circumcision nor uncircumcision makes a difference, only a new creature. Peace be to all those who walk in accordance with this rule, and mercy upon the Israel of God.

Brothers and sisters, I don't want to have to deal with this issue again. Consider this –
the stigmata I bear in my body are those of the Lord Jesus. May the grace of our Lord Jesus Christ be with your spirit,

Amen.

TO THE EPHESIANS

Paul, an apostle of Christ Jesus through the Will of God, to the saints in Ephesus and to the faithful everywhere in Christ Jesus: grace to you and peace from God our Father and the Lord Jesus Christ.

Blessed is the God and Father of our Lord Jesus Christ, who blessed us with all blessings of the Spirit in the Heavenly Places by virtue of our union with Christ and who, according to his Will, chose us in him before the foundation of the world in order that we be holy and without blemish before his Presence in Love, having likewise preassigned us for Adoption to himself through Jesus Christ according to the pleasure of his Will and to the praise of the Glory of his Grace, by which he blessed us in the Well-Beloved – in whom we have redemption through his Blood, the forgiveness of transgressions according to the Richness of his Grace, which he shed abundantly on us in all wisdom and counsel in making known to us the Mystery of his Will, whereby in his good pleasure he purposed in himself that in the ordered fullness of the appointed times he might sum up all things, gathering together into the Christ all things in Heaven and on the Earth – in whom we were also taken for his Inheritance, having been delineated according to the Purpose of the one who energizes all things according to the Counsel of his Will, in order that we who first hoped in the Savior should be to the praise of his Glory – in whom you also, once you heard the Word of Truth and believed the good news of

your Salvation were sealed by the Spirit of Promise, the Holy One who is the first installment of our Inheritance until the full redemption of his possession to the praise of his Glory.

On that account I as well, having good report of your faith in the Lord Jesus and the love you show toward all the saints, have not ceased giving thanks for you, remembering you in all my prayers to the end that the God of our Lord Jesus Christ, the Father of Glory, might give you the Spirit of Wisdom and Revelation in the full understanding of him, having the eyes of your heart enlightened that you might know what is the Hope of his Calling, what are the Riches of the Glory of his Inheritance in the saints and what is the surpassing Greatness of his Power toward us who believe in accordance with the outworking of the Power of his Might which he energized in Christ when he raised him from among the dead, seated him at his Right Hand in the Heavenly Places high above all rule and authority and power and dominion and every name that is named not only in this age but in the age to come, subjected all things under his feet and presented him as Head over all things to the Church, which is his Body, the Fullness of him who fills all in all.

And you once were dead in the sins and transgressions of your past way of living, conforming yourselves to this world's ways under the rule of the Prince and Power of the Air (the same spirit now at work in the Sons of Disobedience) – with whom we ourselves once disported, indulging our carnal desires, obeying the wishes of our bodies and our thoughts, and were by nature children of wrath as also were the rest of our companions. But God, being rich in Mercy on account of his great Love by which he loved us even when we were dead in our sins brought us to Life with Christ (by Grace you are saved), raised us up with him and seated us in the Heavenly Places together with Christ Jesus in order that he might demonstrate in the coming ages the overflowing Richness of his Grace in showing kindness toward us in Christ Jesus. It is by Grace that you are saved through faith and this not of yourselves but rather by the Gift of God, not by virtue of your efforts, lest anyone should boast. And so we are God's handiwork created in Christ Jesus for good deeds which God prepared beforehand, that we should walk in them.

Keep in mind that having been born Gentiles (uncircumcised in the flesh and therefore treyf to the circumcised) you were once without Christ, alienated from the Commonwealth of Israel, strangers to the Covenants of Promise, living in the world without hope and without God. But now in Christ you who once were far off were brought near by the Blood of Christ - for he is our Peace, who has made both one and torn down the dividing partition wall, destroying that enmity with his own flesh. He nullified the Law of decretal commands in order to forge the two into one new being in himself, thereby making peace and reconciling both in one Body to God through the cross, having slain the enmity on it.

And once he had arisen he preached peace to you who were far off and peace to those who were near so that through him both we Jews and you Gentiles might have access in one Spirit to the Father. You are therefore no longer strangers and sojourners but fellow citizens with the saints and members of the Household of God, having been built upon the foundation of the apostles and prophets, Jesus Christ himself being the Chief Cornerstone, in whom the whole building carefully framed together is growing into a Holy Temple in the Lord and in whom you are being built together with us into a dwelling place for God in the Spirit.

That's the reason that I, Paul, serve as Christ's prisoner for the sake of you Gentiles by the Grace of God, it having been granted to me in the Wisdom of God's ordered revelation to understand the Mystery that was unknown to prior generations of God's children but has now been revealed by the Spirit to his holy apostles and prophets, that is, that the Gentiles are fellow heirs, members of the same Body and equal participants in the Promise through the gospel of Christ Jesus, of which I have been made a minister according to the Gift of the Grace of God given to me through the working of his Power - to *me*, though I am less than the least of all saints! - that I should preach to the Gentiles the unsearchable Riches of Christ and bring to light for all peoples the system and structure of God's Mystery (which had been hidden from the beginning of the Time by God, the Creator of all things) in order that by means of the Church the multifaceted Wisdom of God should now be made known to the spiritual rulers and authorities in the Heavenly Places in accordance with his Timeless Will for the ages, which he ordained in Christ Jesus our Lord - whom we approach boldly and with full assurance and confidence, having free access to him through our faith.

And I want to urge you not to be fainthearted about the things I'm now suffering for your sake. Rather, let it be your source of pride, since it's because of your place in God's Plan that I bow my knees before the Father, from whom all kith and kin in Earth and Heaven are named, that he might grant you according to the Riches of his Glory to be strengthened in power through his Spirit in your innermost selves; that Christ might find his home in your hearts through faith; that being rooted and grounded in love you may be able to comprehend with all saints what is the Breadth and Length and Depth and Height; and that you may know the Love of Christ, which passes knowledge, in order that you be filled with all the Fullness of God. Now unto him who is able to do exceeding abundantly above all that we ask or think according to the Power that works in us, unto him be glory in the Church and in Christ Jesus throughout all ages, world without end, amen.

I, the bondservant of the Lord, therefore urge you to walk worthily of the calling by which you were called – with all humility and gentleness, with forbearance yielding to one another in love, zealously guarding the Unity of the Spirit in the Bond of Peace. There is one Body and one Spirit just as you have also been called in one Hope of your calling – one Lord, one Faith, one Baptism, one God and Father of all who is over all and through all and in all. Even so, Grace has been given to each of us as God has apportioned in accordance with the Gift of Christ, which is why the Scriptures say,

> When he ascended on high he took the
> captors captive
> and gave gifts to mankind.[1]

What's the implication of saying that "he ascended?" It's that he first *descended* to the lower depths of the Earth. He that descended is therefore the same as he that ascended above all the Heavens that he might fill all things. And he himself appointed some as apostles, some as prophets, some as evangelists, some as pastors and teachers, all to train the saints for the task of serving others in order to build up the Body of Christ until together we reach the Unity of the Faith and Knowledge of the Son of God, to perfect completion, to the measure of maturity of the Fullness of Christ, that we no longer be children tossed about on the waves, carried thither and yon by every crosswind of false doctrine and card-shark teaching foisted by crafty methods of deception, but rather speaking the truth in love should increase in all things

---

1   *Psalms* 68:18.

in him who is the Head, namely Christ, from whom the whole Body derives, every ligament and joint supplying strength in its own measure, each part energizing all, that as the Body grows it builds itself up in love.

I therefore testify and charge you in the Lord not to conduct yourselves any longer as do the Gentiles in the vanity of their minds – having their understanding darkened, alienated from the Life of God through the ignorance that dwells in them by virtue of the hardening of their heart, people who have become callous, having given themselves over to debauchery, greedily engaging in every form of uncleanliness. But that is not how you have learned Christ, if indeed you have hearkened to his Voice and been taught in his Ways according to the Truth that is in Jesus. Rather, let your old nature waste away with its passion for deceit, abandoning your former ways to the past and renewing your mind in the Spirit, clothing yourselves in the New Man created in the image of God in Righteousness and Holiness of Truth.

Having shed yourselves of lies let each of you speak truth with his neighbor,[2] because we are members of one another. And sin not in your anger[3] – let not the sun go down on your wrath, giving no space to Satan's wiles. Whoever steals must steal no more but rather work using his own two hands not only to earn a living but also to gain enough to share with those who are in need. Don't let any slander leave your lips but only those words that are helpful and constructive, giving spiritual grace to those who hear you. And grieve not the Holy Spirit of God, in whom you were sealed unto the Day of Redemption. But let all bitterness and rage and anger and clamor and reviling be put away from you, together with all wickedness. Be helpful and tenderhearted to one another, forgiving one another as God in Christ forgave you.

Be therefore imitators of God, as well-beloved children, and walk in love even as Christ also loved us and gave himself up for us as an offering and sacrifice to God for a sweet-smelling savor – but don't tarnish the Church's witness by getting involved in casual sex or strange worship practices or any sort of greedy behavior. Don't revel in dirty jokes or gossip or mocking sarcasm, none of which has any place in your midst, but instead enjoy the true gladness and joy that come from thanksgiving. And you can be sure that no lecher or purveyor of filth or greed-filled idolater

---

2   *Zechariah* 8:16.

3   *Psalms* 4:4.

has any share in the Kingdom of Christ and God.

Don't let anyone trick you with smooth talk – it's on account of these things that the Wrath of God falls on the Sons of Disobedience. Don't mix with them. You were indeed once darkness but now you are Light in the Lord. Therefore walk as Children of Light, shining forth in all that is pleasing to God, letting the spiritual light that is in you bear fruit in every way that is good and righteous and true. Steer clear of the desolate works of darkness – don't even speak about the shameful things done in hidden places, it being sufficient to expose them to the light. Everything exposed to the light is revealed and what is revealed is light. As Isaiah said in the Spirit,

> Wake up, you sleeper!
> Rise up from the dead,
> and the Anointed One will shine upon you![4]

Be sure that you conduct yourselves as those who are wise, not as fools, redeeming the time (for the days are evil) and understanding what God's Will is for your lives. Don't get carried away with wine in dissipation but be filled with the Spirit, speaking to one another in psalms and hymns and spiritual songs, singing praise to the Lord in your heart, always giving thanks for all things in the Name of our Lord Jesus Christ to God the Father.

Yield to one another in godly reverence. Thus wives to their own husbands as to the Lord – what I mean is, think of the man as the head of the woman in the same sense that Christ is Head of the Church, himself Savior of the Body, so that as the Church yields itself to Christ so also should wives to their husbands. But *equally* so must husbands love their wives as Christ loved the Church and gave himself for her that he might sanctify her, having purified her in the baptismal font of the Word to present to himself a glorious Church without spot or wrinkle, holy and blameless. Husbands therefore ought to love their own wives as they do their own bodies. Whoever loves his wife therefore loves himself, since no one hates his own body but rather nourishes and cares for it.

---

4   *Isaiah* 60:1.

And just so does the Savior nourish and care for *his* Body, the Church, because we are members of his Body, flesh of his flesh and bone of his bones.[5] Thus we perceive by allegory that a man shall leave his father and mother and be joined to his wife, and the two shall become one flesh.[6] Listen – this is a great mystery. I speak concerning Christ and the Church, but nevertheless you men must love your wives as yourselves and a wife should give her husband due respect.

Children, obey your parents – that's only right! More than that, this is the first commandment that comes along with a promise: Honor thy father and mother, that it may be well with thee and thou mayest live long on the Earth.[7] Parents – don't drive your kids crazy with unreasonable demands but raise them up in the proper discipline and instruction of the Lord. Slaves, servants and employees – obey your mortal bosses with fear and trembling in sincerity of heart, just as you would if serving the Lord himself. And do your work without pretense – don't stand at your post just to look good in other people's eyes but work with enthusiasm, as servants of the Lord not of men, doing the Will of God from deep in your heart in the sure knowledge that whatever good thing you do will earn its full reward from the Lord, whether you be bound or free. Overseers, treat those who labor for you with the same kind of respect – don't threaten or terrorize them – knowing you both have the same Master who dwells in Heaven and is not swayed by anyone.

Finally, my brethren, be strong in the Lord and in the Power of his Might. Put on the whole Armor of God, that you may be able to stand against the wiles of the Devil. For we wrestle not against flesh and blood, but against principalities, against powers, against the rulers of the darkness of this world, against spiritual wickedness in high places. Wherefore take unto you the whole Armor of God, that you may be able to withstand in the evil day, and having done all, to stand. Stand therefore, having your loins girt about with Truth, and having on the Breastplate of Righteousness; and your feet shod with the preparation of the Gospel of Peace; above all, taking the Shield of Faith, wherewith you shall be able to quench all the fiery darts of the wicked. And take the Helmet of Salvation, and

5   *Genesis* 2:23.
6   *Genesis* 2:24.
7   *Exodus* 20:12; *Deuteronomy* 5:16.

the Sword of the Spirit, which is the Word of God: praying always with all prayer and supplication in the Spirit, and watching thereunto with all perseverance and supplication for all saints; and for me, that utterance may be given unto me, that I may open my mouth boldly, to make known the Mystery of the Gospel, for which I am an ambassador in bonds: that therein I may speak boldly, as I ought to speak.

In closing, I want to be sure you have a complete picture of how things are going with me and what my plans are. I am therefore sending Tychicus, beloved brother and faithful servant in the Lord, for this very purpose and to encourage your hearts. Peace to all the brethren and love with faith from God the Father and the Lord Jesus Christ. May Grace Incorruptible be with all who love our Lord Jesus Christ.

TO THE PHILIPPIANS

1

From Paul and Timothy, bondsmen of Christ Jesus, to all in Philippi who are pure and holy in him, servants and overseers together: grace to you and peace from God our Father and the Lord Jesus Christ.

I think of you everywhere I go all the time I'm there and I give thanks to God in all my prayers for your fellowship in the gospel from the very first days until now because I fully trust that God will finish in you the good work he began, bringing it wholly to completion at the coming of the Lord Jesus Christ. It should be no surprise that I think of you in this way because I know you also have me on your hearts, sharing in my grace despite the chains that hold me – sharing, in other words, in both the confession and comfort of the gospel. And God is my witness how deeply I long for you, even as does Jesus in his inner heart. I pray that as you grow toward perfect knowledge and insight so too may your love abound to overflowing. Put everything to the test and hold to what is constant and true – your character thus made sunlight-clear, refined, filled with the fruits of righteousness, confident at his coming, all to the praise and glory of God.

Here's an illustration from my own life of what I am trying to say. Yes, I now suffer hard times, but the outcome of my trials is a further spread of the gospel. For one thing, everyone in the barracks of the praetorian guards as well as those beyond it know I'm in prison for the Savior. Moreover, many of our brethren in the Lord, trusting in my example, have become exceedingly bold, fearlessly speaking the Word. Now it *is* true that some people are simply envious and go about trying to create strife through their preaching. Others, of course, preach in good faith. And again, some go about scheming, acting impurely even though they preach Christ, thinking they are somehow adding pain to my imprisonment. But the others preach out of love, knowing that I am being held here for the defense of the gospel.

What's my point? Basically, it actually doesn't matter whether Christ is preached in pretense or in truth so long as the gospel is spoken. For me it's something to rejoice about and I *do* rejoice, because I also know that this will result in my salvation[1] through your prayers and the added supply of the spirit of the Anointed Jesus. My greatest wish is simply not to be ashamed of anything I've done with my life. Instead, I aim for Christ to be greatly exalted in my very body, whether through life or through death. For me life is Christ. As for death? It's gain.[2] So long as I live in this body I do of course see good come from my labors. But on the other hand I'm caught between two desires - preferring to break camp and be with Jesus (our better and ultimate goal), but also confidently persuaded that I need to abide by the flesh, standing by you to the increase and joy of your faith.

So, when next I come be sure to let your glorying in Christ overflow to me. And in the meantime, conduct yourselves worthily of the gospel of Christ as good citizens of his kingdom, that whether I'm with you or away I will always hear that you hold your ground in one spirit, one united soul, competing for the faith of the gospel, not startled by your enemies. That's a sign from God to them of their destruction, but it's also a sign of salvation to you because you've been given the gift not only to believe in the Lord but also to suffer for him, fighting the same contest you've seen and heard to be the case with me.

---

1   *Job* 13:16.
2   Euripides, *Phyrixus*, Fr. 638 N².

2

My own joy will be to know you are of one mind, one in love, one in spirit, forsaking faction and pride, in humility each thinking better of the other than she does of herself. I long to know that your conduct is such – if so it will be for me as soothing words of love, a comfort in Christ, sealing our communion in the Spirit, a sign of God's mercies and compassion. And keep your priorities straight, not worrying about your own problems but helping your brothers and sisters. Just think about what Jesus did in that regard: timelessly subsisting as he did in the form of God he had no need to seize equality with God as a prize.[3] Rather than maintain his divine prerogatives he emptied himself of them and took on the form of a servant, appearing among us in human similitude.[4] And more than that, being found in outward form as a man Jesus humbled himself in obedience all the way through to death, even the death of the cross. Therefore God exceedingly exalted him and gifted him the Name that is above every name, that at the Name of Jesus all things in Heaven all on Earth and all below should bow their knees and with their tongues proclaim with thanksgiving that he is Lord, to the glory of God the Father.[5]

Therefore my beloved ones, as you have always obeyed not only when I was with you but now just as much in my absence: carry out your own salvation with fear and trembling, knowing that God is the one who creates in you the desire and strength to fulfill his good purpose. Do all that you do without murmuring or conniving and so you will be faultless, undefiled, the blameless children of God in the midst of a crooked and twisted generation,[6] in which you appear like bright lights in the Heavens. Offer the word of life freely. I want to be able to boast at the Lord's coming that I neither ran nor toiled in vain – but even if I am poured out as a libation on the sacrificial altar of your faith I myself rejoice and rejoice with you, just as you should rejoice yourselves and rejoice with me.

I do hope to send Timothy to you shortly. That way, when he returns he can cheer my soul with the latest news about you. No one else is as close to my heart as he is. Moreover, he is well able to care for your needs

3   *John* 1:1.
4   *Isaiah* 53:2-3.
5   *Isaiah* 45:23; *Romans* 8:22; *Revelation* 5:13.
6   *Cf. Deuteronomy* 32:5.

in my stead. I'm afraid all the rest seem to have gone off on their own, not following the ways of Christ. But you know Timothy's character, that as a son serves his father he has served alongside me in the gospel. Therefore I hope to send him at once (as soon as I see how things stand with me, that is).

I also trust in the Lord that I myself can come visit you soon. Until then, I also thought I'd better send you my brother Epaphroditus. He's my co-worker and fellow soldier. Indeed, you yourselves commissioned him and he's been faithful to help meet my needs. But I want you to know that he yearned for you all and was distressed because you had heard that he was sick. And indeed he *was* sick, nearly to death – but God had mercy on him and not only on him but on me too, that I not suffer more grief upon grief. I've therefore sent him back to you out of concern for you because seeing him again you'll be joyful and thus I less sorrowful. Be sure to receive him in the Lord with all joy, and hold all who are like him in the same honor, because it was on account of the work of Christ that he came near to dying, showing no regard for his life in order to make up for your lack of service to me.

3

As far as everything else is concerned, rejoice in the Lord. But here are some cautions: beware the impure, evildoers who mutilate the flesh.[7] We are the true circumcision, our hearts and lips made pure,[8] worshiping in the Spirit of God, boasting in Christ Jesus, not trusting in our own merits. As I'm sure you know, at one time I did put my faith in who I was and what I did. And well I might have since if there was anyone who had reason to rely on his inborn gifts and family background it was I – born a Hebrew of the Hebrews, circumcised on the eighth day, a son of the House of Israel, a member of the tribe of Benjamin.[9] And more than that I was a Pharisee, a doer of the Law. Does anyone think he can compete with me in terms of energy? Well, I was so zealous that I even persecuted the Church! And if anyone could have been found righteous before God by observing the Law then I was that person

---

7   *Leviticus* 21:5; 1 *Kings* 18:28; *Isaiah* 15:2; *Hosea* 17:14.
8   *Leviticus* 26:41; *Deuteronomy* 10:16, 30:6.
9   See *Genesis* 49:27.

- blameless. But whatever things I gained by obedience to the Law's commands were a loss as far as Jesus is concerned. Indeed, I consider everything
as nothing compared to the excellency of the knowledge of Jesus my Lord, for
whom I've willingly suffered the loss of all things, mere scat flushed away in
order to gain Christ.

My goal is to be found justified in the end through faith in the Savior,
not by whatever vindication I could obtain from the Law. So how will I be
made righteous before God? By God's act, not mine. And it's by faith that I
know him and the power of his resurrection, sharing in the fellowship of his
sufferings, conforming my heart and soul and mind to his death with all my
strength – if so be I may attain the resurrection from among the dead.

Don't get me wrong – I haven't gotten there yet nor am I perfect by any
means. But I *am* pressing ahead because I want to live up to all that Jesus
seeks for me. Brothers and sisters, believe me, I haven't arrived! Indulge me
a minute if I use a sports analogy: I'm not thinking about the prior set of
downs. I'm just focused on the goal line. And at this point in my life I know
I'm in the red zone, rushing forward, aiming to win the prize of the heavenward calling of God in Christ Jesus. So if any of you wish to perfect your own
faith, keep that same focus. God will let you know if you've stepped out of
bounds. But the most important thing is that we not lose the ground we've
gained. Instead let's stand together all of one mind, one purpose, one will,
one accord.

Imitate me, brothers and sisters, and also take a good look at those
among you who conduct themselves the way I do. They are your mentors and
examples. As I've told you before but say it now with tears in my eyes: there
are many others around who are enemies of the cross of Christ. Yet their end
is destruction, their god their bowels,[10] their glory their shame,[11] their minds
set only on the things of this world. But *your* citizenship is in the Heavens,
whence we expect our Savior the Lord Jesus Christ, who will change the bodily form we bear in low estate, transforming it to the likeness of his glorious body by the same power by which he will subject all things to himself.

---

10   *See* Euripides, *Cyclops* 335; Seneca, *On Benefits* VII.26.
11   *Hosea* 4:7.

4

Therefore stand fast in the Lord, my beloved brethren, my crown, my joy, whom I long to see.

And Euodia and Syntyche – I beg you, be of one mind in the Lord. And I urge you, true yokefellow, to assist these women, inasmuch as they strove alongside me for the gospel along with Clement and my other co-workers. All their names are written in the Book of Life.

Rejoice in the Lord always! And again I will say, rejoice! Let all men see your gentleness, because the Lord is near. And don't worry about mere things: simply let God know your needs in all your prayers and petitions with thankfulness; and the peace of God, which surpasses all understanding, will keep your hearts and minds through Christ Jesus.

More than that, my brothers and sisters: whatever is true, whatever solemn, whatever just, whatever holy, whatever speaks of kind affection, whatever is gracious – if anything excel and if anything be praised, think on these things. And whatever you have learned, received, heard and seen from my life, these things do. And the God of peace will be with you.

And I rejoice greatly in the Lord because you flourish in your care for me. Not that you didn't care about me before, of course, but you didn't have the same opportunity you do now. I'm not saying this because I need anything from you – on the contrary, I've learned to be content whatever comes my way. I know how to have nothing. I know how to have more than enough. In all ways and in all places I've learned the secret of how to be filled and how to be hungry, how to deal with having more than I need and how to do without what I do need. And I am only able to do all that I do because my strength is in Christ.

However, it was a good thing you did when you kept in fellowship with me in my time of suffering. And indeed you Philippians know that when I left Macedonia in the early stages of my gospel mission you were the only church that shared with me in giving and receiving. Even when I was in Thessalonica, you sent me what I needed not just once but twice. Again, it's not that I'm asking for a gift but rather seeking credits that will overflow to your account. But now I have everything I could want and indeed am overflowing myself, having received your gifts from the hands of Epaphroditus, a sweet-smelling savor, a fit sacrifice, well-pleasing to God. And my God will provide all your needs according to his riches in glory in Christ Jesus. Therefore to our God and Father be glory age upon age. Amen.

Greet each saint in Christ Jesus. The brethren who are with me greet you. All the saints greet you, most of all those in the household of Caesar.

The grace of the Lord Jesus Christ be with you all.

Amen.

TO THE COLOSSIANS

Paul, an apostle of Christ Jesus in accordance with the will of God, and Brother Timothy - to the saints in Colossae, steadfast brothers and sisters in Christ, we send grace and peace from God our Father and the Lord Jesus Christ.

1

We give thanks always to God the Father of our Lord Jesus Christ in our prayers for you, having heard of your faith in Christ Jesus and the love you have toward all the saints on account of the hope stored up for you in Heaven, that hope of which you've heard before in the word of truth of the gospel present among you - as it is in fact in all the world, constantly bearing fruit and increasing just as it also has been in you from the very first day you heard and fully understood the grace of God in truth even as you were instructed in it from Epaphras, our beloved fellow laborer. He is Christ's faithful servant on your behalf and has also made plain to us your love in the Spirit.

Therefore we too from the time we first heard about you haven't ceased in our prayers for you, imploring God that you be filled with perfect knowledge of his will in all wisdom and spiritual discernment, that you might conduct yourselves in a manner worthy of the Lord in all things, seeking to please him, bearing fruit in every good work, increasing in the knowledge of God, strengthened with all power according to the might of his glory – all this so that you may endure to the end with all patience, giving thanks with joy to the Father, who enabled us to share in the inheritance of the saints in the realm of light having rescued us from the tyranny of darkness and translated us to the kingdom of his beloved Son, in whom we have redemption through his blood, the forgiveness of sins.

He is the Radiant Image[1] of the Invisible God,[2] the Offspring of Heaven, the Firstborn[3] of all creation – because in him[4] all things in Heaven and on Earth collectively were created,[5] whether seen or unseen, thrones or dominions, rulers or powers.[6] All things were created by him and for him.[7] He himself is before all things and all things cohere in him.[8] He is the Head of the Body, the Church, its source and beginning, firstborn from among the dead in order that he himself have preeminence in all things[9] – because it was pleasing to God that the totality of the pleroma of divine perfection[10] should take up its dwelling in him[11] and that having made peace through the blood of the Savior's cross he would through him reconcile all things back to himself, whether things on Earth or things in Heaven.

And you too, you Gentiles who once were estranged and at enmity with God both by your thoughts and the wicked things you did have now been reconciled by his material body through death so that he may present you holy and unblemished and irreproachable in his sight – *if*, that is, you hold steadfast in faith, well-grounded and seated, not shifting away from the hope afforded by the gospel you've heard, that which has been

---

1   *Wisdom* 7:26.
2   *John* 1:18.
3   *Exodus* 4:22; *Psalms* 89:28; *Psalms of Solomon* 18:4; *4 Esdras* 6:58.
4   *John* 1:4; *Acts* 17:28.
5   *Genesis* 1:1, 2:1 and 14:19; *Revelation* 10:6.
6   *See, e.g., Jeremiah* 52:32; *Ezekiel* 1:26, 9:3, 10:1 *et seq.*, 11:22; *Psalms* 18:10.
7   *John* 1:3, 10; *Hebrews* 1:2, 2:10; *Revelation* 22:13.
8   *Exodus* 3:14; *John* 8:58; *Hebrews* 1:3; *cf.* Philo, *Concerning Noah's Work as a Planter* II (9).
9   *Revelation* 1:5.
10 *Cf.* Hippolytus of Rome, *The Refutation of All Heresies* VII.31; Irenaeus, *Against Heresies* XVII.2.
11 *2 Maccabees* 14:35.

heralded to every creature under Heaven and of which I Paul am become a servant.

I rejoice now in the things I suffer for the sake of the Body of Christ, his Church, supplementing what still lacks in my body of the Savior's afflictions. In God's ordered plan I was made a servant of his Church, gifted with the privilege of fulfilling God's word toward you, the mystery that was hidden in past ages and generations but has now been revealed to his holy ones, those to whom God wished to make known the richness of the glorious manifestation of this mystery – Christ within you Gentiles. He is the hope of glory, the one whom we proclaim as we admonish and initiate every person into all wisdom in order to present each perfected[12] in Christ.[13] And this is the same goal to which I also strive, battling in the arena by virtue of his energy working powerfully in me.

2

I want you to know how much I've agonized over you and your neighbors in Laodicea and all others who haven't yet seen me in person – that with your hearts made one in love you may be confirmed in all richness of the full assurance of knowledge and gain a thorough understanding of the mystery of God, even our Savior, in whom lie all apocryphal treasures of wisdom and knowledge.[14] I say this so that no one leads you astray with casuistry and seemingly clever reasoning – for while I may not be there in person I am present with you in my spirit, rejoicing as I behold you in ordered ranks, shoulder-to-shoulder in defense of the faith of Christ.

Live your lives in just the way you've received Christ Jesus the Lord: solidly rooted and built up in him, strengthened by the faith as you were taught it, overflowing therein with thanksgiving. But *watch out* for anyone who tries to lead you down the primrose path, taking you captive

---

12   *Cf.* Plato, *Phaedrus* 249c, 250b-c.
13   *1 Corinthians* 2:6-7.
14   *Isaiah* 55:3; *1 Macabees* 1:23; *see* Augustine, *Against Faustus* XI.2.

through empty and deceitful philosophy[15] or mundane rituals.[16]   None of these come from the Savior, in whom all the plenitude of Deity dwells corporeally.[17]

And so your fulfillment is in him who is the Fountainhead of every potentate and power, in whom you were circumcised with the circumcision not made by human hands,[18] that is to say, with the circumcision of Christ by the stripping off of the whole body of your carnal affections. You were buried with him in the act of baptism, by which you also were raised up through faith in the energizing power of God, who raised him from among the dead – because though you were dead in your transgressions and the uncircumcision of your corrupted self yet he made you alive with him, having forgiven us all our sins and cancelled the graven decrees that stood in hostility against us,[19] erasing our debt once and for all, having nailed it to the cross and through the cross divesting all sovereigns and dominions, exhibiting them boldly in his triumph over them.

Therefore don't let anyone take you to task for what you eat or what you drink[20] or how you deal with feast days or new moons or Sabbaths,[21] all of which are a shadow of things to come while that which is typified by them, the true substance, belongs to Christ alone.[22]   In the same way don't let anyone cheat you of your prize by insisting you abase yourselves in pompous worship of angels[23] – such a person is suffused with vanity in his carnal mind, treading the void[24] of mystical sights[25] rather than clinging to the Head, from whom the whole Body derives, with every joint and ligament providing nourishment and strength as it knits together growing in godly increase.

---

15   *See, e.g.,* Philo, *That Every Good Man Is Free,* XI (74), XIII (88);
     see generally Hippolytus of Rome, *The Refutation of All Heresies* I.
16   Josephus, *Antiquities of the Jews* XVIII.1.2-4.
17   *John* 1:1, 14; *cf.* Irenaeus, *Against Heresies* I.26.1, III.11.1.
18   *Cf. Leviticus* 26:1; *Isaiah* 21:9.
19   *Deuteronomy* 27:14-26;
20   *Mark* 7:14 *et seq.*
21   *See, e.g.,* 1 *Chronicles* 23:31; 2 *Chronicles* 2:4, 31:3; *Numbers* 28:11; *see also Galatians* 4:10.
22   *Hebrews* 10:1.
23   Josephus, *The Wars of the Jews* II.8.7; Hippolytus of Rome,
     The Refutation of All Heresies V, VII.21.
24   See generally Irenaeus, *Against Heresies* I.4.1-2, II.3.1
25   Philo, *On Dreams* II (2); *cf.* Aristophanes, *Clouds* 225; Plato, *Apology* 19c.

So why, if you died with Christ to childish things do you still subject yourselves to man-made dogmas as though living worldly lives - "don't handle, don't taste, don't touch" - all concerning foods that perish in the eating?[26] These are but human commandments and teachings.[27] So while some people think it's "spiritual" to deny their natural passions with self-imposed asceticism and fleshly mortification, none of this properly honors the body.

3

If then you were raised up together with Christ seek now the things that are above, where Christ is seated at the right hand of God, setting your minds on heavenly not earthly things: for you died and your life is hidden with Christ in God. When Christ (who is our life) appears, you also will appear with him in glory.

Therefore put to death all that is earthly in your lives - licentiousness, impurity, passion, lust, but especially greed (which is idolatry) - because it's on account of these that the wrath of God will be visited on the children of disobedience. These are, of course, behaviors in which you too reveled in times past. But now you must set them all aside along with any kind of anger, wrath, wickedness, blasphemy, obscene mockery. Don't lie to one another either, now that you've cast off your old nature with its practices and clothed yourselves with the new, that which is ever being renewed into perfected knowledge according to the image of its creator[28] - where there can neither be Greek nor Jew, circumcised nor uncircumcised, privileged, untouchable, labor or capital, but Christ is all and in all.

As the Elect of God, holy and beloved, immerse yourselves in depths of mercy, kindness, humility, gentleness, patience. Forbear and forgive one another (even if you have cause for blame), because just as the Savior forgave you so must you forgive one another. But above all

---

26   Josephus, *The Wars of the Jews* II.8.5; Tertullian, *Against Marcion* V.19.
27   Matthew 15:1-20; Mark 7:1-23.
28   *2 Corinthians* 4:16; *Ephesians* 4:24; cf. *Genesis* 1:26.

this clothe yourselves in love, which is the bond of perfection. Let the Lord's Peace hold sway in your hearts, because to this you've been called in one Body. And be thankful. Let the Savior's Word dwell richly among you, teaching and encouraging one another with all wisdom, singing to God with grace in your hearts in psalms and hymns and spiritual songs. And whatever you do in word or in deed do all in the Name of the Lord Jesus, giving thanks to God the Father through him.

Wives, yield the right of way to your husbands, as becomes members of Christ. And husbands, you'd better love your wives – don't even *think* of treating them harshly! Children, always listen to your parents, because this is pleasing to the Lord. Fathers, don't provoke your children, lest they feel beaten down.

Workers, obey those who over you as far as worldly things go, not just to look good in their eyes but with sincerity and in godly fear. Whatever your task labor heart and soul as for the Lord, not men, knowing you'll receive the inheritance from the Lord as your reward – you serve the Lord Christ! But whoever works injustice will reap what he's sown because the Lord's no respecter of persons. Bosses, treat your employees with fairness and equity and know that you as well as they have a Boss in Heaven.

4

Devote yourselves to prayer. Stay vigilant in your petitions, with thanksgiving. Pray for us as well that God might open a door for us to proclaim the mystery of Christ – on account of which I'm now in prison – that I may manifest the Word to all, as I am always bound to do. Conduct yourselves sensibly to those outside our fellowship. And make the best use of your time you can, letting your speech be always gracious, seasoned with salt,[29] so you'll know how to answer each person.

Tychicus – a beloved brother, faithful servant and my fellow bondsman – will fill you in on my situation. It's for that very reason I've sent him. You'll be comforted in your hearts once you know how things are

---

29   Cicero, *On Oratory* I.34 (159).

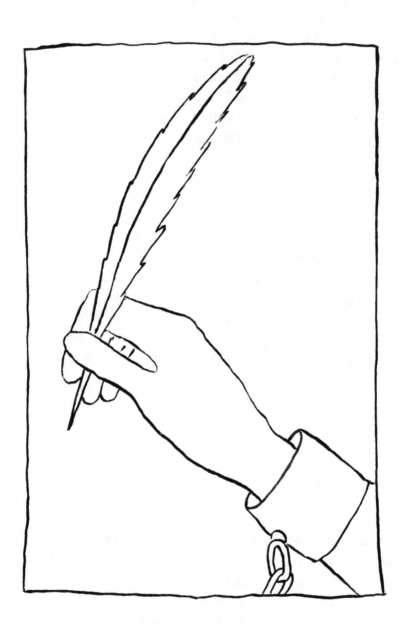

with us and how things are going here. To that end I've also sent Onesimus along with him. He is a faithful and beloved brother as well as being one of your own people.

My fellow prisoner Aristarchus greets you as does Barnabas' cousin Marcus. You've already gotten letters from me about him, so be sure to welcome him when he arrives. He and his fellow Jew Jesus (the one also called Justus) are now my only co-workers for the kingdom of God and they've been a great comfort to me. Epaphras a servant of Christ Jesus greets you – he's also your landsman – always toiling on your behalf in his prayers to the end that you stand perfected, fully settled in all the Will of God. And I can testify how much he's labored for you and for those in Laodicea and Hierapolis. Lucas the beloved physician hails you, as does Demas.

Salute the brothers in Laodicea along with Nympha and the congregation that meets in her house. After this letter has been read by you make sure it gets to the church in Laodicea for them to read as well. Likewise I want you to read the letter left for you at Laodicea. And one more thing – let the assembly say to Archippus, "See that you fully discharge the ministry you received from the Lord."

I write this last salutation with my own hand:
Remember my chains. Grace be with you,

Paul

FIRST LETTER TO THE THESSALONIANS

P aul, Silvanus and Timothy to the assembly in Thessalonica in God
the Father and the Lord Jesus Christ - grace to you and peace!

We give thanks at all times for you our brethren, beloved by
God, his very elect. We never cease to mention you in our prayers, putting
God and our Father in membrance of your acts of faith shown in charitable labor even as you patiently await our Lord Jesus Christ, understanding
as you do that our gospel came to you not only in word but also with the
power and full conviction of the Holy Spirit. You also know the way we
conducted ourselves among you, acting always on your behalf. And having received the word in much affliction you patterned yourselves on us
- and not just us, but the Lord! - and thus became examples to the whole
company of believers in Macedonia and Achaia.

Indeed, the word of the Lord and the testimony of your faith toward
God pealed out from you not only to them but to all parts elsewhere, such
that we need say no more than that in commending your faith toward
God. They themselves have declared the kind of reception we had among
you, how you turned to God from idols to serve the true and living God,
awaiting his Son from Heaven, he whom he raised from the dead, Jesus,
who rescues us from the coming wrath.

And brethren, you yourselves know well it was not by adventition that
we came to you, for despite having suffered already at Philippi (where we

were quite outrageously beaten) we took courage in our God to preach the good news to you in the midst of such struggles. We've stayed true to our calling. Our lives are pure. We lay no snares. Instead, we speak as those approved by God to be entrusted with the gospel. We're not out to please people but God alone, he who tests our hearts. And as God is our witness we neither lured you with flowery words nor used our ministry as a cover for greed nor sought obeisance from you or others. And even though as missionaries for Christ we might well be entitled to such honor, yet we were as gentle among you as a mother nursing her babes. We were so earnestly desirous for you to grow that we were willing to offer you not only the gospel but our own souls – yes, you had become that precious to us!

You'll recall, brothers and sisters, how we suffered wear and tear toiling night and day with our own hands so as not to burden any of you with our material needs, even as we preached to you the gospel of God. Both you and God are our witnesses how holy and righteous and blameless we behaved ourselves among you who believe and how, as would a father his children, we exhorted, encouraged, even implored each one of you to walk worthy of God, he who calls you into his own kingdom to partake of his glory.

On this account we give unceasing thanks to God that when we delivered the word of God in your hearing you took it in not as the word of men but as the true word of God that it is and is now at work in you who believe. You therefore followed the lead of the assemblies of God in Christ Jesus that are in Judea, suffering the same things at the hands of your own countrymen as they did from theirs – I speak of those who killed Jesus and the prophets, who drove us out by persecution, who displease God in their hostility to all mankind, hindering us from speaking to the Gentiles that they might be saved, thereby filling up the measure of their own sins such that God's anger is fully come upon them.

Ever since we were torn away from you, brethren (albeit for a short while and even then only in presence not in our heart), we've redoubled our efforts to return, being greatly desirous of seeing you face to face. We had made plans to come not once but twice – I Paul included – but the Adversary hindered us. Why my persistent desire to see you? It's because you are our hope, our joy, our crown of rejoicing in the presence of our Lord Jesus Christ at his coming – for who is our glory and joy if not you?

And when I could no longer bear your distance from us I decided

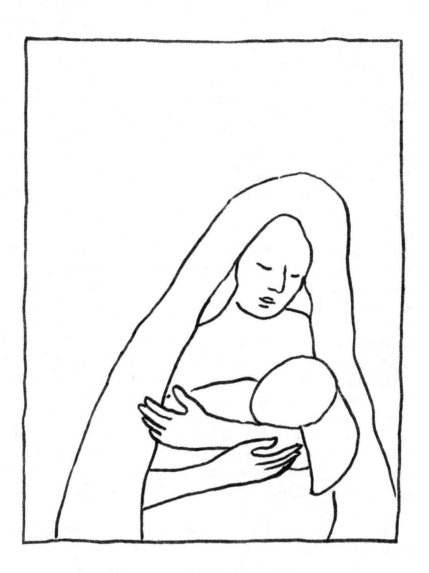

to stay behind in Athens by myself and send Timothy, our brother and co-worker in the gospel of Christ, to strengthen and encourage you, lest any be shaken in their faith on account of these afflictions. You yourselves know this is what we Christians must expect. Recall that when we were with you we told you we are destined for persecution, even as now befalls. Yet when I couldn't endure the silence I sent him to learn firsthand the state of your faith, apprehensive as I was that the Serpent might have tempted you and our labors turn to dust.

But Timothy has just now arrived with glad tidings of you, telling us of your faith and love, how you have our well-being always in your thoughts, how you long to see us just as we long to see you. My brethren, your faith comforts us in all our distress and sorrow: for now we live, if you stand fast in the Lord. And what thanksgiving are we able to give back to God for you for all the joy in which we rejoice over you before our God, as we pray without measure to see you face to face and supply anything that may be lacking in your faith?

Now may our God and Father himself and our Lord Jesus lay a straight path for us to you and may the Lord make you increase to overflowing in love for one another and for all, even as we for you, to the strengthening of your hearts unblameable in holiness before our God and Father at the coming of our Lord Jesus with all his saints, amen!

Beyond that, brethren, we call upon you, entreating in the name of the Lord Jesus that just as you received from us how you ought to live your lives conducting yourselves in a manner pleasing to God – as indeed you do now – so too may you advance in the same all the more, because you know the precepts we have given you on the authority of the Lord Jesus. And this is God's will and your sanctification: that you abjure ritual prostitution; that each treat his own body with respect in holiness and honor, no longer being mired in passionate lust like Gentiles who don't know God; and that no one cross the line, defrauding his neighbor, coveting his wife – as we've told you before and testified solemnly, God will avenge such cases. God has called you to sanctity, not sexual license. Anyone who rejects this rejects not man but God, who gives you his own Holy Spirit.

But as far as love of the brethren goes you hardly need us to write anything to you because you yourselves have been taught by God to love one another and already so do toward your brothers and sisters throughout all Macedonia. Even so, we urge you to excel yet more: aspiring to live quiet lives, managing your own affairs, working with your own hands as we've instructed you, having no need to depend on anyone, to the end that you be well regarded by those outside the fellowship.

Something else – I don't want you to be wondering what happens to those who sleep death's sleep lest you grieve like those who have no hope. After all, if we believe Jesus died and rose again so too will God bring back with Jesus those who've fallen asleep through him. Let us share this word with you from the Lord: we who remain alive at the Second Coming will not get ahead of those who have died. The Lord himself will descend from Heaven with a commanding shout, the voice of an archangel and the trumpet of God. The dead in Christ shall first arise, then we who remain alive will be caught up together with them on clouds to meet the Lord in the air, and thus united we shall unendingly be with the Lord. Therefore console one another with these words.

But I have nothing more to write concerning the exact time or season when all this will occur because, as you well know, the Day of the Lord comes as a thief in the night. Just when people are saying, "Peace and safety," that's when doom will fall on them suddenly much as birth pangs seize the womb, and they will find no escape. Don't be in the dark about this and find yourselves caught napping when the thief comes, for you are all children of light, children of the day. And because we are neither of night nor darkness let us sleep not as the rest but rather watch with all soberness.

Those who sleep, sleep in the night and those who are drunk are drunk in the night, while we who are of the day are sober, clothing ourselves with the breastplate of faith and love, taking for our helmet the hope of salvation – because God has not appointed us to wrath but to gain salvation through our Lord Jesus Christ, who died for us that whether awake we watch or whether we rest we enter life together with him. Encourage yourselves with these words and continue to build one another up.

I want you to pay attention to those who toil among you, caring for you and exhorting you in the Lord – you should hold them in highest esteem in love on account of their work.

Be at peace among yourselves.

We call on you, brethren, to warn those who are disorderly. Cheer up the faint-hearted. Support the spiritually weak. Show forbearance to all.

Be sure that no one repays evil with evil but rather pursue the good not only for yourselves but for all.

Rejoice always. Pray without ceasing. Give thanks in all things – because this is the will of God in Christ Jesus for you.

Do not suppress the Spirit. Do not reject prophecies. Put all things to the test. Hold fast to the good. Abstain from all appearance of evil.

May the God of peace himself sanctify you in perfection and may your spirit, soul and body be preserved whole, blameless at the coming of our Lord Jesus Christ. Faithful is he who calls you, who also will accomplish it.

Brethren, make us the subject of your prayers.

Greet all the brethren with a holy kiss.

I charge you before the Lord: have the letter read to the gathered brethren.

The grace of our Lord Jesus Christ be with you.

SECOND LETTER TO THE
THESSALONIANS

Paul, Silvanus and Timothy to those assembled in Thessalonica in God our Father and the Lord Jesus Christ – grace to you and peace from God our Father and the Lord Jesus Christ.

It is very meet, right, and our bounden duty that we should at all times and in all places give thanks to God for you, my brethren, seeing that your faith is on the constant increase, with your love each for the other abounding so much so that we ourselves brag about you to all the congregations of God. We give thanks especially because of the patience and faith you've shown in the face of all the trials and afflictions you endure. This itself gives proof of the justice of God's counsel: as he finds you worthy in suffering for the kingdom of God, he also finds it just to recompense those who persecute you with crushing afflictions of their own while granting relief to you who are pressed along with us – all this when the Lord Jesus is revealed from Heaven in fiery flames with messengers of his might,[1] wreaking vengeance on those who know not God and obey not the gospel of our Lord Jesus. They will suffer the just penalty of endless doom, shut out from the presence of the Lord and the glory of his might when

---

1   *Daniel* 7:9-10.

he comes on that Day to be glorified in his saints and marveled at by all those who have believed.

Just as our witness to you was believed so we pray for you always, petitioning our God to consider you worthy of your calling and by his power to bring to fullness your every good work and generous purpose as they spring from your faith, that the Name of our Lord Jesus may be glorified in you and you in him, according to the grace of our God and Lord Jesus Christ.

Keep a weather eye open for the Lord's return and our gathering up to him. At the same time don't let your minds be quickly shaken neither confused into thinking that the Day of the Lord is at hand – no, not even if someone says they *think* they heard us say so in some prophecy or teaching, or *think* they read it in a letter come from us. Don't be fooled! That Day won't come before the great apostasy reveals the Lawless One, that Son of Perdition, opposing and exalting himself beyond measure against all that is worshipped and called divine, going so far as to seat himself in God's own Temple, declaring himself to be God.[2]

Don't forget that I've told you about all this before! Indeed, you well know what's presently holding him back, lest the Son of Perdition be revealed before his appointed time. Yes, the mystery of iniquity is already in motion. But the one who restrains it will do so until removed, at which point the Lawless One will be revealed – whom the Lord will slay by the breath of his mouth[3] and annihilate at the Shine of his Coming.[4] This is that Man of Sin by the Fiend enabled to perform every kind of false power and sign and miracle in all wicked craft for those on the Highway to Hell. Because they refused to accept the love of the Truth (that they be saved), God sends them the delusive power of evil (that they believe the Lie) – to the end that all who reject truth and take pleasure in iniquity might be called to account.

But we are bound to give thanks to God always for you, brethren beloved of the Lord, because God chose you from the beginning and appointed you to salvation by sanctification of the Spirit and faithful acceptance of the truth, having called you through our gospel to obtain the glory of

---

2   *Daniel* 11:36.
3   *Isaiah* 11:4.
4   *Cf.* Milton, *Paradise Lost*, VI:768.

our Lord Jesus Christ. Therefore stand fast, my brothers and sisters, and safeguard the traditions you've been taught by our speech or letters. And may our Lord Jesus Christ himself and God our Father who loved us and gave us never failing assurance and good hope through grace comfort and confirm your hearts in every good word and deed.

As for the rest, pray for us, my brethren, that the word of God may quickly advance and be glorified elsewhere as it has been among you, but also that we be rescued from sidewinding evildoers. Not everyone shares our faith, as you know, but God is faithful who will strengthen you and safeguard you from the Wicked One. And, to be sure, we are fully persuaded that you act and will act in accordance with all we have preached to you. May the Lord direct your hearts to the love of God and the patience of Christ.

Now we call upon you, brethren, in the name of our Lord Jesus Christ to keep at arm's length any brothers or sisters who have fallen into sloth against the guidelines we've given you. You yourselves know well the pattern we set for you, because we were hardly slackers when we were with you. We didn't take the bread off of anyone's plate but worked night and day with toil and care so as not to burden any of you - not that we couldn't insist on your support if we had wanted to, of course, but rather to give you an example to follow in your own lives. That's why when we were with you we could credibly command that anyone unwilling to work would just have to go without food. But we're still hearing that some among you are freeloading, refusing to work and spending their time meddling in other people's business. Therefore we direct and exhort them in the Lord Jesus Christ to work in quietude, enjoying the fruits of their own labor. Don't be weary, brethren, but persist in going good.

Take note of anyone who refuses to obey the things we write. Shame him by keeping your distance yet don't treat him as an enemy - instead, warn him as a brother in the hope of restoring him to the fold.

May the Lord of peace himself always give you peace in every way.

May the Lord be with you all.

As you can see from the size of the letters, I'm writing
this last greeting myself!
May the grace of our Lord Jesus Christ be with you all.

Paul

FIRST LETTER TO TIMOTHY

1

Paul, one of those sent out by Christ Jesus according to the will of God our Savior and our hope Christ Jesus, to Timothy, true child in the faith: grace, mercy and peace be with you from God the Father and our Lord Jesus Christ.

I'm writing to reiterate the instructions I left for you on my way to Macedonia: stay in Ephesus to rein in that group of heterodox teachers! Press them to give up their obsession with proto-Gnostic myths and mind-numbing genealogies, all of which foster worthless speculation, when they should instead be focused on managing the household of God in all faith. We've set the goal of our gospel commandment against that kind of false teaching – we aim instead for love that grows from a pure heart, a clear conscience and faith unfeigned.

Now, some have wandered from the gospel, turning to vain fables. They hold themselves out as teachers of the Law when in fact they don't know what they're talking about and probably don't even believe the things they say. But we know the Law is precious to someone who makes right use of it. The Law isn't placed to judge the righteous but rather to condemn the lawless and unruly, the impious and sinners, the unholy and profane – I'm talking about pedophiles, patricides, pederasts and perjurers; man-stealers, matricides, miscreants and murderers; or anything or anyone opposed to sound teaching that accords with the gospel of the glory of the blessed God, with which I was entrusted.

I give thanks to the one who empowered me, Christ Jesus our Lord, in that he deemed me faithful, appointing me to his service - me! - even though I used to be an insolent and violent blasphemer, persecuting God's people. But he showed me mercy because I acted in ignorant unbelief. And the grace of our Lord increased in me with faith and love to overflowing, which are God's good gifts in Christ Jesus. Here is a trustworthy saying that all can accept - the Savior Jesus came into the world to save sinners, with me at the top of the list. That's really why I found mercy - in other words, so that Christ Jesus might demonstrate in me the completeness of his longsuffering, making me an example for those who should come to believe on him to endless life. Now unto the king eternal,[1] immortal, invisible, God alone, be honor and glory forever and ever, amen!

Timothy my son, hold close to your heart the prophetic words sent out ahead of you, soldiering on valiantly with faith and a clear conscience. Sad to say, some have shipwrecked their souls setting these things aside - like Hymenaeus and Alexander, whom I have left open to the Adversary so that, once chastised, they may learn not to blaspheme.

2

I'm therefore urging first and foremost that people offer petitions, prayers, intercessions and thanksgivings for all mankind, especially for kings and those holding higher authority in order that we live out our lives peacefully and undisturbed, in all godliness and reverent dignity. This is right and pleasing before the face of God our Savior, who wills that all people should be saved and come to full knowledge of the truth, there being but one God and one Mediator between God and mankind, the man Christ Jesus, who gave himself a ransom for all, the testimony promised in God's proper time. And I'm telling you straight out that this is why I was appointed God's herald and apostle, teaching the Gentiles his faith and truth.

---

1   *Psalms* 144:13.

I therefore wish the men in every local church to pray lifting holy hands without anger or self-doubt and so too the women, adorning themselves not with coiffure and couture, gold rings and pearls but with good deeds done decently and with self-discipline, characteristics of those who profess to be pious. In first learning the faith, women ought to listen quietly and humbly. I personally don't think it helps to have women in a place of authority teaching the basics to men – after all, it's worth keeping in mind that Adam was first formed, then Eve, and that Adam himself wasn't deceived but rather Eve crossed the line when seduced by deceit (even so, of course, God promised Eve salvation to come through a good and faithful woman raising her holy child in holiness and self-control).

3

More importantly, here's something you can count on – anyone aspiring to serve as an overseer of the flock is aiming for a noble task. Just remember that such a person must be unimpeachable in character, monogamous, clear-headed, thoughtful, modest, a friend to strangers, given to teaching and not out to get rich. Not a boozer, bully or brawler but gentle instead. Let him have an orderly household, a reverent family, the kids not running wild – because if someone doesn't know how to run his own household how is he supposed to take charge of the people of God? He also can't be too new to the faith lest he begin to think too highly of himself and fall by pride, as fell Satan. And he should also have a good reputation among those outside the assembly, lest he fall into the Tempter's snare and reproach.

Just the same should men who wish to be deacons be grave, not double-tongued, not overly taken with wine, not greedy of gain, holding the mystery of the faith in pure conscience. But before being ordained to this office let them first be tested. If found irreproachable then let them serve in that ministry. And it's the same with deaconesses – they should be respectable, not gossips, sober, faithful in all manner. In all such cases they should be monogamous, well-managing their household affairs and their children, because those who've served faithfully in the diaconate preserve for themselves a good place to stand at the Great Day and much assurance in the faith that is in Christ Jesus.

I'm writing all this to you hoping to be there sooner rather than later – but in case I'm delayed I want to be sure you know how to handle yourself in the house of God, the very assembly of the living God, the pillar and support of the truth. And beyond doubt great is the mystery of godliness: God was manifest in the flesh, justified in the Spirit, seen of angels, preached to the Goyim, believed on in the world, received up into glory.

4

Yet the Spirit speaks plainly that in later times some will be seduced by false spirits, distancing themselves from the faith and chasing after doctrines of demons falling from the lips of liars whose consciences have been seared with hypocrisy's hot brand. They prevent people from getting married and shun food that God created – food that should instead be received with thanksgiving by those who are faithful and fully understand the truth that everything God created is good, none to be rejected, because food so received is sanctified by the Word of God and prayer.

As long as you lay these things out before the brethren you'll be a worthy servant of Christ Jesus, training yourself in the words of the faith and the sound doctrine you've followed. But reject godless and anile myths, exercising yourself instead with a view to godliness. Physical training isn't bad but it also doesn't amount to much in the end, while piety is of benefit in all things because it holds promise for this life *and* that which is to come – and that's another guideline you can trust and adopt. Indeed, it's to that end we labor and struggle, our hope fixed on the living God, the Savior of all mankind and most of all those who believe.

Command these things and teach them – but don't let anyone say you're too young to do so, just be an example for the believers to follow in word, demeanor, love, faith and purity. While you're waiting for me to arrive pay attention to the public reading of Scripture, to exhortation and to teaching. And don't neglect the charismatic gift that's in you, which was given through prophecy and endowed with the laying on of hands by the elders. Work on these things and absorb them so that your growth may be evident to everyone. Get a grip on yourself and spend time on your teaching – in doing so you'll save both yourself and those that hear you.

5

Don't reprimand the older men in your congregation but encourage them as you would a father. Likewise, treat younger men as brothers, older women as mothers and younger women as sisters, in all purity.

Provide care for widows who are truly destitute. But if any widow has children or grandchildren let these in the first instance learn to honor their own household, caring for their forebears, as is right in the sight of God.[2] Widows who are alone and impoverished have their hope fixed on God, remaining constant in prayers and supplications daytime and night, while those who though widowed live in luxury are bereft of life in the Spirit. Therefore give instructions on this matter in order that they escape reproach, because if anyone refuses to care for his own, even those of his own household, he's denied the faith and is worse than a heathen.

You may enroll in the ministry a widow over 60, wed but once, with a reputation for good deeds, one who has raised children, taken in the homeless, washed the feet of the saints, given comfort to the afflicted, a follower of every good work. But decline to ordain younger widows – once their passions arise they'll turn from Christ and seek to marry again, incurring judgment as they set aside their first faith, learning to idle about from house-church to house-church, spreading gossip, getting into other people's business and generally speaking things they ought not. That's why I would prefer that younger widows marry again, and soon – that they bear children, manage households and thus give our opponents no room to slander (and I'm afraid the truth is that some have already turned toward Satan). And if any believing woman has widows among her relatives let her care for them so as not to burden the church, but rather leave the church to care for those who are widows indeed.

Church elders who oversee well are entitled to double honors, especially those who studiously preach and teach. As the Scriptures say, don't

---

2   *Exodus* 20:12.

muzzle the ox while he's treading[3] and the laborer is worthy of his pay.[4] Moreover, don't take an accusation against an elder lightly but insist on the testimony of two or three witnesses. If any in fact are found to do wrong then rebuke them in the presence of the whole congregation so that the people may fear.[5] I charge you in solemn witness before the presence of God and Christ Jesus and the chosen angels that you heed these instructions, staying free of prejudgment, leaning to no one's favor.

And don't be too quick about commissioning people with the laying on of hands, lest you become party to the sins of others. Stay pure![6] Keep in mind that some people's sins are obvious to everyone, leading straight to condemnation, while others' aren't known for a while. It's the same with good deeds – some are done out in the open but those that aren't won't be hidden forever.

6

Those who are slaves under the yoke of bondage should look on their masters as worthy of respect in order that the name of God and the teaching not be blasphemed. And those who have masters who are also brothers in the faith shouldn't despise them, given that they're fellow brethren. Instead, they must serve them that much more heartily, because the beneficiaries are believers and beloved.

Teach and exhort these things. But if someone preaches contrary doctrine, refusing to accede to the sound words of our Lord Jesus Christ and precepts that accord with godliness, then he's just a swellhead, understanding nothing, sickened and diseased by conflicts and controversies over words, out of which arise envy, strife, slander, ill suspicion and grating debates among people corrupted in mind and devoid of the truth, who claim that prosperity is a fruit of the gospel. But godliness with contentment is great gain – we brought nothing into this world and it's

---

3   *Deuteronomy* 25:4.
4   *Luke* 10:7; see *Leviticus* 19:13; *Deuteronomy* 24:14.
5   *Deuteronomy* 13:11.
6   This reminds me. I know you have a weak stomach and are prone to all sorts of illnesses. Try drinking some wine instead of the local water – after all, who knows what's in it?

certain we'll carry nothing out. Therefore having food and raiment let us be content. The truth is that people who aim for riches fall headlong into temptation and snares, a world of thoughtless desires plunging them to destruction and ruin – because the love of money is the root of all evils, which some running after have wandered from the faith and pierced themselves through with multiple sorrows.

But you, O man of God, flee these things and follow instead after righteousness, godliness, faith, love, patience, gentleness. Fight the good fight of faith and seize hold of unending life, into which you have been called, having confessed the good confession in front of many witnesses. And I enjoin you in the presence of God, who gives life to all things, and of Christ Jesus, who witnessed his good confession before Pontius Pilate, blamelessly to keep the commandment free of reproach until the appearance of our Lord Jesus Christ when revealed in his due season – he who is the only blessed Potentate, the King of kings and Lord of lords, who alone has immortality, dwelling in light inaccessible, whom none among mortals has ever seen nor could see, to whom be all honor and power forevermore, amen.

Now, instruct this world's rich not to think too highly of themselves neither stake their hopes on the uncertainties of wealth but rather on God, who supplies us with all things abundantly for our enjoyment, and to do good, as those who would be rich in good deeds, generously and cheerfully sharing with all – thereby storing up treasure for themselves, a foundation for the future, laying hold of that which is true life indeed.

And Timothy, guard closely what's been placed in your hands, turning aside the vain babble and contrarian ways of so-called *gnosis*, professing which some have missed faith's mark.

May the grace of God be with you all.

SECOND LETTER TO TIMOTHY

1

Paul, an apostle of Christ Jesus by the will of God with a view to the promise of the life that is in Christ Jesus, to Timothy, beloved child: grace, mercy and peace from God the Father and Christ Jesus our Lord.

I give thanks to God, whom I worship with a clear conscience in descent from my forebears, because unceasingly I remember you in my prayers both night and day, longing to see you, even as I recall your tears, in order that I may be filled with joy. And I bring to mind the sincerity of your faith, springing first as it did from your grandmother Lois and your mother Eunice and finding its dwelling, I am persuaded, in you as well. I therefore remind you now to rekindle the gift of God vouchsafed to you by the laying on my hands – because the Spirit God gave us is one not of cowardice but boldness, love and self-discipline.

Don't be ashamed of the testimony of our Lord or of me his prisoner but suffer evil together with me for the sake of the gospel according to the power of God, who saved us and calls us with a holy calling, *not* by virtue of our own deeds but in accordance with his own purpose and grace given us in Christ

Jesus before time began but now revealed through the appearing of our Savior Jesus Christ, who set death to naught and brought endless life to light by the preaching of the good news, all for which I was ordained a herald, apostle and teacher of the Gentiles and on account of which I now suffer. But I am not ashamed, because I know whom I have trusted and am persuaded he is able to safeguard my soul until that Day.

Use as templates of sound teaching the words you've heard from me, words I shared in the faith and love that are in Christ Jesus, and guard by the indwelling Holy Spirit all that has been committed to you. As you know, everyone in the Asian district has deserted me, including Phygelus and Hermogenes. Yet I pray the Lord to shower mercy on the household of Onesiphorus, who many times revived my soul. He was not ashamed that I'd landed in jail but on the contrary, when he came to Rome he promptly sought and found me – and indeed, you know better than anyone the many ways he ministered to me while I was in Ephesus – so may he find mercy at the Lord's side in that Day.

2

Therefore, my child, grow strong in the grace that is in Christ Jesus and commit to faithful stewards the things you've heard from me in front of many witnesses so that they may pass the same along to others in turn. Suffer wrongs like a good soldier of Jesus Christ! No soldier on duty lets himself be distracted by the affairs of life but focuses all his energies on pleasing the one who recruited him to the service. No Olympian wins a medal unless he plays by the rules. And it's the weary farmer who ought to taste the harvest's first fruits. Turn all this over in your mind and let the Lord shed light on my meaning.

Don't lose sight of my gospel's core – that Jesus Christ, born of David's seed, has been raised up from the dead. It's for the gospel's sake I now suffer evil, shackled in chains as though I were a criminal. But the word of God is not bound! I therefore endure all things for the sake of the elect, that they too may with unending glory obtain salvation in Christ Jesus.

And here's a reliable set of maxims:

> If we died with him we shall also live with him.
> If we endure we shall also reign with him.
> If we deny him he will also deny us.
> If we are unfaithful to him, he remains faithful
> and will not break faith with us.

Remind them of these things, warning them before God not to fight over words - something that benefits no one but can well spell disaster for the listeners. You, on the other hand, should strive to present yourself before God a tested laborer, unashamed of his work, rightly construing the word of truth. But reject the kind of godless blather foisted by Hymenaeus and Philetus - they've gone off the rails, spreading the gangrenous doctrine that the general resurrection has come and gone, turning the faith of some upside down. Yet God's firm foundation remains, having this seal:

> The Lord knows his own people
> and
> Let all who bear the Lord's name turn from iniquity.[7]

In every great house there are not only vessels gold and argent but also wooden and clay, some of special value and others of humbler use. If any member of the congregation shall have purified herself among these she'll be a vessel fit for honorable service, sanctified and useful to the Master, made ready for every good work.

Flee the cravings of your youth, following instead after righteousness, faith, love and peace with those who call upon the Lord out of a pure heart. And stay away from foolish and ignorant speculations, knowing that they cause nothing but strife. The Lord's servant must not quarrel but rather be gentle toward all, ready to teach, patient when suffering wrong, humbly correcting those mired in self-contradiction, if ever God might grant them repentance yielding knowledge of the truth, with the

---

7   *Isaiah* 52:11; *Numbers* 16:26.

goal that they come to their senses and awake sober, freed from the snare of Satan - in which in their drunken spiritual state they'd been taken captive, though only so far as God's will allowed.

3

Be sure you keep this in mind: in the Last Days harsh times will impend, mankind naught but narcissistic moneygrubbers, bombastic braggarts, filled with contempt, impious, disdaining their parents, ungrateful, unholy, unloving, intractable, undisciplined, unmerciful, hating the good, traitors, impetuous, conceited puffballs, lovers of pleasure more than lovers of God, masked in a form of godliness yet having repudiated its power. Stay away from such people! These are the kind who worm their way into house-churches, taking captive polypassionate women sinfully led astray - always looking for the latest fad but never coming to a full knowledge of the truth. These are men after the fashion of Jannes and Jambres, who withstood Moses[8] just as these withstand the truth, with minds corrupted, vain as concerns the faith - yet they shall go no farther, their madness bared before all just as with those two of old.[9]

But you've been able to follow my teaching, guidance, goals, faith, longsuffering, love and steadfastness, as well as the persecutions and suf-

---

8   *Exodus* 7:11, 22.
9   *Exodus* 8:18, 9:11.

fering I endured in Antioch, Iconium and Lystra, the Lord delivering me from all of them. Indeed all those who wish to live a holy life in Christ Jesus will suffer persecution, while frauds and charlatans will go from bad to worse, deceiving and being deceived. But you, hold steady in the things you've learned and absorbed, understanding from whom you learned them - that from your childhood you've known the Holy Scriptures, which are able to grant you wisdom leading to salvation through the faith which is in Christ Jesus. And all Scripture is inspired by God, beneficial for teaching, for refutation, for on-course correction, for instruction in righteousness, all to equip the people of God for every good work.

4

I charge you before God and Christ Jesus, the coming Judge of the living and the dead, and by his appearing and his reign: proclaim the word of God (standing ready to do so whether you feel like it or not), reprove, warn, encourage with all patience and attention to instruction, because there will come a time when even people professing to be Christians won't want to put up with sound doctrine anymore. Instead, giving free rein to their own desires they will load themselves up with teachers who will tell them what they itch to hear, blocking out the voice of truth as they ramble off to fables and myths.

You, however, keep a clear head, endure hardship, do the work of an evangelist, filling up the full measure of your appointed service. I myself am already being poured out as a sacrificial libation and my days now close upon me. I have fought the good fight. I have finished my course. I have kept the faith. Henceforth there is laid up for me the crown of righteousness which the Lord, the righteous Judge, shall give me at that Day - and not to me only but also to all them that love his appearing.

Come see me quickly if you possibly can. Demas has gone back to Thessalonica because of his love for this present world. Crescens is off to Galatia. Titus to Dalmatia. I've only got Luke here with me, having now sent Tychicus to Ephesus. But if you can find Mark and bring him with you he would be of great use to me in my ministry. Oh also, when you do come, grab the cloak I left with Carpus at Troas along with my scrolls and - most importantly - the parchments with the copies of my letters.

I need to tell you that Alexander the coppersmith did me much evil, greatly opposing our proclamation of the word. Yet what goes around comes around and the Lord will repay him for what he's done. Even so, watch out for him.

The first time I had to appear in court no one stood up in my defense - they all deserted me, but I pray God not to hold it against them. But I had the Lord by my side giving me strength, that I might yet fully share my gospel message with the Gentiles. And thus was I delivered from the lion's mouth - and indeed the Lord will rescue me from *every* wicked work and bring me safe to his heavenly kingdom, to whom be the glory from age to age, amen!

Greet Prisca and Aquila and the house of Onesiphorus. Erastus has stayed on in Corinth. I had to leave Trophimus in Miletus because he was ill. And do try to get here before winter prevents a voyage! Eubulus salutes you, as do Pudens, Linus and Claudia, along with the rest of the brethren.

The Lord be with your spirit and the grace of God be with you all.

TO TITUS

Dear Titus, my true son in our shared faith, I, Paul, send you this letter with grace and peace from God the Father and Christ Jesus our Savior, because I am God's servant and Jesus' apostle in accordance with the faith of those chosen by God. You and I hold in common our knowledge of the truth in all godliness, secure in our hope of timeless life, which God – who is Truth – declared before time began. And he seasonably revealed that life through the preaching of his Word, which has also been entrusted to me by the command of God our Savior.

I had you remain in Crete while I went on ahead so you could put right some things that were out of kilter, ordaining elders from city to city in just the way I directed you, picking only those who conduct themselves blamelessly. And just to remind you, no polygamists! Moreover, an elder's children should themselves be faithful, not running riot or out carousing all the time. The reason is that those who take on responsibility as elders to oversee the church have to be irreproachable guardians of God's household. They can't be arrogant, hot-headed or bullying. They can't have a drinking problem or be out to get rich. No, they should instead be hospitable to strangers and focus on the things that are good, not those that are bad. They should be level-headed, just, pious, self-disciplined. And they must hold fast the doctrine they've received, keeping it in faithfulness to God – that way they'll be able to use sound teaching to counter anyone who takes an opposing view.

I'm sad to say there are a number of people out there, including many of my fellow Jews, teaching shameful things - they are disobedient, empty-headed babblers, deluded in their own minds - and they've turned whole house churches upside down. One of their own prophets said it well: "The Cretans are vicious brutes, lazy gluttons, and they lie all the time."[1] This is a true statement - that's why you must rebuke them sharply in the hope they'll turn back to faith in godliness.

You also need to ignore bubbe-meises as well as any manmade commandments that lead people from the truth. Everything is clean for those who are cleansed. But as for those who disbelieve and defile themselves? Nothing is pure for them - even their minds and consciences are stained. They *say* they know God but they deny him by their deeds, being abhorrent, disobedient and useless for any worthwhile task.

So it's your job to be sure you are well grounded in your teaching. Among other things, instruct grown men to be temperate, grave and prudent - sound in their faith, charity and obedience. And likewise let the women be reverent in demeanor, free from gossip or too much wine, teachers of good things, encouraging younger women to be faithful in their marriages, caring for their children and managing their households well in harmony with their own husbands so that the word of God not be slandered. And as far as the younger men and women are concerned, instruct them to be sober minded.

Above all set yourself as an example of good deeds - your teaching solid, your demeanor serious, your speech above reproach. That way anyone who is against you will be put to shame, unable to find anything bad to say about us. Let those who serve be properly obedient to their own masters, tractable, not back-talkers or embezzlers but showing integrity in everything so as to adorn with their goodness the teaching of our God and Savior.

Now, the grace of God has been revealed, bringing salvation to all people and teaching us that rejecting all ungodliness and worldly passions we should live modestly, justly and piously in this present age, waiting expectantly for our blessed hope - the coming in glory of our great God and Savior Jesus, who gave himself for us to redeem us from the curse of lawlessness and purify for himself a people zealous of good works. Teach and preach these things, encouraging people in all your instruction. And

---

1   Epimenides, *Cretica* (hypothetical); *see* Callimachus, *Hymn to Zeus* v.8.

don't let anyone scorn you.

Remind your people to keep themselves obedient in an orderly way to the governing authorities, ready to put their hands to any good task, not slandering anyone, not brawling, considerate of others, showing kindness to all mankind. We ourselves were once foolish, disobedient, deceived, slaves to all sorts of hedonistic passions, consumed with evil and envy, loathsome, hating one another. But when God's gentleness and love for mankind was revealed through our Savior we found salvation not by observing right rituals but by his mercy. And thus he saved us by the washing of new birth and the renewal of the Holy Spirit, which was poured out on us richly through Jesus Christ our Savior, that having by that grace been made righteous in his sight we should become heirs through hope of unending life.

This is a true saying and I want you to insist on it – that those who have believed in God should lead the way in charitable deeds, because this is right and beneficial to all. But avoid the kind of silly controversies, endless genealogies, strife and debates that people get into over fine points of the Law – these are useless and a waste of time. If someone wanders off into heresy warn him once, then twice if need be. If he still ignores you there's no choice but to exclude him from your midst: such people have turned to sin, twisting themselves in a knot.

When I send Artemas or Tychicus to you, make a beeline to come to me in Nicopolis, because I plan to spend the Winter there. Send Zenas the lawyer and Apollos speedily on their journey – don't let them lack for anything. And let the people in your care learn to do good works that they not be unfruitful.

All those with me greet you. Greet those who share our love in the faith.

Grace be with you all.

TO PHILEMON

From Paul (now in chains for the sake of Christ Jesus) and Timothy to our beloved fellow laborer Philemon, Apphia our sister, Archippus our fellow soldier and the fellowship gathered in your house – grace to you and peace from God our Father and the Lord Jesus Christ.

I thank God for you always, Philemon, remembering you in my prayers even as I hear of the love and faith you have toward the Lord Jesus and all his faithful ones, to the end that as you share your faith with others it may become yet more effective in perfect knowledge of every good gift that is in us through the Savior.

And I have been given much joy and comfort because of your love – by it you have refreshed the hearts of the saints.

My brother, I have enough confidence of my standing with the Lord that I know I could order you to do the right thing – but I'd much rather appeal to you as a matter of love. I'm an old man now, serving time for Jesus' sake. But I come to you seeking a favor

concerning my child Useful, whose spiritual father I've become
during my time in bonds. I'm well aware that in past times he was
useless to you; yet now he's useful to both you and me, and not only
in name! I'm therefore sending him back to you, although he's my
very heart and soul.

In truth I had a mind to keep him by my side so he could
minister to me in your stead (being, as I say, stuck inside of prison
for the gospel's sake again). But I didn't want to do so without your
consent – because I want your kindness toward me to be voluntary
and not something I've made you do.

If you think about it, this may well be why he was separated
from you for a little while, only to be later received by you for all
time not as a runaway slave but as a beloved brother. And so he is to
me but even more so for you – a partner in the things of this world
as well as in the Lord.

If you consider me your comrade in the faith accept him as you
would me. If he's cheated you out of anything in the past, put it on
my tab. I wrote and signed this with my own hand – so count on it,
I will repay you. Now, I need hardly mention that you owe me your
very self. Regardless, my brother, do let me have this favor from you.
I promise, it will bring some joy to my heart!

I've written to you in full confidence in your obedience. Indeed,
I know you'll even go above and beyond what I'm asking of you.
Please also hold a guestroom for me ,because I still hope that through
your prayers I will be delivered to you free from these bonds.

Epaphras, held captive with me, sends his best to you, as do
Mark, Aristarchus, Demas and Luke, all of whom are my co-workers.

The grace of the Lord and Savior Jesus be with your spirit.

HEBREWS

1

From Ancient Days at multiple times in multiplex manner God spoke to our fathers through the mouths of his prophets. But now in these Last Days he spoke to us in the Son – the Radiance of his Glory, the very Impress of his Being, timelessly appointed Heir of all things, maker of Time and Space, sustaining the universe by the Word of his Power – who having once made purification for Sin sat down enthroned at the right hand of God's Exalted Majesty, having become as far superior to the angels as his inherited Name is to theirs.

Indeed, to which of the angels did God ever say,

You are my Son, this day have I begotten you?[1]

Or again,

I will be to him as a Father and he will be to me as a Son?[2]

---

1   *Psalms* 2:7.
2   *2 Samuel* 7:14.

So too, placing the world beneath the Firstborn[3] he said,

> Let all God's angels worship him.[4]

In contrast the Scriptures tell us,

> He made the angels winds, his servants a fiery flame.[5]

But to the Son he said,

> Your throne, O God, is unending
> > and the scepter of righteousness
> the scepter of your kingdom.
> > You have loved righteousness
> and hated lawlessness:
> > Therefore God, your God
> has anointed you with the oil of rejoicing,
> > above and beyond your companions.[6]

And

> O Lord, in the beginning
> > you laid the foundations of the Earth
> and the Heavens are the works of your hands:
> > they will all be destroyed,
> but you remain;
> > they will wear out like old coat,
> be folded up and put away,
> > exchanged for a new one –
> but you are always the same,
> > your years never-ending.[7]

---

3   *Psalms* 89:27.
4   *Deuteronomy* 32:43.
5   *Psalms* 104:4.
6   *Psalms* 45:6-7.
7   *Psalms* 102:25-27; *cf. Genesis* 1:1; *Psalms* 8:3.

Or to which of the angels did he ever say,

> Sit at my right hand
> until I set your enemies
> as a footstool beneath your feet?[8]

Aren't the angels ministering spirits, dispatched to serve the heirs of unending life?

2

And that's all the more reason for us to pay careful attention to everything we've heard lest we be deflected from our course. If the word that came by way of messengers was binding – each misstep and mishap finding meet punishment[9] – how shall we escape if we neglect so great a salvation, coming to us first from the Lord himself and then confirmed by those who heard him, God bearing joint witness to their testimony with signs and miracles and diverse other gifts of the Holy Spirit, all apportioned according to his Will?

Listen, we're speaking about the world to come! Do you think God has subjected it to angels? Not at all. But this is what the Scriptures attest –

> What is mankind,
> that you should pay it the least attention?
> Or men and women, that you should watch over them?
> You created them inferior,
> a little lower than angels,
> yet you've crowned them with glory and honor,
> giving them rule over the works of your hands,
> setting all things under their feet.[10]

---

8   *Psalms* 110:1.
9   *Exodus* 21:29, 33-34; *Numbers* 15:27, 30.
10   *Psalms* 8:4-6.

Inasmuch as God subjected all things to mankind's rule he left nothing unsubdued. But though we don't yet see everything subject to mankind we *do* see Jesus, who was himself diminished, entering the world a little lower than angels but crowned with honor and glory through suffering and death that by the grace of God he might taste death for all – because it seemed fitting to God, for whom and through whom all things exist, to perfect through suffering the author of salvation of the many sons he is leading into glory in order that both he who sanctifies and those who are sanctified should be made holy through one and the same sacrifice. Therefore he is not ashamed to call them brothers, as it is written,

> I will declare your name to my brethren;
> > in the midst of the congregation
> will I praise you.[11]

And,

> I will put my trust in him.[12]

And again,

> Here I am along with the children God has given me.[13]

Since the children share in blood and flesh so too did Jesus partake thereof that through his bodily death he might destroy the one holding death's power – the Devil, that is – and thereby free those who all their lives had been in bondage through fear of death.

Jesus didn't take on the form of angels but that of the seed of Abraham. That's also why he had to become like to his brethren in every respect, thus to serve as a faithful High Priest to God in making atonement for the sins of the nation. And he himself having suffered when he was tempted is able to aid those who now suffer temptation.

---

11   *Psalms* 22:22.
12   *Isaiah* 8:17.
13   *Isaiah* 8:18.

3

Therefore, holy brethren, partakers in a heavenly calling, think closely on Jesus, the Apostle and High Priest of our confession, who is faithful to the one who appointed him as was Moses in his own lineage. This man Jesus was counted worthy of greater honor than Moses because the one who establishes a royal dynasty has more honor than the dynasty itself. Now, every family line is established by someone but the one who founded all things is God. To be sure, Moses was faithful to God's whole house as a servant and witness of things to be spoken of in the future;[14] but now Messiah is faithful as Son over his own house.

And we are members of his household as well – if, that is, we hold fast to the confidence and hope of which we boast. As the Holy Spirit cautioned,

> If only you would hear his voice today,
>> not hardening your hearts
> the way your ancestors did in the Wilderness,
>> rebelling against me, testing me,
> even though they saw my works for all those 40 years.
>> But because that generation provoked
> me to anger
>> I said, "They have a wandering heart
> and have not come to know my ways."
>> So I swore in my wrath,
> They shall not enter into my Sabbath Rest."[15]

Therefore watch out, my brothers and sisters, lest there be in any of you a faithless and wicked heart, apostate from the living God. Encourage one another daily while we are still in the Present Age so that none of you be hardened by the deceitfulness of sin, seeing as we have become partakers of the Savior – if, that is, we hold fast to our

---

14   *Numbers 12:7.*
15   *Psalms 95:7-11; see Exodus 17:7 and Numbers 14:21-23, 20:2-5*

first assurance strong to the end.

Again as it is said,

> Today, if you will but hear his voice,
> not hardening your hearts
> as you did in the time of provocation.[16]

Who are we talking about when we refer to those who heard but rebelled? Wasn't it all those who came out of Egypt with Moses? And who angered him those 40 years? Wasn't it those who went astray, their dead bodies parched in the Wilderness? And about whom did he swear they would fail to enter the Promised Land if not those who disobeyed? Hence we perceive it was their unbelief that kept them from entering in.

4

Let us therefore fear lest with a promise being left for us of entering into his Rest any of you should appear to fall short of it. We've received a message of good news just as they did. But they didn't obtain the benefits of the word they received because those who heard it didn't take it in by faith. Yet those of us who *do* believe will enter his Rest. When he spoke, I swore in my anger, "They will not enter into my Sabbath Rest,"[17] it was already plain that God's works were complete as from the foundation of the world. Thus it is said that God rested on the Seventh Day from all his works[18] and elsewhere, lest they enter into my Sabbath Rest.[19] Since (a) it was left for some to enter into that Rest, yet (b) those who first received that good news did not enter in because of disobedience, then (c) he fixed a time for us - Today - David speaking of that time so much later when he prophesied, Today, if you will listen to my voice, not hardening your hearts.[20]

---

16 *Psalms* 95:7-8.
17 *Psalms* 95:11.
18 *Genesis* 2:2.
19 *Psalms* 95:11.
20 *Psalms* 95:7-8.

It's therefore clear that if Joshua had led the people into God's Promised Land there would've been no need to speak through the Psalmist of *another* Day. Accordingly, there remains a Sabbath-keeping for the people of God whereby the person who enters into God's Rest has ceased from his own works, just as God rested from his. Let us hasten to enter into God's Sabbath Rest lest anyone fall into that prior generation's pattern of unbelief.

Now, the Word of God is alive, forceful, sharper than any double-edged sword, penetrating as far as soul and spirit, joints and marrow, parsing the thoughts and imaginations of the heart, such that no creature is veiled from his presence but all lie naked and exposed to the sight of him with whom we have to do. Seeing as we have Jesus – the Son of God, our great High Priest passed through the Heavens – let us stand firm in our confession. For this is not a high priest unable to sympathize with our weaknesses but rather one who was in all manner tested in our similitude, yet remained apart from sin. Let us therefore approach with boldness the throne of grace, receiving mercy and grace in time of need.

5

Every high priest taken from among mankind is appointed to act on mankind's behalf in its relation to God by offering gifts and sacrifices in expiation of sins. And such high priests can temper their anger toward the wayward and ignorant since they too are touched by weakness, having therefore to make offerings for themselves as well as the people.[21]

No one dares take this role to himself but only those called by God – as for example was Aaron.[22] Even the Savior didn't elevate himself to the office of High Priest but rather he who spoke to him in timeless generation saying, You are my Son – this day have I begotten you.[23] And in another place he said, You are a priest forever after the

---

21 *Leviticus* 9:7, 16:6.
22 *Exodus* 28:1.
23 *Psalms* 2:7.

order of Melchizedek[24] – this man who in the days of his fleshly life offered up prayers and supplications with strong cries and tears to the
one who was able to save him from death and was heard because of
his reverent submission. Son though he was yet learned he obedience
through the things he suffered[25] and having been perfected he became
the source of unending salvation[26] to all who obey him, thus named
before God a high priest after the order of Melchizedek.

   We have many things to say about this man – but we're having a
hard time explaining them to you because it seems you've become lazy
listeners. So despite how long you've been believers and even though
you should now be teaching others you still need someone to run you
through the catechism! The point is, you're nursing when you should be
on solid food: you're still babes, feeding on milk, lacking the skills you
need to handle the word of righteousness. But solid food is for grownups,
those who through exercise and discipline have had their senses tuned to
distinguish true from false doctrine.

6

It's time for you to move along to maturity – building on the first
principles of Christ, to be sure, but not laying again the foundation
of repentance from dead works and faith toward God, or the basic
teaching about baptisms, laying on of hands, the resurrection of the
dead and aeonian judgment. And this we will do, God willing.

   Of course, we're unable to restore again to repentance those who
have once come to the Light, tasted of the heavenly Gift, shared in the
Holy Spirit and tasted the pure Word of God and the powers of the
world to come but have then fallen away, seeing as they purposefully
crucify to themselves the Son of God, making him an open spectacle.
They are like land that has drunk the rain falling oft upon it, yielded crops for the benefit of those who tended it and thereby received
God's blessing – but then sprouted thorns and thistles and soon be-

---

24   *Psalms* 110:4.
25   Aeschylus, *Agamemnon*, 177.
26   *Isaiah* 45:17.

came useless, cursed, threatened with fiery destruction.

But listen here, beloved, we're persuaded much better of you, even of things that pertain to salvation though thus we have spoken! God is not so unjust as to let your labors and love go unnoticed, all of which you've made manifest for his Name's sake in your past and continuing service to the saints. It's therefore our devout wish that each of you shows the same diligence in carrying your hope through to the end, that you not become dullards but rather imitators of those who through faith and persistence inherit the promises.

Take Abraham as an example. When God made promises to him he swore by himself (there being none greater by whom he could swear) –

> In blessing I will bless you,
> and in multiplying will increase you.[27]

And so Abraham, having endured with patience, obtained the promises. When people make an oath they always swear by someone greater than themselves, thus confirming the oath and avoiding any contradiction. But God, wishing to demonstrate to the heirs of the promise the immutability of his Will, interposed himself as Mediator between himself and mankind and confirmed the promise by an oath to himself in order that we who for refuge to Jesus have fled might lay hold with certainty on the hope set before us, trusting the twofold unchangeable witness of God, who cannot lie. We therefore have that hope as a safe and sure anchor for our souls, secured behind the Inner Veil through which Jesus entered as forerunner for us, having become our eternal High Priest after the order of Melchizedek.

7

Now, this Melchizedek, King of Salem and priest of God Most High, remains a priest without end. When he met Abraham returning from the slaughter of the kings he blessed him; and Abraham gave him a

---

27   *Genesis* 22:16-17.

tithe of all.[28] His name by interpretation means King of Righteousness and being King of Salem he is also King of Peace. He is shown
in the Scriptures without father or mother or any genealogy, with no
beginning of days or end of life, thus likened to the Son of God.

See how great this man was that the Patriarch Abraham gave him
a tenth off the top of his spoils! Under the Law the Levitical priests
are commanded to collect tithes from their brethren, all of whom
spring from Abraham's loins. But he whose descent is never linked to
theirs received tithes *from* Abraham and then blessed him as the one
who has God's promises – and we know that the lesser is always blessed by the greater. Moreover, normally it is mortal men who receive
tithes but here it is testified that he who received them yet lives.[29]
Even Levi, who receives tithes from the people, himself paid tithes
through Abraham (so to speak), being yet in his forefather's sperm
cells when Melchizedek met him.

Again, if mankind could find perfection through the ministry of
the Levites – a priesthood that was established under the Law – then
why was there any need for another priest to arise in the manner of
Melchizedek, one not spoken of in the Law concerning the priestly
order of Aaron? But if the priesthood changes the rules must change
as well and he of whom these things are spoken is member of another
tribe, none of whose members ministered at the altar – for beyond
doubt our Lord has arisen out of Judah, about which Moses spoke
nothing concerning the priesthood. And to be clearer still, another
priest arising after the similitude of Melchizedek is appointed not
according to mortal command but by the power of an indestructible
life. And so it is witnessed, You are a priest forever after the order of
Melchizedek.[30]

Although the former commandment is set aside for its weakness
and inefficacy – because the Law perfected nothing – a better hope
is then introduced by which we draw near to God. And given that
Jesus' priesthood was ordained by oath he is become the guarantor
of a better covenant. In other words, while the former priests were
ordained without an oath Jesus became High Priest by the oath of

---

28   *Genesis* 14:17-20.
29   *Psalms* 110:4.
30   *Psalms* 110:4.

the one who said, The Lord has sworn and will not repent, "You are a priest forever."[31]

Moreover there had to be multitudes in the former line of priests because death ended their ministries. But Jesus remains High Priest forever, having an unchangeable priesthood. He is therefore able to save to the uttermost those who approach God through him, ever living as he is to make intercession for them. And because the former priests were frail they had to make daily offerings – first for their own sins and then for the people's – but this Jesus did once and for all when he offered up himself. Our High Priest is therefore holy, innocent, undefiled, separate from sinners and made higher than the heavens. And so it is that the Law made high priests of men in their infirmity but the word of God's oath, given after the Law, perfected the Son for evermore.

8

Here's the main point: we have as our High Priest the one who took his seat in Heaven at the right hand of the Throne of Majesty as liturgist of the Holy Places and the True Tabernacle, which the Lord pitched, not men. Now every high priest is appointed to offer gifts and sacrifices – hence this High Priest also had need of something to bring. If he were still on Earth he wouldn't be a priest at all because the Law has priests of its own appointment. Yet they minister typologically in foreshadow of the heavenly sanctuary as was revealed to Moses when he was to complete the tabernacle – See that you make everything in accordance with the pattern shown you on the mountain.[32]

It follows that he has attained a more excellent ministry in that he is Mediator of a superior covenant, ordained by better promises. If the first covenant had been faultless there would've been no reason to seek space for a second one. But finding blame with the Children of Israel he says,

---

31   *Psalms* 110:4.
32   *Exodus* 25:40.

Behold, the days come, saith the Lord,
     that I will make a new covenant
with the house of Israel, and with the house of Judah:
     Not according to the covenant that I made
with their fathers in the day that I took them by the hand
     to bring them out of the land of Egypt;
which my covenant they brake, although
     I was an husband unto them, saith the Lord:
But this shall be the covenant
     that I will make with the house of Israel;
After those days, saith the Lord,
     I will put my law in their inward parts,
and write it in their hearts;
     and will be their God, and they shall be my people.
And they shall teach no more every man his neighbor,
     and every man his brother, saying,
Know the Lord: for they shall all know me,
     from the least of them unto the greatest of them,
saith the Lord: for I will forgive their iniquity,
     and I will remember their sin no more.[33]

In speaking of the new he renders the first one old – and what is old and worn out will soon disappear.

9

The first covenant had its own ordinances governing forms of worship and the earthly sanctuary. The tabernacle consisted of an outer tent, referred to as the Holy Place, in which were the candlestick[34] and the table[35] and the bread of presentation.[36]   Then there was an inner part behind the Veil, known as the Holy of Holies.[37]   It held a golden

---

33   *Jeremiah* 31:31-34.
34   *Exodus* 25:31-39, 26:35, 37:17-24.
35   *Exodus* 25:23-30, 26:35, 37:10-16.
36   *Exodus* 25:30, 35:13.
37   *Exodus* 26:31-33.

censer[38] and the ark of the covenant,[39] covered on all sides with gold,[40] together with a golden jar containing the manna,[41] Aaron's budding rod[42] and the engraved tablets of the covenant.[43] Glorious cherubim[44] overshadowed the ark's cover, the place of atonement.[45]

Without going into greater detail the essential point is that these things were arranged to allow the priests to perform their daily rituals in the Holy Place, whereas the High Priest entered the Holy of Holies alone and but once a year. There he went with blood to offer for his own sins done in ignorance as well as for those of the people.[46] By means of these typological offerings the Holy Spirit made clear that the path into the Holy of Holies was not yet opened as long as the first tabernacle's Holy Place remained standing – because the gifts and sacrifices made under those corporeal rubrics could not with perfection sanctify the conscience of the worshipper, consisting as they did in food and drink and various sorts of ritual ablutions. The former tabernacle therefore functioned parabolically with reference to the present time of reformation, when access to the heavenly place has been revealed.

The Savior having now appeared as High Priest of good things to come thereby passed once and for all time through the greater and more perfect tabernacle – the one not made by mortal hands – and into the Holy of Holies, obtaining ageless redemption not by the blood of goats and bulls but by his own blood. Consider this: if a sprinkling of the blood of goats and bulls and the ashes of a red heifer on those who had been defiled sufficed to make them ceremonially pure, how much more shall the blood of the Anointed One who by the Everlasting Spirit offered himself without spot or blemish to God cleanse our conscience from dead works to serve the living God?

And because he died as a ransom for transgressions under the first covenant he is become Mediator of a new covenant, in order that

---

38 *Exodus* 30:1,6, 27; *Leviticus* 4:7.
39 *Exodus* 25:10 *ff.*, 26:34, 37:1 *ff.*
40 *Exodus* 25:11.
41 *Exodus* 16:32-34.
42 *Numbers* 17:1-11.
43 *Exodus* 25:16, 31:18; *Deuteronomy* 10:1-5.
44 *Exodus* 28:18-20.
45 *Exodus* 25:17, 21.
46 *Leviticus* 16.

those who are called might receive the promise of an unending inheritance. It is plain that where there is a last will the death of the testator must be proved before it can take effect. In other words, a will has no force while the testator lives but only takes hold at his death. Therefore the first covenant was itself dedicated with blood when Moses, having spoken all the commandments of the Law to the people, drenched scarlet wool and hyssop with the blood of bulls and goats mixed with water[47] and sprinkled it over the Scroll and all the people, saying

> This is the blood of the covenant
> which God has commanded you.[48]

And he likewise sprinkled blood upon the tabernacle with all its furnishings and instruments of worship.[49] Indeed, under the Law nearly everything is cleansed with blood and without the shedding of blood there is no remission of sin.[50]

It was therefore also necessary that the patterns of the heavenly things be cleansed in this manner – but the heavenly things themselves with a better sacrifice than these because Messiah did not enter into man-made representations of the Holy Place, mere copies of the true, but into Heaven itself, now to appear before the face of God on our behalf. Nor did he need to offer himself on multiple times (much as a mortal high priest makes repeated offerings by entering the Holiest of Holies year-in and year-out, presenting not his own blood but that of another) because then the Savior would needs have suffered often from the foundation of the world. But now he has appeared once, close to the End of Time, to put away sins through his sacrifice. And as it is appointed to mankind once to die and after that judgment so too the Anointed One having once been offered to bear the sins of many will appear a second time, not to bear sin but to bring salvation to those that wait for him.

---

47   *Numbers* 19:6, 17.
48   *Exodus* 24:7-8; *Deuteronomy* 4:13.
49   *Cf. Leviticus* 8:30.
50   *Leviticus* 17:11.

10

Because the Law does not contain the true form of good things to come (but only their reflected shadow) it cannot perfectly purify the consciences of those who draw near to the Holy of Holies continuously offering an atonement sacrifice year after year. If the Law had been able to do so then logically those sacrifices would have ceased, the worshippers' consciences having been purified once and for all from the contamination of sins. But on the contrary, the yearly offerings themselves call continuing sins to mind.

In truth, it is impossible for the blood of bulls and goats to take away sins, which is why when he came into the world he said,

> You have no desire for gifts and sacrifices,
>   neither take pleasure in burnt offerings –
> but instead you've prepared a body for me –
>   So I said, "Behold, I come to do your will, O God,
> as it is written of me in the scroll of your Word."[51]

So when he says in the first instance, You have no desire for gifts and sacrifices, neither take pleasure in burnt offerings, he refers to the sacrifices of the Law. And when he then says, "Behold, I come to do your will, O God," he does away with the first covenant in order to establish the second – and in accordance with that will and purpose we have been sanctified through the offering of the body of the Anointed Jesus once and for all time.

Every high priest performing the Temple worship brings to the altar again and again the same sort of sacrificial offerings – even though these can never strip away sins. Yet this man, having made his offering for sin one time only, sat down timelessly enthroned at the right hand of God until his enemies be made his footstool,[52] by his one gift unendingly perfecting those who are sanctified. The Holy Spirit testifies to us likewise because after saying,

---

51   *Psalms* 40:6-7, 51:16-17; *Isaiah* 1:11; *Jeremiah* 6:20, 7:21-23; *Hosea* 6:6; *Amos* 5:21 *ff.*; *Micah* 6:6-8.
52   *Psalms* 110:1.

> This shall be the covenant
> > that I will make with the house of Israel:
> After those days, saith the Lord,
> > I will put my law in their inward parts,
> and write it in their hearts,[53]

he goes on to say,

> > their sins and their iniquities
> > I will remember no more.[54]

And it follows that when sins are forgiven, sacrifices cease.

My brethren, we have confidence to enter the Holy Places by virtue of the blood of Jesus, who opened a new and living path for us when he passed through the veil, that is to say, his own flesh. Therefore, because we have a Great Priest over the House of God let us approach with true hearts in fullness of faith, our hearts sprinkled free from an evil conscience, our bodies washed with pure water,[55] holding firm to the profession of our hope without wavering – because he is faithful who promised – motivating one another to good and noble works, not failing to gather ourselves together in assembly (as has become the habit of some) but rather encouraging one another and that all the more as you see the Day approaching.

But if we continue to sin deliberately after receiving the knowledge of the truth, does any sacrifice remain for sins? Or isn't what remains nothing but a fearful expectation of God's fiery jealousy consuming all enemies? If anyone set aside the Law of Moses she was doomed without mercy on the testimony of two or three witnesses.[56] So how much worse punishment do you think someone deserves if despite having been sanctified he then stomps on the Son of God, treating the blood of the covenant like trash, acting with hubris toward the Spirit of Grace? We all know the words spoken – Vengeance is mine,

---

53   *Jeremiah* 31:33.
54   *Jeremiah* 31:34.
55   *Ezekiel* 36:25-27; *cf. Leviticus* 16:4.
56   *Deuteronomy* 17:2-7.

I will repay[57] and again, The Lord will judge his people.[58]

It is a fearful thing to fall into the hands of the living God. But call back to mind the earlier days when you first came to the Light and endured the suffering of great affliction, sometimes exposed to public humiliation and abuse, other times sharing in sympathy with others when they were ill-treated – comforting them in prison and even accepting the loss of your own goods with joy, knowing that you have a greater treasure in store for you. Therefore cast not aside your confidence, which has great hope of reward, but endure, that having done the will of God you may receive what is promised, for yet

> a bare little while[59] and he who is coming will come
> and not delay.
> Now the righteous shall live by faith;
> and my soul has no pleasure
> in someone who draws back.[60]

We do not cringe to our destruction but are faithful, securing our souls.

11

Faith gives substance to our hopes and evidence of things seen not. It grounds our knowledge that Time and Space were spoken into existence by the Word of God[61] – the visible thus invisibly framed. And so by faith did the elders give witness:

By faith Abel offered God a greater sacrifice than that of Cain and by his faith thereby obtained the testimony of righteousness, God accepting his gifts, and by that same faith though he died yet he speaks.[62]

By faith Enoch was assumed into Heaven – he was not found be-

---

57 *Deuteronomy* 32:35; *cf. Romans* 12:19.
58 *Deuteronomy* 32:36; *Psalms* 134:14.
59 *Isaiah* 26:20.
60 *Habakkuk* 2:3-4.
61 *Genesis* 1; *Psalms* 33:6-9.
62 *Genesis* 4:10.

cause God had taken him[63] in order that he not see death, his corruptible putting on incorruptible, his mortality immortality – because before his translation it was testified that he pleased God. But without faith it is impossible to please God because whoever comes to God must believe he exists and is a rewarder of those that seek him out.

By faith Noah had divine revelation of things not yet seen and, planning ahead, prepared the ark, saving himself and his family, condemning the world and becoming heir to that righteousness which is according to faith.[64]

By faith when Abraham was called he obeyed, emigrating to a land he was to inherit, traveling without knowing exactly where he was headed.[65] Yet by faith he sojourned in the Promised Land as a bedouin, making his home in a tent with Isaac and Jacob as fellow heirs of the same promise – because in truth he sought a city with firm foundations whose architect and master builder is God. And by faith Sarah herself, though barren in her youth and now well past menopause, received strength in her womb to conceive a child by the seed of Abraham because she reckoned faithful him who had promised. Thus from one man – and him as good as dead – sprang generations numerous as the stars of the sky, numberless as the sands of the shore.[66]

These all died in faith, not having received the promises.[67] Even so, seeing them afar off they embraced them, confessing they were but strangers and pilgrims upon the Earth.[68] And people who speak like that demonstrate that they still seek a home, because if they'd been pining for the place they came from they would've had plenty of chances to return. But now they reach for someplace better, that is, a heavenly home – which is why God is neither ashamed of them nor the least embarrassed to be called their God but has instead prepared for them a city.

By faith Abraham being put to the test offered up his only begotten

---

63 *Genesis* 5:24; *Sirach* 44:16.
64 *Genesis* 6:8 *ff.*; *Ezekiel* 14:20; *Sirach* 44:17-18.
65 *Genesis* 12:1 *ff.*, 13:3, 18:1 *ff.*
66 *Genesis* 13:16, 21:17; *Sirach* 44:19-21.
67 *Genesis* 17:5-8, 26:13-14, 49:18.
68 *Genesis* 47:9; *cf. Psalms* 118:19; *Ecclesiastes* 12:5.

son Isaac[69] even though God had promised him, Your descent shall be through Isaac,[70] judging that God is able to raise the dead – thus receiving Isaac back in his own person from the death he suffered in the figure of the ram.

By faith Isaac bespoke future blessings upon Jacob and Esau; by faith Jacob blessed both sons of Joseph, worshiping even as he leaned on his deathbed;[71] and by faith Joseph when he lay dying foresaw the redemption of the Children of Israel, giving commands concerning his bones.[72]

By faith Moses' parents defied the king's command[73] and kept the child hidden for three months after he was born, perceiving him to be well-favored of God.[74] By faith when he was grown Moses refused to be called the son of Pharoah's daughter, choosing shared hardship with the people of God over the short-time pleasures of sin – he kept his eyes on the prize, valuing the abuse he would suffer for Messiah's sake more than all the gold in Egypt.[75] By faith he fled Egypt in the face of the king's wrath after slaying a taskmaster, not fearing his sojourn in exile but enduring as one who sees the unseen.[76] By faith he kept the Passover, striking the blood on the posts and lintels of the doors lest the Destroying Angel should touch Israel's firstborn.[77] By faith he crossed the Red-Weed Sea as through it were dry land – while the Egyptians were swallowed up attempting the same.[78]

By faith the walls of Jericho fell after being encircled seven days.[79] By faith the whore Rahab escaped destruction with the disobedient because she received the spies to her home in peace.[80]

And what else can I say? I don't have the time here to recount

---

69   *Genesis* 22:1 *ff.*
70   *Genesis* 21:12.
71   *Genesis* 47:30-31, 48:1-20, *cf.* 49:1 *ff.*; *Sirach* 44:22
72   *Genesis* 50:24-25.
73   *Exodus* 1:22.
74   *Exodus* 2:2.
75   *Sirach* 45.
76   *Exodus* 2:14.
77   *Exodus* 12.
78   *Exodus* 14.
79   *Joshua* 6.
80   *Joshua* 2.

the stories of Gideon,[81] Barak,[82] Samson,[83] Jephthah,[84] David[85] and Solomon[86] or those of the prophets – people who by faith conquered kingdoms, worked righteousness, obtained promises, stopped the mouths of lions,[87] quenched the power of fire,[88] escaped the edge of the sword, were made strong in their weakness, waxed powerful in battle, stormed the barricades of enemies. Women received their dead back to life.[89] Others were tortured, rejecting deliverance in order to gain a better resurrection. And others were scorned, tested by whips, bonds, prison.[90] They were stoned to death,[91] sawn asunder, slain by the sword, wandered about clothed in the skins of sheep and goats, destitute, afflicted, suffering evil, wandering in deserts and mountains and caves and dens.[92] The world was worthy of none of them. Yet even though attested in their faith, they did not obtain the promise, God foreseeing something better for us such that their perfection depends on ours.

12

Therefore having so great a cloud of witnesses about us we should lay aside every superfluous weight and entangling sin and through patience run the race laid before us, keeping our eyes on Jesus, the leader and perfecter of our faith, who for the joy set before him despised the shame of the cross and is now set down enthroned at the right hand of God. Just compare his situation to yours: look at the rebellion of contrary sinners *he* endured and you won't let your souls faint or give out because, after

---

81 *Judges 6-8.*
82 *Judges 4-5.*
83 *Judges 13-16.*
84 *Judges 11.*
85 *1 and 2 Samuel; 1 Kings; 1 Chronicles; Psalms; etc.*
86 *1 Kings; 1 Chronicles; Proverbs; Ecclesiastes; Song of Solomon; etc.*
87 *Daniel 6:16-23.*
88 *Daniel 3.*
89 *1 Kings 17; 2 Kings 4.*
90 *2 Chronicles 36:15-16; Jeremiah 20:2, 37:15*
91 *2 Chronicles 24:20-21.*
92 *1 Kings 18:4, 19:10; Jeremiah 26:21-23.*

all, you haven't yet resisted sin to the point of shedding blood. Or is it the case you've forgotten that the Lord speaks to you as his children when he says,

> My son, don't disdain the Lord when he punishes you
> > or brush him off when he criticizes you –
> he only disciplines those he loves,
> > scourging every child he embraces.[93]

Don't you see that God cares for you as children even as he corrects you? Is there any child who doesn't need a parent to punish him from time to time? And if God *doesn't* punish you the way he does his other children aren't you then bastards, not sons at all? We all had fathers in the flesh who chastised us and we honored them – how much more should we subject ourselves to the Father of spirits and live? They corrected us a bit in whatever way seemed best to them; but he strives to keep us on the straight and narrow for our own benefit in order that we might share in his holiness. Now admittedly, no one finds pleasure in punishment. But remember – no pain, no gain. And in due course godly discipline yields the peaceable fruit of righteousness to those who learn from it.

Therefore pick up those drooping hands, strengthen those weak knees and make straight paths for your feet[94] so that whatever's been out of joint not go lame but rather be healed.

Follow peace with all and sanctification, without which no one will see the Lord, watching out lest any fall short of the grace of God, lest any root of bitterness grow up and torment you[95] causing many to become defiled, lest there be in your midst a godless glutton like Esau who sold his rights as first-born son for one lousy meal.[96] And you know that afterwards he longed to recover that blessing but was rejected, unable to change the past even though he begged his father

---

93 *Proverbs* 3:11-12.
94 *Proverbs* 4:26.
95 *Deuteronomy* 29:18.
96 *Genesis* 25:29-34.

for help, shedding many tears.[97]

But you have not drawn near that untouchable mountain spewing forth fire, filled with glowering storm and doom, trumpets blaring and a voice speaking words striking fear in those who heard it, such that none could not bear the command touch not this mountain, where even a trespassing beast must be stoned to death[98] – indeed, the sight was so terrifying that Moses himself confessed I tremble in fear.[99] No, you have come to Mount Zion; to heavenly Jerusalem, city of the living God; to ten thousands of angels in joyful throng; to the church of the firstborn enrolled in Heaven; to God the Judge of all; to the spirits of the righteous now perfected; to Jesus, Mediator of a new covenant; and to the sprinkled blood that speaks more excellently than did that of Abel.

So see to it you don't refuse the one who speaks! If those who refused God's oracle on Earth did not escape much less can we escape if we turn our backs on the one who speaks from Heaven. And in those days his voice shook the Earth[100] but now he has promised, Yet once more will I shake not only the Earth but Heaven itself.[101] This phrase yet once more makes clear that what is shaken will be put away – in other words, he means to remove the created order – so that only those things that cannot be shaken should endure. And since we are receiving a kingdom that cannot be removed let us give thanks to the Lord, for it is meet and right so to do, and worship him acceptably with reverence and godly fear, which is our reasonable service – for our God is a consuming fire.[102]

---

97   *Genesis* 27:38.
98   *Exodus* 19:12-13.
99   *Deuteronomy* 9:19.
100 *Exodus* 19:18.
101 *Haggai* 2:6.
102 *Deuteronomy* 4:24.

13

Let brotherly love continue – but also don't forget to welcome strangers because some have taken in angels as guests without realizing it.[103] Remember those in prison as if you were bound with them and those who are mistreated, because you are also liable to bodily suffering. Honor your marriage and keep its intimacies pure, because God will judge the adulterous and immoral. Live a life free from greed and be content with what you have – he has said, I will never abandon or leave you behind,[104] such that we now can say with confidence

> The Lord is my helper –
> I shall not fear,
> for what can anyone do to me?[105]

Remember those who led you, because they spoke the Word of God to you. Now that they've died, survey the course of their lives and faith and pattern your own on theirs.

The Anointed Jesus is the same yesterday, today and forever: therefore don't be swept away by strange and varied doctrines. It's enough for the heart to be founded on grace and not on teachings about what to eat or what to drink, none of which ever helped anyone. Instead, we now have an altar from which those who still serve the former Tabernacle have no right to eat – what we mean by this is that just as the bodies of those animals that had been brought into the Holy of Holies by the high priest in order to shed their blood in atonement for sin were taken outside the city to be burnt,[106] so too Jesus suffered outside the gate in order to purify the people by his own blood.[107] Let us therefore go to him outside the camp, bearing his reproach, because we have no constant abode here but rather seek the

---

103 *Genesis* 18.
104 *Deuteronomy* 31:6; *1 Chronicles* 28:20.
105 *Psalms* 118:6.
106 *Leviticus* 6:30 *and* 4:5-7, 12:16-21, 16:27.
107 *Cf. Exodus* 33:7.

abiding city to come. And let us offer a continual sacrifice of praise to God,[108] the fruit of our lips giving thanks to his Name,[109] with charity sharing the things we have – because these are sacrifices that truly please God.

Obey your overseers, yield to them. They watch for your souls as those who must give account. Thus may they perform their office with joy without having to sigh over your disobedience, something that will do you no good.

Pray for us. We are fully persuaded that our conscience is clear, always desiring to conduct ourselves with all propriety. But pray especially that I may swiftly be restored to your midst.

Now may the God of peace – who by the blood of the everlasting covenant[110] brought up from the dead our Lord Jesus, the Great Shepherd of the sheep – make you fit to perform every good work in accordance with his will, working in you that which is pleasing in his sight through Jesus Christ, to whom be the glory forever and ever, amen.

Finally I call on you brothers and sisters to take this message of encouragement to heart. The truth is, I've written it to you in but a few words.

Know that our brother Timothy has been set free! It's my goal to come with him to see you soon. Greet all your overseers together with all the saints. The brothers in Italy greet you, whence this letter is sent.

Let grace be among you all.

---

108 *Leviticus* 7:12.
109 *Hosea* 14:12.
110 *Zechariah* 9:11.

JACOB'S LETTER

From Jacob, a servant of God and the Lord Jesus, to the Twelve Tribes of Israel living in the Diaspora - *Greetings!*

1

My brothers and sisters, count it manifest joy when you fall into manifold trials! Think of it like this - when your faith is put to the test the good result is patience. And let patience have its perfect work in you, so that being whole and complete you'll lack for nothing.

But if any of you lacks wisdom simply ask God for it. He won't criticize you for asking but will give to you generously, as he does to all. Just be sure that you ask in faith, not second-guessing yourself.[1] But if you waver you're like the billowing seas, driven and tossed by the wind. People like that are double-minded and unstable in everything they do - they can't expect to receive anything from the Lord.

If any of you be poor and afflicted rejoice when you are exalted. And if any be rich rejoice when you're laid low. Why? Because riches are a passing bloom, fading like wildflowers scorched by the rising sun, their blossoms

---

1   *Matthew* 21:22.

falling, their beauty perishing.[2] It's the same with riches - they too will fade.

Blessed are those who hold steady when tested because once tried they will receive the crown of life that God has promised to those that love him. But let no one who faces temptation say, "God is tempting me!" God stands apart from evil and tempts no one. Make no mistake, my beloved brethren, each person is tempted when seduced and enticed by his own harlot passion. When passion conceives it gives birth to sin. And when sin has its way it gives birth to death.[3]

But every good and perfect gift descends from above from the Father of Heavenly Lights,[4] who neither shifts nor casts an eclipsing shadow and in his will gave birth to us by the Word of Truth to the end we should be a kind of first fruit of all his creatures.

Knowing all this, beloved brethren, it falls to each of you to listen attentively, to think first before speaking and think twice before getting angry - because the wrath of man worketh not the righteousness of God. Sift instead the soil of your souls, ridding them of choking weeds of evil excess, and in mildness receive the implanted Word, which is your salvation. And don't just listen to the Word - do it! If you're hearers but not doers you're deceiving yourselves and are like the man who reflected on himself and his ways but then let his mind drift, conveniently forgetting the kind of person he was. In contrast, someone who looks closely into the perfect law of Christian liberty and abides there - not becoming a forgetful hearer but a doer - that person will find blessing in all she sets her hands to.

If anyone thinks of himself as a "religious" person but can't hold his tongue, he's deceiving his heart and his worship is worthless. True and pure religion in the sight of God and our Father is this: that you visit orphans and widows in their distress and keep yourselves unstained by the world.

---

2   *Isaiah* 40:7.
3   *See* Milton, *Paradise Lost*, II:648-883; J. Gower, *Mirour de l'Omme*, II:205-37.
4   *Genesis* 1:14, 16.

2

My brothers and sisters, don't be snobby about your faith and don't play favorites as you worship our Lord and Savior Jesus, the Lord of Glory. Suppose a rich man walks into your church wearing a nicely tailored suit and sporting gold rings on his fingers while a poor man follows him pretty much in rags. Would you tell the first, "Come, sit in the best seat so you can see and hear well," while you say to the other, "Go sit in the back or maybe down by my feet?" If so, aren't you now discriminators, setting yourselves up as arbiters, wicked in thought?

Listen to me - didn't God choose the poor of this world to be rich in faith, heirs of the kingdom he's promised to those who love him? But you have scorned the poor. Don't you know that the rich exploit you and drag you into court? And aren't they the same people who mock the Name that's been given you?[5]

You're in a good place if you fulfill the royal law set forth in the Scripture - Thou shalt love thy neighbor as thyself[6] - but if you favor one person over another you're actively doing wrong, violating the Law just like any other sinners. Trust me, you don't want to find yourselves judged under the Law again, because it's a seamless whole, summed up in that one verse. What I mean is that if you get tripped up and violate one commandment you become guiltily liable for all of them - he who said Thou shalt not commit adultery[7] also said Thou shalt not commit murder.[8] So even if you don't commit adultery but murder someone you've transgressed the whole Law since both concern your obligations to your neighbor. Therefore you need to speak and act as those who would be judged by the law of liberty - because judgment under the Law shall be without mercy to those who show no mercy, but mercy prevails over judgment.

What good is it, my brethren, if someone says she has faith but does no good deeds? Can her faith save her? It's as if one of your brothers or sisters hadn't a stitch to wear or a morsel to eat and one

---

5   *Amos* 9:12; *Acts* 15:17.
6   *Leviticus* 19:18.
7   *Exodus* 20:14; *Deuteronomy* 5:18.
8   *Exodus* 20:13; *Deuteronomy* 5:17.

of you were to say, "Go in peace my friend, be warmed and filled," but didn't give them any clothes or food. What good does that do them?? So too faith standing alone and without works is dead. Therefore one might well say to such a person, "You say you have faith, as do I, but I also do good deeds. Show me your faith without works (if you can) and I will show you my faith *by* my works." Do you believe that the Lord is One?[9] That's nice, but so do the demons – and they tremble.

Don't you know, you empty-headed fool, that it's pointless to have faith without works? Isn't it true that our father Abraham was found righteous in the eyes of God when he perfected his faith by bringing his son Isaac to the altar? Can you see how faith worked together with his actions and how his faith was therefore made perfect by deeds? And so the Scripture was fulfilled – Abraham believed God and it was imputed unto him for righteousness.[10] That's why he was called God's friend, showing us that a person is justified in God's sight through his perfecting works, not by an isolated faith. And wasn't it the same with the whore Rahab, who found redemption when she let the spies into Jericho and then sent them safely away?[11]

Therefore just as the body is dead without the spirit so too is faith unquickened by works.

3

Brothers and sisters, I don't want you to think you can all be teachers – you need to realize that teachers will be held to a higher standard and that teachers are often bound to slip up. Of course, if anyone is able to speak without stumbling he is fully mature, able also to rein in his whole body. Think of how we put bits in the mouths of horses to bridle their whole bodies, and even a great ship powered by mighty winds can be steered with a small rudder as the helmsman wills.[12]

So too the tongue is a small member yet boasts of great things.

---

9 *Deuteronomy* 6:4.
10 *Genesis* 15:6.
11 *Joshua* 2:1-15.
12 *See* Pseudo-Aristotle, *Mechanical Problems,* 851A; Philo, *Against Flaccus,* Ch. V, § 25.

And indeed how great a fire is lit by so small a spark! For the tongue is a flicker ready to ignite the whole body, a world of evil enflaming the cycle of life – and the tongue itself is set ablaze by the fires of Hell.

You know that all sorts of beasts of the field, birds, reptiles and even sea creatures can and have been subdued throughout human history – yet no one can tame the tongue. It is elusive, corrosive, wicked, filled with the sting of death, the same tool we use to bless our Lord and Father and yet curse those created in his likeness. But my brethren, how can it be that both blessing and curse flow from the same mouth!? Does a rock spring run bitter and sweet? Does a fig tree yield olives? A grape vine figs? Salt water sweet?

Any who are wise and knowledgeable among you should live in such a way as to demonstrate the humility of their wisdom through good deeds. But don't withstand the truth – if you harbor bitter jealousy and strife in your hearts that's not the kind of wisdom that descends from above but instead is earthly, base, even demonic. Why? Because wherever there's envy and strife there is chaos, revolt and every evil deed. But the wisdom that comes from above is first of all pure, then peaceable, gentle, tolerant, full of mercy and good fruits, steadfast, unpretentious – and thus the fruit of righteousness is sown in peace by those who make peace.

4

Do you think wars and battles come from some external source? Not so – they proceed from the hedonistic passions encamped within you.[13] You want something you don't have so you kill someone to get it. You covet something but can't get it so you start a war to seize and plunder. But the reason you lack is because you don't ask. And even when you *do* ask you don't receive because you ask for the ill purpose of satisfying your own lusts. Adulteresses![14] Don't you know that friendship with the world is enmity toward God? Whoever wishes to be the world's friend therefore makes herself God's adversary.

---

13   Plato, *Phaedo* 66C.
14   *Hosea* 9:1; *Ezekiel* 16:15 ff.

Do you think it's for nothing the Scriptures say that God is a jealous God,[15] and all the more so with his Spirit now dwelling in us?[16] But he gives all the grace that is needed, or as the Spirit says,

> God resists the proud
>> but gives grace to the humble.[17]

Submit yourselves to God. Resist the Devil and he will flee from you. Draw nigh to God and he will draw nigh to you. Cleanse your hands, ye sinners and purify your hearts, ye double-minded. Be afflicted, and mourn, and weep: let your laughter be turned to mourning, and your joy to heaviness. Humble yourselves in the sight of the Lord and he shall lift you up.

And don't slander one another, brethren, because whoever slanders or judges his brother speaks against the law of liberty, determining who is complying and who isn't. But if you're deciding who's right and who's wrong you are not a doer of the law but acting as its keeper. And yet there is but *one* Lawgiver and Judge - he who is able both to save and to destroy - so who are you to judge your neighbor?

What's up with you who say, "We'll go to this town today or tomorrow and spend the next year buying and selling and taking our profits"? You don't know what tomorrow will bring or what a wisp your life is, a mist, appearing for a bit then vanishing as quickly as it came. What you *should* say is, "We'll go to such-and-such a place and do this-and-that ... if the Lord wills." Yet now you boast in your pretentions. But all such boasting is wicked - and it's sinful for someone who knows what is good to go ahead and do wrong anyway.

5

Hear me, you wealthy! Go now and weep wailing for the woes soon coming upon you! Your riches are decayed, your clothes moth-eat-

---

15   *Exodus* 20:5, 34:14; *Numbers* 35:34; *Deuteronomy* 5:9, 6:15, 32:10 *ff.*
16   *Ezekiel* 36:27; *John* 20:22; *Acts* 2:4.
17   *Proverbs* 3:34.

en, your silver and gold corroded.[18] And their rust shall be a witness against you, consuming your flesh as by fire. You've hoarded treasure in these Last Days but the wages withheld by fraud from your fieldworkers[19] cry out against you and the cries of the harvesters have entered the ears of the Lord of Hosts. You've enjoyed your life on Earth, luxuriating in every indulgence, feeding your hearts in the day of slaughter. You condemned and murdered the righteous, yet he did not resist you.

So be patient, my brothers and sisters, until the coming of the Lord. Take a lesson from the farmer who waits with patient expectation for the precious crop from the soil until it has received both the early and the latter rain. Therefore you be patient as well and steady your hearts, because the coming of the Lord draws near.

Don't grumble against one another, lest you be judged yourselves, because the Judge of all stands at the gates. And if you need more examples consider the patience and suffering of the prophets of old who spoke in the Name of the Lord. We count those blessed who have endured – and surely you've heard about the patience of Job. See how the Lord stays faithful to the end, multiplying mercy, full of compassion.

And above all, as our Lord said, "Don't swear any kind of oath, not 'by Heaven' and not 'by the Earth.' When you give your word just let it be 'yes, yes' or 'no, no.'"[20] Anything else will simply lead you into judgment.

If anyone suffers hardship, let him pray; if joyful, let him sing psalms. If anyone is sick let her call for the elders of her congregation and they will pray over her, anointing her with oil in the Name of the Lord – a prayer of faith will heal the sick and the Lord will raise her up. And if she has committed any sins they shall be forgiven her – that's why you should confess your sins to one another and pray for one another that you may be healed, because the effectual fervent prayer of a righteous man availeth much. You know that Elijah was someone just like us and he prayed with focused prayer that it should

18   *Matthew* 6:19-20.
19   *Leviticus* 19:13; *Jeremiah* 22:13.
20   *Matthew* 5:34-37.

not rain – and the rains ceased for three and a half years. Then he prayed again, the heavens opened and the earth yielded its fruit once more.[21]

My brothers, if anyone retrieves another from the error of his ways he will save that soul from death itself and cover a multitude of sins.

---

21   1 Kings 17-18.

PETER'S FIRST LETTER

From Peter, a missionary of the Anointed Jesus, to the elect pilgrims scattered in the Diaspora, especially those living now in the Roman districts of Pontus, Galatia, Cappadocia, Asia and Bithynia: may grace and peace overflow in you, you who have been chosen in the foreknowledge of God the Father, sanctified by the Holy Spirit for obedience, vouchsafed by the sprinkling of Jesus' own blood.

Blessed be God and the Father of our Lord the Savior Jesus, who brought us to new life according to his great mercy, giving birth in us to a living hope when he raised up Jesus from among the dead that we might receive an inheritance that can never perish, unfading and pure, safeguarded for us in Heaven by the power of God - even as we are safeguarded on Earth by faith leading to salvation ready to be revealed in the Last Days.

And so you will rejoice, though until now as need be you've been afflicted with manifold trials. Yet know this: your faith thus tested and purified by fire is more precious than perishable gold and will redound in praise and glory and honor at the revelation of the Anointed Jesus, who though you've not seen you love and who not yet seeing you trust, rejoicing with inexpressible joy, obtaining as the goal of your faith a share in his glory, even the salvation of your souls.

Keep in mind that the prophets of old diligently sought to understand when and for whom the Spirit was testifying through them as it foretold the sufferings of Messiah and his ascension into glory. And it was revealed to them that they spoke this good news not for themselves but in service to you, to whom it is now proclaimed through the Holy Spirit sent from Heaven – these things being a mystery that even angels longed to glimpse.

Therefore pull yourselves together, focus your minds with all sobriety, expectantly hoping for the grace that will soon be brought to you by Jesus Christ at his coming again. And, as children of obedience, don't pattern yourselves on the passions of your prior ignorance but just as the one who called you is holy, be holy as well in all you set your hands to, even as it is written,

> Be a holy people, because I am holy.[1]

If you call upon him as Father – he who judges all people without regard to their outward appearance or status but each according to his deeds – make your pilgrimage here with godly fear, knowing that you were redeemed from your ancestors' worthless ways not with perishable things, not silver coins or gold, but with precious blood, even the blood of the Savior as of a lamb without spot or blemish. He was chosen before the foundation of the world but revealed for your sakes in these Last Days, you who now have faith through him in God who raised him from the dead and gave him glory, in order that your faith and hope be grounded in God.

Having purified your souls by obedience to the truth extend yourselves in love to one another with true brotherly love because you were not born again to new life from perishable seed but the imperishably living and timeless word of God. In truth,

> All human life is grass
> > and its glory as the blossom on a flower –
> the grass fades and the blossom falls
> > but the word of God endures forever.[2]

And this is the very word of the gospel preached to you.
Ridding yourselves of all wickedness, all deceit, hypocrisy, envy and

---

1   *Leviticus* 11:44-45, 19:2, 20:7.
2   *Isaiah* 40:6-8.

slander, as newborn babes yearn for the purest of spiritual milk that by it you may be nourished to the fullness of salvation - if, that is, you have tasted that the Lord is kind. You come to him as to a living stone - rejected by men, it is true, but chosen and precious in the sight of God. Therefore as living stones be built up into a spiritual building, a holy priesthood to offer up through Jesus Christ spiritual sacrifices acceptable to God. As is also contained in Scripture,

> Behold I lay in Zion
>> a chief cornerstone, chosen and precious,
> and whoever trusts in him
>> will never be put to shame.[3]

For you who believe he is therefore precious, but to the disobedient the stone the builders rejected has become the headstone of the corner[4] and a stumbling stone, a rock of offense.[5] And they stumble in being disobedient to the Word, having been appointed to that end.

But you are a chosen race,[6] a royal priesthood,[7] a holy nation,[8] God's own people, that you might publish to all the excellence[9] of him who called you out of darkness into his wondrous light - you who once were not a people but are now the people of God,[10] who were outside his mercy but to whom mercy has now been shown.

Beloved ones, I call on you as the strangers and pilgrims you are to keep your distance from sensual desires, because they battle against the soul. Let your lives be an open book among the Gentiles so that even though they speak about you as if you were evildoers, they will see your good deeds and give God the glory in the Day of his coming.

For the Lord's sake, allow yourselves to be subject to established institutions, whether a president as one holding power or governors as those sent by him both to punish evildoers and to honor those who do good. It is God's will that by doing what is right you may silence the willful igno-

---

3   *Isaiah* 28:16.
4   *Psalms* 118:22.
5   *Isaiah* 8:14.
6   *Isaiah* 43:20.
7   *Exodus* 19:6.
8   *Exodus* 19:6.
9   *Isaiah* 43:21.
10   *Hosea* 2:23.

rance of foolish men. You are a free people, but don't use your freedom to cover up evil deeds. Rather use your freedom in slavery to God. Show honor to all – love the brotherhood, fear God, reverence the queen.

You who are domestic servants, be subject with due respect to the household masters, not only to the kind and considerate but even the crooked ones. It will be to your credit if, with God in mind, you endure hardships, even suffering unjustly. After all what virtue is there in suffering blows when you have done something wrong? But if you endure suffering having done right, this is thankworthy in the sight of God. Indeed, this is your very calling, the Messiah having also suffered for you, leaving behind an example to follow in his footsteps.

As it is written, he committed no sin neither was there any deceit found in his mouth;[11] when reviled he didn't rail back; though suffering he didn't threaten in return but committed himself to the one who judges in righteousness. And he himself bore our sins in his own body on the cross so that now having died to sins we might live unto righteousness – for you were healed by his wounds. You were as sheep that wandered astray but have now returned to the shepherd and guardian of your souls.

Wives, in like manner yield to your own husbands so that even if any are disobedient to the Word they may be won over without words by your manner of life, seeing how you maintain purity with reverent respect. And let your adornment not be found in the cosmetics of coiffed hair, gold bangles and *haute couture* but in that which is incorruptibly yours within, the adornment of a gentle and peaceful spirit, a prize of great worth in the sight of God. That was, after all, the manner of the holy women of old, who placed their hope in God and graced themselves by submission to their own husbands just as Sarah obeyed Abraham, calling him Lord – whose daughters you've become in well-doing, not shaken by fears of frightful things.

And the same goes for you husbands: live together with your wives in grateful appreciation, supportive of them when they are weak, always honoring them as joint heirs with you of the gift of life unending, lest your prayers be hindered.

The point of all this is that you must be like-minded toward one another, sympathetic and understanding, compassionate, filled with brotherly love,

---

11 *Isaiah* 53:9.

humble in spirit, not paying back evil with evil or insults with insults but blessing, just as you've been called to inherit a blessing.

> Anyone who wants to enjoy life
> > and come to a good end
> should hold his tongue from speaking evil,
> > seal his lips from any deceit,
> turn aside from evil and do what is right,
> > seek peace and follow after it –
> because the eyes of the Lord are upon the righteous
> > and his ears are open to their prayers,
> but his face is dead set against those who do ill.[12]

Who will do you evil if you are zealous for what is good? But even if you suffer for righteousness' sake, consider yourselves blessed. Don't let their terrors frighten or trouble you but let Christ rule as Lord in your hearts, ready in defense to all who seek reason for the hope that is in you. Yet do so with gentleness, reverently and with a clear conscience, so that those who slander or abuse you may be put to shame by your sound manner of living in Christ. It's better, if it be God's will, that you suffer as well-doers than as wrong, because the Savior also suffered in sacrifice for sins – once, the just for the unjust, that he might bring us near to God having been put to death in the flesh but made alive again in the spirit.

And in this new spiritual life he went and proclaimed his triumph to the spirits held in prison, spirits who once were disobedient back in the days of Noah, when God held his temper while the ark was being built. Though just a few people entered that ark – eight souls all told – they were saved, being borne upon the waters. And thus their rescue foreshadowed yours, where baptism now seals your salvation, cleansing you not by the mere washing away of dirt but the securing of a clear conscience toward God through the resurrection of the Anointed Jesus – who having gone into Heaven sits enthroned at the right hand of God, angels, rulers and dominions being made subject to him.

Christ suffered in his fleshly body. Therefore you too should arm yourselves with his attitude, for having suffered in the flesh you have been loosed from sin so as not to live out your time under the sway of human

---

12   *Psalms* 34:12-16.

passions but rather in the doing of God's will. It should be more than enough that you wasted away the past doing what pagans do – chasing women, piling up goods, guzzling wine, reveling at orgies, trading shots, serving unholy idols. And it should be no surprise that your boon companions now mock you for not running with them toward the flood of damnation. But they will give account to him that is poised to judge the quick and the dead. Indeed, that's why even the dead were preached to – that even though judged as people in the flesh yet might they live to God in the spirit.

The end of all things is at hand. Therefore keep yourselves in check and be sober minded in order that your prayers may be fruitful. Above all be unfailingly charitable toward one another because love covers a multitude of sins.[13] And be hospitable, welcoming one another in without grumbling. Each of you has been graced with a gift from God – use your gifts to serve one another, being faithful stewards of God's manifold grace. If anyone speaks, let her do so as one inspired by God. If anyone serves, let it be with the strength he is given. The goal is that everything be done so that God is glorified through Jesus the Christ, to whom be the glory and the power through all ages, amen.

Beloved, do not be astonished at the fierce and fiery trials coming upon you as though something unexpected were occurring, but rather rejoice insofar as you share in the Savior's sufferings that you may likewise exult when his glory is revealed. And blessed are you when you are reviled and abused for confessing Jesus' name, because the Spirit of God and his glory rests upon you. Just be sure that none of you suffers as a murderer or thief or evildoer or peeping Tom!

But if any of you suffers as a Christian don't be ashamed in the least. Instead, give the glory to God for being so named. It's now time for judgment to begin at the house of God. If it first begin with us, what will the end be of those who disobey the gospel of God? And

> if the righteous scarcely be saved,
> where shall the ungodly and the sinner appear?[14]

---

13   *Proverbs* 10:12.
14   *Proverbs* 11:31.

Let those who suffer according to the will of God therefore entrust their souls in well-doing to a faithful Creator.

I call upon the elders among you, not only as a fellow elder but also a witness of Christ's sufferings and one who will share in the glory about to be revealed – tend God's local flock, overseeing it not because you have to but because you eagerly desire to honor God's call to do so, never for the sake of money but in a spirit of generosity, not lording it over your people but being an example to them. And when the Great Shepherd appears you will receive an unfading crown of glory.

Likewise for the rest of the congregation, keep everything in order under the elders' care and clothe yourselves with humility the one toward the other, because God resists the arrogant but gives grace to the humble.[15] Therefore humble yourselves under the mighty hand of God that he may exalt you when the time comes. And cast all your cares upon him – because he cares for you.

Keep a sober mind and stay alert. Your Accuser – the Devil – prowls about like a roaring lion seeking prey to devour. Stand strong against him, knowing that these very same sufferings are taking their toll among your brethren in the world. But after you have suffered a little the God of all grace, who has called you to unending glory in Christ Jesus, will himself confirm, support, strengthen and establish you. To him be dominion through age upon age, amen.

I have written these few words to you by the hand of my faithful brother Silvanus, confirming and testifying that the things I write are the true grace of God, by which you stand.

She who is in Babylon, chosen together with you, sends greetings as does Marc, my own son. Greet one another with a kiss of love. Peace be to all you that are in Christ.

---

15   *Proverbs* 3:34.

PETER'S SECOND LETTER

S imeon Peter, a servant and apostle of the Anointed Jesus, to all those chosen to receive a faith as fully valuable as ours by virtue of the righteousness of our God and Savior Jesus – may grace and peace be multiplied to you in the full-grown knowledge of God and of our Lord Jesus, seeing that his divine power has granted us everything we need for life and godliness through the knowledge of him who called us by his own glory and excellence, by which he has also given us glorious and most precious promises that by means of these you may become partakers of his divine nature, having fled the corruption that fills the world with craven desires.

Be all you can be, incorporating within your faith what the ancient Greeks called *areté* – a quality of character exemplified by nobility/excellence/moral virtue[16] – adding to it self-knowledge, self-restraint, patience, piety and both godly and brotherly love. If these graces subsist in you, constantly increasing, you'll be neither slothful nor unfruitful as you move toward the perfect knowledge of our Anointed Lord Jesus. But if someone lacks these things he's become shortsightedly blind, having somehow forgotten the purification of his old sins. But you, brothers and sisters, should make it your life's work diligently to pursue an excellence of faith, confirming your calling and election. As you provide your part God will provide his, ushering you richly into the everlasting kingdom of our Lord and Savior, the Anointed Jesus.

That's also why I always make it a point to remind you of these things.

---

16   *E.g.,* Plato, *Meno* 89a3-5, 89c2-4; Aristotle, *Nicomachean Ethics*, 1105b4-8, 1144b27-30.

Of course, I realize you already know all this and are well planted in the truth professed among you. Even so, it seems to me a good idea to cheer you on while I'm still with you – the fact is, the Lord Jesus has made it clear to me that it won't be long before I'm gone. I've therefore taken steps to make sure that once I've left the house you'll have at hand everything you need to keep in mind the things I've told you.

You can be confident, in this regard, that we weren't pursuing some cleverly-crafted myths[17] when we revealed to you the power and coming of our Lord Jesus, the Messiah, having ourselves been made eyewitnesses of his majesty when we were with him in the holy mountain and heard a voice carried to him from Heaven – then and there we heard a voice divine from Heaven bearing the Father's glory and honor as it spoke, This is my beloved Son, in whom I am well pleased.[18] But we have a prophetic word yet firmer than this, to which you do well to pay attention as to light piercing twilight as dawn disperses dark, the Day Star arising in your hearts. Understand first and foremost that no one has a private right to interpret prophecies. Why? Because no prophecy ever came by human invention but only through men sent from God who spoke as they were moved by the Holy Spirit.

Even so there were false prophets among the nation just as there will be false teachers in your midst, people who will import destructive heresies, going so far as to deny the Master who bought them. They will bring swift destruction on themselves and many will be led astray by their debaucheries, on account of whom the word of truth will be defamed. They will buy and sell you as a matter of greed, seducing you with lying doctrines.

But their judgment descends from ancient times and neither slumbers nor sleeps: for if God was unsparing when angels sinned, driving them headlong from the pitch of Heaven to the gloom of Tartarus deep,[19] held fast until the Judgment Day; if he gave no reprieve to the ancient world, loosing cataclysm on the ungodly and saving only Noah, that herald of justice, along with seven in his family; if he condemned the Cities of the Plain, reducing them to ashes as an example to the future ungodly; and if he rescued righteous Lot, worn down as he dwelt surrounded by

---

17   *Cf.* Aristophanes, *Clouds,* 543.
18   *Matthew* 17:5.
19   Milton, *Paradise Lost,* II:772, 858.

lives of lawless lust, his just soul tormented day after day by the sights and sounds of sinful men – if all that be the case then the Lord knows how to rescue the godly from temptation and reserve to the Great and General Doom all those who wickedly despise lordship, swept as they are by the unceasing winds of carnal desires.[20]

These are arrogant and audacious people, unafraid to defame those with excess of glory obscured[21] even though the holy angels themselves, greater than they in power and might, do not blaspheme them in judgment before the Lord. Such people speak ill of things they don't understand. They will perish in their own corruption, earning the wages of sin for their injustice. They are much like mindless beasts born in the wild, subject only to capture and destruction, finding their fondness in daytime revels. Yet they are cursed children, spots and stains, feasting with you while they bathe in their deceptions with eyes full of adultery, unsated by sin, enticing wayward souls, their hearts naked with greed. Having now abandoned the straight and narrow they've wandered off with Bosor's son Balaam – who coveted unrighteousness' gain but was rebuked for his own lawlessness when a mute beast of burden spoke in human voice and forbade the prophet's madness.[22]

They are waterless wells, wind-driven mists for whom the gloom of darkness is reserved: with silken voice and sensual wile they lure into lust those not long escaped from their entanglements in that same morass, promising freedom while they themselves are slaves to corruption (because you are enslaved by whatever masters you). And if, having fled the world's pollutions through the knowledge of our Lord and Savior Jesus, they are again enmeshed and defeated, their last state is worse than the first.[23] It would've been better for them never to have known the way of righteousness than, having known it, to turn back from the holy commandment given to them. What has happened to them is as written in Proverbs: A dog returns to its own vomit.[24] Or as is now commonly said, "A sow having bathed wallows back in the mire."

---

20 Dante, *Inferno,* Canto V:30-46.
21 Milton, *Paradise Lost,* I:593-94.
22 *Numbers* 22:22 *ff.*
23 *Matthew* 12:43-45; *Luke* 11:24-26.
24 *Proverbs* 26:11.

This is already the second time that I'm writing to you, beloved ones. My aim in both my letters is to stir up your pure mind so that you'll remember the things foretold by the holy prophets and the commandment of the Lord and Savior given through your apostles. Know this first of all: in the Last Days scoffing mockers will come, led by the passions of their own desires. They will say, "What ever happened to that promise of Jesus' coming? Nothing has changed since the fathers fell asleep – everything's been the same since the beginning of Creation."

They only say this because they've purposefully closed their minds, ignoring that the Heavens were from old and the Earth was composed when darkness was upon the face of the deep and the Spirit of God moved upon the face of the waters, set a firmament in the midst of the waters to divide the waters under the firmament from the waters above the firmament and gathered the waters below the firmament into one place so that the dry land appeared – all by means of the Word of God – and that by such waters the world then-existing was flooded and destroyed. But by this same Word the Heavens and Earth that now exist are reserved for fire, being kept until the Day of Judgment and the destruction of ungodly people.

My beloved ones, don't make the mistake of thinking that the Lord is subject to the constraints of Time – in his sight one day is as a thousand years and a thousand years as one day.[25] The Lord is not late in delivering on his promise in the way that some consider late. Instead, he is longsuffering toward you, not willing that any should perish but that all should find a place of repentance. And yet the Day of the Lord will come as a thief in the night[26] – the Heavens imploding in a rushing roar, the Earth and its Elements dissolving in a maelstrom of fire.[27] And since all this will thus pass away what sort of lives do you think you should live?! Shouldn't you conduct yourselves in holiness and pious expectation, hastening toward the coming of the Day of the Lord on account of which the Heavens will dissolve aflame and the Elements burning will melt, all while we look for a new Heaven and a new Earth according to his promise, where righteousness dwells?[28]

---

25   *Psalms* 90:4.
26   *1 Thessalonians* 5:2.
27   *Psalms* 97:5; *Ezekiel* 38:19-22; *Zechariah* 14:12; *Matthew* 24:29-30, 36-44.
28   *Isaiah* 65:17-25.

But beloved, seeing as you *do* have this expectation make it your goal to be found at his coming spotless and without blemish, in peace in his sight, accounting the longsuffering of our Lord as your salvation. Consider as well the things our beloved brother Paul has written to you, how God's kindness and forbearance comfort you, leading you to turn from your old ways.[29] And thus he speaks in all his epistles according to the wisdom given to him. While it's true he sometimes writes things about the Last Days that are difficult to grasp[30] it's only the unlearned and unstable who twist them to their own destruction, as they also do with the rest of the Scriptures.

Since you know all this ahead of time be on your guard, my beloved, lest you be swept along with the deceptions of the lawless and lose your footing. Instead, increase all the more in the grace and knowledge of our Lord and Savior, the Anointed Jesus – and to him be the glory from now till the Dawn of Eternity.

---

29   *Romans* 2:4; *1 Corinthians* 1:7-9; *1 Thessalonians* 4:13-5:11; *cf. Hebrews* 9:26 *ff.*, 10:25, 37.
30   *See, e.g., 2 Thessalonians* 2:1 *ff.*

JOHN'S FIRST LETTER

We proclaim to you what we have seen and heard concerning the Word of Life. This Life was from the beginning with the Father and has been revealed to us – and we ourselves have heard and gazed upon and seen it with our eyes, even touched it with our own hands. And the Life which was with the Father and we have seen is the Life Everlasting we now testify and declare to you, in order that you may share in our fellowship – because our fellowship is with the Father and with his Son, the Anointed Jesus. We therefore write these things to you that our mutual joy may be full, even to overflowing.

And this is the message we have heard from him and bring back to you – that God is Light and in him there is no Darkness at all. If we say we have fellowship with him yet continue to walk in Darkness we are lying and not acting in Truth. But if we walk in the Light – as he is in the Light – we have fellowship with one another and the Blood of his Son Jesus Christ cleanses us from all sins. Just so, if we say we have no sin we deceive ourselves and the Truth is not in us. But if we confess our sins he is Faithful and Just to remove our sins and cleanse us from all Unrighteousness. If we say we have not sinned we make him a liar and his Word is not in us.

My little children, I write to you that you sin not. But if anyone sins we have an Intercessor before the Father – our Savior the Righteous Jesus, himself the Sacrificial Offering for our sins and not for our sins only but those of the whole world. And this is how we know that we know him: if we keep his

Commandments. Whoever says, "I know him!" but doesn't keep his Commandments is a liar and the Truth is not in him. But truly the Love of God is perfected in those who keep his Word and in this way we know we are in him. Whoever says he dwells in him should therefore walk as he himself walked.

Beloved, what I'm writing to you is not a new Commandment but the one you had even at the outset of your faith. This Commandment is the Word you have heard. And yet the Commandment I write to you is also full of newness - it is True in him and in you because the Darkness is passing away and the True Light now shines. Therefore whoever says he is in the Light but hates his brother is in Darkness until now, but whoever loves his brother dwells in the Light and causes no one to fall. Whoever hates his brother is in the Darkness and walks in Darkness not knowing where he goes, because Darkness has blinded his eyes.

I write to you, little children, because your sins have been forgiven for his Name's sake. I write to you, fathers, because you have known him who was from the beginning. I write to you, servants, because you have overcome the Wicked One. I wrote to you, children, because you have known the Father. I wrote to you, fathers, because you have known him from the beginning. I wrote to you, servants, because you are strong and the Word of God dwells in you and you have overcome the Wicked One.

Love not the world neither the things that are in the world. If anyone loves the world the Love of the Father is not in him because everything that is in the world - a sensual appetite, a lustful eye, life's false pretension - none of that comes from the Father but comes from the world. And the world and its desires are passing away but whoever does the Will of God remains forever.

Children, these are the Last Days and as you have heard, an anti-messiah comes. Indeed, many who oppose the Lord's Anointed have already now appeared - that's how we know these are the End Times. They went out from among us but they were not of us because if they had been of us they would have remained with us - but they were revealed to make it clear that not all among us are of us. Yet you have an Anointing from the Holy One and you know all things. I have not written to you because you do not know the Truth but because you *do* know it and that no lie is of the Truth. Who is a liar but he who denies that Jesus is the Savior? He who denies the Father and the Son - that's Christ's enemy. No one who denies the Son has the Father. Whoever confesses the Son also has the Father. Hold fast to that which you have heard from the beginning because if that which you have heard from the beginning remains in you you will remain in the Son and in the Father. And this is the Good News he himself has promised to you, even Life Unending.

I have written these things to you concerning those who would deceive you. But the Anointing you received from him remains in you. You do not need anyone to teach you because the same Anointing will teach you concerning all things – and it is True and is not a lie. So just as he has taught you, remain in him.

And now, little children, abide in him so that when he appears we may stand in complete assurance at his Advent, not shrinking from his presence in shame. If you know he is Righteous then you know that everyone doing righteousness has been born of him.

See how great is the Love the Father has shown us, that we should be called Children of God – and so we are. That is why the world has not known us, because it did not know him. Beloved, now we are the Children of God and it has not yet been revealed what we shall be. But we do know that when he appears we shall be like him because we will see him as he is. And everyone who has this Hope grounded on him purifies himself, just as he is Pure. Everyone who continues in sin acts in lawlessness because sin is lawlessness. You know that he appeared in mortal flesh in order to take sin away and in him there is no sin. Everyone who continues in him continues not in sin and whoever continues in sin has neither seen nor known him.

Little children, let no one deceive you. Whoever does righteousness is righteous just as he is Righteous. Whoever continues in sin is of the Evil One because the Evil One has been sinning from the start. For this reason the Son of God was revealed – that he might destroy the works of the Evil One. Everyone who is born of God does not continue in sinful habits because God's seed dwells in him – he is not able to lead a sinful life because he has been born of God. In this way it is clear who are the Children of God and who are the children of the Evil One. Everyone who does not continue in Righteousness is not a Child of God, neither he who loves not his brother.

This is the Truth you have heard from the beginning, that you should love one another – not like Cain, who was on the side of the Evil One and slaughtered his brother. And what was the reason he slew him? Because his own deeds were evil and those of his brother were righteous. My brothers and sisters, do not be surprised if the world hates you. We know we have crossed over from Death into Life because we love the brethren.

Whoever loves not remains in Death. Everyone who hates his brother is a murderer and you know that no murderer has Unending Life dwelling in him. This is how we know Love, because he laid down his life for us. So we too should lay down our lives for the brethren. Whoever has this world's goods and sees his brother in need yet locks him out of the door to his heart, how can the Love of God dwell in him? Little children, let us not love in mere word or speech but in deed and in truth.

In this way we shall know we are in the Truth and reassure our hearts in his sight – because even if our heart condemns us God is greater than our heart and knows all things. Beloved, if our heart does not condemn us we have complete confidence toward God and whatever we ask of him we receive because we keep his Commandments and do those things that are pleasing to him. And this is his Commandment, that we believe in the Name of his Son Jesus, the Anointed One, and that we love one another just as he has given us command. Whoever keeps his Commandments dwells in him and he in him. And by this we know that he dwells in us – by the Spirit he has given us.

Beloved, do not trust every spirit but test the spirits to see whether they come from God, because many false prophets have gone out into the world. This is how you will know whether a spirit comes from God: every spirit that confesses Jesus Christ come in the flesh is from God and every spirit that does not confess Jesus is not from God – and this is the Enemy of God, the one you have heard is coming and is now already in the world. You belong to God, little children, and have overcome them, because greater is he that is in you than he that is in the world. They are of the world and for this reason they speak as of the world and the world listens to them. We are of God. Whoever knows God listens to us and whoever is not of God does not listen to us. This is how you can tell the spirit of Truth from the spirit of Deceit.

Beloved, let us love one another, because Love is from God and everyone who loves has been born of God and knows God. Whoever loves not has never known God – because God is Love. This is how the Love of God has been revealed to us, in that he sent his Only Begotten Son into the world that we might live through him. Herein is Love – not that we have loved God but that he loved us and sent his Son into the world a sacrificial offering for our sins. Beloved, if God so loved us we too ought to love one another. No one has ever beheld God – but if we love one another God dwells in us and our love toward God is made complete in us.

This is how we know we dwell in him and he in us – because he has given us of his Spirit. We have seen and testify that the Father has sent the Son to be the Savior of the world. If anyone confesses that Jesus is the Son of God then God abides in him and he in God. And we have known and believed the Love God has for us. God is Love and whoever abides in Love abides in God and God in him.

This is how Love is perfected with us, so that we might have full confidence in the Day of Judgment – that such as he is, so are we in the world. There is no fear in Love but perfect Love casts out fear. Fear lives under the shadow of punishment and whoever lives in fear has not been perfected in Love. We love because he first loved us. Whoever says, "I love God" but hates his brother is a liar – because how can someone love God whom he has not seen yet hate his brother whom he has seen? And we have this Commandment from him, that whoever loves God should also love his brother.

Everyone who believes that Jesus is the Anointed One has been born of God and everyone who loves the progenitor loves the offspring. In this we know that we love God's Children, because we love God and follow his Commandments. This is the Love of God, that we keep his Commandments – and his Commandments are not burdensome. All that is born of God overcomes the world. And this is the victory that overcomes the world, even our Faith. Who overcomes the world if not the one who believes that Jesus is the Son of God?

This is he who came by means of Water and Blood – not by Water only but also by Blood. And it is the Spirit that testifies to this because the Spirit is Truth. There are Three who testify: the Spirit and the Water and the Blood and these Three are united as One. If we receive testimony from men, God's testimony is greater, and this is the testimony of God he has given concerning his Son. Whoever believes in the Son of God has this testimony within himself. Whoever does not believe God would make God a liar because he has not believed the testimony that God has given concerning his Son. And this is the testimony – that God gave us Eternal Life and this Life is in his Son. Whoever has the Son has Life. Whoever has not the Son of God has not Life.

I write these things to you who believe in the Name of the Son of God that you may know you have Life without end. And this is the confidence we have toward him: that if we ask anything according to his Will he hears us. If we know he hears us whatsoever we ask then we know we have the things we have asked of him.

If anyone sees his brother committing a sin not leading to Death he must petition on his behalf and by doing so grant him Life - that is, for those who sin not unto Death. There *is* sin that leads to Death but I'm not directing that anyone petition in that regard. All injustice is sin and there is sin that does not lead to Death.

We know that everyone who has been born of God does not continue leading a sinful life because the Only Begotten Son of God guards him and the Evil One does not touch him. We know we are of God and that the whole world lies under the power of the Evil One. We know the Son of God is come into the world and has given us understanding minds in order that we know the One who is True and that we are in the One who is True, in his Son Jesus Christ. He is the True God and Life Imperishable.

Little children, keep yourselves away from idols.

JOHN'S SECOND LETTER

The elder to the elect lady and her children, whom I love in truth and not I alone but all those who have known the truth, for the sake of the truth which dwells among us and will be with us forever. Grace, mercy and peace will be with us from God the Father and Jesus Christ, Son of the Father in truth and love.

I rejoiced greatly that I found you and your children walking in truth, just as we have received command from the Father. And now I pray you, dear lady, not as one writing a new commandment to you but that which we have had from the outset, that we should love one another. And this is love, that we walk in accordance with his commandments - this is the commandment and just as you have heard it from the beginning, so also walk in it, because many deceivers are out and about in the world, those who do not acknowledge Jesus Christ having come in the flesh. Such a one is the Deceiver and the Antichrist.

Watch out for yourselves that you do not lose the things you have gained, but rather that you obtain a full reward. Anyone who goes out on his own and does not remain in the teaching of Christ does not have God. Whoever remains constant in the teaching, he has the Father and the Son. If anyone comes to you and bears not this teaching don't receive him into your household – don't even greet him, because I tell you anyone who welcomes him shares in his evil deeds.

Though I have many things to write to you I prefer not to commit them to paper. Rather, I hope to come to you and speak face to face in order that our joy be made full. The children of your elect sister greet you.

JOHN'S THIRD LETTER

The elder to the beloved Gaius, whom I love in truth.

Beloved, I pray more than anything that you prosper and continue in good health, just as your soul prospers. I rejoiced greatly at the coming of the brethren who witnessed to the truth in you, just as you also walk in truth. I have no greater joy than to hear that my children walk in the truth.

Beloved, they have testified before the whole assembly to your faithfulness in performing good deeds for the brethren and for strangers. You especially do well in helping them along in their journeys in service to God because they have gone out for the sake of his Name, accepting nothing from the Gentiles. We therefore ought to support such ones, so as to be their co-laborers in the truth.

I have written something to the assembly but their self-important leader Diotrephes refused to recognize our authority. For that reason when I do get there I will focus them on what he has done - spreading foolish gossip about us and, as if that weren't enough, refusing to welcome in the brethren, going so far as to hinder those who wished to do so, even kicking them out of the congregation.

Beloved, don't mimic the bad but follow what is good. Whoever does good is from God. Whoever does ill has not seen God. Demetrius has been testified to by all and by the truth. We endorse him as well and we know our testimony is true.

I had many things to write to you but I did not wish to set them down with pen and ink. Yet I look forward to seeing you soon and speaking face to face. Peace be upon you. The friends greet you. Greet the friends by name.

JUDAS' LETTER

J udas, Jacob's brother and a servant of Jesus Christ, to those beloved
and called by the Father, safeguarded by Jesus Christ – may mercy,
peace and love overflow to you.

Beloved, I have been eager to write to you concerning our mutual salvation but find myself compelled more urgently to write concerning your need to battle for the faith once delivered to the saints. Why? Because certain people have now snuck inside – irreverent people whose judgment has been long foretold, turning the grace of our God into an occasion for lasciviousness, denying the only Ruler, our Lord Jesus Christ.

I want to remind you, knowing all things as you do, that although Jesus first saved the people out of the land of Egypt he afterwards destroyed those who disobeyed. And he has with unbreakable chains imprisoned in darkest gloom until the Great Judgment Day the angels that held not to their proper place of power. They left their own dwelling behind – just as Sodom and Gomorrah and the Cities of the Plain like them went way outside the bounds of normal sexuality, chasing after other types of creatures, and remain to this day an example of judgment punishable by unconsuming fire.

They have similarly defiled their bodies under the spell of trances, disdaining authority and blaspheming angels in glory. Yet even when the Archangel Michael contended with Satan over the body of Moses he didn't presumptuously curse judgment upon him but simply said, "The

Lord rebuke you." These people, on the other hand, curse things they know nothing about and, having no more understanding than unreasoning beasts, are destroyed in pursuit of their passions.

Woe to them, because they have travelled the path of Cain, run headlong after Baalam's deceit in pursuit of filthy lucre and perished in Korah's rebellion. They are spots at your communion table, shamelessly feasting together with you but caring only for themselves – dry clouds blown aside by the winds, twice-dead rootless trees bereft of late harvest fruit, wild sea-waves, their shame a roiling foam, wandering stars doom-destined for ageless darkness.

But Enoch, seventh in descent from Adam, prophesied about them when he said, "Behold, the Lord comes with his myriads of angels to render judgment against all and to condemn the ungodly for all their ungodly deeds godlessly committed and for all the vicious things ungodly sinners have spoken against him." They are murmurers, complainers, self-absorbed in their own passions, their mouths filled with self-glorying, playing favorites to get ahead.

Beloved, keep in your minds the sound doctrine earlier spoken to you by the apostles of our Lord Jesus Christ when they told you that in the Last Days there will be scoffers following after their own ungodly desires. These are schismatics, worldly and sensual people, having no spiritual life. But you, beloved, keep yourselves in the love of God – building yourselves up in your most holy faith, praying in the Holy Spirit, looking with expectation for the mercy of our Lord Jesus Christ unto life unending. But on some have mercy, convicting them of error where they are disputatious. Others save, snatching them from the fire. And show compassion on others still, but with fear, hating even the clothes stained by the flesh.

But to him who is able to keep you from falling and establish you blameless in the presence of his glory with exultation, to the only God our Deliverer through our Lord Jesus Christ, to him be glory and majesty and power and might before all ages, now and forever, amen.

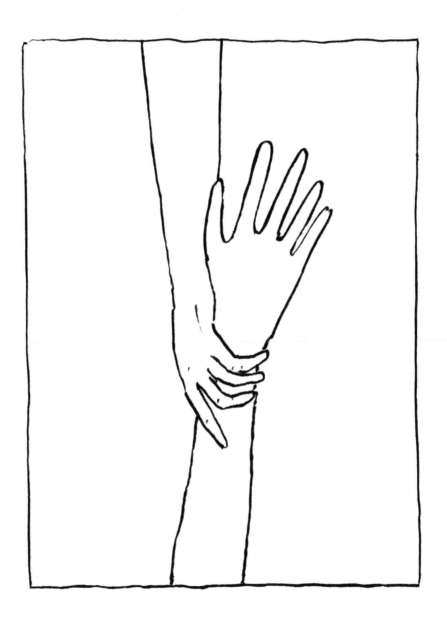

REVELATION

Hidden things are now revealed – God putting it in Jesus' hands to disclose these secrets to his servants so they'll be ready for what's to happen. And God himself sent this revelation to me, his servant John, confirming it by way of an angel messenger. I write this now from the island called Patmos, an exile for the Word of God and my testimony concerning the Savior. And I your brother share not only in your suffering but also in the kingdom and patience of Jesus.

As I worshipped there on the Lord's Day I was caught up to see things unseen, hear things unheard, being filled with the Spirit and a vision of Heaven. I therefore here bear witness to the Word of God and the testimony of Jesus Christ and to all that I learned by sight and by sound. Anyone who reads or hears the words of this prophetic book – and guards it safe in her heart – will be multiply blessed, because the very moment is upon us.

So watch!

He comes with clouds and all will look on him, even those who pierced him, and all the tribes of the Earth will beat their breasts because of him. Listen to me – that's just how it will happen.

"I am Ἄλφα and Ωμέγα, he who was and is and is to come, the Almighty God," says the Lord.

Let me start with the message I was given to the seven churches in the Asian Province, bringing grace and peace from God who is and was and is to come and from the seven Spirits in perfect plenitude before his throne and from Jesus Christ, the faithful witness, first-born from among the dead and ruler of all the kings of the Earth. Now to him who loved us and redeemed us from our sins by his own blood and made us kings and priests to God and his Father, to him be everlasting glory and power. Amen.

The first thing I heard seemed to be a great voice behind me sounding as if it were a trumpet saying, "Write what you are seeing on a scroll and send it to the seven churches, even to Ephesus and to Smyrna and to Pergamos and to Thyatira and to Sardis and to Philadelphia and to Laodicea."

Turning around to see the voice speaking I gazed on gilt candlesticks seven where among the candlesticks I saw someone seeming like the Son of Man tall in copious white of Zahar wool standing belted with the gold of Uphaz across his chest his head and hairs white like snow his eyes as wheels two flames flashing his feet fine brass fresh from the furnace his voice a flood surrounding me like rushing streams seven stars within his right hand a keen two-edged sword issuing from his mouth his countenance like the dawn fair as the moon radiant as the sun majestic as the stars in procession – and I fell at his feet as though dead.

But he his right hand laid upon me said, "Don't be afraid! I am the First and the Last, the Living One. Though I died, look! I am now forever living and hold the keys of Doom and Destruction. Write down now what you've seen – things that are and things that will be. Listen first to the secret of the seven stars seen in my right hand and the seven golden candlesticks – the seven stars are the angel messengers of the seven churches, the seven candlesticks the seven churches themselves.

"Therefore write this to the messenger of the church at Ephesus: Hear what the one holding seven stars fast in his right hand says, the same one walking in the midst of the seven golden candlesticks – I know your deeds, your toil, your patience, your intolerance for the wicked. I know you have tested the spirits of those who call themselves apostles but are not and found them to be liars. And I know you have endured and labored for my name's sake and not grown weary. But still I've put a mark against you in my book because you've left behind your first love. Remember those earlier days, think whence you've fallen – and then turn back and tend to first things first, lest failing I come swiftly to seize your candlestick from its holder. But I grant you this: you hate those who oppress the people, those I too despise. Let all who have ears hear what the Spirit says to the churches. To her who overcomes will I grant to eat from the Tree of Life, the Tree in the Paradise of my God.

"Write this to the messenger of the church at Smyrna: This is what the First and Last says, he who was dead and is alive – I know your deeds, your pains, your poverty (and yet you are rich!) and I know the sacrilege of those contesting for Israel's heart even as they worship her foe. Though the Accuser stands guard at the gates of your prison ten days of torment held in his hand, yet fear not the things you'll suffer. Be faithful if need be even to death and I'll hand you the Crown of Life. Let those who have ears hear what the Spirit says to the churches. Whoever conquers will never be harmed by the second death.

"And write this to the messenger of the church in Pergamos: This is what the one who holds the sharp and double-edged sword says – I know your deeds and where you dwell, even in the Tempter's own home town. Yet you've held fast to my name not denying my faith in the days when my faithful martyr Antipas was murdered in your midst, yes, right there where Beelzebub thinks he's safe. But even so, I have a few things against you because some of you hold to Balaam's doctrine, he who taught Balak to cast a snare on the children of Israel – that they should eat things sacrificed to idols and commit adultery. And you also have some among you siding with the people's oppressors, something you know I hate. I tell you turn away from all that, lest failing I come swiftly to fight against them with the sword of my mouth. Let those who have ears hear what the Spirit says to the churches. To him who overcomes will I grant to eat of the Hidden Manna – and I will give him a white stone with a new name written on it, a name no one knows but the one who receives it.

"And to the messenger of the church at Thyatira write: This is what the Son of God says, whose eyes are like a flame of fire, whose feet are like fine brass fired in a furnace – I know your deeds and love and faith and service and patience, yes, and your latest deeds, which are even greater than your first. Yet I still have something against you because you tolerate that woman Jezebel – she calls herself a prophet even as by wiles she leads my servants into lechery and idolatry. I gave her space to repent but she would not, so mired she was in her own whorishness. Therefore I will toss her to a bed – and her adulterous partners with her – there to suffer great torment unless they turn away from her deeds; and I will also put her children to death. Let all the churches know that I pierce to the innermost thoughts and soul – I will reward each of you according to your deeds. But I say to you and the rest in Thyatira – all who abhor her teaching, who have not plumbed the deep things of the Evil One – I will not cast any greater burden on you than this: hold fast to what you have until I come. To him who overcomes and guards my works till the end I give the nations to be his inheritance and he will break them with a rod of iron and dash them to pieces like a potter's vessel - just as I have received power from my Father - and I will give him the Morning Star. Let those who have ears hear what the Spirit says to the churches.

"And to the messenger of the church at Sardis write: This is what the one who holds the seven Spirits of God and the seven stars says - I know your deeds, that you have the reputation of being alive, but are dead. Wake up! Strengthen what's left and is about to die, because I've found your deeds wanting before the face of my God. Call to mind all you've received and all you've heard - guard it closely and turn from your ways. If you will not awake, if you will not watch, I will come as thief - you won't even know the hour I come for you. Even so, there are some named among you in Sardis who have not stained their robes - they will walk with me in white, for they are worthy. I will drape fair garments on those who overcome and never wipe their names from the Book of Life but will confess their names before my Father and before his angels. Let those who have ears hear what the Spirit says to the churches.

"And to the messenger of the church at Philadelphia write: This is what the Holy One says, the True, who keeps the Key of the House of David, who having opened no one closes and having closed no one opens - I know your deeds and behold, I have opened a door before you, one that no one can close. I know you have but little strength left and have kept my word and never denied my name. And what of those who pretend to be true Children of Israel but lie and aren't? They're the Devil's own parishioners - I will make them lie prostrate at your feet so they know I have loved you. But because you have patiently endured, guarding my word with steadfastness, I - even I - will keep you safe from the hour of trial, that time soon to fall on the whole world to try those who dwell upon the Earth. I will come swiftly. Hold tight to what you have. Let no one steal your crown. She who overcomes will be a pillar in the temple of my God. She will dwell there agelessly and I will write on her the name of my God and the name of the city of my God - the new Jerusalem, which comes down from my God in Heaven - and I will write upon her my new name. Let those who have ears hear what the Spirit says to the churches.

"And to the messenger of the church at Laodicea write: This is what the Amen says, the Faithful and True Witness, the Beginning of the Creation of God – I know your deeds, that you are neither frigid nor hot, and yet I wish you were one or the other. But because you are merely tepid – not hot, not cold – I'm about to spit you out of my mouth. Yet you say 'I am wealthy, I've gotten rich, I need nothing.' You have no idea you are in fact wretched, miserable, poor, blind and naked. I urge you to buy from me gold, pure, refined (then you will truly be rich) and white robes (then will you be well-clothed indeed, covering the shame of your nakedness) and salve to anoint your eyes (then you will truly see). I only reprove and chasten those whom I love, so be zealous and turn from your ways. Look! I stand striking at the door – if anyone hears my voice and opens the door I will enter and dine with him and he with me. Whoever overcomes will sit with me on my throne – I myself also conquered and am now seated with my Father on his throne. Let those who have ears hear what the Spirit says to the churches."

Looking again – behold! – I saw an open door appear in Heaven and the first voice I heard speaking to me sounding something like a trumpet said, "Come up here and I will show you things yet to happen."

Then!

As in night visions even in an instant I was in the Spirit seeing before me a throne at Heaven's Gate the countenance of him upon it appearing clear as jasper blood-red as Sardian stone an emerald iris encircling the throne encircling again twice twelvefold thrones on them two dozen elders sitting wrapped radiant in purest white robes gleaming upon their heads crowns of gold and from the throne lightning bolts and thunder peals beneath the throne seven burning lamps blazing – these the seven Spirits of God – before the throne a glass sea shimmering as if it were rock crystal in the midst of the throne circling about it four living creatures eyes covering them front and back the first like a lion the second an ox the third a man the fourth a soaring eagle each creature having six wings with eyes wheeling within wheels ceaselessly singing day and night

> Sanctus, Sanctus, Sanctus
> Dominus Deus omnipotens –
> qui erat, et qui est, et qui venturus est.

And as the four living creatures gave endless glory and honor and praise to the one endlessly living sitting upon the throne so too the four and twenty elders fell down before the Ancient of Days timelessly worshiping him who timelessly lives casting crowns woven of amaranth and gold before the throne singing

> You are worthy O Holy Lord and our God
> > to receive glory and honor and power,
> for you created all things
> > and by your word they are and were created.

Then!

I saw lying on the open right hand of the one seated on the throne a scroll fully written inside and out but tightly sealed with seven seals just as a mighty angel cried with a loud voice, "Who is worthy to open the scroll and to loose its seals?" But no angels in Heaven no people on the Earth nor dead below the Earth had the power to open the book or even to gaze upon it. So I for my part cried, shedding no end of tears when I heard there was none found worthy so much as to look upon the scroll let alone loose it from its seals. But one from among the elders said to me, "Weep not but look! The Lion of the Tribe of Judah has prevailed, the Root of Jesse, the Branch of David - and he will break open the seven seals, revealing all that is in the scroll."

Then there appeared to me standing in the midst of the throne amidst the four living creatures amidst the twenty-four elders a Lamb as sacrifice slain throat sliced having seven horns and seven eyes - these the seven Spirits of God sent through all the Earth - approaching taking the scroll from the one seated on the throne the four living creatures the four and twenty elders falling before the Lamb each having a stringed instrument and golden bowls filled with incense - these the prayers of the Holy Ones - this new song singing

You are worthy to take the scroll
        and break open its seals
because you were slain
        and with your own blood redeemed
from every tribe and tongue and race and nation
        a people for God
e ne hai fatto per il nostro Dio un regno e dei sacerdoti –
        e regneranno sulla terra.

Watching still I heard the sound of myriad angels surrounding the throne and the creatures and the elders their number ten thousand ten thousands a thousand thousands over again in choral voice praising as they sang with might

Worthy is the Lamb that was slain
        to receive power and riches
and wisdom and strength
        and honor and glory and blessing![1]

Even still again I heard all angels in Heaven all people on the Earth and the dead below the Earth and every creature upon the sea and all those in Earth and sea answering saying

Soient louange et honneur,
        glory and power
al que está sentado en el trono
        y al Cordero in sæcula sæculorum.

And I heard once more the four living creatures say "Amen" and saw the elders fall upon their faces worshiping.

Still watching I saw the Lamb open one of the seven seals and one of the four living creatures speaking as thunder roars said "Come!" as I beheld

---

1   http://hdking.mobi/download/ngSsaSimi8A

a white horse one on it with a bow given power to go conquering that he might conquer then the Lamb opened the second seal and the second living creature said "Come!" I saw another horse this time red and on it one with a mighty sword taking peace away from the Earth men murdering men then the Lamb opened the third seal and the third living creature said "Come!" and I saw a black horse upon it one with a pair of scales in his hand while a sound from the midst of the four living creatures said "A day's pay for a pound of wheat, a day's pay for three pounds of barley, yet leave no shortage of oil and wine" then the Lamb opened the fourth seal and the sound of the fourth living creature said "Come!" and I saw a horse green in pallor one atop it having the name Death all Hell following him with power killing a quarter of Earth's people with slashing Thracian blade famine death ravaging wild beasts and even so the Lamb opened the fifth seal and looking I saw below the altar the souls of all slaughtered for the sake of the Word of God and his testimony crying out together with great voice "How much longer Holy Master and True until you judge vindicating our blood on all who dwell on the Earth?" each one wearing a lustrous long white robe told patiently to wait a little while longer until their ranks be complete continuously filling up with their fellow servants' souls the souls of their brothers and sisters slain as were they but when the Lamb opened the sixth seal seismic shudders seized the Earth the sun as sackcloth darkening the whole moon turning to blood the stars of Heaven falling to Earth as wind-shaken late Summer figs the whole Heaven splitting apart rolling up as a scroll every mountain and island upended from its roots the kings of the Earth the rulers the captains the rich the strong all slaves and all free hiding themselves in mountain dens and stone grottos shouting to the mountains and rocks "Fall upon us and hide us from the face of the one who sits on the throne and from the wrath of the Lamb because the Great Day of his wrath is come and who can withstand it?"

Yet again transfixed I saw four angels standing at the four corners of the Earth holding fast the Four Winds lest they blow on the land or the seas or even any tree while another angel rising with the rising of the sun holding the seal of the living God with great voice calling to the four angels having power to ravish land and sea said "Touch not the land nor sea nor even any tree until we have sealed the servants of our

God upon their foreheads." I heard the number of those being sealed, 144,000, sealed from every tribe of the sons of Israel: from the tribe of Judah 12,000, from the tribe of Reuben 12,000, from the tribe of Gad 12,000, from the tribe of Asher 12,000, from the tribe of Nephtali 12,000, from the tribe of Manasseh 12,000, from the tribe of Simeon 12,000, from the tribe of Levi 12,000, from the tribe of Issachar 12,000, from the tribe of Zebulon 12,000, from the tribe of Joseph 12,000 and from the tribe of Benjamin 12,000.

And watching I saw a vast crowd from all nations and tribes and peoples and tongues numberless uncountable by anyone standing before the throne and before the Lamb together robed gleaming white palm branches in their hands waving in joyous shout proclaiming

> Salus Deo nostro
> qui sedet super thronum et Agno.

So too the angels gathered about the throne the elders the four living creatures all falling face down before the throne worshiping God singing

> Amen! Praise and glory and wisdom
> and blessing and honor and power and strength be
> to our God for all endless ages, amen.

Then one of the elders asked me, "Who are these gathered in glistering white robes and whence have they come?" But I answered, "My lord, do you know?" So he told me, "These are they who have passed through the great suffering and washed their garments and made them white in the blood of the Lamb. Therefore they stand day and night before the throne of God worshiping him in his temple and he who sits upon the throne has his tabernacle among them. They no longer hunger nor thirst and the sun's scorching heat falls not upon them – because the Lamb in the midst of the throne is their shepherd, leading them beside the still waters – and God himself blots away every tear from their eyes."

But when the Lamb broke open the seventh seal silence held Heaven as if for half an hour and looking I saw the seven angels who stand before

God holding seven trumpets and another angel standing by the sacrificial altar before the throne holding a golden censer filled with incense offering it together with the prayers of the Holy Ones upon the auric altar before the throne smoke rising up before God from the hand of the angel offering the incense the angel also taking the censer filling it with fiery ashes from the altar casting it upon the Earth – and there came thunder, roaring, lightning, quakes.

Then the seven angels with the seven trumpets poised to sound.

The first sounded his trumpet and hail and fire mingled with blood showered the Earth burning a third of the Earth and a third of all trees and all green grass the second angel echoed and as it were a great mountain smoldering lit with fire was hurled to the sea the third part of the sea turning to blood killing the living creatures sinking the ships as the third angel blew his trumpet a great and glowing star like to a torch fell from the Heavens on a third of the rivers and springs of waters – this star has a name and its name is Absinthe – and a third of the waters turned to wormwood myriads dying from the embittered waters the fourth angel trumpeting blotted out the third part of the sun and the third part of the moon and the third part of the stars eclipsing their light the day blackening a third so also the night.

As I looked I heard an angel soaring like an eagle through the midst of Heaven crying aloud "Woe, woe, woe to those who dwell on the Earth, because of the blasts of the three angels' trumpets yet to sound."

Then when the fifth angel sounded I saw the star fallen as lightning from Heaven to Earth holding in his hand the key to Hell's wide well uncovering that pit of gloom soot rose up the shaft as through the stack of an iron furnace veiling the sun even the air itself with the infernal smoke while locust-like creatures emerged from the cloud shrouding the Earth with power to sting as a scorpion stings – but they were told not to harm the grasslands or any pale plant or any tree only those men who bore not God's seal on their heads yet neither should they kill but rather torture them five months tormenting with a scorpion's burning strike. Men will seek death rather than suffer those days of travail but not find it, yearn to die but find death fled from them. Now the shapes of these swarming creatures were as horses ready for war but with faces like men their heads seemingly crowned in gold yet with hair like women teeth as a lion's breasts covered with iron plates – or so was the likeness – with the semblance of wings, wings making a sound as would horse-drawn chariots massed and rushing to battle. And they had scorpions' tails – or what appeared to be stingers – able to plague men for five months with their fiery strikes. Their king was the messenger of the Abyss, whose name in Hebrew is אֲבַדּוֹן and in Greek Ἀπολλύων but in English – the Destroyer. One woe is past but two remain.

When the sixth angel sounded his trumpet, I heard a single voice come from the four horns of the golden altar that stands before God saying to the sixth angel holding its trumpet, "Release the four angels who lie bound in the great River Euphrates!" And so these four angels were set free, having been prepared for this very hour and day and month and year, prepared to kill a third of all mankind. Their horsemen numbered twice ten thousand ten thousands – I heard their number – seemingly breast-plated in fire dipped in sulphur the color of blue-blooded Hyacinth their horses having lions' heads mouths vomiting fire and smoke and sulphur with breath three times a plague of burning brimstone blotting out a third of human life – because the horses' power lay in their mouths and in their tails a viper's sting.

And yet the rest of mankind, all those who survived these woes, still did not turn from their evil deeds, not from their worship of demons and idols – things made of gold and silver and bronze and wood and stone that cannot see or hear or walk – not even from murder, sorcery, perversion and theft.

I saw another angel, powerful, descending cloud-clothed from Heaven the brightness around him as the image of God's bow appears in light rain his face a solar blaze his feet two flame pillars holding in his right hand a small scroll unrolled placing his right foot on the sea his left on the land shouting with a voice loud as if a lion's roar – and as he cried out seven thunders spoke. When they finished speaking I was poised to write down their words but heard a voice from Heaven command me, "Seal up what the seven thunders spoke and write it not!" Then the Colossus straddling land and sea lifted his right hand to Heaven and swore by him who lives all ages unending he who created Heaven and all that is in it and Earth and all that is in it and the sea and all that is in it and said, "Time shall be no more – but in the days of the seventh angel's voice when he is about to sound his trumpet God's hidden mystery shall be complete, the good news foretold by God to his servants the prophets."

The voice I heard from Heaven spoke to me again, "Go, take the opened small scroll from the hand of the angel spanning land and sea." So I went to the angel and said, "Hand me the small scroll." He said to me, "Take and eat – it will be sweet as honey in your mouth but bitter to your stomach." Then I took the small scroll from the angel's hand and ate it whole. It was sweet-tasting to my mouth but when I was done, bitter to my belly. He told me, "You must prophesy again to many peoples and nations and tongues and kings."

He gave me a measuring rod, something like a staff, and said, "Rise up and take measure of the temple of God and the altar and those who worship there. But do not measure the court outside the temple, because it has been given to the Gentile nations and they will trample the holy city for 42 months. Yet I will give power to my two witnesses and they will prophesy for 1,260 days, clothed in sackcloth. These are the two olive trees and the two candlesticks that stand before the Prince of this World. Should anyone have a mind to harm them fire from their mouths will burn their enemies to a crisp – and anyone seeking to injure them must be killed in that manner. They have power to lock the doors of Heaven and stop the rain from falling all the days of their prophecy. So too they have power to turn the waters to blood and to strike the Earth with every sort of plague, so often as they wish. And when their testimony is complete the beast ascending from the Depth will go to war with them and defeat them and kill them.

"Their corpses will lie on the main boulevard of the great city, spiritually named Sodom and Egypt, where also their Lord was crucified. And for three and a half days people from all regions and tribes and tongues and nations will gaze at their bodies and not let anyone bury them in a tomb – Earth's inhabitants will rejoice in their deaths and celebrate, sending presents to one another, because these two prophets tormented those who dwell on the Earth.

"But after three and a half days God breathed upon the slain and they stood on their feet – and a vast terror fell on all who saw them. Then they heard a mighty voice from Heaven speak to them saying, 'Come up here!' And they ascended to Heaven in a cloud, their enemies watching. In that same hour the Earth shook and a tenth of the city collapsed, the quake killing seven thousand souls. But the rest in fear gave glory to God in Heaven."

Two woes have passed but one remains. When the seventh angel boomed his trumpet deep voices vast spoke from Heaven.

> The kingdom of the world is now become
>> the kingdom of our Lord and his Anointed –
> and he shall reign agelessly and ever.
>> And the four and twenty elders who sit on their thrones
> before God fell upon their faces and worshipped God
>> We give thanks to you, Lord God Almighty
> אֶהְיֶה אֲשֶׁר אֶהְיֶה,
>> because you have seized your great power
> and taken rule.
> The nations were angered
> but the time of your wrath has come
>> and with it judgment over all who have died –
> rewards to your servants the prophets
>> and to all holy ones,
> those who fear your name both small and great,
>> but destruction to Earth's destroyers.

The temple of God was opened in Heaven and in it the Ark of his Covenant – and there appeared lightning, voices, thunderclaps, tremors, hailstones.

Then too appeared a marvelous sign in Heaven – a sun-draped woman, the moon below her feet, her head crowned with twelve stars, at full term crying out in her birth pains. And another sign appeared, immense, a fire-red dragon with seven crowned heads and ten horns his tail sweeping a third of the stars casting them down to Earth. He stood before the woman as she was abouta to give birth in the hope of devouring the child when it was born. And she did give birth, to a male child, one destined to rule all nations with an iron scepter. But the child was snatched away to God and his throne while the woman fled to the desert where she has a place prepared for her by God, being nourished there 1,260 days.

There was war in Heaven, Michael and his angels battling the dragon. The dragon and his angels fought back but they were no match and forfeited their place in Heaven. So the great dragon was cast out, the one they call Old Harry, El Diablo, the whole world's deceiver - he was hurled down to Earth and his legions with him.

Then a voice resounding in Heaven said

> Now is come the salvation and power
>   and kingdom of our God
> and the power of his Anointed
>   because the Accuser of our brethren is cast down,
> he who slandered them before God day and night -
>   they have triumphed over him by the
> blood of the Lamb
>   and the word of their testimony
> and they loved not their own souls, even to death.
>   Therefore rejoice O Heavens and all who
> dwell therein.
>   But woe to the land and sea
> because the Devil comes down to you in fiercest rage,
>   knowing his days are numbered.

So the dragon being cast down to Earth persecuted the woman who gave birth to the male child. On wide eagle wings the woman flew to her safe place in the desert, where she was nourished for a season and seasons and half a season from the face of that serpent. But the viper spewed water from his mouth like a flood, pursuing the woman, hoping to sweep her away in the tide. Yet the land gave her succor, opening its mouth and swallowing up the water the dragon had cast from its mouth. And again the dragon fumed against the woman and battled the rest of her line -

these are they who guard the commandments of God and hold fast their witness an Tiarna Íosa.

And as I stood at the shoreline I saw a beast ascend from the sea with ten crowned horns and seven heads and on each head an ungodly name written, this beast in form like a leopard – save for its bear's paws and lion's mouth. The dragon gave its own power and throne to the beast, granting him great sway. It appeared as though one of the beast's heads had been slain, but the deathblow healed and the whole Earth marveled at the beast, kneeling to worship the dragon because it had given authority to the beast. So too they bowed down before the beast and said, "Who is like unto the beast and who is able to fight against him?"

The Lawless One was given space for his blasphemies, holding power for 42 months, opening his mouth to belch curses against God, profaning his name and his tabernacle and all those who dwell in Heaven. And the Antichrist went to war against os santos de Deus, defeating them, ruling over every tribe and people and tongue and nation, all worshiping him – those, that is, whose names were not written in the Lamb's Book of Life, he who was slain from the beginning of the world.

If anyone has ears, let him hear.

Anyone who takes a captive will be taken captive and anyone who lives by the sword will die by the sword. Herein lies the faith and patience of the saints.

Yet another beast I saw rising up from the Earth. He had two horns that looked like a lamb's but he spoke with a dragon's voice. He had all the authority of the first beast, wielding it in his presence, and he made all the inhabitants of the Earth worship the first beast, the one whose seemingly mortal wound was healed. This second beast performed great wonders, even making fire fall on men from Heaven, deceiving Earth's people by the signs he did in the beast's name, commanding them to fashion an image of the beast – who though wounded with a sword still lived. And he gave breath to the image of the Son of Perdition so that it spoke, and he had power to put to death any who would not worship the image. Then he forced all, small and great, rich and poor, free and slave, to be sealed on the right hand or the forehead with the graven image of the beast. Without that mark they could neither buy nor sell. And the mark is the name of the beast, or the number of his name. But mark this wisdom and let anyone with his wits about him count the number of the beast, because it's a man's number – 666.

Again I turned and saw the Lamb, this time standing on Mount Zion with 144,000 souls and written on their foreheads I saw his name and the name of his Father. Then I heard a voice from Heaven as a noise of roiling waters rumbling on like rolling thunder while these souls lyric as minstrel bards lifting their voices in chorus sang a new hymn before the throne and before the four living creatures and before the elders – and no one could learn the song save the 144,000 souls rescued from the Earth, chaste youths following the Lamb wherever he might go, redeemed as first-fruits harvested of mankind for God and the Lamb, blameless, in whose mouths no lies were found.

Then I saw an angel of the endless evangel winging through the midst of Heaven spreading the good news to all those dwelling upon the Earth and upon the sea and to every nation and tribe and tongue and people heralding with deeply sonorous voice, "Stand in awe of God and give him glory because the hour of his judgment is come: worship therefore him who made Heaven and Earth and the sea and all springs of water."

Yet again another angel this second one following said, "Alas, Babylon – Babylon that great city is fallen because she poured out to every nation the raging wine of her adultery."

And another following them this third cried out, "If anyone should worship the beast and his image and take on his forehead or on his right hand the mark of the beast he, even he will drink the unadulterated wine of judgment poured into the goblet of God's wrath and be tormented in sulphur and smoke before the holy angels and the Lamb. The smoke of their torment shall rise up ages without end – day and night they have no surcease of sorrow, those who worshipped the beast and his likeness, those who took to themselves the image of his name."

Herein lies the patience of the saints, who guard the commandments of God keeping the faith of Yeshua. Then I heard a voice from Heaven spoken, "Write! Blessed are the dead, all who die in the Lord henceforth." The Spirit too said, "Amen, so may they rest from their labors and their deeds shall follow them."

I gazed, and behold!

A white cloud one seated on the cloud seeming like the Son of Man a golden crown worn on his head in his hand a sharp sickle borne while another messenger emerged from within the temple with loud voice calling to the one seated on the cloud, "Put forth your sickle and reap because the harvest time is come and the crop is about to wither!" So he who sat upon the cloud thrust his sickle into the Earth and the Earth was harvested.

Yet another angel emerged from Heaven's temple and he too had a sharp sickle while yet another angel came from the altar having power over fire and cried with a loud voice to the first one holding the sharp sickle, "Lay out your sickle and gather in the grapes from Earth's vines because the clusters are ripe!" So that angel thrust his sickle into the Earth and cast the grapes into the great winepress of God's anger and as the grapes of wrath were trampled down blood flowed from the press spreading 200 miles beyond the city, even reaching the height of horses' bits.

Then passing wondrous I saw a sign in Heaven seven angels holding seven last plagues wrapping in full the wrath of God. And I saw as it were a sea of glass laced with fire and on it standing those victorious over the beast and the number of his name bearing in their hands God's lyres singing the song of Moses the servant of God and the song of the Lamb

> Great and wondrous are your deeds
> > O Seigneur Dieu, Tout-Puissant,
> just and true are your paths
> > O Rei de la Nacío!
> Who dares not reverence you, Señor,
> > who dares not give you the glory?
> For you alone are holy
> > so the Goyim shall come
> and worship before you,
> > because your righteousness has been
> fully revealed.

After this my view was opened to the Sanctum Sanctorum where the tabernacle stood witness to God's presence as the seven angels seven plagues holding emerged from within the temple clothed in purest linen

glimmering cinches of gold girding their chests – and when one of the four living creatures handed the seven angels seven golden vials filled with the last wrath of hwhy the temple filled with the smoke of the glory and power of God, none allowed to enter until the seven angels' seven plagues come to an end.

I heard a voice speak from within the temple saying to the seven angels, "Go! Pour upon the Earth the seven vials filled with the wrath of God." So the first departed and poured his vial on the Earth. Grievous canker sores broke out on all who had the mark of the Son of Perdition and all who worshipped his image. The second poured his vial into the sea and it became as a dead man's blood such that every soul died that dwelt upon the sea. The third angel poured his vial into the rivers and the springs and they too turned to blood.

Then I heard the angel of the waters say

> O Heilige, you are just in these your judgments,
> you who were and truly are,
> because they spilled the blood of saints and prophets
> and you gave them blood to drink,
> their just deserts.

And I heard the altar say,

> Yea, Domine Deus Omnipotens,
> just and righteous are all your judgments!

Then!

The fourth angel poured his vial over the sun and the sun scorched people with fire – but though blistered by the heat they cursed God's name for his power to plague them, turning not from their ways, not giving him glory. And so the fifth angel poured his vial right onto the throne of the beast plunging his kingdom to pitch darkness people gnawing their tongues in distress. Yet they swore at God in Heaven for their suffering and sores, still turning not from their ways. The sixth angel drained his vial over the great River Euphrates, its waters drying up to make a pathway for the kings of the

East. And I saw slytherin from the mouths of the serpent and the beast and the false prophet three spirits frog-green and foul. These are the spirits of sign-working demons spreading throughout the whole world gathering the kings of the Earth together for war in that great and terrible day of El Shaddai. Yet he says, "Behold, I come as a thief in the night. Blessed is she who keeps watch, who holds fast her garments, lest she be found walking naked and they see her shame." And thus they gathered themselves together near the place called in Hebrew הַר מְגִדּוֹן – which in English means Mount Megiddo.

Finally the seventh angel poured out his vial, this one into the air, and a voice boomed out from the temple and out from the throne declaring, "It is done!" And together there came lightning bolts voices thunder and a quaking tremulous roar such as never was no not from the ancient time man first walked the Earth now splitting in three the great city cratering the cities of the nations because Babylon the Great has come up for remembrance before God, her time come to drink from the cup of wrath, the Tyrian-dark wine of his anger. All the islands fled; no mountain remained. Hailstones like crags fell grievous from the sky and the people cursed God for the harsh hailstone blows.

Now one of the seven angels having the seven flasks approached me and spoke, "Come here and I will show you the judgment passed on the great slut sitting on many waters, in whose bed Earth's kings reveled, Earth's people drunk with the wine of her lust." Then he carried me in the Spirit to the wilderness, where I saw a woman seated on a crimson beast. The beast was covered with curses and it had seven heads and ten horns. The woman was clothed in purple and scarlet encrusted with gold and gems and pearls. She clutched in her hand a chalice brim-filled with abominations and the filth of her desires and on her head was this name writ: "Mysterium, Babylon the Great, Mother of Whores and All Earthly Abominations." And I beheld the woman drunk with the blood of the saints, the blood of those martyred for Jesus.

I was dumbstruck at the sight of her but the angel said to me, "Why do you marvel? Let me explain to you the secret of the woman and of the beast with seven heads and ten horns that bears her. The beast you saw was but is no more and yet will rise from Hell's deep hollow to be destroyed. And all who inhabit the Earth seeing him will stand in awe – all those whose names have not been written in the Book of Life, even from the foundation of the world – because he was but is not and yet will come. Let this wisdom sink into your mind: the seven heads are the seven hills on which the woman sits. And the hills are seven kings. Of these five have fallen, one still lives and one is yet to come – and when he comes he must remain for some little time. And the Antichrist who was and is no more even he himself is the eighth. He springs from the seven – but he goes to destruction. Then too the ten horns you saw are ten kings. They have not yet come into their kingdoms but when they do they will reign as kings along with the beast for the space of one hour. They will be of one mind and one heart. They will yield their power and authority to the beast and they will wage war against the Lamb. But the Lamb will crush them to pieces because he is Lord of Lords and King of Kings and those with him are called and chosen and faithful."

Again he spoke to me, "The waters you saw, where the great whore sits, are peoples and kin and nations and tongues. The beast as well as the ten horns you saw will loathe the whore and lay her waste, leaving her naked, devouring her flesh, burning her with fire because it is God who put it in their hearts so to unite in purpose, handing their kingdoms over to the beast, so that God's own purposes might be fulfilled. And the harlot you saw is that great city, the one that holds sway over all the kings of the Earth."

After these things I saw another angel descending from Heaven, overwhelming in power, the Earth resplendent with his glory. He cried out with a voice of matchless strength

> Babylon is fallen! Babilônia that mighty city fallen
> > is now become a den of demons
> guardhouse of every foul spirit
> > nest of every unclean bird
> lair of every vile and hated beast –
> > because Babylon was an aurelian cup in
> the Lord's hand
> > and the nations drank the raging wine of
> her adultery,
> > Earth's kings, her lovers, reveling with her,

Earth's merchants gorged with the fat of her wealth,
    auri sacra fames.
But another voice from Heaven said,
    Come out from her my people
that you share not in her sins
    neither in the woes she must suffer,
because her sins are piled up to Heaven
    and God now calls her to account for her injustice.
Give back to her as she has given,
    pay her double according to her works,
fill double the cup she herself has filled.
    As much as she gloried in her own delights,
just so let her measure be of torment and sorrow.
    Because she said in her heart, "I reign as queen,
no widow am I,
    I know no grief,"
so shall her sorrows come in a moment, a day –
    death, grief, famine –
and she will be consumed with fire,
    because the Lord God judging her is mighty.

The kings of the Earth, they who shared the delights of her bed, now shall weep and beat their breasts seeing her aflame and shall mourn wailing standing far off in fear lest they share her torment, saying

    Alas, Babel, Βαβυλών, mighty city and strong,
        laid low in but an hour!

So too shall Earth's merchants wail over her and grieve because no longer will any buy their wares – cargoes of gold from Ophir, silver from Tipperary, damask from the looms of Antrim, Limerick lace, Foxford tweeds, Huguenot poplin, dyed robes silken and crimson, scented woods from the East, horns of ivory and ebony, gemstones and pearls, white flint glass, choice vessels of wood, iron and brass, Helbon wine, olives from Qana, market wheat of Minnith and Pannag, Connemara marble, cinnamon and spice, myrrh and frankincense, the cattle on a thousand hills, sheep and horses,

Persian chariots, slave girls – and the souls of men. The very fruits your heart craved are wrenched from you, your fashions and splendor, all gone, not a feather to be found. And the traders and dealers enriched with these goods keep themselves far apart from her now, trembling wailing weeping in terror of her woes with nothing more to say than

> ¡Ay, ay, great Babilonia,
>> dressed in fine satin and lace
> purple and crimson
>> encrusted with gold
> gemstones and pearls –
>> sic transit gloria mundi!

They that go down to the sea in ships, that do business in great waters, they too stood afar off and cried seeing the smoke as she burned as they said, "What city was ever like this great city?" Then they cast up dust upon their heads, wallowing themselves in the ashes, deep grieving, mourning, sighing in lamentation

> Hélas, Hélas Babylone la grande,
>> prospering ships' captains and crew,
> in one hour your wealth is come to naught.

But the angel said, "Rejoice ye, O Heaven and saints, apostles and prophets, because God has brought judgment on her for your sakes." And another mighty messenger lifted a stone, as it were a millstone, saying as he cast it into the sea

> Thus with violent rush
>> is that great city Babylon
> cast down to rise no more.
>> Taken away are the voice of mirth
> and the voice of gladness,
>> the voice of the bridegroom

and the voice of the bride,
   the grinding of the millstones
and the light of the candle:
   the rest is silence.
For your merchants were Earth's great ones,
   yet by your sorcery all the nations were deceived.
And so in her was found the blood of prophets, holy ones
   and all those slaughtered upon the Earth.
After this the Music of Heaven assembled singing
   Salvation and glory and power be to our God.
True and just are his judgments
   because he judged the great harlot,
she who seduced the whole world with her wiles.
   He has avenged the blood of his servants
spilled by her hand.

And again they sang, "Hallelujah!" – as her smoke rose up ages on endless ages while the twenty-four elders and the four living creatures fell down and worshipped before God seated upon his throne saying, "Aamen! Allelujah!" At that a voice came forth from the throne

Lodate il nostro Dio,
   voi tutti suoi servitori,
voi che lo temete,
   piccolo e grandi.

Then!
I heard at once in myriad throng a multitude sing with streaming thunder

הַלְלוּיָהּ

for the Lord God Omnipotent reigneth![2]
Gocémonos y alegrémonos y démosle gloria
porque son venidas le nozze dell'Agnello
and his bride se ha aparejado
robed in radiant linen, fine and pure –
car le fin lin, ce sont les oeuvres justes des saints.

The angel said to me, "Write! Blessed are those who are called to the Lamb's wedding banquet." And again, "These are God's true words." At that I fell at his feet to worship him. But he abjured me, "Gott bewahre! I am but one of your brothers. We are fellow servants sharing the same witness to Jesus, to whom all prophecy testifies through the Spirit. Therefore worship not me, but God alone."

Then!

I saw Heaven opened and beheld one faithful and true seated on a white horse judging justly battling in righteousness eyes flaming as it were with fire on his head crowns and crowns engraved with names but written on his brow a new name known to him and none other his garment dipped in blood his name Ὁ Λόγος τοῦ Θεοῦ the Host of Heaven following on white horses armies draped in linen gleaming pure as from his mouth with curved and slashing blade he goes subduing the nations ruling them with iron scepter trampling down the grapes of wrath stored in the winepress of the fury of God Almighty and on his garment and thigh this name writ "King of Kings and Lord of Lords" – and before my eyes I saw within the sun an angel standing summoning all winged creatures flying through Heaven's midst with loud voice crying "Venez, rassemblez-vous! Gather yourselves on every side to God's great sacrifice on the mountains of Israel to feast on the flesh of captains and kings men of power horses riders the flesh of men both free and slave great and small."

I watched as the Antichrist the kings of the Earth their legions gathered together to war against the one seated on the throne and against his armies. But the beast was taken and with him the false prophet, the

2   https://www.youtube.com/watch?v=IUZEtVbJT5c

one who worked wonders wielding the beast's powers, deceiving all those sealed with the mark of the beast, worshiping his image - these two were tossed alive into a fiery lake burning with sulphur. The rest were slain by the thrusting blade of the one seated on the white horse - and the birds gorged themselves with their flesh.

Yet another angel I saw descending from Heaven holding in his hand the key to the Deep Abyss and a mighty chain. He grabbed hold of the dragon, Old Scratch, that snake Satan, bound him for a thousand years, cast him into the Bottomless Pit and sealed it with lock and key, barring him for a thousand years from deluding the nations, until the millennium be passed. But after that he must be loosed for a short while.

I also saw thrones and those seated on them given authority to judge. I saw too the souls of all beheaded for their witness to Jeziš and for the word of God and the souls of all those who had not worshipped the beast or his image neither taken his seal upon their foreheads or their hands - these all rose from the dead to reign a thousand years with Messiah. But the rest of the dead did not live again until the millennium had passed. This is the first resurrection. Blessed and holy are those who have a share in the first resurrection - the second death has no power over them but they shall be priests of God and his Anointed and reign a thousand years with him.

Yet when the thousand years are up the Wicked One will be freed from his prison and go out to deceive the nations in the four corners of the Earth, even Gog the prince of Magog, to gather them together to war, their number as the sands of the sea coming like a storm cloud shadowing the land, encircling the camp of the saints and the beloved city - but fire streamed down on them from Heaven, consuming them utterly. And that Father of Lies, the Serpent of Old, he was cast into the lake of fire burning with sulphur tormented with the Man of Sin and the false prophet day and night without age.

I saw a great white throne. Earth and Heaven fled from the presence of him that sat upon it - there was no place for them any longer. Then too I saw the dead both great and small standing before the throne. The books were opened, and another book, Bók Lífsins, and the dead were judged according to all that was written in the books, according to their deeds. The

sea yielded up its dead and Death and Hell yielded up the dead in them. Each one was judged according to his deeds. Then Doom and Destruction themselves were cast into the flaming lake. This is the second death. But if anyone was not found written in the Book of Life he too was pitched into Gehenna's blaze, where maggots die not and unconsumed sulphur unendingly burns.

A new Heaven and a new Earth came into my view – because the first Heaven and the first Earth had disappeared, and the sea was no more. I saw New Jerusalem, the holy city, coming down out of Heaven, from God himself, prepared as a bride is adorned for her husband. I heard a voice in might from Heaven say, "Behold, God's tabernacle is with mankind and he shall abide in their midst and they will be his people and God himself will be with them. He will wipe away every tear from their eyes, he will swallow up death in victory, there will be no more pain or weeping or suffering – because the things that were no longer are."

The one that sat upon the throne said, "Look!   I have made everything new."

And, "Write! For these words are faithful and true."

Then he said to me, "It is done. Eu sou o Alfa e o Ômega, no início e no final. I will give to all who are thirsty freely to drink from the fountain of the Water of Life. Whoever overcomes will inherit all things: I will be his God and he will be my son. But the cowardly and faithless, the hateful and murderers, lechers, sorcerers, idolaters – and all who lie – these have their share in Gehenna's brimstone basin. This is the second death."

One of the seven angels who had one of the vials with one of the seven last plagues came and spoke to me, "Come up here! I will show you the Bride, the wife of the Lamb." He carried me on in the Spirit to a towering lofty peak and showed me the holy city, Jerusalén, coming down out of Heaven from God himself and having his splendor, her radiance like that of crystalline jasper, her roof in grandeur soaring. There were twelve gates to the city with twelve angels watching and the names graven on the gates were the twelve tribes of Israel – three gates in the East three gates in the North three gates in the South three gates in the West. And in the wall of the city twelve foundation stones were laid and upon them were etched the names of the Lamb's twelve apostles.

The angel who spoke to me held a golden measuring rod to measure the city and her gates and her wall. The city lay foursquare, length and width the same. He measured the city with the rod - fifteen hundred miles per side - length and breadth and height all equal. He measured the depth of the wall as well, 144 cubits in a man's terms (also that of the angel), some 200 feet. The wall seemed built of green jasper, the city itself pellucid gold, transparent, pure, the foundation stones adorned with jewels - the first jasper, the second sapphire, the third chalcedony, the fourth emerald, the fifth sardonyx, the sixth carnelian, the seventh tourmaline, the eighth beryl, the ninth topaz, the tenth green agate, the eleventh jacinth, the twelfth amethyst - and the twelve gates twelve pearls each fashioned from a single pearl opening to golden streets pristine as glass.

But I saw no temple in the city because the Lord God, Ὁ Παντοκράτωρ, he is its temple, he and the Lamb. Neither was there sun nor moon in its vaulted sky because the city is lit by God's lambent glory, the Lamb its everlasting radiance. The nations come to its brightness bringing the wealth of the seas. The city's gates are not shut by day and there is no night. Within it rest all nations' praise and honor. Nothing unclean or detestable shall be found in it neither any lie and those alone may enter whose names are written in the Lamb's Book of Life.

Then he showed me a river of living water lucent as polished glass flowing from the throne of God and the Lamb. In the midst of the city's street and on both sides of the river stood the Tree of Life. It bore twelve kinds of fruit, yielding its fruits every month. The leaves of the tree were for healing of the nations. There will be nothing cursed in the city because in it is the throne of God and the Lamb and there will his people serve him. They will see his face. His name will be on their foreheads. Night shall be no more neither shall they need any lamp nor the light of the sun - because the Lord God himself shines upon them. And they shall reign agelessly and ever, ages without end.

He said to me, "These words are faithful and true: The Lord God sent his messenger imbued with the spirits of the prophets to reveal to his servants the things that soon must be."

"Behold, I am coming quickly. Blessed is she who guards the words of the prophecy of this book."

It was I John who heard and saw these things. And when I had seen and heard I fell down to worship at the feet of the angel who showed me all this. But he said to me, "God forbid! I am just one of your brothers, a fellow servant with you and the prophets and all those who keep safe the words of this book. Therefore worship God alone." Then he said, "Seal not the prophetic words of this book – because the moment is upon us. Let him who does wrong yet do wrong; let him who is foul yet be foul; but let him who is just yet do what is right; and let him who is holy yet be holy."

"Behold, I am coming quickly and I have everyone's pay, to give to each according to his deeds. Ik ben alfa en omega, het begin en het einde, de eerste en de laatste. Blessed are those whose long robes have been cleansed, so shall they eat of the Tree of Life and enter the holy city. Outside are the treyf – sorcerers libertines assassins idolaters – and all those who love to tell lies. I Jesús have sent my messenger to testify these things to you for the sake of the churches. Io sono la radice e il ramo di David, inizio splendente dell'alba."

The Spirit and the Bride say "Come" and let all who hear say "Come" and let all who are thirsty come to the river and all who desire drink freely the Water of Life.

I charge you now, you who hear the words of the prophecy of this book: If anyone adds to these words God will heap on him the plagues here written and if anyone takes away from the words written in the book of this prophecy God will take away his share of the Tree of Life, out from the holy city. The one who bears witness to these things says, "Truly I come quickly."

Veni, Domine Jesu and may God's grace be with all the saints.

Amen.

CPSIA information can be obtained
at www.ICGtesting.com
Printed in the USA
FSHW020213160519
58154FS

9 781532 648762